ADVENTURES OF A BYSTANDER

Books by Peter F. Drucker

Adventures of a Bystander
The Unseen Revolution
Management: Tasks, Responsibilities, Practices
Men, Ideas, and Politics
Technology, Management, and Society
The Age of Discontinuity
The Effective Executive
Managing for Results
Landmarks of Tomorrow
America's Next Twenty Years
The Practice of Management
The New Society
Concept of the Corporation
The Future of Industrial Man
The End of Economic Man
Managing the Non-Profit Organization

Peter F. Drucker

ADVENTURES

OF A

BYSTANDER

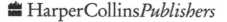 HarperCollins*Publishers*

THIS BOOK IS DEDICATED TO

AMY MARIS DRUCKER

(1975–1978)

WHO GAVE SO MUCH JOY AND LOVE IN SO SHORT A LIFE

Portions of this work originally appeared in *The Atlantic Monthly, Human Nature, Industry Week*, and *Quest*.

A hardcover edition of this book was originally published in 1978 by Harper & Row, Publishers. A paperback edition was published in 1979 by Harper & Row, Publishers.

First HarperCollins edition published 1991.

LIBRARY OF CONGRESS CATALOG CARD NUMBER 90-55533

ISBN 0-06-016565-0

91 92 93 94 95 RRD 10 9 8 7 6 5 4 3 2 1

Contents

Preface to the
New Edition

I taught religion once, many years ago, and I greatly enjoyed it. But I never had much use for theology. There are, I am told, some thirty-five thousand different species of flies. But if the theologians had their way, there would be only one, the right Fly. The Creator glories in diversity. And no species is more diverse than those two-legged creatures, Men and Women. Even as a small child I marvelled at their diversity. And I have never met a single uninteresting person. No matter how conformist, how conventional, or how dull, people become fascinating the moment they talk of the things they do, know, or are interested in. Everyone then becomes an individual. The most conventional person I can recall, a banker in a small New England town, who seemed to know nothing but the most hackneyed clichés, became fascinating when he suddenly started talking about buttons throughout the ages—their invention, their shapes, their materials, their functions and uses—with a fire and passion worthy of a great lyrical poet. The subject did not interest me much; the man did. He had become an individual. And individuals in their diversity are portrayed in this book.

It is this belief in diversity and pluralism and in the uniqueness of each person that underlies all my writings, beginning with my first book more than fifty years ago. During most of these fifty years centralization, uniformity, and conformity were dominant. The total-itarian regimes in which everybody was to conform, to think the same, to write and paint the same, to be centrally controlled—the Nazis called it "switched onto the same track" (*gleichgeschaltet*)—were but the head of a universal current. It swept over the democracies as well. But every one of my books and essays, whether dealing with politics, philosophy, or history; with social order and social institutions; with management, technology, or economics, has stressed pluralism and diversity. Where the prevailing doctrines preached control by big government or big business, I stressed decentralization, experimentation, and the need to create community. And where the prevailing approaches saw government and big business as the only institutions and as the "countervailing powers" of a modern society, I stressed the importance and central role of the non-profit, public-service institu-

vi

tions, the "third sector"—as the nurseries of independence and diversity; as guardians of values; as providers of community leadership and citizenship. And I pointed out how much of society is organized and informed by non-business, non-governmental institutions, the universities, for instance, or the hospitals, each with very different values and a different personality. But I was swimming against a strong current.

Now, at last, the tide has turned, and it has turned my way. The flag-bearer of the collectivist, centralizing, uniformity-imposing parade, Communism, has proven a sham, incompetent even to provide the mere rudiments of effective government, functioning economy, citizenship, and community. And in the West too we are now rapidly decentralizing, indeed uncentralizing. For a generation after World War II, we believed that any sickness was best treated in a centralized hospital, the bigger the better. We are now moving patients into "outreach" facilities as fast as we can. During the last fifteen years America's large corporations have been shrinking steadily. All the phenomenal employment growth in this period—the fastest growth in jobs in peacetime history anywhere—has been in small and middle-sized enterprises. In the decades following World War II, America built ever-bigger consolidated schools—one cause, I believe, of our educational malaise. Now we are moving towards diverse, decentralized schools, the "magnet schools," for instance. "Small is beautiful" is, of course, as much stifling dogma as "big is best"—and equally stupid, as one look at the diversity of God's creation will show. We surely will not return to the nineteenth-century society, which knew only the smallest and weakest of governments and few institutions except the local church and school. The knowledge society into which we are moving so fast is going to be a society of organizations. But of organizations—plural—that will be diverse, decentralized, multiform. And within these organizations, we are moving away from the standardized, uniform structures that were generally accepted in public administration and business management, "the one right structure for the typical manufacturing company," for instance, or the "model government agency." We are moving toward organic design, informed by mission, purpose, strategy, and the environment, both social and physical—the design I began to advocate forty years ago in *The Practice of Management* (which came out in 1954).

But while my writings for fifty years have been stressing organic design, decentralization, and diversity, they deal with ideas, that is, with abstractions. They draw heavily on my work with people as a teacher and as a consultant. And I always try to bring in people to exemplify and to illustrate. But still, these individuals are being used to exemplify and to illustrate concepts. I myself have always been more interested in people than in concepts. But I have known all along that as a writer I do better with concepts than with people.

Adventures of a Bystander is thus a book I wrote for myself. It is a book about people. Not about myself; the subtitle of the British edition describes my intention: *Other Lives and My Times*. No book of mine has had a longer gestation period; for twenty years I lived with the characters in my head, ate, drank, walked, talked with them, awake and in my dreams. But no book of mine has come into the world faster—it took less than a year to complete once I sat down at the typewriter. It is surely not my "most important" book. But it is the one I enjoy the most.

And so apparently do my readers. That the book has had success—more than enough to justify reissuing it in this new edition—is, of course, gratifying in itself. But what is even nicer are the readers who write or who tell me when I encounter them in a meeting: "I have read many of your books, have learned a great deal from them, and use them constantly in my work. But of all your books I *enjoy* most *Adventures of a Bystander*." And then they often add: "I enjoy it so much because the people in it are so diverse."

I chose the people in this book because of their diversity and because I enjoyed their stories the most. But as an early reviewer pointed out, they also "signify." They were not picked because they were "great and famous." Indeed, most of them were totally obscure; the telephone directory was the only "reference book" ever to list them. What holds them together is pure chance: they crossed my path. But still, I think, their individual tales create a tapestry. In a subjective, eclectic way, they convey, I hope, something of the atmosphere, the ambience, of a time that is rapidly fading even in the recollection of older people: that very peculiar half-century between pre-World War I Europe and post-World War II America. Each story is separate. Each was picked because it made a good story. But together, I believe, they show that history is, after all, composed of stories.

Memorial Day, 1990
Claremont, California

Prologue:
A Bystander Is Born

Bystanders have no history of their own. They are on the stage but are not part of the action. They are not even audience. The fortunes of the play and of every actor in it depend on the audience whereas the reaction of the bystander has no effect except on himself. But standing in the wings—much like the fireman in the theater—the bystander sees things neither actor nor audience notices. Above all, he sees differently from the way actors or audience see. Bystanders reflect—and reflection is a prism rather than a mirror; it refracts.

This book is no more a "history of our times," or even of "*my* times*," than it is an autobiography. It uses the sequence of my life mainly for the order of appearance of its dramatis personae. It is not a "personal" book; my experiences, my life, and my work are the book's accompaniment rather than its theme. But it is an intensely subjective book, the way a first-rate photograph tries to be. It deals with people and events that have struck me—and still strike me—as worth recording, worth thinking about, worth rethinking and reflecting on, people and events that I had to fit into the pattern of my own experience and into my own fragmentary vision of the world around me and the world inside me.

I was still a week shy of my fourteenth birthday when I discovered myself to be a bystander. The day was November 11, 1923—my birthday is on the nineteenth. November 11 in the Austria of my childhood was "Republic Day," commemorating the day, in 1918, on which the

1

last of the Habsburg emperors had abdicated and the Republic was proclaimed. For most of Austria this was a day of solemnity, if not of mourning—the day of final defeat in a nightmare war, the day in which centuries of history had crumbled into dust. But in Vienna, with its solid Socialist majority, Republic Day was a day of victory and celebration. Everything was closed firmly until the early afternoon— no streetcar ran, no train moved, and only ambulances, fire engines, and police cars could drive the streets. The city was given over to the workers of Vienna who, red banners aloft, marched from every quarter and every suburb into the big square in front of the City Hall—to sing the old revolutionary songs, to renew the faith, and to listen to their leaders retell the myths of oppression and of a future of classless bliss.

Republic Day in Vienna—even before May Day in Russia—was the first of the "spontaneous demonstrations" that have become the peculiar public art form of this century. Mussolini, Stalin, Hitler, even Mao and Perón, largely imitated the Viennese Socialists. Indeed the organizer of Hitler's first great "spontaneous demonstration" after his coming to power on January 31, 1933, the "March on Potsdam," was a former Viennese Socialist who had for years been in charge of Vienna's Republic Day.

The first to march—hours before the workers began to assemble in the industrial suburbs of Hernals and Ottakring—were the youth auxiliaries, something both Stalin and Hitler copied, by the way. And on that November 11, 1923, the first youth auxiliary to march (for the honor rotated each year) was that of the 19th District, Doebling, the district where I lived. The lead troop of the youth auxiliary of the district was the raggedly-taggedly band of "Young Socialists" from the Gymnasium, the "humanist" and college-preparatory high school of the district. And the youngest "comrade" in the troop, the newest recruit—given the honor of marching first and of carrying the big red banner that proclaimed to all that we were "Doebling's Students for Freedom and Equality Under Socialism"—was I, of course. Legally, I was not permitted to take part, nor were the Young Socialists permitted to have me; legally, a high-school student had to be fourteen to take part in any political activity. There was not much risk in my marching eight days before the statutory age. I knew this; yet the illegality of my marching, however riskless and trivial, added spice. It was certainly one reason why I let myself be recruited. But then I was also a rather lonely boy and far from popular with my classmates. And so when the formidable organizer of Doebling's Young Socialists—a muscular medical student of whom I remember nothing, not even her name, except that she had a mustache—asked me to lead the procession, I accepted eagerly.

Earlier that fall, when school began, I had moved out of the children's room I had until then shared with my younger brother and into a big room of my own, under the eaves, with two high mansard windows that looked out over the main roof into the vineyards and beyond to the hills of the Vienna Woods. I had also been given the symbols of adulthood in the Vienna of my time—an alarm clock of my own and a house key. But I had not yet used either. The maid still knocked on my door each morning shortly after half-past six—school began at eight and it was a long walk—and a maid was there to let me out and to open the heavy gate for me when I came back. Now I was going to use both, alarm clock and key, for the first time. When the alarm clock rang at 4:30—maybe even earlier—I raced to the window. It had been raining heavily when I went to bed and I was afraid we would be hauled ingloriously in streetcars, which was the arrangement for really bad weather. It had not exactly cleared but the rain had stopped and stars were showing through the scudding clouds.

Our group met outside the school. But the familiar streets that I walked every day looked and felt different. Even the boring school looked different, mysterious and secretive. We began to march to the first major street junction where the high-school troops from the neighboring districts joined up and fell into line behind us. Then we began to sing—and I proudly unfurled the huge red flag. The youth groups of apprentices and young workers joined us, all falling in line behind me; and so we marched down one of the city's main streets twelve abreast—I alone marching by myself at the head of what rapidly became a multitude. I thought it was the happiest day of my life —maybe it was.

But as we moved off the main radial street and across a big square, behind which loomed the pseudo-gothic monster of City Hall, I saw in front of me, directly in my path, a long, narrow, but deep puddle of water left by last night's downpour.

I liked puddles—I still do. I know few more satisfying sounds than the squoosh-squoosh of a good puddle. Normally I would have gone out of my way to wade through a puddle like this. But I had not chosen *this* puddle; it was being forced on me by the crowd. I fought with all the will I could muster to make myself swerve. But the rhythmic

pounding of the feet of my followers behind me, the press of mass
man, the physical coercion of mass movement overpowered me. I
waded through the puddle from one end to the other. At the far end
I thrust the banner, without saying a word, into the arms of the hefty
medical student in back of me, dropped out of the ranks, and turned
toward home. It was a long walk, two or three hours. Throughout, the
massed ranks of Viennese Socialists, marching twelve abreast and
carrying their banners, passed me going the other way. I felt terribly
lonely and yearned to join them. But I also was lightheaded and elated
beyond words. When I got home, I let myself in—the first time—with
my own key. My parents, who were not expecting to see me until late
afternoon, were concerned. "Aren't you feeling well," they asked? "I
never felt better in my life," I answered truthfully. "I only found out
that I don't belong."

But, of course, I only found out that I was a bystander on that cold
and blustery November day. Bystanders are born rather than made.
At least I was well on the way to becoming one by the time I was eight,
at a children's Christmas party during World War I. That fall, the first
of the big "war-profiteering" scandals broke and occupied the head-
lines for weeks on end. The owner of one of Vienna's best hotels and
restaurants—I still remember his name, it was Kranz—was arrested
and indicted for black marketing. The real hunger years in Vienna
were then still in the future. But meat already was very scarce, even
the tiny allowance to which the ration book entitled each adult could
almost never be found in the shops, and what there was was all but
inedible. Kranz, who had never served anything but the best, bought
decent meat for his restaurant at black-market prices, was promptly
denounced, and became a popular villain. He had not charged a penny
more for the meat dishes than the law allowed, had not served bigger
portions than the ration books permitted, and had properly collected
the ration coupons. The law only fixed prices for sellers of meat—no
one in drafting the regulations had envisaged a buyer eager to pay
more. But as the prosecutor pointed out, to the applause of press and
public, Kranz had "constructively" sold at black-market prices by
raising his charges for unregulated items such as the overnight stay at
his hotel or the cover charge in the restaurant so as to absorb the
higher costs for the meat.

We were all sheltered upper-class children at the Christmas party,
none more than eight or nine years old, yet it was hardly surprising

that we talked about the Kranz affair. The war and its news was never very far away those days, even from sheltered upper-class children and even at a Christmas party. All of us had relatives and friends at the front. All of us saw our parents each morning turn furtively in dread to the newspaper's second page, where the casualty lists were printed. Indeed all of us—my playmates and I—had taught ourselves to read by scanning the casualty lists and the obituaries with the big black borders, looking for names we knew, names of people we loved and missed. And that year, while I went to third grade in a public school in the neighborhood, I spent two or three weary hours each day under the supervision of an even wearier ancient (back from retirement to take the place of a teacher who had been called up) pasting stamps into ration books, fending off the emaciated women who tried to slip us money to get a few extra stamps, or being told: "I'm entitled to extra stamps. My husband just got killed at the front." None of us children was old enough to remember much of the "prewar" the adults talked about. None of us could imagine that the war would ever end. Indeed every boy my age *knew* that "When I grow up" meant "When I get drafted and am sent to the front." Of course we talked about the Kranz affair, even at the Christmas party. So did our parents in the next room. I found myself asked by one of the other children to explain it, and launched, to my own surprise, into an impassioned speech defending, nay praising, Kranz the arch-villain. Whether he had broken the law as everyone debated seemed to me trivial. He had tried to do the honorable thing. He gave his guests what they had come to expect, what he had promised them and what they were paying for.

There was silence when I stopped. The other children were embarrassed. My friend and playmate, Bibi, in whose house we met, reproached me for years thereafter for spoiling her Christmas party. The adults who had come in while I was orating smiled indulgently. But Bibi's father, an old friend of my parents in whose honor the party was being held—he had just been invalided out of the army, having been wounded near-fatally after three years in the trenches—took me aside and said: "This is certainly an interesting point of view, and one none of us has heard before—at least no one expressed it when we talked about this business at our dinner table in the other room. Peter, don't think I'm being critical. It may be you're right about Kranz. But you're certainly the odd man out. And then one has to be a little tactful

and a little careful. To watch and think for yourself is highly com-
mendable. But to shock people by shouting strange views from the
rooftops is not."

This is the admonition the bystander always hears, for it is his lot
to see things differently. The admonition is well taken. But I have
rarely heeded it—nor does this book.

REPORT

FROM

ATLANTIS

Grandmother and
the Twentieth Century

I had not been back for almost twenty years when I visited Vienna in 1955 to give one or two lectures. And even earlier, before I last stopped over in 1937 en route from England to America, I had been in Vienna only infrequently. I had left as soon as I finished the Gymnasium, in 1927, not quite eighteen, and returned later only to spend Christmases with my parents, rarely for more than a week at a time.

In 1955 I was going to stay only long enough to give my lectures. But as I was walking outside my hotel the morning after my arrival, I passed a food market that had been a byword for choice delicacies in my childhood. I remembered that I had promised my wife back in America a bottle of a particular Austrian liqueur, so I went into the store to buy it. I did not remember ever having been there—certainly I had not been a regular customer. But as I went through the door, the ancient lady who, according to old and by then thoroughly outmoded custom, presided over the store from the cash register, recognized me at once and hailed me by name. "Mr. Peter," she said, "how nice of you to visit us. We read in the papers that you were coming here to lecture and wondered whether we'd see you. We were very sorry to hear last year that your dear mother had passed away; and of course your dear Aunt Anna has been gone a long time now. But I hear that your esteemed father is still alive and well. Is it true that we can expect him in Vienna next year to celebrate his eightieth birthday? Your Aunt Greta was here only a few years ago when your Uncle Hans got the honorary doctorate. Being suppliers to the family from the old days,

9

we didn't think it would be presumptuous for us to send a hamper of fruit and a note of congratulations to their hotel, and we got such a gracious letter back from your Aunt Greta. Those were lovely ladies. The young people here," and she nodded toward the sales personnel in the store, "don't know real quality any more. But, begging your pardon, Mr. Peter, none could compare with your grandmother. What a wonderful lady she was; there was no one like her. And," she began to smile, "she was so funny! Do you remember the story of her telegram to her niece's wedding?" She broke into loud cackling laughter and I joined her.

Of course I knew the story of Grandmother's telegram, even though it was sent well before I was born. Unable to attend the wedding of a niece, Grandmother had wired:

> Since it is considered proper and good form to confine oneself to the utmost brevity in sending a telegram let me only wish you on this solemn day MANY HAPPY RETURNS.

Then, according to family legend, Grandmother had complained bitterly that they charged so much when she was only wiring three words.

Grandmother was tiny and small-boned and had been beautiful in her youth. When I came to know her there were hardly any traces of youth and beauty left—except for her abundant curly hair, still a warm red-brown, of which she was very proud. Shortly after her husband died and left her a widow when barely forty, she had had a long siege of illness: the serious infection then called rheumatic fever that left her with permanent heart damage and perennially short of breath. She was badly crippled by arthritis, and all her bones, especially in the fingers, were swollen and painful. As the years went by she also became increasingly deaf.

Yet nothing stopped grandmother from being on the go all the time and in every weather. She would visit all over the city, by streetcar or, more often, on foot. She was always armed with a big black umbrella that doubled as a cane, and lugged an enormous black shopping bag that weighed as much as she did and was full of tiny mysterious packages, individually wrapped—a few ounces of herb tea for an ailing old woman, a few postage stamps for a schoolboy, half a dozen "good" metal buttons from a discarded frock as a present for a dressmaker, and so on. Grandmother was one of six sisters, every one of whom in turn had had at least four daughters, so that there were innumerable nieces. Most of them had been brought up by Grandmother at one time or another and were closer to her than to their own mothers. But there were also old family servants and retainers, elderly ladies in reduced circumstances and former fellow music students, old shopkeepers and craftsmen, and even old servants of long-dead friends. "If I don't visit her, who will do it?" Grandmother would say when she set out for a long trip to some outlying suburb to look up "Little Paula," the elderly widowed niece of her cousin's long-deceased housekeeper. And everyone, including her daughters and her nieces, had come to call her "Grandmother."

She spoke to everybody the same way, in the same pleasant friendly voice, and with the same old-fashioned courtesy. She always remembered what was important to everyone she met even if she had not seen them in a long time. "Tell me, Miss Olga," she would say to the governess of the children next door to us, whom she had not seen for months, "how is that nephew of yours coming along? Has he passed that final engineering exam by now? Oh, you must be so proud of him." Or to the old cabinetmaker whose father had made the furniture for her trousseau and whom she dropped in to see once in a while for old time's sake: "Have you been able to get the city to cancel the increase in the real estate tax on your shop, Mr. Kolbel? You were upset about it the last time we met."

Grandmother spoke the same way to the prostitute who had her stand at the street corner next door to the apartment house where she lived. Everyone else would pretend not to see the woman. But Grandmother would always wish her a good evening and say, "It's a cold wind tonight, Miss Lizzie. Do you have a warm scarf and is it wrapped tight?" And one evening when she noticed that Miss Lizzie was hoarse, Grandmother crawled up the five flights to her apartment— this was postwar Vienna and elevators rarely functioned—rummaged in her medicine cabinet for cough drops, then painfully crawled down again to give them to Miss Lizzie. "But Grandmother," remonstrated one of her stuffier nieces, "it's improper for a lady to talk to a woman like her." "Nonsense," Grandmother said, "to be courteous is never improper. I am not even a man; what that's improper could she want with a stupid old woman like me?" "But Grandmother, to bring her cough drops!" "You," Grandmother said, "always worry about the horrible venereal diseases the men get from these girls. I can't do anything about that. But I can at least prevent her from giving a young man a bad sore throat."

One of Grandmother's nieces—or maybe a grandniece—had become a starlet of film and musical comedy whose love affairs were forever being reported in the more lurid Sunday papers. "I wouldn't mind," said Grandmother, "if I never heard another word about what goes on in Mimi's bedroom." "Oh, Grandmother, don't be a prude," a granddaughter said. "I know," said Grandmother, "she has to have these affairs and I know she has to get them in the papers. It's the only way she can get a decent part; she has no voice and can't act. But I wish she wouldn't name those awful men in her interviews." "But Grandmother," the granddaughter said, "the men love it." "That's just what I object to," snapped Grandmother; "pandering to the vanity and conceit of those dirty old lechers. I call it prostitution."

Grandmother's marriage had apparently been very happy. To her dying day, she kept her husband's portrait in her bedroom and went into seclusion on the anniversary of his death. Yet he had been a notorious philanderer. When I was about seventeen and walking down one of Vienna's main streets, an ancient chauffeur-driven automobile passed me, then stopped. A hand waved at me out of the rear window. I went up and saw two women sitting inside, one heavily veiled, the other a maid, judging by her apron. The maid said to me: "My lady thinks you might be Ferdinand Bond's grandson." Yes, I was. The maid said: "He was my lady's last lover"—and the car drove off.

I was terribly embarrassed, but apparently not embarrassed enough to keep quiet. The story got to Grandmother, who called me in and cross-examined me about the veiled lady in the car. Then she said, "It must have been Dagmar Siegfelden. I can well believe that your grandfather was *her* last lover—poor woman, she was never very attractive. But you can take it from me, she was *not* your grandfather's last mistress." "But Grandmother," I said—we were forever, it seems, saying, "But Grandmother"—"didn't his having mistresses bother you?" "Of course it did," said Grandmother. "But I would never have a husband who didn't have mistresses. I'd never know where he was." "But weren't you afraid he might leave you?" "Not in the least," said Grandmother. "He always came home to eat dinner. I am only a stupid old woman, but I know enough to realize that the stomach is the male sex organ."

Grandmother's husband had left her a large fortune. But it all went in the Austrian inflation, and Grandmother had become poor as a churchmouse. She had lived in a big two-story apartment with plenty of servants; now she lived in a corner of her former maids' quarters and kept house all alone. Her health grew steadily worse. Yet the only thing she ever complained about—and that rarely—was that arthritis and deafness increasingly prevented her from playing and listening to music. In her young days she had been a pianist, one of Clara Schumann's pupils and asked by her several times to play for Johannes Brahms, which was Grandmother's proudest memory. A girl of good family could not become a public performer, of course. But until her husband died and she fell ill, Grandmother often played at charity concerts. One of her last performances had been under Mahler's baton shortly after he had taken over as conductor of the Vienna Opera in 1896. She had no use for the big romantic sensuous sound that the Viennese loved. She called it "stockjobbers' music," and considered it vulgar. Instead, Grandmother anticipated by half a century the dry, unadorned, precise "French" style that has become popular in the last twenty years. She never used the pedals. Altogether she disliked sentiment in music. When she sat with us children while we practiced, she would always say, "Don't play music, play notes. If the composition is any good, that will make music out of it." She had on her own discovered the French Baroque masters—Lully, Rameau and, above all, Couperin—who were then totally out of fashion. And she played them with a dry, even, harpsichord-like sharpness rather than with the sonority of the "grand piano" which, of course, had not been invented when the music was written. She had a remarkable musical memory. I once practiced a sonata. Grandmother came in from the next room and said, "Play that bar again." I did so. She said: "That should be a D flat; you played a D." "But Grandmother," I said, "the score says 'D.' " "Impossible!" Then she looked at the score and found that it did say "D." Whereupon she called up the publisher— he was of course the husband of one of her nieces—and said, "On this or that page of your second volume of Haydn Piano Sonatas, in bar so-and-so, there is a misprint." And he called back two hours later to tell her that she had been right. "How did you know this, Grandmother?" we would say. "How could I not know it?" she came back. "I played the piece when I was your age and in those days we were expected to know our pieces."

We all adored her. But we all knew she was very funny indeed. Like the lady in the delicatessen, we smiled when her name came up, then broke out laughing when we remembered this or that "Grand-

mother story." For we all knew that she, with all her wonderful qualities, was the family moron. Every member of the family, from the
oldest to the youngest, dined out on "Grandmother stories." They
could make even the dullest and most tongue-tied of us the life of the
party. Our playmates, when we were still quite small, would clamor:
"Do you have any new Grandmother stories?" and would break out
in guffaws of laughter when we told them. As for instance:

After years of being badgered by one of her sons-in-law, Grandmother finally set to work cleaning up her kitchen cabinet. She then
proudly displayed the new order. Tacked onto the top shelf was a card
on which Grandmother had written in her Victorian hand: "Cups
without Handles." Beneath it, on the next shelf, the card read: "Handles without Cups."

The day came when Grandmother couldn't keep all her stuff in
the two tiny rooms to which she was finally reduced. So she packed
everything she didn't need into enormous shopping bags and took off
for the bank in the center of the city where she kept her account, by
then down to a few pennies. Her husband had started the bank and
had been its chairman until he died, and she was still treated with the
consideration due his widow. But when she appeared with her shopping bags and asked to have the contents put on her account, the
manager balked. "We can't put *things* on an account," he said, "only
money." "That's mean and ungrateful of you," said Grandmother;
"you only do this to me because I am a stupid old woman." And she
promptly closed her account and drew out the balance. Then she went
down the street to the nearest branch of the same bank, reopened her
account there, and never said a word about her shopping bags.
"Grandmother," we'd say, "if you thought the bank was unfriendly,
why did you reopen your account at another branch?" "It's a good
bank," she said; "after all, my late husband founded it." "Then why not
demand that the manager at the new branch take your stuff?" "I never
banked there before. He didn't owe me anything."

Grandmother's troubles over her apartment were a never-ending
source of stories. She sublet it to a dentist who used one floor to live
in and one floor for his office, with Grandmother keeping a few rooms
in the back for herself. But she and the dentist soon began to quarrel
and engaged for years in a running fight—suing each other, claiming
damages, and even filing criminal charges against one another. Yet
Grandmother kept on going to Dr. Stamm to have her teeth treated
and her dentures made. "How can you patronize a dentist you just had

arrested for criminal trespass?" we would ask. "I am only a stupid old woman," Grandmother would reply, "but I know he's a good dentist or else how could he afford those two big floors? And he is convenient; I don't have to go out in bad weather or climb stairs. And my teeth are not part of the lease."

There was the story of how she threw a waitress out of her own restaurant. She was traveling with four or five of us grandchildren— to take us to a summer camp, I believe. When we changed trains we went into the station restaurant for lunch, and Grandmother noticed the slovenly waitress. As the girl came close to our table, Grandmother hooked her with her umbrella handle and said quite pleasantly: "You look like an educated, intelligent girl to me. You wouldn't want to work in a place where the staff doesn't know how to behave, would you? Go out that door," Grandmother gave her a mighty shove with the umbrella toward the exit, "come in again and do it properly." The girl went meekly; and when she came in, she curtseyed. We were terribly embarrassed and protested: "But Grandmother, we aren't going to be in this place ever again." "I hope not," said Grandmother, "but the waitress has to be."

And there was the cryptic advice she always gave to her grand-daughters: "Girls, put on clean underwear when you go out. One never knows what might happen." When one granddaughter, half amused and half offended, said to her: "But Grandmother, I'm not that kind of a girl," Grandmother answered: "You never know until you are."

Grandmother held fast to "prewar." But her standard was not 1913; it was the time before her husband had died—especially in regard to money. Austria had had a silver currency for most of the nineteenth century, the Gulden, which contained 100 Kreuzer. Then in 1892, when Grandmother was a young woman of thirty-five or so, Austria switched to a gold currency, the Krone, with 100 Heller—each Gulden being exchanged into 2 Kronen. Thirty years later inflation destroyed the Krone. When it had depreciated to the point where it took 75,000 Kronen to buy what one had bought before the war, a new currency came in—the Schilling, each exchanged for 25,000 of the old Kronen. Within a year or less everybody thought only in terms of the Schilling, except for Grandmother. She stayed with the Gulden when she went shopping. She would laboriously translate prices from Schilling first into Kronen before the exchange, then into Kronen before World War I, and finally into Gulden and Kreuzer. "How come the

eggs cost so much?" she'd say. "You ask thirty-five Kreuzer a dozen
for them—they used to cost no more than twenty-five." "But, gracious
lady," the shopkeeper would reply, "it costs more these days to feed
the hens." "Nonsense," said Grandmother, "hens aren't Socialists.
They don't eat more just because we have a Republic."

My father, who was the economist in the family, tried to explain
to her that prices had changed. "Grandmother," he said, "you have to
realize that the value of money has changed because of war and
inflation." "How can you say that, Adolph?" Grandmother retorted. "I
am only a stupid old woman but I do know that you economists consider money the standard of value. You might as well tell me that I am
suddenly six feet tall because the yardstick has changed. I'd still be
well below average height." My father gave up in disgust. But because
he was as fond of Grandmother as we all were, he tried to help her.
At least he could relieve her of the chore of computing all those prices
—multiplying by 25,000 and then by 3 and then by 2, or whatever it
was Grandmother had to do to get back to what eggs had cost in 1892.
He made a conversion chart and presented it to her. "How sweet of
you, Adolph," she said. "But it doesn't really help me unless it also tells
me what things did cost back in those years." "But Grandmother," my
father said, "*you* know that—you always point out what eggs or lettuce
or parsley used to cost in Gulden." "I am only a stupid old woman,"
replied Grandmother, "but I have better things to do than stuff my
brain with trivia like the price of parsley thirty years ago. Besides I
didn't shop in those days; I had a housekeeper and a cook to do that."
"But," my father argued, "you always tell the shopkeepers that you
know." "Of course, Adolph," said my Grandmother; "you have to
know or they'll cheat you every time."

But Grandmother was at her best—or worst—when dealing with
officialdom and politics.

Before 1918 no one had a passport and no one had even heard of
a visa. Then suddenly one could not travel anywhere without both,
and especially not from one part of what used to be the old Austria to
another. But also, in those first few years after the break-up of the old
Austria, each of the successor states tried to make it as difficult and
disagreeable as possible for the citizens of its neighbors to come in and
for its own citizens to get out. To get a passport one had to stand in
line for hours—and then usually come back again because no one had
the right papers, or even knew what papers were needed. To get a visa
one had again to stand in line for hours—and again, usually, come

back. And of course one had to go in person, accompanied by every member of the family who might go along on the trip. At the new border stations everybody had to go out and stand in line in the open for hours, regardless of weather, then do the same all over again for the customs. So when Grandmother announced in the summer of 1919 that she was going to visit her oldest daughter who, a year earlier, had married and moved to Budapest in Hungary, everybody tried to argue her out of the harebrained idea. But no one ever changed Grandmother's mind once it was made up.

My father was then the senior civil servant at the Austrian Ministry of Economics. So Grandmother, without telling him, went to the ministry's messenger and had him get her the *passports* and the visa. And she got passports, where everybody else had a hard enough time to get one. Her late husband had been a British subject—that he had died twenty years earlier one did not need to tell anyone; and so she got a British passport. She herself had lived all her life in Vienna, so she got an Austrian passport. While her husband was alive he had an apartment in Prague, where he often went on business; of course the apartment had been sold when he died, but one doesn't have to volunteer information to authority—and so she got a Czech passport. Next she wrote her daughter in Budapest to get a Hungarian passport for her. And she got the needed visas into each of these four passports the same way.

When my father heard all this, he exploded. "The ministry's messenger is a public servant and must not be used on private business," he shouted. "Of course," said Grandmother; "I know that. But am I not a member of the public?"

She had me put into the passports and visas as a minor accompanying her. "Why should Peter come with you to Budapest?" my parents asked. "You know very well," said Grandmother, "that he only practices the piano when I sit with him; and he has so little talent he can't afford to miss two weeks of practicing."

When we got to the border, the police ordered everybody out with their luggage. But Grandmother stayed in her seat until the last person had entered the small shed at the end of the platform in which passports were inspected. Then she hobbled to the passport office, black umbrella and shopping bag on one arm, me on the other. The official was about ready to close up and had already taken down the sign. "Why didn't you come earlier?" he snarled. "You were busy," said Grandmother. "You had people standing in line." With that she plonked the four passports on the table in front of him. "But no one," said the man, taken aback, "can have four passports." "How can you say that?" said Grandmother. "Can't you see I have four?" The clerk, thoroughly beaten, said meekly, "But I can only stamp one." "You are a man, and educated, and an official," said Grandmother, "and I am only a stupid old woman. Why don't you pick the one that will give me the best rate of exchange for Hungarian currency?"

When he had stamped one passport and she had safely stowed all four of them back into her shopping bag, she said: "You are such an intelligent young man; please get my bags and take them through customs for me. I can't lift them myself and," nodding at me, "I have this boy to look after, to make sure he does his piano exercises." And the surly, supercilious clerk obeyed.

As the twenties wore on, Austria steadily drifted toward civil war. The Socialists held the only big city, Vienna, with an unshakable majority. The Catholic Conservatives held the rest of the country with an equally unshakable majority. Neither side would give an inch. Instead both built up private armies, brought in weapons from abroad, and prepared for a showdown. By 1927 everybody knew it was imminent, and indeed everybody knew the fighting would start at a demonstration at the conclusion of some long, drawn-out legal trial. The only question, apparently, was who would shoot first—which only depended on which side lost the lawsuit and took to the streets in protest. When it was announced that the Supreme Court would hand down its verdict on a certain day, everybody got off the street, went home, and locked the door—everybody, that is, except Grandmother. She sallied forth on her usual rounds. But when she passed by the University— a block or two from her apartment house—she saw something unusual on the building's flat roof. As it was the middle of the summer vacation, the doors were locked. But Grandmother knew, of course, where the back door was and how to get to the back stairs. She climbed up all six or seven stories, umbrella and shopping bag in hand, until she came out on the roof. And there was a battalion of soldiers in battledress with guns trained on the Parliament Square just below. (The precautions were not altogether frivolous. Riots started a few hours later. The mob burned down the law courts and tried to set fire to the Parliament Building, and there was heavy fighting all over Vienna for another week or so.) But Grandmother went straight up to the commanding officer and said, "Get those idiots out of here double-quick, and their guns with them. They might hurt somebody."

The last time I saw Grandmother, already in the early 1930s, a big pimply youth with a large swastika on his lapel boarded the streetcar in which I was taking Grandmother to spend Christmas with us. Grandmother got up from her seat, inched up to him, poked him sharply in the ribs with her umbrella, and said, "I don't care what your politics are; I might even share some of them. But you look like an intelligent, educated young man. Don't you know this thing"—and she pointed to the swastika—"might give offense to some people? It isn't good manners to offend anyone's religion, just as it isn't good manners to make fun of acne. You wouldn't want to be called a pimply lout, would you?" I held my breath. By that time, swastikas were no laughing matter; and young men who wore them on the street were trained to kick an old woman's teeth in without compunction. But the lout meekly took his swastika off, put it in his pocket, and when he left the streetcar a few stops later, doffed his cap to Grandmother.

The whole family was aghast at the risk she had run. Yet everybody also roared with laughter at her naïveté, her ignorance, her stupidity. "Nazism just a form of acne, ha-ha-ha-ho-ho-ho," roared her niece's husband, Robert—the one who, as Undersecretary of War, had ordered the battalion onto the roof of the University and who had not been a bit amused when he heard of what he called "Grandmother's feeble-minded interference with law and order." And "ha-ha-ha-ho-ho-ho" roared my father, who was then trying unsuccessfully to have the Nazi Party outlawed in Austria; "if only we could have Grandmother ride all streetcars, all the time." And "ha-ha-ha-ho-ho-ho" roared the (former) husband of a niece—she had died—who was suspected of having Nazi sympathies, or at least of making a very good thing out of stamping swastikas in his metalworking plant: "Grandmother thinks politics is a finishing school!"

I laughed too, just as hard as the others. But it was then that I first began to wonder about Grandmother's reputation as the family moron. It wasn't only that her stupidity worked. She did get through the postwar boundaries without having to stand in line for days on end; she made the grocer reduce his prices; and she got the lout to take off his swastika. Yet that, I reflected, might still be stupidity, for as an old Latin tag has it, even the gods fight in vain against stupidity. But I had been arguing with Nazis for years and never seen the slightest results. Facts, figures, rational argument—nothing availed. Here was Grandmother appealing to manners, and it worked. Of course I knew the lout had put back the swastika as soon as he was out of Grandmother's sight. But for a moment he might have felt a little bit ashamed or at least embarrassed.

Grandmother was not "bright," of course. She was not an intellectual. She was simple-minded and literal. She read little, and her tastes ran to gothic tales rather than "serious" books. She was shrewd in a way, not a bit clever. Yet, as I came to suspect slowly, maybe she had wisdom rather than sophistication or cleverness or intelligence. Of course she was funny. But what if she were also right?

To approve or disapprove of the twentieth century would never have occurred to her—that was beyond a "stupid old woman." Yet she intuitively understood it long before anyone else. She understood that in an age in which papers mean more than people, one can never have too many papers. What papers one has does indeed determine the rate of exchange when currencies are controlled. When bureaucrats get power, "public servants" become public masters, as Grandmother knew intuitively, unless they are made to serve the real "public," that is, the individual. And the one compelling argument against guns is, of course, that they hurt people.

We thought it very funny that Grandmother did not understand money and inflation. But we have learned since that no one really understands them, least of all the economists perhaps. Trying to relate everything to the one stable currency Grandmother had known, even though it was past history, is no longer quite so funny. When the Securities and Exchange Commission prescribes "inflation accounting" for businesses, it does exactly what Grandmother tried to do in her primitive way; we "index" wages, pensions, and taxes, and express revenues and expenditures in "constant dollars." Grandmother had sensed a basic problem of the twentieth century: if money is money, it must be the standard of value. But if government can manipulate the standard at will, what then is money? The price of eggs in 1892 Kreuzer is not the measure of all value, yet it may be better than no measure at all.

To approve or disapprove of the status of women or of the relationship between the sexes would never have occurred to Grandmother—that was beyond a "stupid old woman." But she knew that it was a man's world and that women needed to be prepared for it, even though all they could do was put on clean underwear before sallying forth into a world that had little pity on them. She did not have much use for the things men took seriously. When her husband started talking economics or politics at the dinner table, Grandmother, I was told by my mother, would say, "Stock Exchange—if you gentlemen want to discuss things like Stock Exchange at the dinner table, you'd better do it without me," and would get up and leave. But she accepted that men are needed and that one has to put up with them—with their having stupid affairs with every stupid woman who makes eyes at them, with their not practicing the piano unless one sits with them (and I suspect that the piano was more important to Grandmother than sex, marriage, or mistresses), and that they made the rules, which a "stupid old woman" could then manipulate without too much difficulty.

What these bright nieces and grandchildren and sons-in-law and nephews of hers—and the shopkeepers as well—saw as proof of her being a moron, though a lovable one, was that Grandmother believed in and practiced basic values. And she tried to inject them into the twentieth century, or at least into her sphere within it. A wedding was a serious affair; one could not just shrug it off. Maybe the marriage would turn out disastrously—Grandmother would not have been surprised. But on that one day of the wedding, bride and groom were entitled to be fêted, to be made much of, to be taken seriously. One could not, of course, disregard the conflicting demand of a modern age "to confine oneself in a telegram to the utmost brevity," but one must explain this before sending the perfunctory greeting.

The term "bourgeois" in its contemporary, and especially its English, meaning does not fit Grandmother. She belonged to the earlier Age of the Burgher, the age that preceded the commercial and industrial and business civilization of the "Stock Exchange" to which she would never listen. Her ancestors had for generations been silk weavers and silk dyers and ultimately silk merchants—originally probably from Flanders or Holland, then settled in Paisley near Glasgow when it emerged as the great textile center in the seventeenth century. Ultimately, in the 1750s, they had been recruited to come to Vienna, to the new Imperial Austrian Silk Manufactory. Theirs was a world of skilled craftsmen, of responsible guild members; a small world but one of concern and community, workmanship and self-respect. There were no riches in that world, but modest self-reliance. "I am but a stupid old woman" echoed the self-limitation of the skilled craftsman who did not envy the great ones of this world and never dreamed of joining their ranks; who knew himself to be as good as they, and better at his trade. It was a world that respected work and the worker. The poor prostitute forced to sell her body to get enough to eat was an object of pity; but she was entitled to be treated with courtesy. The starlet who used her body to get acting roles and publicity and a rich husband—as Mimi ultimately succeeded in doing—deserved only contempt and had no "glamour." The waitress who did not respect her job enough to do it well was going to be unhappy—it was for her sake, not for that of the customers, that she should be forced to learn manners. And however laughable Grandmother's approach to the Nazi swastika, there was wisdom in it too. Abandoning respect for the individual, his creed, his convictions, and his feelings, is the first step on the road to the gas chamber.

Above all, what that parochial, narrow-minded, comical old woman knew was that community is not distribution of income and social services and the miracles of modern medicine. It is concern for the person. It is remembering that the engineering nephew is the apple of Miss Olga's eye, and rejoicing with that dried-up spinster when he passes his examination and gets his degree. It is going out to some remote suburb to visit the whining "Little Paula" whom a long-dead family servant had raised and loved. It is dragging arthritic joints up five flights of stairs and down five flights of stairs to bring cough drops to an old whore who has become a neighbor by soliciting men on the nearby street corner for years.

This world of the burgher and his community was small and narrow, short-sighted and stifling. It smelled of drains and drowned in its own gossip. Ideas counted for nothing and new ones were rejected out of hand. There was exploitation in it and greed, and women suffered. Like Grandmother's silly feud over the apartment, it could be petty and rancorous. But the values it had—respect for work and workmanship, and concern by the person for the person, the values that make a community—are precisely the values the twentieth century lacks and needs. Without them it is neither "bourgeois" nor "Socialist"; it is "lumpen proletariat," like the young lout with the swastika.

But what about those "Handles without Cups" and "Cups without Handles"? How do they fit into the twentieth century, and what do they have to tell us? I must admit that I could not fit them in for a long time. Then ultimately, around 1955 or so, it dawned on me: Grandmother had had a premonition of genius! In her primitive and unsophisticated way, she had written the first computer program. Indeed her kitchen cabinet, with its full classification of the unnecessary and unusable, is the only "total information system" I have seen to this day.

Grandmother died as she had lived—creating a "Grandmother story." Running around as usual in every kind of weather, she stepped off the curb in a heavy rainstorm directly in the path of an oncoming car. The driver managed to swerve around her but she fell. He stopped the car and rushed to help her up. She was unhurt but obviously badly shaken. "May I take you to a hospital?" the driver said. "I think a doctor should look at you." "Young man, you are very kind to a stupid old woman," Grandmother said. "But maybe you'd better call an ambulance. It might compromise you having a strange woman in your car—you know how people talk." When the ambulance came, ten minutes later, Grandmother was dead of a massive coronary.

Knowing how fond I had been of her, my brother phoned me to give me the news. He began in a somber tone: "I have something very sad to tell you: Grandmother died earlier this morning." But when he began to tell me about her death, I heard a change come into his voice. Then he started to laugh. "Imagine. Only Grandmother could say that —a woman in her seventies compromising a young man by being in a car with him!" I laughed too. Then it occurred to me: a living seventy-five year old woman doesn't compromise a young man—but how would he have explained an unknown old woman *dead* in his car?

Hemme
and Genia

I owe to Hemme and Genia that I did not become a novelist. I knew fairly early in my life that writing was one thing I was likely to do well —perhaps the only one. It certainly was one thing I was willing to work on. And the novel has all along been to me the test of the writer. I was always more interested in people than in abstractions, let alone in the categorical straitjackets of the philosopher. People are to me not only more interesting and more varied but more meaningful precisely because they develop, unfold, change, and become. And I knew early that Hemme and Genia—or, to give them their full names, Dr. Hermann Schwarzwald and his wife, Dr. Eugenia Schwarzwald *née* Nussbaum—were the most interesting people I was ever likely to meet. If I was to write stories, they would have to be in them.

Yet I also knew early that I was unlikely to succeed in making believable, living characters out of Hemme and Genia. Their foibles would be easy. But their characters and personalities were far too shimmering, too ambivalent, too complex. They attracted and fascinated me endlessly; they also disturbed, repulsed, and bothered me. And whenever I tried to embrace them I embraced empty air.

At first glance there was nothing so very difficult or complex about Hemme or Genia, the prodigy civil servant and the prodigy woman educator. Even their life stories differed from those of many others of their generation only by their greater, or at least earlier, worldly success.

Hemme was all bone and sharp angles. He was completely bald, had been apparently since student days, with a pointed shiny bony knob at the top of the head, with bony ridges above deep-set eyes, bony pointed ears, and a sharp outthrust chin. He had long bony hands with big knuckles and big wrists protruding from coat sleeves that always appeared much too short. He was of medium height and powerfully built, though lean as a scarecrow. His mouth was tiny, prim, with narrow lips, usually clamped tightly shut. His speech was a high-pitched bark and came out in short staccato bursts. He said very little, and then usually something unpleasant. My mother once came back from a trip to Paris with a wondrously fashionable dress, bought at high cost from one of the great couturiers. She was very proud of it and saved it for the first big occasion—a reception at the Schwarz-walds', perhaps the Christmas party, since children were invited too. Hemme took one look at my mother and said: "Go back home, Caroline, and take off that dress. Give it to your maid—it looks as if you had borrowed it from her." And my mother—my strong-willed, argumentative, independent mother—went back home, took off the dress, and gave it to the maid. Yet she was one of Hemme's great favorites among the young women he called "Genia's children."

This angular, biting, bony man also was capable—though rarely—of great intuitive kindness. Totally encapsulated in his own shell, he still sensed when to say the redeeming word, and what it had to be —and forced himself to say it. I was in my mid-twenties and had long left Vienna when I came back to spend Christmas 1933 with my parents. The spring before, when Hitler came to power, I had left Germany, gone to London, and found a job of sorts as "trainee" in a big insurance company for a few months. But the job had come to an end by Christmas, I had no other and no prospect of one, and was deeply discouraged. I knew I was not going to move back to Vienna —I had known since I was fourteen that I was not going to live there and had left at the earliest moment, when I finished high school. I had also met in London a young woman—later to become my wife—and with every day away from her it became more apparent to me that I wanted to be with her and had to be where she was.

Still, I was being lulled into inertia by the comfort and ease of life at home, and I was besieged on all sides with arguments for staying and offers of cushy jobs—as a press officer in the Austrian Foreign Office, for instance. I knew perfectly well that I did not want to stay, but I lingered. Finally around early February I made up my mind to leave—eventually. And so I began to postpone my departure by mak-

ing farewell calls, among them to the Schwarzwalds. Genia was kind
and sympathetic and asked all sorts of questions about my job pros-
pects in London (dismal), my finances (even more dismal), and the
well-paid jobs and their opportunities that Vienna seemed to offer.
Suddenly Hemme came in, listened for a few seconds, and then spoke
sharply—something he had never done to Genia in my hearing before:
"Lay off the lad, Genia. Don't act the foolish old woman!" And turning
to me, he said: "I've known you since you were born. I have always
liked your willingness to go it alone and your refusal to run with the
crowd, even with ours. I was proud of you when you decided to leave
Vienna and make your own career abroad as soon as you finished high
school. I was proud of you last year when you decided to quit Germany
when the Nazis came in. And you're right not to stay in Vienna—it's
yesterday and finished. But, Peter," he continued, "once one decides
to leave, one leaves; one doesn't make farewell calls. Kiss Genia goodbye, get up"—and he pulled me out of the chair—"go home and pack.
The train for London leaves tomorrow at noon and you are going to
be on it." Roughly and with considerable force he dragged me out the
door and pushed me down the stairs. When he saw that I had reached
the bottom and was making for the front door, he shouted, "Don't
worry about getting a job—there always are jobs, and better ones than
you'd find here. When you have it, drop us a postcard—and don't
altogether forget us."

I did leave, on the noon train the next day. I got a job within six
hours after arriving in London—and an infinitely better one than any
Vienna could possibly have offered—as economist to a London merchant bank and executive secretary to the partners. And I did send
Hemme the postcard he had asked for. But I knew that I owed him
more—much more—and I sensed what helping me must have cost
that retiring, withdrawn man. I did want to write him a warm letter.
But I was afraid of being laughed at for being sentimental and didn't
write it. I have never forgiven myself. For I never saw Hemme again,
never could tell him. I did indeed revisit Vienna every Christmas until
my wife and I moved to New York, three years later. And I did then
call on Genia each time. But Hemme could not be seen on any of these
visits. He suffered a stroke the summer of 1934, recovered fully physically but became senile mentally. He had lucid days, many of them,
apparently, but never when I chanced to be there. I was told years
later that he would often during these lucid, or half-lucid, days ask:
"Why haven't I heard from Peter Drucker?"

Adults tended to be afraid of Hemme, resentful of his bitter, biting tongue and put off by his refusal to let anyone come close. He was just as rough with children—indeed he treated small children exactly the way he treated everyone. For this reason, perhaps, they adored him and were totally unafraid of him. Even in his later years he was always surrounded by seven or eight year olds, at whom he barked and who barked right back. Yet he had the one physical char- acteristic that frightens small children, for Hemme Schwarzwald was a cripple. One leg was much shorter than the other and ended in a grossly deformed clubfoot. The hip twisted to the outside so that the thigh stood at a sharp angle to the body. Then, below the knee, the leg twisted sharply back in again. Without his cane Hemme could not move at all; and with the cane he could only slither, almost crabwise. Stairs and slopes were difficult for him, although he managed and refused all offers of help. On level ground, however, he moved so fast that even sturdy young men had a hard time keeping up with his loping shuffle. According to rumor, Hemme's deformity was the result of an early childhood accident. He had been dropped in infancy, some said; he had fallen out of a window, said others; the most popular version had young Hemme in the way of a runaway horse or thrown by one. Hemme himself never mentioned his handicap. But then he never mentioned anything about his childhood, his family, or his early life.

It was well known that he had been born, the youngest of several sons, around 1870 or a few years earlier in the easternmost part of Austrian Poland, just a few miles from the Russian border. The family was dirt-poor, living at the margin of subsistence—the father was said to have been a shiftless peddler whose wife supported him by working as a midwife. But the family had already made the big step toward assimilation into the successful bourgeoisie. An uncle—the mother's brother—had moved to Vienna and become one of the city's leading lawyers and the first Jew to head the Vienna Bar Association. The uncle had no children of his own and undertook to look after his nephews, especially young Hemme, who showed intellectual bril- liance and high promise at an early age. He put the nephews through secondary school. Hemme's next brother then moved to Vienna and went to the University as his uncle's guest—he later became a re- spected lower court judge in Vienna. So when Hemme, a year or two later, graduated from the local Gymnasium two years ahead of his age group, everyone including the uncle expected him to follow his brother.

Hemme cannot have been more than seventeen then. But both

his gift for doing the unexpected and inexplicable and his willpower
had matured. He refused to go to Vienna; he chose the University of
Czernowitz instead. Czernowitz was the German-speaking university
of Austrian Poland (of the two others, Krakow spoke Polish and Lem-
berg, or Lwow, Ukrainian). And this meant, of course, that its student
body was solidly Jewish—only Jews in Austrian Poland spoke German
(or Yiddish). But even Polish Jewish boys did not go to Czernowitz
unless they absolutely had to. They scrounged and finagled to make
it to a university in "the West," such as Vienna or Prague. For while
a fully accredited state university, Czernowitz was unacceptable socially and hardly the right place to launch a career. In some ways
Czernowitz's position in Austria-Hungary was similar to New York's
City College in American academia during the 1920s and 1930s: renowned for the competitive ardor of its students, but shunned by
anyone who had the chance to go anyplace else.

When Hemme announced his decision to go to Czernowitz, the
pressures on him to change his mind were tremendous. The uncle—
or so my father, who got to know the uncle quite well, once told me
—offered to rent a separate room for the young man if only he would
come to Vienna. He offered to pay for a long study trip to Germany,
Switzerland, France, and England—the dream of every young Austrian. He even threatened to withdraw his financial support. But
Hemme stood his ground and went to Czernowitz. He graduated first
in his law-school class and in record time. Now he was ready to move
to Vienna. The uncle pulled all the strings to get him the best government job Austria could offer a young law-school graduate (especially
one who was Jewish rather than a son of the landed aristocracy): a
position in the counsel's office of the Ministry of Finance. Yes, Hemme
answered, he had decided to enter the civil service, but not in the
Ministry of Finance. He was entering the Department of Foreign
Trade.

If choosing Czernowitz rather than Vienna was the whim of a boy,
turning down the Ministry of Finance in favor of the Department of
Foreign Trade was both folly and deliberate manifesto. To be sure, the
Department of Foreign Trade was the oldest of Austrian government
agencies, having been founded in the mid-eighteenth century before
any of the "modern" nineteenth-century ministries. It still bore the
quaint name the eighteenth century had given it, being known as the
"Commercial Museum," since it had been founded originally to pro-
mote Austria's export trade through permanent and traveling trade

fairs. It was autonomous, though precariously balanced between Foreign Office and Ministry of Economics. It ran and controlled the consular service, independently of, and often in competition with, the diplomatic service. The Commercial Museum also operated two institutions of university status, the Oriental Academy and the Consular Academy; and soon after Hemme joined it, it started the first university-level business school in Austria, the present Vienna University of World Trade, originally called the "Export Academy." It was thus an interesting place and full of interesting people. But it had no prestige and offered no opportunities. It was a backwater. The Ministry of Finance, by contrast—and especially its counsel's office—practically controlled the top positions in Austria's government and in the top rungs of Austrian business, or at least those that were open to non-aristocrats since the other three "prestige" ministries, Agriculture, Interior, and Foreign, were by and large reserved for barons and counts. Those officials in the counsel's office who did not get to the top in Finance moved into the senior positions in the prime minister's office, into the top jobs in the "lesser" ministries, such as Commerce and Justice, or into the chairmanships of the major banks. But worse than folly, choosing Foreign Trade over Finance was a political manifesto. Finance was the official "liberal." Educated, tolerant, judicious, it was, so to speak, the "loyal opposition" in a heavily conservative Austrian establishment. But the Department of Foreign Trade was "subversive." Austria was protectionist; Foreign Trade was avowedly free-trade. Austria was primarily agricultural; Foreign Trade industrialized. Trade unions were, of course, frowned upon officially if not suppressed by the police. But Foreign Trade believed in them, encouraged the workers' university-level courses started by the unions and furnished teachers for them. It preached industrial safety, child labor laws, and a shorter work week. Worst of all, from its inception as a child of Austrian Enlightenment in the eighteenth century, the Department of Foreign Trade had had close though surreptitious ties to Austrian Freemasonry—and Freemasonry in Austria was always political rather than social or philanthropic, even when the Vienna Grand Lodge was headed by an emperor as it was in the eighteenth century. Freemasonry was anti-clerical if not anti-Catholic, opposed to big landholders and big landholdings, and above all, deeply anti-military. Whether this subversive element was tolerated within the bosom of government because Austria was tolerant or because it was disorganized, I leave to the historians. But it was only tolerated. To join

Foreign Trade, especially when one had the choice to go to Finance, was worse than being eccentric; it was a slap in everybody's face—and clearly meant as such.

Hemme, it soon transpired, did not even decide for Foreign Trade over Finance out of conviction, as my father did for instance, about ten years later, and as most of the officials in Foreign Trade had done. He went to Foreign Trade to break with his family once and for all, and in a way most calculated to hurt them. The solicitous uncle not only got Hemme the Finance Ministry job. He sent him a first-class railway ticket—at that time in the early 1890s only generals and bank directors traveled in such luxury. And since the young man had never been in a big city, the uncle went down to the railroad station at an ungodly morning hour to meet him after the long trip from the Eastern provinces. He was shocked by the young man's deformity—he had, of course, known about it but had not realized how bad it was. But he was pleased when the nephew asked how far it was to the uncle's apartment and then suggested that they might walk in the early sun of a lovely spring morning. That, thought the uncle, would give him a chance to tell all about the job he had lined up for him, the living arrangements—he had invited the young man to stay with him, but tactfully offered to put him up in a nearby hotel should he prefer to be alone—and the important and influential people to whom the brilliant nephew had already been introduced by name.

He was somewhat disconcerted that the young man did not say one word the whole way during a walk of over an hour. But finally when they came to the quiet residential street in which the uncle and aunt had their apartment, the nephew asked to be excused for a few minutes. "I thought to myself," recounted the uncle: "How nice. He is going to get some flowers for an aunt he has never seen and with whom he is going to live for some time." An hour went by—and no nephew—then two hours, three, four. Finally in mid-afternoon when the aunt was in hysterics and the uncle ready to call the police, a messenger arrived with a note: "I have accepted a position with the Commercial Museum; please hand bearer of this my trunk." That was the last the uncle and aunt ever heard or saw of Hemme. When, during the first years, these good people invited him—for New Year's, for holidays, or for a weekend—their letters were returned unopened. Nor did Hemme call on his brother or respond to his letters or calls.

This may be called eccentric; ultimately it degenerated into what can only be called contemptible. Some ten years after Hemme had moved to Vienna, Hemme's mother died and his father, the incompetent peddler, gave up. Uncle thereupon brought the father to Vienna and procured a sinecure for him, the monopoly on peddling in the building of the Ministry of Finance. Officially, of course, peddlers were strictly forbidden in government buildings. But actually there was always one who, by purchase or influence, was allowed the free run of the building where he peddled small items from ties to razor blades, ran errands for civil servants such as getting a corsage or theater tickets when the younger ones went out on a date, or a picnic hamper when the older ones took their families out for a Saturday afternoon, went down to the store to buy stationery against a 10 percent discount and, in general, supplied the large bureaucracy with small needs and amenities. This "in-house peddler" was by no means an Austrian specialty. He can be found in the English government departments of Trollope's novels of the 1850s, and in stories of Bismarck's Germany. He was still very much alive in the office buildings of New York in the 1930s and 1940s—each of which had a shoeshine "boy" with a secure turf of his own, a vendor of ties, shirts, notions, and so on; perhaps they still have them, for aught I know. The in-house peddler was considered a kind of upper servant and his social position was not very high. But it was higher, and certainly more secure, than that of a small shopkeeper. There was no competition and, above all, the in-house peddler did not "degrade" himself by running an "open store." So old man Schwarzwald was at least guaranteed a modest living and a job he could hold. Then Hemme moved to the Ministry of Finance. His first act was to order the old man thrown out; and when the father pleaded for an interview with his son, Hemme refused to see him.

Alfred Adler, Freud's erstwhile disciple and later rival, who knew Hemme well, considered this story a classical example of "overcompensation" for a debilitating physical deformity. He was convinced that Hemme blamed his parents, if only subconsciously, for being a cripple. But the behavior toward his family was by no means Hemme's only "eccentricity." He had chosen the Department of Foreign Trade over the Ministry of Finance. Yet he had no use for the department's basic policies and convictions. On the contrary. The department believed in free trade. Hemme did not believe in trade at all, and would permit it only if completely controlled. The department believed in industrialization, if only to find jobs for a rapidly growing population. Hemme was an agrarian; and he would have exposed babies to prevent population growth. The department had been created to help merchants. Hemme despised merchants and all middlemen, consider-ing them parasites. Altogether his ideal was the China of the Manda-rins; and the only thing he ever wrote was an encomium on Chinese bimetallism. For Hemme also totally repudiated the gold standard and the economic theory of his day. In retrospect it is clear that he was a Keynesian forty years before Keynes, believing in demand manage-ment where the received wisdom did not believe in political manage-ment of the economy at all, or only in management of supply; in government manipulation of currency, credit, and money where the received wisdom considered such manipulation to be both futile and self-defeating; and in creating consumer purchasing power as the cure for most economic ills. Only neither the theoretical tools nor the data for such revolutionary theories were available in 1890—and anyhow Hemme was a prophet who talked in tongues rather than a systematic thinker. But again in his economics there was the strange twist, the quirk that had showed in the way he treated his father. For Hemme had a hero in economics—and his name was Eugen Dühring.

If Dühring is known to economic history at all, it is as the target of Friedrich Engels's powerful attack on him, the *Anti-Dühring* which is one of the canonical books of Marxism. One need not be convinced of Engels's position after reading this book. But for everyone who has ever read the book, Dühring is finished—for everyone, that is, except Hemme Schwarzwald. Reading the book as a student in Czernowitz, he became a lifelong admirer of Dühring's. Until World War I he journeyed every year to Jena, the small German university where his hero is buried, to deposit a wreath on his grave. But what attracted Hemme was not the man's economics—Hemme had much too good a mind not to know Dühring to be thoroughly muddle-headed. What attracted him was that Dühring alone among all known nineteenth-century economists had been ardently, indeed violently, anti-Jewish.

Of course this was long before Hitler, when being anti-Jewish was not seen as necessarily having practical consequences. Also Hemme was by no means the only European Jew who turned anti-Jewish to resolve his own inner conflicts. Marx held very much the same opin-ions. And both Freud in Vienna and Henri Bergson in France—Hemme's contemporaries—could only come to terms with their own Jewish heritage by turning against it, Freud in *Moses and Monotheism,* one of his last major works. Hemme also—unlike Marx—had no per-sonal feelings about Jews. His wife was Jewish. His only truly close friend was the one among Viennese bankers—most of them Jewish in origin—who was a practicing orthodox Jew to the point where his son, a classmate of mine, was the only one among many Jews in the school who did not read, write, or recite on Saturdays; even the rabbi's child, who was also in our class, did so. And Hemme, of course, never pretended that he himself was of any but pure Jewish origin. Still, he considered the Jew the source of all evil in the modern world and the poisoner of society through his bourgeois, acquisitive, rationalist spirit. Only, being Jewish to him was not a matter of race or religion but of attitude and spirit. And he himself, he knew, had sloughed off the Jew long ago and was as completely un-Jewish as one could be.

Anyone less likely to succeed in the tight, cliquish, and jealous world of Austrian officialdom than Hemme Schwarzwald is hard to imagine. Abrasive, rude, tactless, obnoxious; from Czernowitz rather than from Vienna, and the Commercial Museum rather than the counsel's office in the Ministry of Finance; married to an equally aggressive Jewish outsider; without money or family connections but with loudly voiced opinions on all and every subject that would have been considered laughable had they not been so offensive; and with a tongue that made enemies out of most of the people he encountered—he sounds almost like the anti-hero in one of Sholem Aleichem's or Isaac Bashevis Singer's tragi-comic stories of Jewish failure.

Hemme also did everything in his power to trip himself up. There is, for instance, the story of his almost destroying his chance of becoming a privy councillor or "Hofrat," the highest title in the official hierarchy, roughly comparable to the German "Geheimrat." Long before Hemme got into a senior position Jews had become accepted, had indeed gradually taken over the top rungs of the Austrian civil service. Still, in the "prestige" ministries the fiction was maintained that the top positions were filled by Christians. In fact that meant that Jewish civil servants in these ministries, when promoted to "Hofrat," would quietly undergo what was quaintly but accurately called a "formality of baptism," either by being baptized as Catholics without publicity at some such hour as five in the morning by one of the Emperor's chaplains, or by having the old pastor of Vienna's main Lutheran church visit them quietly in their homes with the pastor's wife and son—also a pastor—as the sole very discreet witnesses.

Hemme was to be a "Hofrat" in the Ministry of Finance, which was, of course, a "prestige ministry." But when it was suggested to him that he undergo the "formality of baptism," he balked. "I don't mind the formality," he said; "to a Confucian like myself it's meaningless.

But I will not do it in order to stop being considered a Jew. I am not a Jew and have not been one for years, ever since I cleansed myself of my Jewish spirit as a student." The officials, knowing Hemme's reputation for being stubborn, gave up and withdrew the nomination. But this piqued the curiosity of the Emperor—then already in his seventies—who asked for a report; after all he, rather than the ministers, supposedly appointed a Hofrat. The old man sat down and wrote Hemme a personal letter—my father saw it before Hemme, deeply offended by it, burned it. "My dear Dr. Schwarzwald," it read, "I have never dictated the choice of religion to any of my subjects and respect all religious beliefs. But I took a coronation oath to maintain a Christian country and, old-fashioned as this may well seem to you, this means that I prefer the gentlemen who have official access to me and work with me to profess a Christian religion. I am a much older man than you—and you might yield, if only to old age." But Hemme said no. After six months of sulking on both sides he was promoted to Hofrat and the "formality of baptism" was quietly dropped for good. Whereupon Hemme lodged an official protest. For now Jews were to be promoted who were *Jews*; and he urged that they be required to slough off their Jewish spirit before getting to the top!

And yet Hemme achieved a great career, indeed one of the greatest careers in the annals of any civil service. "How could it happen?" I asked my father when I first became interested in the phenomenon of Hemme Schwarzwald, at a time when both Hemme and my father had already left government service and I was about fourteen or fifteen years old. "He was needed," was my father's reply. "Whenever there was a really nasty job, one that required absolute fearlessness and so complicated that no one really understood it, it went to Hemme —and he always delivered. He had the ability to see the central point and the willingness to face up to the unpalatable.

"Do you remember," my father continued after a few moments, "that we went to the Adriatic seashore one summer when you were a very small child, not quite five years old?" I nodded—I did have a dim memory of a beach and sand and of my building a sandcastle with my mother in a funny bathing suit. "But do you remember that we didn't stay long?" asked my father—of course I didn't. "Well," he continued, "that was the summer the war broke out. Your mother and I had long planned the trip. I had saved up vacations for years and was going to stay with you and Mother and your brother all summer. But no sooner had we settled on the beach than the Archduke Francis

Ferdinand, the heir to the Austrian throne, was assassinated in
Sarajevo. We were shocked, of course, but not too upset. What was one
more diplomatic crisis? My boss at the office agreed and wired me to
stay put. But Hemme immediately saw that this was not just another
crisis. He realized that the Austrian military would do everything it
could to push us into war—with the Archduke dead they were otherwise going to be out of power in no time. He understood that the
military's idea of a limited, nice, riskless war against Serbia was folly
and that the war would escalate. And he summoned me and a few
other senior civil servants—the known 'liberals' and pacifists—back to
Vienna to join him in a systematic though futile effort to stop the
military. We were to lobby our ministers, buttonhole politicians, try
to get to the old Emperor through the wall of equally old courtiers,
reach bishops, businessmen, labor leaders, and the press—even mobilize the old generals, then retired, who had been pushed out by the
Archduke's 'hawks.' Of course it was futile. Nobody believed Hemme's
warnings, not even I, or Hemme's other colleagues. Until the day of
mobilization we thought he saw burglars under the bed. But he was
right—he usually was. And he had the courage to throw himself into
a totally hopeless cause and fight for it."

Whatever the reason, Hemme did achieve a great career. He got
to be Hofrat earlier than any commoner in Austrian civil service history—indeed earlier than anyone but princes of the blood. For even
counts and "ordinary" princes usually had to wait until they were past
forty; commoners almost never got the title before they were fifty.
Hemme had it by the time he was thirty-five when he moved over to
his old enemy, the Ministry of Finance, as head of fiscal and monetary
policy. And when World War I broke out, he was almost immediately
promoted to "Sektionschef"—Undersecretary—and put in charge of
all monetary and financial affairs with almost dictatorial powers.

That Austria-Hungary, torn by explosive internal discontent and
bitter strife between a dozen discordant "nationalities"; with almost
no foreign exchange or gold reserves; with a narrow industrial base
and a backward agriculture; and with totally incompetent political
and military leadership—beginning with a senile Emperor—could
fight effectively for four long years before collapsing, was largely
Schwarzwald's doing. For it was he who kept Austria solvent for four
years of war. He financed the war without raising taxes, that is, by
voluntary bonds; he kept the value of the Austrian currency stable
both at home and abroad during these years; and he even—a supreme

joke on an enemy of the gold standard—managed to add to Austria's
gold reserves during the time.

But though Hemme was the great success, he ultimately became
the great failure. As soon as Austria was defeated, Hemme left the
Ministry of Finance and took over what now would be called the
Veteran's Administration—he was especially interested in the
rehabilitation of crippled veterans. Then the currency collapsed and
postwar inflation set in. And when the Austrian currency, the Krone,
had fallen to about one-thousandth of its prewar value, in the summer
of 1921, Hemme was recalled and put again in charge of finance—this
time with even broader powers. He was an absolute disaster. Maybe
nothing much could have been done; politically it was then considered
impossible to stop the printing press and thereby increase already
catastrophic unemployment. But Hemme's cure was to print ever
more money and to bolster "purchasing power"—he was, after all, a
pre-Keynesian. Six months later the Krone had fallen to one ten-
thousandth of its prewar value and Hemme was out of a job.

His successor failed just as badly, it should be said, even though
he was Austria's—and probably Europe's—greatest economist, Joseph
Schumpeter. Schumpeter, unlike Hemme, knew perfectly well what
needed to be done. But even though he was Minister of Finance rather
than a mere civil servant, he could not do it. Austrian politics was then
still dominated by the Socialists, who refused to sanction any cut in
public spending. And so Schumpeter also left a year later. He went
first to the University of Bonn in Germany and then, in 1929, to
Harvard. By the time he left in 1922, the Krone had depreciated to
the point where it took 75,000 Kronen to buy what 1 Krone had
bought in 1914—and still bought, by and large, in the spring of 1918.
Schumpeter quit, convinced that stopping inflation is a matter of political will rather than of economic theory or policy, but also deeply
skeptical about the ability of a free society to take the politically
necessary decisions. His pessimistic conclusion, reached in the classic
Capitalism, Socialism and Democracy (1946), which predicted that
democracy would ultimately be destroyed by its inability to forego or
to stop inflation because of the lack of political will—a prediction that
alas sounds far more prophetic today than it did in 1946—was squarely
based on his traumatic experience as Hemme's successor in charge of
Austrian finances in 1922. And indeed, after Schumpeter, Austria's
inflation was stopped by a reactionary politician-priest, Monsig-
nor Ignaz Seipel, who knew no economics but dared risk high un-

employment and sharply reduced welfare expenditures.

By that time Hemme had failed once more, and for the last time. From being Austria's financial czar, he went to the chairmanship of one of Vienna's largest banks, the Anglo-Austrian Bank. The bank had been headed by Hemme's only close friend—the orthodox Jewish banker mentioned earlier. That man had committed suicide, some said because he had brought the bank to the brink of ruin by betting on Schwarzwald to stop Austria's inflation. Hemme, so the story went, felt it his duty to redeem his friend's memory and to save his friend's bank. Probably no one could have done this. Vienna, after all, was grotesquely overbanked, since it housed the headquarters of twelve or fifteen banks that had served the old Austro-Hungarian Empire with its almost 60 million people, now shrunk to a small Alpine republic of barely 6 million. Within a few years one Viennese bank after the other folded until, by the early thirties, only two were left, and one of those only because it was taken over by the government after its collapse. But the Anglo-Austrian Bank was the first one of the old big solid banks to go—less than a year after Hemme had moved into the chief executive's job—and the shock was tremendous. As the name indicates, the bank had been founded by English capital and had major London banks among its leading shareholders. The Bank of England therefore took it over and guaranteed officers and employes, including Hemme, their retirement pensions, but moved in its own people to liquidate and salvage what could be salvaged. Hemme, not yet sixty, was retired and disappeared altogether from public view.

He did not turn bitter; and the only comment anybody ever heard from him was that if he did not deserve all the blame for the collapse of the Krone or of the Anglo-Austrian Bank, he also did not deserve all the praise for enabling Austria to fight a war it should never have provoked. But though outwardly serene, he was a beaten man. He stayed home, played chess or, if alone, worked on chess problems, played pool, listened to classical records—he had a huge collection of early records which he loved, scratchy and distorted though they were —and he talked less and less. But when he spoke his tongue was as tart, as cutting, as pungent as ever.

Where Hemme was all angles and bone, Genia was all roundness. She was not fat, although inclined toward plumpness; she was round. Where Hemme reminded me of an old snapping turtle, Genia always made me think of a red squirrel.

Genia was a little less than medium height. Her figure was unfortunate—a big head set on a short neck, and a big rump on very short legs which, of course, made her look even plumper than she was. And her features were coarse. But neither figure nor face would have mattered had Genia not been so conscious of both. She had extraordinarily attractive eyes, the eyes of a serious child, which registered every emotion—surprise, affection, hurt—and held the beholder like a magnet. But she did everything to distract from them by overusing the heaviest eye makeup. Similarly she had lovely hair, chestnut brown, with red lights in it and a soft natural wave. But since her student days she wore it cut very short so that it accentuated the coarseness of her features rather than softening them. She wore the most expensively wrong clothes I have ever seen—clothes designed for the long-limbed slender ballet dancer Genia so obviously wanted to be, clothes that only accentuated her bullneck, heavy hips, and stubby legs. It was altogether clear that Genia would have traded all her attainments and successes—and probably her intellectual brilliance—to be a conventional beauty.

And this got worse as she grew older. Hemme was ageless. In a photograph taken when he graduated from the University at age twenty—it stood on Genia's dresser and was the only photograph of Hemme ever taken—he already looked exactly the way he would forty-five years later in the very evening of his life. But Genia aged early and very badly. She had been a teetotaller all her life, yet her nose and cheeks began to show distended red-blue veins before she was forty. And the skin, never very healthy, turned sallow, sagged, and wrinkled. Genia overreacted—she always did; but the heavy application of unsubtle cosmetics to which she resorted only made her look older and even more haggard. So did her taking lovers—a whole slew of them for a few hectic years, all men much younger than she and all rather effeminate and futile. Every one of these petty affairs was loud, public, raucous. Every one of them ended in a violent row, after which Genia would find a wife for the young man, usually among her rather spinsterish secretaries and administrative assistants who could at least support the ex-lover.

All told Genia had the gift of making the most of her worst points. She had neither ear nor voice, lacked all musical taste, and could not carry the simplest tune. But she loved to lead a community sing and always chose the songs with the tritest words and most trivial tunes. She kept secret, however—or tried to—a genuine gift for drawing, especially children and animals. When asked once why she hid her drawings from all but old and close friends, she said, "In what I do well I have to excel"—and that was perhaps the key to Genia's personality.

For in what Genia did well she did indeed excel. And her achievements were, in many ways, greater than Hemme's, more impressive and certainly more imaginative.

Genia, like Hemme, came from the far end of Austrian Poland, close to the Russian border. But her father, a timber merchant, had been as rich as Hemme's father was poor. Genia, it was said, was his illegitimate child, the offspring of a casual affair with a Polish maid whom the merchant married only on his deathbed to legitimize a daughter who was almost grown up. What lent credence to this story was the slight Polish accent in Genia's Viennese German—a soft lilt quite different from the harsh guttural trace of Yiddish that characterized the Polish or Russian Jew in the Vienna of my childhood; Hemme still had it, for instance, after forty years among the Viennese. Genia surely spoke Polish as a child rather than Jewish-German or Yiddish. And her features too had a pronounced Slavic cast, especially the high cheekbones, the generous mouth, the snub nose, and arching full eyebrows. Whatever the truth of the story, Genia apparently was in her late teens when she found herself on her own with a substantial fortune. She immediately left for Zurich—at the turn of the century the only German-speaking university that freely admitted women students. A few years later—it must have been 1903 or 1904—Genia, with a doctorate in German literature, though still only in her early twenties, made straight for Vienna, determined to bring down the walls of the Austrian university system that were keeping out women.

Legally, there was no barrier to the entry of women students at any Austrian university. Any student, male or female, who had passed the university entrance examination, the so-called Matura, had the right to attend any Austrian university of his or her choice. In practice, women were excluded. The first barrier was the resistance of "good families" to university attendance by their daughters. When my mother, for instance—born a few years after Genia and therefore of college age when Genia appeared in Vienna—showed signs of wanting to prepare herself for the university entrance examination, her guardian (she was an orphan) hired the university professor of Sanskrit to give her private lessons. This way, he argued, she could not complain that she was prevented from learning, yet she also would not learn anything of use in the entrance examination. "You aren't going into teaching," said the guardian to my mother, "you don't have to. You are pretty and you have money. And you'd better not frighten off every eligible young man, which a university education most assuredly would do." Yet this was a certified, grade-A liberal, and indeed considered such a dangerous radical that his appointment as guardian for my grandfather's minor children was strongly opposed by the aunts and uncles.

Those young women who managed to overcome family opposition and pass the entrance examination were subjected to constant harassment. Vienna's leading pediatrician in the decades before the Nazis was a woman, my beloved "Aunt Trudy" (who was no relation at all but had been a close friend of my father's since their childhood). Aunt Trudy was the only European woman doctor of my time who became chief of staff and medical director of a major hospital. But she was also the only chief of staff of a major hospital in Austria who did not get the coveted title of "Professor" that otherwise came automatically to the "Primarius," or chief physician. She was admitted to medical school—there was no way of keeping her out. But she was told always to sit in the last row, never, never to ask a question or make a comment, and to dress during her entire years as a student and intern as a man—that is, in shirt, tie, jacket, and trousers, "so as to be less conspicuous." She was always addressed meticulously as "Mr. Bien" though it must have been hard to mistake the sex of the strikingly handsome Aunt Trudy. And her doctor's diploma was made out in the name of "*Herr* Doktor Gertrude Bien"! The inventor of these rules was not an anti-feminist and pettifogging bureaucrat; he was her own uncle, the university's distinguished professor of anatomy, who had encouraged Trudy from childhood to aim at medicine and who had himself coached her in mathematics and physics, the two subjects in the university entrance exam in which women were least prepared as a rule.

But the greatest barrier to access to university for women students was the absence of a school to prepare for the entrance examination. There were secondary schools for women. But they stopped two years short of the Matura, that is, at age sixteen; after that there were only private finishing schools teaching "culture" and deportment. And the girls' schools did not teach the subjects the university entrance examination featured. They taught modern languages, literature, music, and art, with a little botany thrown in. The university entrance examination required Latin, Greek, mathematics, and physics, with a little history thrown in. As long as the school system stayed the way it was, women were effectively debarred—and both an all-wise ministry and enlightened public opinion were determined to keep it that way.

Genia proposed to open a college-preparatory girls' school. She charged head-on—there never was any subtlety to anything she did. Like all successful activists, she lived the old Irish definition of a peace-lover: a person who is willing to listen after having knocked the opponent unconscious. She rented a big apartment in a fashionable district. Then came teachers. It took her a few days to find out that there were workers' education courses, taught by earnest young liberal civil servants. She enrolled, listened for a few sessions, then went and signed up the men who, in her opinion, did the best job teaching and did not talk down to their students. My father was the first teacher she hired; Hemme the second. "What in the world did Genia say to persuade you?" I once asked my father when he told me that story. "You know her better than to think she *persuaded* me," said my father; "she *told* me. I was sitting in my office one day when a 'Dr. Nussbaum' was announced, and in stomped a chunky young woman with a boy's haircut and loud Scotch tweeds, who said without a word of greeting: 'Would you rather teach Monday and Wednesday evenings or Tuesday and Thursday evenings?' I stammered that I had an engagement most Monday evenings, and Genia said, 'All right, Tuesday and Thursday from 6:30 to 9—dinner is included.' " That was Genia all right. I had seen her in action myself.

Still nobody quite believed in her plan. Where would the students come from? And how, given the resistance of their families, would they pay? Genia took out the first full-page advertisement ever seen in Viennese newspapers to announce courses for the university exam, "open to both sexes." In small print it added: "Don't worry about fees. They can be arranged." My mother, who saw the ad just after one of the odious Sanskrit lessons imposed upon her, took her paltry jewels, broke her piggybank, packed a few clothes, and went to the address given. She had her first class that evening and Genia went to see my mother's guardian. He refused to pay—but Genia had her fortune and could advance the money to my mother against her inheritance. And when a girl had no money coming to her, Genia could and did give her a scholarship.

There were, I was told, 300 applicants the first two weeks, including about 100 men. The men were told where other courses could be found and sent away. Of the 200 girls who applied, 50 or 60 were accepted. Two years later about thirty of them passed the university entrance exam, most with honors. And Genia celebrated by marrying Hemme. Another two years later she got her school approved by the ministry and accredited as the first genuine full-scale woman's Gymnasium in all Austria—several years before there was such an institution in Germany, by the way, and ten years or more before the French accepted it. A year later a coeducational primary school was added. By 1910 Genia had 600 students and moved into her own school—again shocking the Viennese by renting the top four floors of the city's first tall office building rather than putting up the traditional Austrian education barracks. It was the only school I have ever known that smelled neither of urine nor floor wax.

Genia had just turned thirty.

The Schwarzwald School continued to thrive until Hitler shut it down after taking over Austria. But Genia gradually withdrew from it. She did want to continue to teach—she needed to teach. She satisfied this need in characteristic direct fashion by reserving to herself the right to substitute for any teacher absent, sick, or on leave so that she got several hours each week.

And Genia was a powerful, compelling teacher. Of all those I have seen over many years, only Martha Graham, teaching a class of beginners in the modern dance, radiated similar power and held the students in the same iron grip. But Martha Graham, to the best of my knowledge, never taught anything except modern dance. Genia taught every subject and on every level, from the lowest, the first grade, to the highest, the thirteenth. I did not of course myself attend the Schwarzwald School as a high-school student; it was for girls only. But I spent as much time as possible there during my own high-school years, for I was for years constantly and hopelessly in love with Schwarzwald School girls—never fewer than three at a time and never the same ones for more than a few weeks, but hopelessly and constantly in love nonetheless. Yet whenever I heard that Genia was substitute-teaching, I forgot the girls of the moment and sneaked in to listen to her. She had the gift of holding twenty third-graders spellbound while drilling them in multiplication tables, without jokes, without telling a story, but by making demands and more demands on them. "You can do better," she'd say; or, "You need more work on the seven-times table"—and her commitment to perfection infected the eight year olds. But I also heard her read Aeschylus' *The Persians* with the eighteen year olds preparing for the university entrance examination. Genia would insist on their translating verbatim, the way they were going to be examined; then, fifteen minutes before the end of the hour, she would stop the drill and start reading in a quiet but hard voice the Greek lines of the final dialogue between the beaten, broken Xerxes and the Chorus with their terrible grief and despairing compassion. And suddenly everyone in the room would be seized by the holy awe of the Great Pan and sit transfixed.

But apart from these few hours of occasional teaching, Genia detached herself from the school that bore her name. She incorporated it as a foundation with its own board of trustees (of which my father was chairman until Hitler). She put in professional administrators. And she herself resigned every office—she never had taken a salary. She was not much interested in education as such, and most definitely not in running a school. She had to found a school because it was the one way to open up the universities to women. That objective achieved, the school held little further interest for her.

Instead, she first went in for all kinds of social actions to remedy or assuage specific problems. To help the young wives with small children whose husbands were in uniform during World War I, and to get them out of their anxious loneliness, Genia started, in 1915, "family camps"—and at one time, toward the end of the war, ran eight or ten of them in the summer. Then there were the Russian prisoners of war—hundreds of thousands of them, as Russian armies surrendered wholesale; they swamped every facility Austria had or could possibly organize. But there were also the Austrian middle-class and upper-class women with husbands at the front, who were left feeling sorry for themselves and with time heavy on their hands. So Genia beat down the strenuous opposition of the generals and organized a volunteer social service for Russian prisoners of war. Then came children's camps—the first known in Europe—especially for children whose fathers had been killed in the war. When the famine years hit, beginning in 1917, Genia organized co-op restaurants where a family, paying a modest sum, could get a simple but nourishing lunch; there were fifteen or twenty of those in Vienna at the worst famine time, in 1919. And early in 1923, when Austria had already stabilized its currency while Germany was writhing in the worst inflationary paroxysm, Genia expanded beyond Vienna to start a massive program of co-op restaurants in Berlin.

But after she had closed the Berlin restaurants when they had done what they were founded to do, Genia increasingly switched what might be called her "public" activities toward being an unpaid and unofficial but highly effective "ombudsman," battling red tape and bureaucratic callousness on behalf of individuals. Those were the years in which "papers" first became important—it is hard today to realize that before World War I nobody needed or had a passport, an identity card, a work permit, a driver's license, and often enough not even a birth certificate. All of a sudden a person without papers was a non-person; and all papers had to be in the right order. Vienna was full of people without papers: refugees from the Russian Revolution by the thousands, refugees from the Communist terror in neighboring Budapest and from the white "anti-terror" that followed it, prisoners of war who couldn't go home, returning soldiers without proper discharges, and many many more. The most hapless and helpless of these casualties of the onward march of twentieth-century civilization were apt to end up in Genia's tiny, cramped office in the Schwarzwald School, in which four telephones rang incessantly. Genia would listen, ask questions, and then have a secretary make a few phone calls to check out the supplicant's story. She had a good ear for phonies, frauds, and hard-luck stories. But she also knew that she had to be absolutely sure of her ground before interceding for anyone. "Everybody," she said, "is waiting for me to fall for the first con artist. That would be the end of my effectiveness." While the secretary checked, Genia would sit for a few minutes with her eyes closed, mapping out strategy. But then she would be in action and on the telephone.

Of course by that time she was known, at least by name, to most of the top people—and a good many of them, in government, in the professions, and in business, were by that time either married to one of "Genia's children" or had daughters or nieces who had been or were Schwarzwald students. But whether she knew a person or not, Genia always went straight to the top. She never called unless she knew exactly what action she wanted. "Never ask a person what to do; always tell him or her," was her motto. "If it's the wrong thing to do or if there is a better way, they'll come back and tell you. But if you don't tell them what to do, they won't do anything but make a study." Finally Genia never, never asked for help. She was doing the person a favor by telling him (or her) how to solve what surely must be a bothersome problem for authority.

"I think I have worked out the answer to a problem that, I know, must concern you," Genia would begin. "You are so busy, you may not be able to recall Mrs. So-and-So, the young war widow with her three sons of high-school age who are entitled to tuition remission, remember? Her husband was a Russian prisoner of war in one of those camps that got swept away in the Russian Revolution and the Civil War. Some of his fellow prisoners report that he died there; but of course there are no records. I know you've been put in a nasty position—if he were alive and back home the boys would be entitled to tuition refund as children of a war veteran had he signed the application; and if there were records attesting to his death, they'd be entitled to it as war orphans with the application signed by their mother. I know, though, what we do—order the refund pending investigation—I'll send Mrs. So-and-So over to your office with a letter for your signature. One of my assistants (you know her, she went to school with your niece Susy) will come with her so that you don't have to bother getting the letter to the right office. They'll be over in twenty minutes. I'm *so* glad I could help you out on this one."

Many years later, in the 1950s and 1960s, I found myself in a position where I could test Genia's methods. I was at that time professor of management at the Graduate School of New York University— and suddenly whole swarms of middle-aged ex-officers descended on me for advice and help. These were the years when the armed services chopped off officers who had signed up during World War II and had reached the age at which, unless promoted, they had to retire. They came to see me because they suffered from the delusion that they should get a doctor's degree and go into teaching. But what these middle-aged men needed was a job, and one that would quickly restore their confidence in their own ability and manhood. Most of them had never worked for anyone but the Army, Navy, or Air Force. Being tossed out as "unfit for further promotion" at age forty-five was a pretty rude shock.

I did exactly what Genia had done. I found out what each man had done and could do. I checked out every story. At first I was embarrassed to call up former superior officers or colleagues while the men were across the desk from me, but I soon learned that it had to be done. Then I thought through what job the man should be placed in, turned to the telephone, and called up. And I too always started out by saying: "I'm coming to you with something that will help *you*. I understand that you're having problems with your computer" (since everyone then had problems with the computer, this was a perfectly safe thing to say). "I know the man who can straighten them out—and

I think you can get him if you move fast. He's Commander So-and-So and he just finished putting in the computer for the Navy at Mare Island Navy Yard. Yes, I think he can be in your office in an hour—I'm *so* glad I can be of help to you." This hardly ever failed; and when it did, the person I called would invariably say, "Hey, wait a minute— he sounds exactly like the man my friend, the business manager at Columbia University, told me last night on the train they'd need there to straighten them out. Can you hold while I call him on the other line?"

Genia certainly did better than I, and with more difficult cases. But even I placed most of the men by following her method, and most of them on the first call. I also learned how much self-discipline Genia had exercised. The hardest thing of all, I found, was to be scrupulously honest about the applicant's qualifications and disqualifications. Yet it was absolutely crucial. It is not easy to say in a man's presence: "All he can do is set up a computer. Don't use him for anything else"; or: "He works very well if you tell him exactly what to do. But don't expect him to think or to use his imagination; he doesn't have any." Yet one has to say it, or one immediately loses all faith and credit. I also learned that once in a while I had to say to a man: "Yes, you should probably spend three years sitting on your backside to get an advanced degree; at least I cannot recommend you to a prospective employer."

But while Genia battled valiantly with the paper dragon who began to devour humanity with World War I, she also gradually moved out of the public sphere in which she had been active since she came to Vienna, as a young Ph.D., in the very early years of the century. Since she first married Hemme, Genia had had a "salon"; but it had been a sideline. In the 1920s it became the center of her life. And where earlier she had held her salon one or two afternoons a week during the winter months, she now ran it five days a week all the year round. For nine months it remained in the Schwarzwalds' home in Vienna. Then Genia bought an old resort hotel on a lake near Salzburg, rebuilt it to house a fair number of invited (but paying) guests, and could run her salon year-round.

Salons are virtually unknown in America. Even in England only two spring to mind immediately: the one Mrs. Thrale ran for the "Great Panjandrum," Dr. Samuel Johnson, in the late eighteenth century, with Boswell acting as the first war correspondent; and the salon that figures so frequently in the novels of Henry James (especially *The*

Awkward Age) that there must have been a real-life model to be written up. Salons were equally rare in the northern European countries, especially the German-speaking ones. They have only flourished in the country of their origin, France. Genia's was thus an exception. And it flourished precisely because Genia knew that a salon is not private but public. It flourished because Genia understood that a salon is performing art, just like opera and ballet, the other performing arts of the bourgeois, post-Renaissance age. She also knew, I am convinced, that the salon is the only performing art of the bourgeois age that does not serve the male ego and male vanity and does not manipulate women for the sake of male gratification—as do both opera and ballet. Salons are run, managed, molded by women, serve to enhance women and put them in control. Indeed the salon, it seems to me, served the role the Mysteries served in antiquity, where in otherwise male-dominated cultures the Priestess of the Eleusinian or the Minoan Mysteries—anonymous, behind the scenes, and seemingly offstage—controlled the souls while mere men controlled bodies and minds. Until the modern dance emerged in the opening years of this century, the salon was the only performing art that served women and that women controlled.

Genia knew what even so astute an observer as Henry James only glimpsed: a salon means work—and the more work, the more it looks spontaneous, free-flowing, improvised. This is something our generation has learned, of course. We know that the "spontaneous" movie needs the most work and the best-prepared scenario, precisely because it does not have a script. We know that an "unrehearsed" radio or television program has to be thought through and prepared twice as carefully as the scripted, staged, rehearsed one. We have learned the hard way the difference between the "improvised" event, with its discipline behind the scenes, and the disaster of the unprepared "bull session." Genia's salon was unrehearsed, spontaneous, free-form, flexible, and fast. It must have involved an unbelievable amount of hard work to make it into such a successful public performance.

It was a performance all the way, beginning with the stage setting. The Schwarzwalds lived in a lower-middle-class district of Vienna which, as late as 1830, had still been semi-rural although it was quite close to the Inner City. But then, in the middle of the century, it became built up with six- to eight-story apartment buildings housing respectable but humble folk—small shopkeepers, customs inspectors, piano teachers, bank clerks, dental technicians, and the like. One went

into an undistinguished almost grimy building. But instead of climbing
up one of the four or six staircases that led from a cold, drafty, dank
foyer, one went out again into a back court. And there suddenly stood
a small eighteenth-century villa, the summer house of a lesser noble
or wealthy merchant built in the days of Haydn and Mozart out of the
eighteenth century's favorite yellow sandstone and still set off by a
high ornamental iron fence.

When the gate was opened, the caller entered a big hall, totally
empty, from which a wide staircase led upstairs. At the foot of the
stairs stood Martha, the Schwarzwalds' cook, adopted daughter, and
general-manager-downstairs. Martha was petite and pretty, with a
cheerful milkmaid face and raven-black hair. She kissed everyone
except bashful adolescent boys, who had to kiss her first before they
got a kiss. She took hats and coats, explaining who was already there
and who was still expected. Then the caller went up about ten steps
to a mezzanine, where the staircase split into two curved courses that
reunited at the top. And there stood Mieze, the Schwarzwalds' other
maid, other adopted daughter, and general-manager-upstairs. Mieze
—a Schwarzwald affectation for the common Austrian "Mitzi" or little
Mary—was as tall as Martha was petite, and as blond as Martha was
dark. But where Martha was pretty, Mieze was beautiful. Both women
had been with the Schwarzwalds for years—I think well before World
War I. But both, fifteen years later, still looked like picture-postcard
peasant girls. Mieze also kissed everybody, including the adolescent
boys, who never resisted; for she had the widely set eyes that folklore
believes indicates extreme sensuousness in a woman, and that certainly make a woman's kisses acceptable to even the most bashful
fourteen-year-old male. Mieze always said something nice—"Caroline, you look stunning," she would say to my mother; "you ought to
wear that shawl more often." Or, to me, "Peter, you like Couperin,
don't you? Helge Roswaenge, the tenor, is here today. He'll sing a little
later and I've asked him to choose a few Couperin songs for you."
Then one went up another fifteen steps to the top—and there stood
Annette.

If Martha was pretty and Mieze beautiful, Annette was truly gor-
geous. Tall, willowy, with gray gold-flecked eyes, she was also the most
elegant and best-dressed woman I have seen in my life. Where Martha
was friendly and Mieze come-on-ish, Annette was as cool as freshly
starched lime green linen. She didn't kiss anyone, but shook hands in
a firm, almost masculine handshake. In a lovely, flutelike voice she

would tell you whether Hemme was available playing pool, when he could and should be interrupted, or whether he was playing chess, in which case one had to wait until he stopped. She told you what was going on and who was sitting in the "performer's corner" close to Genia. Then, all too soon, she took the caller in and showed him or her to a seat.

All too soon—for I certainly would have liked to linger. Annette was not only beautiful to look at and a joy to listen to. She was fabulously interesting. She was the daughter of a lieutenant-field marshal, the highest rank anyone but an Imperial prince could reach in the old Austrian Army in peacetime. Like my mother, she had answered Genia's advertisement the first day it appeared and had been a student in Genia's first class. That was not so surprising—there were many daughters of high military officers among "Genia's children," for the military in old Austria were not "aristocracy" nor even "upper-class." They were very much like Army and Navy officers in the England of Jane Austen's day (for instance, the naval captains in *Persuasion*)—near-gentlemen and on the border of the lower middle class. To be sure, once an officer advanced beyond major-general, he got a "von" to put in front of his name. But this was not "aristocracy," only what the Viennese called "triviality" or *"Bagatell."* It ranked close to the title of "Baron" which the coffeehouse waiter bestowed on any male guest in long pants who left a larger-than-average tip (for anything less one got only an honorary doctorate). And the same "von" the lieutenant-general shared with any civil servant who managed to stay in office for ten years after getting the "Hofrat" title, and with any banker who reached retirement age without having been bankrupt more than once.

The true aristocracy had stopped serving in the Army when commoners—and especially Jews—first got commissions, around 1850; it did not suit a count or prince to have to salute a commoner or to say "At your command" to a Jew. And altogether the Army had no money. What they did have they spent on the careers of their sons, so that the daughters of military officers had a hard time finding husbands and were often reduced to earning their living as grammar-school teachers or piano teachers. To most Americans the plot of Richard Strauss's last successful opera, *Arabella* (written in 1930 or 1932) is just a bedroom farce. But to an Austrian of the older generation who could remember "prewar," the plot in which an Austrian Army officer forces his younger daughter to disguise herself as a boy so that the older one has a chance of attracting the rich husband she has to get, was harsh realism. For the daughters of the military the Schwarzwald School, which offered to get them out of being schoolteacher-spinsters and at least into professional work, was therefore highly attractive—and to their parents as well.

So it was not too unusual that Annette should be the daughter of a lieutenant-field marshal. But her subsequent career was highly unusual. For when she had passed her university entrance examination, Annette did not go into medicine or literature, social work or education, as most of the Schwarzwald graduates did. She was the first woman in Austria to go into economics. That was the time—around 1906—when the Austrian School of Economics dominated worldwide. The great men of the school—Wieser, Boehm-Bawerk, and Philipovich—were still alive and teaching. And the students were brilliant; Ludwig von Mises was Annette's classmate. But Annette by common consent was the superstar, equally gifted in theory and in mathematical analysis. Even Mises, who was no feminist and did not suffer from undue modesty, admitted her superiority. Years later in the 1950s when Mises was old and very famous, he and I were colleagues at New York University. We did not see much of each other—Mises considered me a renegade from the true economic faith (with good reason). But one day going down in the elevator together, he turned to me and said: "You knew Annette, didn't you? If she'd been a man and encouraged to go on, she would have been the greatest economist since Ricardo."

Only she wasn't a man and wasn't encouraged. She stayed on as a research assistant, but an academic appointment was unthinkable for a woman. At least at the Commercial Museum and the monetary and financial research department of the Ministry of Finance there were research projects, and in both there were civil servants who were willing to employ women, especially if they did not cost much. And Genia needed an administrator for her growing school—and so Annette grew to be her closest associate as well as her closest friend. When World War I started and Hemme took over the country's financial and monetary management, Annette moved in as his number two. By all accounts she did a brilliant job, especially in smoothing over Hemme's very rough edges, in making this gruff, abrasive man effective, and in carrying out his ideas. And when Genia started her social-action programs, Annette increasingly took over their execution as well.

Then Annette and Hemme became lovers.

When the war was over, Annette was offered two very big jobs. One was as head of research at the newly founded Austrian National Bank—the first woman ever to be offered such a job, and indeed the only woman to be offered such a position anywhere until two students of mine got similar jobs in the 1950s, in the Federal Reserve Bank of New York and the Federal Reserve Bank of the Philippines respectively. The other offer was as financial vice president in one of the major industrial groups of Central Europe, with plants mostly in Czechoslovakia but headquarters in Vienna. And Hemme offered to divorce Genia and to marry Annette. Annette turned down all three offers. She turned down the jobs because she decided that her life was with Hemme. And she turned down Hemme's offer of marriage because she would not humiliate Genia—even though Genia had agreed to the divorce and had, indeed, brought Hemme's offer of marriage to Annette. She moved in with Hemme, taking a bedroom next to his in one wing of the Schwarzwalds' top floor; but she remained Genia's closest friend and the administrator of all Schwarzwald enterprises, from the school to the childrens' camps and the summer resort on the lake.

That was enough to make her interesting, especially to a teenager. But Annette was also known to be bisexual. In addition to the bedroom next to Hemme's, she had an apartment a few streets away which she shared with a well-known woman artist. Small wonder that a fourteen-year-old boy would have liked to linger with so fascinating a person, and one so very good to look at.

But Annette always led the caller firmly into the salon and assigned him or her to a seat, usually at the back at first.

Historically, there have been two kinds of salon. The original one, invented by the "Précieuses," the bluestockings of the Paris of Louis XIV, was managed by women and had women as the actors and conversationalists. This was still the salon in which Henry James apparently spent a good deal of time in the London of 1880 and 1890. The other kind—invented, it seems, by Voltaire's mistress in their retreat in Ferney, on Lake Geneva—has a woman-manager "featuring" a male star, the type of salon Mrs. Thrale ran to make Dr. Johnson roar, and that Anatole France's mistress still ran for him in the early 1920s.

Genia's salon was neither. Indeed it was very puzzling and did not make sense to me until many years later, I encountered the radio or TV talk show, "Meet the Press" or "The Johnny Carson Show." Of course there was no TV camera in Genia's living room. But if Genia asked one of her guests to come and sit next to her in the corner of the settee, the guest knew that he or she was "on camera." Genia was the mistress of ceremonies, and the best I have ever seen. She never humiliated a guest, always brought out the best he or she had to offer, always was kind and considerate. But she also knew how to get rid of a guest who did not shine.

Any guest who did perform was supported by a large, admirably trained cast. There was a "chorus" whose job it was to ask questions, to listen, and to provide light background entertainment. Like any chorus, it consisted mostly of people who had failed to make it in "the big time." There was, for instance, the automotive engineer who had, around 1910, made the great automotive invention—I believe it was the self-starter. But when he was ready to patent it, he found that some dastardly American had gotten there first. Thereupon he became a professional frustrated genius. Then there was the great student of Nordic languages, who was engaged in writing a book that was going to revolutionize Icelandic grammar. Only he was so busy playing chess with Hemme and devising chess problems that he never got around to the book. And there were the three children of an Austrian general —two boys and a very handsome girl—who had become extreme left-wingers and fancied themselves as writers, but could barely hold on to minor jobs as reporters.

There was a solid supporting cast that could always be depended upon to ask the right questions, encourage, and carry a conversation. It consisted of old-time liberals, mostly university professors and their wives of the prewar "progressive" persuasion. First among these were Ludwig Rademacher and his wife Lilly—Germans rather than Austrians, and Protestants, descended from generations of German professors and Protestant pastors. Ludwig Rademacher, who held one of the two chairs of classical philology at the University of Vienna, was the essence of uprightness. He held fast to the basic decencies of pre-Bismarck Germany, had indeed moved to Austria largely because he so deeply despised the Germany of the Kaiser. He was already of retirement age when Hitler came to Vienna, but he resisted the Nazis vigorously and survived imprisonment and concentration camp. In his seventies and eighties, after World War II, he rebuilt the Austrian Academy of Science and the University of Vienna.

Then there were the "stars." But these were rarely "celebrities." For Genia knew what the best TV or radio talk show producer knows:

that you are not on a talk show because you are a celebrity; you are
a celebrity because you are on a talk show. Thus Thomas Mann, whom
I once encountered in Genia's salon—I must have been around sixteen
—was a flop. He was still a few years away from the Nobel Prize but
already The Great Writer. He read out one of his stories—"Disorder
and Early Sorrow." We had, of course, all read it, and most of us
younger ones heartily disliked it as being avuncular and condescend-
ing to young people and full of what now would be called "pop psychology." This miffed Dr. Mann. But worse was yet to come. For the
real "star" of the evening was seated in the performers' corner next
to Genia—a girl of twenty or so who was a graduate of the Schwarzwald School and had spent a year as an exchange student in a well-
known Eastern American women's college. Of course we all thought
that we knew a good deal about American education. But the young
woman's report of courting and mating, Princeton House parties, organized necking, dating, pinning, and well-planned sleeping around,
was news to us. Sex in Vienna was strictly free enterprise. When the
girl had finished telling us her experiences, Genia turned to Dr. Mann
and asked him for his comment. He delivered the conventional educated European male's speech on "American conformism." "Well, I
don't know," said Genia; "after all, I've seen quite a few young women
in their teens. And perhaps the way the Americans do it by organizing
the inevitable causes less stress and anguish at that age than our free-
for-all here, in which there are no rules." Dr. Mann soon took his
departure and did not come back.

   Anybody in the room was exposed to becoming a "star" in Genia's
salon. I myself probably sat in the "performers' corner" for the first
time when I was fourteen or fifteen, though that was rather young
even to be admitted to the salon, I realize. My turn took just a few
minutes—I think I had asked a question following somebody's comment when Genia called to me: "I'm having a little trouble hearing
you. Why don't you sit next to me and tell us what you think?"—and
there I was. But the occasion I remember best came a few years later
when I was in my last high-school year and also my last year of residence in Vienna. I had arrived late. I apologized and explained that
I had been detained looking up stuff in the library for the thesis one
had to write for the university entrance examination in those years.
"What is this thesis about?" Genia asked. She was always interested.
"I'm doing a study of the impact the Panama Canal has had on world
trade. It's only been open ten years and no one has done any work on

it yet," I answered. "That sounds interesting," said Genia. "Do sit next to me and tell us about it." Then she added, raising her voice, "Hemme and Annette, why don't you come in and listen to Peter Drucker? What he's working on might interest you."

When I had finished, Hemme barked out one of the most useful lessons of my life: "In dealing with statistics, remember: never trust them. One either knows the man who invented them or one doesn't —and in either case they're suspect. I ought to know. I was in charge of Austria's export statistics for twelve years." And Annette, in her flutelike voice, perhaps seeing the surprised look on my face, added: "You say no one has published anything on the subject?" I nodded. "Then make sure you publish your paper—here are the names of some of the journals you might send it to."

But in addition to the amateurs and guests among the stars, there were also always a few "fixed stars"—people around whom the salon revolved whenever they were in Vienna or at Genia's resort on the lake. Two stand out particularly in my memory: Count Hellmuth Moltke-Kreisau and Dorothy Thompson.

Hellmuth Moltke, great grandson of Prussia's greatest military hero, was to become the conscience of the German resistance to the Nazis, the center of the attempt to kill Hitler in 1944, and one of the last victims of Nazi terror. Dorothy Thompson was to become the influential American columnist of the thirties and forties. But these fates were well into the future when both were "fixed stars" in Genia's salon. Both—and this is what Genia was always looking for in her stars —combined intellectual incandescence, independence of mind, and radiant beauty. Both were tall, well made, with big leonine heads— Moltke dark, Dorothy Thompson a glowing blonde—with the power, the charm, the magnetism of the born winner and leader. And they embodied—as did Martha, Mieze, and Annette, and indeed everyone in the Schwarzwalds' permanent retinue—what Hemme and Genia believed in and knew that they themselves completely lacked: a physical radiance that goes beyond being physical.

Hemme had enemies galore, but nobody ever considered him a lightweight. Genia, on the other hand, was constantly being underrated. Of course she was a "busybody"—she would have been the first to admit it. She was tactless, coarse, aggressive, and often stepped over the fine line that separates being funny from being comic.

Genia was insensitive. In fact her insensitivity was a source of great strength, for it made her impervious to ridicule and criticism.

But it could lead her into embarrassing blunders, embarrassing, that is, to everyone but herself. Genia was never embarrassed.

The occasion I still remember, because it shamed me so dreadfully, was Genia's *"Greisenhilfe"* which means literally "Help for the Ancients"—the German word *"Greis"* denoting extreme infirmity of old age. The old people in those post-World War I years of hunger and inflation were indeed badly in need of help; and they were totally neglected by all existing programs, public and private. To organize help for them was a good idea. But when Genia announced her program, she could not get any "Ancients" to come forward and register. We have since learned that older people who have all their lives supported themselves shun charity; and, of course, the word *"Greis,"* while making for a catchy title, did not much encourage applicants either. Whereupon Genia had the brilliant idea of mobilizing the middle-class pre-teens of Vienna to find the "Ancients" in need and to bring their names to the headquarters of the crusade. Older highschool students, led of course by the girls from the Schwarzwald School, would then visit them in their homes, find out what help was needed, and largely provide it, in the form of simple homemaker services for example. To get the twelve and thirteen year olds fired up, Genia started a weekly newsletter and announced prizes for whoever could bring in the most "Ancients in need." This was better than collecting football cards or film stars—the crazes of that time. So we thirteen year olds rushed out to hunt down "Ancients in need."

The only ones I could find were three sisters, the daughters of a long-dead Army officer whose wife, also dead, had been a fellow music student of my grandmother's—which of course meant that the three ladies were my mother's age rather than "Ancients." One of the three was my piano teacher, the other two taught junior high school. I badgered them until they agreed to put their names on my sheet, when I promptly got "honorable mention" in the campaign newsletter. But four weeks later we were all invited to the wedding of one of the three, and even an inexperienced thirteen year old could not fail to notice that the wedding took place at the last possible moment. A healthy baby boy was born to my "Ancient" only a few days afterwards. Since this was fairly typical of the events of the *"Greisenhilfe,"* the whole campaign, though started with a good and needed idea, had collapsed into ridicule and red faces all round within a few weeks.

But Genia's reaction was simply: "What needs to be done next?" Her detractors criticized her above all for being "unprincipled,"

which she was. She started a school at a time of tremendous educational ferment, the time of John Dewey and Maria Montessori. But she
had no educational theories and no use for them. She believed in good
teaching and insisted on it, yet a school to her was a means to gain a
little equality for women. I doubt that she ·considered curriculum
terribly important. If the university entrance examination had demanded basket weaving and astrology, Genia would have taught both
and taught them well. Similarly, she had no social or political "isms,"
although she must have been exposed to plenty of them as a student
at Zurich, then the center of all kinds of doctrines from Marxism and
anarchism to theosophy and Zionism. She was interested in specific
needs and in results.

Around 1932 or so, long after Genia had left off the recognized
kind of "social action," she was drawn into public debate and the kind
of publicity she detested and usually managed to avoid. The most
powerful Central European industrialist—head of a Czech conglomer-
ate who lived in Vienna—and the labor unions of his textile plants
were on a collision course. The industrialist saw an opportunity to
destroy the unions he loathed: there was a depression; the unions were
weak; and industry had enough inventory to last out a long strike. The
unions in turn felt the need to assert their militancy, despite their
weak position. These unions of German-speaking workers in Czechoslovakia, which were led by old-time Social Democrats, were rapidly
being undermined by the Nazis, whose main argument was that the
largely Jewish Socialist leaders were selling out the workers to the
largely Jewish bosses, so the unions needed a strike, or felt they did.

When Genia heard this, she was outraged. To throw 30,000 men
out of work for the sake of pride, vanity, and power was ultimate
irresponsibility to her. She thought through what the settlement
should be, then went and "told" both sides. And she mobilized so
much support among businessmen, labor leaders, newspapermen, and
politicians that the two sides had to sit down at the bargaining table
and sign on Genia's dotted line.

She got no thanks. On the contrary, each side blamed her for
forcing it to "betray our principles." A young newspaperman married
to one of "Genia's children" went to interview her and asked her how
she felt about forcing people to abandon their principles. "I have no
use for principles," snapped Genia, "which demand human sacrifice."
This is surely dangerous heresy in a century of absolutes—educational,
psychological, ecological, economic, political, or racial—all of which

glory in human sacrifice for the sake of a utopian future or of that chimera "the good of the greatest number." But however damnable a heresy, Genia's creed was hardly that of a lightweight.

Why did we all feel there was something uncanny about Hemme and Genia? They were interesting people, perhaps larger than life, somewhat quirky, and often petty, yet not in any way mysterious. There was nothing at all other-worldly about them; they were of the earth earthy. Not the slightest whiff of brimstone clung to them. Yet everyone who came close to them—even those who adored Hemme and Genia and would not listen to criticism or ridicule of them—felt a sense of discomfort, of something awry, around the two. It wasn't just that Hemme and Genia were a stage production. No, there was that something that can only be called "not quite canny." It was this feel of a hidden and somewhat sinister dimension that told me at an early age they would have to be characters in any novel that I might write, but also that they would forever elude me.

It was not until many years later that I found the answer, and then in a dream. As a small boy, I read over and over again a book by the Swedish writer Selma Lagerloef called *Nils Holgersson*. It is a charming and gripping children's adventure story which is also, at the same time, so good a history and geography of Sweden that to this day I feel I know the country—which I have rarely been to and never for very long—better than almost any other. One episode in that book fascinated me in particular: a Swedish version of the old myth of Atlantis, the sunken continent. A shipwrecked sailor, in this tale, finds himself in a sunken city at the bottom of the sea. The city was drowned because of the pride, arrogance, and greed of its merchant-inhabitants. And the citizens were punished by not being allowed the rest of the dead. Bells ring on Sundays and they go to their devotions in sumptuous churches, only to forget the Lord the remaining six days of the week, in which they feverishly cheat each other, trading nonexistent merchandise. They wear old-fashioned rich clothes and try to outdo each other in pomp and finery. But they and their city are dead. The young sailor from the world of the living is greatly drawn to them. Yet he also knows that he must not be discovered or else he will be turned into one of these living dead and never allowed to return to earth and sunshine, to love, life, and death.

For years after I had read this tale—probably around the age of ten—I dreamed I was that sailor. I was fascinated by the strange city, but terrified lest anyone would notice me and my different clothes and raise the hue and cry. Yet I was also desperately anxious to see what the inhabitants looked like; and when I thought no one was looking I would peer under their broad-brimmed hats and wide bonnets to see their faces. Then some of them would turn and look hard at me—and I would wake up as from a nightmare. As I grew older the dream became less and less frequent; finally, after I had moved to the United States, it ceased altogether. But about ten years later it recurred once more. Those were the months after the end of World War II when one heard of all the people who had died; but also when the survivors, here and there, crawled out of the rubble. And that last time on which my "Atlantis dream" recurred, it ended differently. The dream was exactly the same. But at its end, in the interval between sleeping and waking, I suddenly knew whose faces were under the broad-brimmed hats and wide bonnets—those of Hemme and Genia.

All of Vienna, indeed all of Europe in those interwar years, was obsessed with "prewar." But Hemme and Genia succeeded in restoring it in their lives; their salon was Atlantis, the sunken city of days gone by, dead but unable to die. That was their attraction; it also made them uncanny and, indeed, frightening.

Few people in the Vienna of the twenties and thirties felt much nostalgia for the old Austro-Hungarian monarchy. Most agreed with Robert Musil, the Austrian writer whose book *The Man Without Qualities*—almost forgotten today, but a literary sensation in the early thirties—called prewar Austria "Kakania." While "Kakania" derived from the official initials of the old Austria-Hungary, "K & K" (Kaiserlich & Koeniglich, or Imperial and Royal), "kaka" is also Austrian babytalk for human feces. "Kakania" meant "Shitland." Yet "prewar" in "Kakania" was the measure of all things.

The Vienna Opera, for instance, was in the early twenties led and conducted by two great musicians, Bruno Walter and Richard Strauss. Both were forced out. They did not conduct the way Mahler had conducted "prewar." Their successors were, at best, mediocre but they knew Mahler's mannerisms if little else. Mahler's singers got old a few years later. A young Danish tenor, Helge Roswaenge, a friend of the Schwarzwalds, got rave reviews whenever he appeared as a guest in *Lohengrin* or *Die Meistersinger.* But he did not get a contract; his tempi were just a little bit different from "prewar." To appease the German Nationalists, on whose support in Parliament a minority Conservative government depended, it was announced that no more Jews would be appointed to full professorships at the University of Vienna. But a weak and in fact incompetent Jewish candidate was then immediately given a full professorship. He had never published anything and was a wretched teacher, but his father had held the chair with distinction "prewar"—and the son owned the complete set of his father's lecture notes. "This way, we'll get the prewar scholarship," said the minister—himself well known for his anti-Semitism—when he was being heckled in Parliament. A large new delicatessen store opened up not far from where we lived. It carried the same brands of wine, preserves, cheese, or sausage as the far more expensive stores "downtown"; and it was an hour closer. Moreover the new store delivered free. For their daily needs the ladies of our neighborhood patronized this store and were well satisfied with it. But when they had "company," the ladies went downtown. "You are buying exactly the same brands, spend more hours doing it, and pay more," their husbands would argue. "But downtown you can be sure of prewar quality," was the answer. When my mother took me to the big "prewar" men's store opposite St. Stephen's Cathedral to buy my one "good" suit, the clerk would always, at the end, lean over the counter and whisper: "I think I have a few suits of prewar quality. I save them specially for our good prewar customers like you." And he would trot out the same clothes he had already shown us, but with a 50 percent higher price tag.

The obsession with "prewar" was not confined to trivia nor to Austria. The 1920s were the years when economic and social statistics first flourished, and the reason for their popularity was that they made it possible to compare the present with the "prewar" standard— whether in respect to the potato harvest ("It's almost back to 'prewar' "), to the number of crimes of violence (alas, for a long time well below the prewar norm in most countries until the rise of Nazism remedied this defect), or the tons of mail carried by the railroads. "Prewar" was like a miasmic smog pervading everything, paralyzing everybody, stifling all thought and imagination. The obsession with "prewar" explains in large measure the attraction Nazism exerted. I was the first, I believe, to point out—in 1939 in *The End of Economic Man*—that there was little resistance to the Nazis anywhere until a country had first been taken over by them. Since then the same phenomenon has been pointed out by a good number of writers, including William Shirer in *Berlin Diary* (1941) and *The Rise and Fall of the Third Reich* (1960), or—most recently—by John Lukacs in his excellent book, *The Last European War* (1976). Nazism was loathsome; but it was, in Charles Lindbergh's phrase, "The Wave of the Future" when everything else was trying to be "The Wave of the Past."

As a youngster, I knew intuitively that I had to escape "prewar." This was, I am convinced, the reason why I knew very early that I would leave Vienna as soon as I could. In the rest of Europe, though, "prewar" was almost as stifling, almost as pervasive a miasmic smog. It was not until I came to the United States in 1937 that I escaped it. There was a "pre" syndrome here too at that time—the period "before the Depression" was norm and yardstick. But primarily in economic events—steel production, employment or stock prices. Otherwise, the America of the New Deal looked ahead. Franklin D. Roosevelt's great contribution was his ability to prevent the "pre-Depression" syndrome from capturing and paralyzing the American imagination as "prewar" had captured and paralyzed Europe's will and vision. This also explains, I think, why my Atlantis dream stopped as soon as I had moved across the Atlantic.

Of course, "prewar" was unobtainable by definition. No one and nothing ever reached it—not even the potato harvest. No one, that is, except Hemme and Genia. What they established, and what Genia's salon tried to live day by day, was naïve fiction. It was the vision of the Liberal Age and of the Cultured City which must have existed in the poor, cribbed Polish-Jewish small towns in which they grew up— towns that looked to the "West" as represented by tales of Vienna, Berlin and Paris, as earthly paradise. There were no sordid economic realities in this version of "prewar"—and indeed businessmen were conspicuous by their total absence in Genia's salon. There Jews and Gentiles met and lived with each other in complete friendship and harmony—as indeed they did in Genia's salon. There were no club feet in the "prewar" and no aging, dumpy women with sagging skins; only the radiance of intellect and body of Genia's "fixed stars"—of an Annette, of a Helmut Moltke, of a Dorothy Thompson.

When Hitler marched into Austria in the winter of 1938 and forever shattered "prewar," Genia was in a hospital in Copenhagen recovering from radical mastectomy. A few weeks earlier she had detected an ominous lump in her breast. She did not want anyone in Vienna to know about it, arranged for a lecture in Copenhagen, and then went to the hospital there for surgery. She never returned to Vienna, but went straight to Zurich. There she was soon joined by

Hemme. He had been retired fifteen years and was almost totally senile. But he was on the Nazi "most wanted" list. A former colleague and protegé whom Hemme had rescued years earlier from a serious bribery indictment—the man later became one of the worst Nazi butchers in Rumania—had denounced him as "dangerous." But Annette got him out on the passport of her own father, the lieutenant-field marshal who had died only a few weeks earlier.

Within the year both were dead.

Miss Elsa and
Miss Sophy

I have observed a good many first-rate teachers in action, and even a few great ones. I myself was taught only by two classroom teachers I would consider first-rate: Miss Elsa and Miss Sophy, both of whom I encountered in fourth grade. And they were not just good, they were outstanding. Yet they failed to teach me what both they and I knew I needed to learn.

Miss Elsa, the principal of the school, was our home-room teacher, with whom we worked four hours every day six days a week—for we had school on Saturday, even though we were dismissed earlier. When the school year started, in September, Miss Elsa told us that we would have two to three weeks of quizzes and tests to see how much we knew. This sounded frightening but turned out to be fun. For Miss Elsa made us grade ourselves or grade each other. At the end of three weeks, she had an individual conference with each of us. "Sit down next to me," she would say, "and tell me what you think you do well." I told her. "And now," she said, "tell me what you do badly." "Yes," she said, "you are right, you read well. In fact reading rats like you don't need work on reading, and I haven't scheduled any for you. You keep on reading what you want to read. Only, Peter, make sure that you have good light and don't strain your eyes. You're reading under the desk when you think I'm not looking; always read on top of the desk. I am moving you to a desk next to the big window so that you have enough light. And you spell well and don't need any spelling drill. Only learn to look up words and don't guess when you don't know. And," she added, "you know you left out one of your strengths —you know what it is?" I shook my head. "You are very good in composition, but you haven't had enough practice. Do you agree?" I nodded. "All right, let's make that a goal. Let's say you write two compositions a week, one for which you tell me what you want to write about, one for which I give you a topic. And," she continued, "you underrate your performance in arithmetic. You are actually good—so good that I would propose that this year you learn all the arithmetic the lower grades teach, that is, fractions, percentages, and logarithms —you'll like logarithms, they're clever. Then you'll be ready to do the mathematics they teach in the upper grades, geometry and algebra."

I was surprised, for I knew I was doing poorly in arithmetic and had, indeed, always been criticized by earlier teachers. I said so. "Of course," she replied. "Your results are poor. But not because you don't know arithmetic. They are poor because you are terribly sloppy and don't check. You don't make more mistakes than the others; you just don't catch them. So you'll learn this year how to check—and to make sure you do, I'll ask you to check all the arithmetic work of the five children sitting in your row and the row ahead of you. But, Peter, you aren't just 'poor' in handwriting, as you think you are. You're a total disgrace, and I won't have it in my class. It's going to hamper you. You like to write, but then no one can read what you've written. It's quite unnecessary; you can write a decent hand. By the end of the year you'll write like this." She whipped out two pieces of paper and put them in front of me. One was a composition I had written; and while the first line was legible, though hardly great calligraphy, the second had already deteriorated into an illegible scrawl. The second sheet of paper carried the same composition, word for word, but in the hand-writing of my first line, legible throughout. "This," said Miss Elsa, pointing to the second sheet, "is how you will write by the end of the year. This is the hand you can and should develop. Don't try to write the way I do"—how she knew I had hoped to do exactly that, I cannot even guess. "Everybody has to write his own hand, and this is *yours.*"

"You agree?" she asked. I did. "Then," she went on, "let's put it down so that you and I know exactly what you are doing. Here are your workbooks—one for each month, and I'll keep an exact copy of each in my desk. See, I haven't put down any goals for you in reading and spelling. But I have given you enough space so that you can put down, if you wish, what you have read, what it was all about, how you liked it, whether you plan to reread it, and what you learned from it.

People who read as much as you will always do often like to do that. You will record each week what compositions you wrote and make sure you write two each week. And here is the arithmetic page. It has two sections: one for quizzes on stuff you already know—addition, subtraction, multiplication, division; one for the new skills: fractions first. Put down each week at the beginning how you expect to do and then how you are actually doing. And here is the handwriting plan. I think you might try each week to write one more line in your compositions in your best, most legible, hand—that shouldn't be asking too much of yourself, I imagine.

"Once a week you and I will look at this together. Of course, come and ask me any time you have a question, and *you* keep your copy of your books. A little later on, if you want to, you may keep mine too —it would help me if you were willing to do that. There are so many children in the room and I also run the whole school and am quite busy."

Miss Sophy taught arts and crafts, to which we devoted one and a half hours each day. She resided in a big, crowded, colorful studio room, which no one ever saw her leave. One side was fixed up for the arts, with easels, crayons, brushes, watercolors, and clay, and with lots of colored gummed paper for cutting out—this was before fingerpaints. Another side was the craft shop, with child-size sewing machines (with foot treadles, of course, if only to make them more attractive to children), and long rows of hand tools, saws, pliers, drills, hammers, and planes in a small but complete woodworking shop. And along a third wall were pots and pans, burners, and a big sink.

For three weeks Miss Sophy would let us try things, always willing to help but never offering advice or criticism. Then she said to me: "You aren't much interested in painting or modeling in clay, are you?" "I'm not good at it," was my reply. "No, you certainly aren't. But by the end of this year you will be able to use simple hand tools. How about starting out by making a milking stool for your mother?" I was somewhat taken aback. "We don't have any cows," I stammered. "Why would my mother want a milking stool?" "Because it's about the only thing you could possibly make," said Miss Sophy tartly. The answer made sense to me, though I doubted whether I could indeed even make a milking stool.

Miss Elsa and Miss Sophy were sisters. A third sister, Miss Clara, taught the fifth grade, the highest grade in Austrian elementary schools. They were as unlike each other as three middle-aged spinsters could be. Clara was built like a Prussian grenadier—broad-shouldered, raw-boned and very tall—she towered over most men. Elsa was middle-sized and plump and dowdy. Sophy was tiny—most fourth-graders looked down on her. Miss Elsa was the youngest—probably three years younger than Miss Clara and five or six years younger than Miss Sophy. At the time when I encountered Miss Elsa in fourth grade, she was in her mid- or late forties and had been principal of the school ever since it had started, twelve years earlier as the elementary and coeducational department of the Schwarzwald enterprises. She was the complete caricature of the schoolmarm-spinster. Clad in shiny black —something called, I believe, bombazine, and extinct by now, I hope —that only showed a little white around the neck and the wrists, she looked like a big beetle. Her dress billowed out in front but was so tight over her buttocks that it crackled ominously whenever she bent forward. On a long black ribbon she wore a pince-nez which never left her nose but always stood askew. And she wore "sensible" high-button shoes.

But she had absolute authority. She would be writing on the blackboard and say quietly without turning her head: "Peter Drucker, stop pulling Libby Brunner's pigtails"; or "Peter Drucker, who gave you permission to walk around? Go back to your seat immediately." We debated for hours how she did it. The rationalists in the class were convinced that she must have a mirror in her hand—or perhaps there was one hidden in the blackboard. But though we searched the blackboard endlessly and all but took it to pieces, we could never find one. The mystics in the class endowed her with magical powers—or at least with eyes in the back of her head, under the meager mouse-colored braids that she wore tightly coiled up on top of her head. She never seemed to check the scores for our work which we recorded in the workbooks. But whenever we cheated, the workbook would come back with the correct score written in her neat, flowing hand. And when we kept on cheating, we'd be called up front and given a tongue-lashing that flayed us alive. But it was always done in private, out of anybody else's hearing.

At the beginning of the year she had told me that she would never praise me for reading and spelling—the things I did well—and she never did. Altogether she praised rarely and then only by saying: "That's quite nice," or, "Better than last week." But she would bear down on us like an avenging angel if we did not improve or advance in areas that needed strengthening, and especially in areas in which we had potential, such as she saw in me for composition. She was not in the least "child-focused," indeed not even much interested in children. She was interested in their learning. Yet she knew every child's name the first day, and every child's characteristics and above all, his or her strengths, within the first week.

We did not love her—she would have considered that an impudent intrusion on her privacy, I imagine. But we worshipped her. When, fifty years later, the Women's Libbers announced that the Lord is really a woman, I was not a bit surprised. The idea that the Lord might look very much like Miss Elsa—black bombazine, pince-nez, high-button shoes, and all—had occurred to me much earlier, and was by no means altogether displeasing. At least it would be a Lord concerned with the strengths of this miserable sinner, unlike the Lord of whom the preacher talked to us on Sunday in church.

Miss Sophy, by contrast, was entirely child-centered. Children always swarmed all over her. I cannot recall one moment when she did not have a girl or boy sitting in her lap; even the big fifth-graders who so much wanted to be "manly" were not a bit ashamed to cry on her shoulder. But they also came running to her with their joys and triumphs; and Miss Sophy was always ready with a pat, a kiss, a word of encouragement or congratulation. But she never, never remembered the name of a child, even though she had most of them as pupils for five years, for arts and crafts were taught in every grade and she was the only arts and crafts teacher in the school. It was always "Child"—I don't think, by the way, that Miss Sophy knew whether she was talking to a boy or a girl; nor did she care, I imagine. For Miss Sophy held the then quite revolutionary doctrine that boys should know how to sew and cook, and girls should use tools and know how to fix things. Sometimes she ran into parental opposition, as when she asked each mother to send a pair of stockings with holes in them to school so that we could learn how to darn, "to teach coordination between eye and hand," as she explained. A good many mothers were offended. "We have no stockings with holes in *this* house," they would write back. "Fiddlesticks," Miss Sophy replied, "in a house with a normal nine year old there are always holey stockings."

It was an altogether quaint idea in the Europe of those days for "good-class" children to learn to use their hands. Art was all right, of course, if kept in its place. And girls were supposed to learn sewing and needlework and knitting. But even cooking was not something "good-class" women ever did themselves, if only because no self-respecting cook would stay if the lady of the house so much as set foot in "her" kitchen. And "everybody" had a cook, of course; "lower middle class," after all, was defined as a family that had no more than two servants. Still, to learn to cook was quite respectable for young women. But shop for girls, or even for that matter for boys—that was carrying things to excess.

For a woman to be handy was actually not too bad. It was eccentric, and that was permissible if one had enough money. No one was greatly scandalized to hear that my mother could and did do home repairs, including a good bit of plumbing and reshingling the roof. And if a man had a "real" hobby, that was all right too—after all, no less than a king of France, Louis XVI, had made and repaired watches (although this probably had something to do with his losing his head). But gentlemen did not *work* with their hands. One did not go quite so far as the Chinese mandarins, who grew 10-inch-long fingernails to show that they did not degrade themselves with manual work, but the Europe of the nineteenth century came close. I once, as a boy, looked at the suits my grandfather had left behind—he had died in 1899 when my mother was fourteen. There was not one pocket in them except for the waistcoat fob pocket for the watch. "Your grandfather was a gentleman," my grandmother explained, "and gentlemen twenty years ago had a servant walking behind them, carrying; a gentleman did not use his hands."

Miss Sophy did not invent her quaint ideas. In fact they had a long though mixed ancestry. They went back to one of the pedagogues of the early nineteenth century, a man by the name of Froebel, father of the kindergarten. Froebel's ideas of craftwork as part of elementary education got nowhere in Europe; however, they were picked up by those great nonconformists, the Shakers in America. From them, in the mid-nineteenth century, they returned to Europe, to Sweden, where they led to a craft-school movement called, I believe, "Skjoeld." Miss Sophy had gone there as a young woman for her training. But though she had an impressive Swedish diploma, there was still something subversive in girls using a plane and boys a darning needle.

Yet no one less subversive-looking than tiny Miss Sophy could be imagined. She looked like a baby mouse—a long quivering red nose, a few stiff stray hairs on her upper lip, and tiny, quick, nearsighted button eyes—but a baby mouse modeled by Bernini or some other Baroque sculptor. She was swaddled from top to toe in multi-hued chiffon scarves—lavender, crimson, cerulean, layer upon layer of them—all fluttering wildly even in a hermetically sealed room (and her room was always hermetically sealed and stifling hot, whereas in Miss Elsa's room every window was wide open even on the coldest days). Out of this cocoon of fluttering chiffon issued a deep, booming bass voice that could be heard over all the noise a hundred children made in school.

Miss Elsa saw each child for a session once a week. In it she discussed last week's work and next week's program, working with the child on anything that caused problems, but always after she had first discussed the things the child was doing well and easily. In between these sessions she was always available if a child had a question or an idea for her approval. She also watched. A child in trouble with work would suddenly feel Miss Elsa's eye on him or her; and when the child looked up, Miss Elsa already knew what the trouble was, and would say: "You forgot to carry forward," or, "You skipped a page—no wonder you are lost." Otherwise Miss Elsa left her students alone to do their own work between weekly review and planning sessions.

Miss Sophy would hover over each child, darting from one to the other, sitting down next to each—always on the floor—but rarely staying with any one child more than a few seconds. She taught non-verbally and indeed soundlessly. She would watch for a moment, then put her tiny paw gently over the child's hand and guide the fingers to the right position to hold a saw or a brush. Or she would take a quick look at whatever the child was trying to draw—a cat, for instance— then take up paper and crayon and draw a purely geometric, nonob-jective figure that yet bore all the elements that make a cat a cat: the rounded rear end, the dip in the back just below the neck, the peculiar angle of the head, and the way in which the ears frame the face. Suddenly even as ungifted a draftsman as I was would see "cat" and break out laughing. When that happened, an answering smile ap-peared on Miss Sophy's face—the only praise she ever gave, but one that was pure bliss to the beholder.

Many years later I encountered another great teacher who worked the same way. Karl Knaats, the painter, taught at Bennington during the mid-forties for two years. In those entire two years no one

heard him say a word. He would stand over a student and grunt—
"humpf, humpf, humpf, brrr"—and the student would turn around
with the same smile of instant enlightenment Miss Sophy's students
had had and the same complete change in performance.

But unlike Karl Knaats, Miss Sophy could, and did, talk. And her
short lapidary sentences, shouted basso-profundo, put across sudden
insights. "Don't draw dogs, they are stooooopid," she would boom,
"draw cats. There has never been a good portrait of a stooooopid
person." Of course, there are the Velasquez and Goya portraits of the
Habsburg and Bourbon kings and queens of Spain to prove her wrong.
But they are the exceptions, as a visit to any museum will show. Or:
"The hardest thing to do in carpentry is to make drawers; they *hide*
things."

Miss Elsa was the very perfection of the Socratic method. But Miss
Sophy was a Zen master. Yet I did not learn from either of them what
I knew I needed to learn and what they set out to teach me: neither
to write a legible hand nor to use hand tools, even poorly.

When I started out on the milking stool for my mother that Miss
Sophy thought I might be able to do, she did the seat and the holes
for the legs. Then she took my hands and led them over the legs of
a stool, making me feel the angle at which the legs have to be cut at
one end so they will stand straight on the other. She had me practice
on a few rods, then showed me how to set up the mitre box to cut the
legs, and we measured them together. But when I sawed, following,
I thought, so carefully the marks we had made together, I came out
with three legs, each a different length—one 17 inches as it was supposed to be, the second 19½, and the third 14. "All right," I said to
myself, "Mother will have to get dwarf cows," and proceeded to cut
all the legs down to 14 inches. But alas I again had three legs of
different lengths. And so it went until I had nothing but stumps—still
of different lengths.

Miss Sophy never scolded, never criticized. When she was truly
horrified, she would sit down next to the miscreant, gently take one
of his hands between hers, and begin to shake her head. She had an
enormous mass of iron-gray hair piled every which way on top of her
head and held together by millions—or so it seemed—of hairpins stuck
in at random. As she shook her head, the hairpins would begin to fall
out and then, as the head-shaking became more vigorous, fly all over
the room. And the hair would come cascading down. Then the children would begin to laugh until they rolled helplessly on the floor.

Finally Miss Sophy would join in the laughter and everyone would scramble to pick up hairpins, to pile the hair back up on her head, and to put the hairpins back in the same crazy random fashion. The offender would go back to work—and usually do a good, or at least a better job. But not I. I tried twice, and both times came out with three legs of different lengths. Twice I went back to work. But when I came out a third time with three uneven legs measuring roughly 5, 7, and 9 inches respectively, each cut to a different bias, Miss Sophy did not shake her head. Instead she sat and looked at my handiwork a long time. Then she turned to me and said—for once in a quiet, funereal voice—"What kind of pen does your mother use?" "A fountain pen," I said. "Are you sure," Miss Sophy asked, "that she never uses a steel nib?" "Positive," I answered; "she hates them." "Good," said Miss Sophy, "then we can have you make a pen wiper. She'll never have to use it." And for years thereafter my mother kept on her desk, unused, a penwiper of my manufacture, made of the tail feathers of a rooster precariously held together by flower wire. Both Mother and I knew that I had reached the limit of my abilities as a craftsman. So did Miss Sophy.

But Miss Elsa was made of different stuff. When it became clear that my handwriting was not improving, she called in my father. In my presence—for she never talked to a parent unless the child was present—she said: "I have sad news for you. I know that the main reason why you took Peter out of public school and enrolled him here was his poor handwriting. It's not improving—I'm afraid it never will. Therefore I propose that you have him apply for immediate admission to the Gymnasium." This was rather stunning. It was possible to apply for the entrance examination to the Gymnasium after the fourth grade, but this was skipping a grade and exceptional reward for superior performance. "I don't understand," said my father. "It's quite simple," said Miss Elsa. "The one thing he needs to learn, he isn't going to learn; so what's the use his wasting a year in the fifth grade when his handwriting isn't going to get any better? I know," she said, "he is young for the Gymnasium. But he was born in November and they take them as long as they were born before December. He will pass the entrance examination—it tests mainly reading and arithmetic, and Peter is fully up to their standards. But," she went on, "the main reason why I tell you to have Peter go straight into the Gymnasium is that I won't have him upset my sister Clara. Her health isn't good and she is a worrier. She won't be able to do a thing about Peter's horrible handwriting—I'm twice the teacher she is and I got nowhere. It will frustrate and upset her, and all to no purpose."

My father argued. But Miss Elsa won, and I became the youngest student in the first grade of the Gymnasium the autumn of that year.

My father, however, had not given up. A few years later—my handwriting getting steadily worse instead of better—he took me to a handwriting school for an intensive course. Mr. Feldman, the handwriting master, lived in a dreary side street in the inner city. Downstairs he had a window display that showed a great number of samples saying: "This is how I wrote before I took Mr. Feldman's calligraphy course" in writing every bit as dreadful as mine. Next to each, in beautiful Spencerian hand or elaborate clerical curlicue, was another sample, signed with the same name, saying: "This is how I write now that I have taken Mr. Feldman's course." In my father's presence, Mr. Feldman had me write: "This is how I wrote before I took Mr. Feldman's course." Then he took the money for the course. After that I went to Mr. Feldman's establishment three times a week after school and sat down on a kitchen chair, writing: "This is how I write now that I have taken Mr. Feldman's course." When I had written a sample good enough to be put in the window downstairs next to my "before" sample, the course was over. After that, even my father gave up.

In the Gymnasium I did not encounter a single one of the sadists and tyrants who, since the days of Dickens, have become standard figures in the schoolday memories of European literary people. But very few of the teachers I had in my eight years in a famous classical Gymnasium—the school which a popular American myth tends to enshrine in the holiest of holies—were of even low-level competence. Most bored their students most of the time and themselves all of the time.

At that they were not a bit different from the teachers I had encountered in my first three years of school before the one year under Miss Elsa and Miss Sophy. Nor were they any different from most of the teachers I later encountered in my university days. Indeed the only good teachers under whom I have worked, except in fourth grade, were two early bosses—first the managing editor of a German afternoon paper and then a wise old merchant banker in London. And most of the teachers I have seen as my colleagues on university faculties since I myself began to teach when barely twenty, have been no better than the teachers under whom I survived in the Gymnasium; the majority ranged from dismal to barely adequate.

But I had been spoiled by the one year under Miss Elsa and Miss Sophy. Or it might be more accurate to say that I had become incurably infected.

I might have gotten into teaching anyhow—there were long years during which I needed a job and an income and could not be choosy. I might have discovered that I liked teaching and am apparently quite good at it. It's unlikely, though; none of the other jobs that I took because I needed money—merchant banking, for instance—turned out to be more than a way to earn a living. But because of Miss Elsa and Miss Sophy I knew that teaching could be something quite different from what it was to the poor drudges who suffered such dreadful boredom while trying to make us learn Latin grammar, the Greek dramatists, or world history. The subjects, I found to my surprise, were not boring at all. Indeed I have not found a subject yet that is not sparkling with interest, and I have taught dozens of subjects, all over the humanities and social sciences, from theology and philosophy through literature and history to government, management, economics, and statistics. I must admit that I did not particularly enjoy Latin—and we had it for two hours each day six days a week. I found it disconcertingly easy and disconcertingly empty. But Greek I thought elegant; yet what a bore the schoolmasters made it to be. The reason was that the poor devils were so dreadfully bored themselves because they were such awful teachers, or because their students were such awful learners. And then I would see Miss Elsa or Miss Sophy in my mind's eyes. Long division, I was quite sure, could not be a less boring subject in itself than Roman history, indeed it was obviously far less stimulating. Yet Miss Elsa was interested, never bored, and made it interesting. So did Miss Sophy when she showed me how to hold a hammer to get a nail in straight, even though I never mastered it.

Without Miss Elsa and Miss Sophy in my memory, I would have resisted teaching myself. Perhaps I would not have minded too much boring others; that is a risk every professional writer takes without thinking twice about it. But I would have hesitated to take the risk of boring myself—and that is what my Gymnasium teachers so obviously did.

Of course I did not think these thoughts consciously until much later. I felt them. But I also knew quite early, and consciously, what

I had learned from Miss Elsa and Miss Sophy, and that it was more important than what they had failed to teach me, and superior to anything the Gymnasium tried to teach me. To be sure, even Miss Sophy could not make a craftsman out of me, just as the greatest music teacher cannot make a musician out of someone who is tone deaf. But I took from her a lifelong appreciation of craftsmanship, an enjoyment of honest clean work, and respect for the task. My fingers have never forgotten the feel of well-planed and sanded wood, cut with rather than against the grain, which Miss Sophy—her hand on mine and guiding my fingers—made me sense. And Miss Elsa had given me a work discipline and the knowledge of how one organizes for performance, though I abused this skill for years. It enabled me to do absolutely no work in the Gymnasium for eight or nine months of the year, during which I pursued my own interests, whatever they were. Then when my teachers were sure that I would at least have to repeat the year, if not be thrown out altogether, I would dust off Miss Elsa's workbooks, set goals, and organize—and I would end the year in the upper third or quarter of the class simply by doing a little work for a few weeks in a purposeful, goal-directed fashion. This is how I still got my law doctorate when I was twenty-one or twenty-two. By that time I was working full time as a senior editor of a newspaper, and had been working full time since the day I graduated from the Gymnasium. I had attended practically no classes though I was already teaching in some law-school areas; and the subjects of the doctoral examination—the typical law-school subjects such as contract, criminal law, or procedure—held very little interest for me. But Miss Elsa's workbook, work plans, and performance sheets were as effective in preparing myself for a grueling three-day oral and/or writing a dissertation as they had been for planning compositions a month ahead in fourth grade.

Finally, Miss Elsa and Miss Sophy taught me that teaching and learning, of high quality and with a high level of intensity and enjoyment, are possible. These two women set standards and they gave examples.

I did not encounter another real teacher until two or three years later. By that time I had almost come to accept the unanimous belief of my classmates, shared by their parents and incidentally by the great majority of students all the world over, that school has to be a bore and teachers have to be incompetent. I had not forgotten Miss Elsa and

Miss Sophy, but they were becoming fairy tale figures in my mind.

Then I had the good fortune to encounter Artur Schnabel. He was never of course my teacher; he taught only advanced pianists of great professional promise. And I only met him once, for two short hours, when—as a result of a mixup in his schedule—I was permitted to sit in while he gave a lesson to a classmate's sister who was a musical prodigy and had already made her professional debut. Schnabel in those years, the early 1920s, was not yet the famous pianist he was to become later, especially after he moved to the United States following Hitler's advent to power in Germany. Indeed in his native Vienna—which he soon thereafter left for Berlin—he was considered far too "austere." But he had already established himself as a master piano teacher.

The first hour of the lesson seemed conventional enough. Schnabel first had my friend's sister play the pieces he had assigned her during the last lesson a month earlier. As I remember it, it was a Mozart sonata and a Schubert sonata. The young woman—she was perhaps fourteen or so—played with what I, even at age twelve, realized was remarkable technique. (She has since become known for her technical proficiency.) Schnabel said nice things about her technique, had her play one phrase over again, and asked questions about another phrase. He wondered whether she might not try playing a passage a little more slowly or with a little more emphasis. But none of this was too different from the way my own totally undistinguished piano teacher taught me.

Schnabel pulled out her assignments for the next lesson, a month hence, and had her sight-read them. Again the technical competence of the young woman was noticeable. Schnabel remarked on it too. Then, however, he went back to the two pieces she had practiced the month before and played earlier. "You know, my dear Lilly," he said, "you played those two pieces very well indeed. But you did not play what *you* heard. You played what you think you should have heard, and that is faking. And if I heard it, an audience will hear it too." Lilly looked at him, totally baffled. "I'll tell you what I'll do," said Schnabel. "I will play the Andante of the Schubert sonata the way *I* hear it. I cannot play it the way *you* hear it. And I don't want to play it as you played it, because *no one* hears it that way. You listen to what *I* hear, and then I think *you* may hear."

He sat down at the piano and played the Schubert Andante the way he heard it. Suddenly Lilly heard. Suddenly she had that same smile of enlightenment I had seen on the faces of Miss Sophy's students. At that moment Schnabel stopped and said, "And now you play." She played the piece with far less competent technique than before, far more like the child she still was, more naïvely—but convincingly. And then I heard it too—at least I must have had the same smile on my face. For Schnabel turned to me and said, "Do you hear it? That's good. As long as you play what you hear, you play music."

I never heard well enough to be a musician. But I suddenly perceived that I myself would always learn by looking for performance. I suddenly realized that the right method, at least for me, was to look for the thing that worked and for the people who perform. I realized that I, at least, do not learn from mistakes. I have to learn from successes.

It took me many years to realize that I had stumbled upon a method. Perhaps I did not fully understand this until, years later, I read—I believe in one of Martin Buber's early books—the saying of the wise rabbi of the first century: "The Good Lord has so created Man that everyone can make every conceivable mistake on his own. Don't ever try to learn from other people's mistakes. Learn what other people do right."

Since the moment of enlightenment in a corner of Schnabel's studio, I have been looking for teachers who teach. I have been going out of my way to find them, to observe them, to enjoy them. Whenever I hear of somebody who has a reputation as a master teacher, I try to sneak into his or her classes or lectures, to listen, and to watch. And if I cannot do this, I try at least to find out from students what the teacher did and what worked.

"Teacher-watching" has been one of my main enjoyments over the years. I can recommend it as a spectator sport that never ceases to hold surprises. I am still at it.

One of the things I learned very early is that students always recognize a good teacher. They may be overimpressed by second-raters who only talk a good game, who are witty and entertaining, or who have reputations as scholars, without being particularly good teachers. But I have not come across a single first-rate teacher who was not recognized as such by the students. The first-rate teacher is often not "popular"; in fact, popularity has little to do with impact as a teacher. But when students say about a teacher, "We are learning a great deal," they can be trusted. They know.

But I also learned that "teacher" is an elusive term. Or rather, I learned that there is no one answer to the question: What makes the effective teacher? No two teachers, I found, do the same things. No two teachers behave the same way. What works for one teacher and makes him first-rate does not seem to work at all for another one—or is never used by another one. It was all very confusing—and still is.

There are the nonverbal teachers, the teachers who teach the way Miss Sophy had taught. Artur Schnabel was a nonverbal teacher. Two other great music teachers of the same generation were strongly verbal. Rosa Lhevinne, who for fifty years was the most effective teacher of pianists in America, taught primarily by talking and rarely by example. So did Lotte Lehmann, the Austrian soprano, who in her old age became a great singing teacher in America.

Of two fine teachers of surgery I have watched, one taught nonverbally. He stood behind the Chief Resident, who was about to perform a major surgical operation, and did not say one word during the entire procedure. But at every move the Chief Resident looked at him, and the surgeon would nod, shake his head, lift a hand ever so slightly, raise an eyebrow; every one of the students in the amphitheater knew by intuition what each signal meant, and so did the Chief Resident. Another surgery teacher of great renown rehearsed the operation in the minutest detail before the patient was wheeled into the operating room. During the operation, he expected to be asked questions and to give answers. Both have taught many successful surgeons. I once mentioned this to a friend of mine, himself known to be a good teacher of surgeons. He laughed and said, "You might be describing Dr. De Bakey and Dr. Denton Cooley, the two Houston heart surgeons who are also great teachers. The fact that one is nonverbal and the other teaches through the spoken word is, I think, one reason why the two men cannot get along. You know," he added, "I'm not old enough to have been a student of Dr. Cushing's at Harvard. But when I trained there, his memory was still green. And he was one of your totally nonverbal teachers, I was told. I myself, incidentally, teach through the word—sometimes I wish I could teach without it."

There are some teachers who do best with advanced students and others who do best with beginners. Two of the great physicists of this century were apparently great teachers: Niels Bohr in Copenhagen and Enrico Fermi, particularly in his last years when he taught in Chicago. But Bohr taught only the "master class." I am told that physics students, even gifted ones, found him almost inaccessible and got little out of his lectures and seminars though he prepared for them meticulously. But practically every one of the great men of the second generation of modern physics—from Heisenberg to Schroedinger and Oppenheimer—did his postgraduate work under Bohr and credited Bohr with his own unfolding as a scientist. Enrico Fermi, by contrast, did his best teaching with undergraduates, especially freshmen, and most especially with students who had no intention of going into physics and never had taken a physics course before. Martha Graham, the modern dancer and a teacher of extraordinary power, was equally effective with both beginners and masters, and taught both exactly the same way.

Some teachers are best in front of a large group, lecturing. Buckminster Fuller holds an audience of 2,000 people in rapt attention for seven hours. Other teachers do their best work with small groups —Lotte Lehmann was apparently one. There are some, like Mark Hopkins, who are effective with an individual. At least the old epigram asserts that the best school would be "Mark Hopkins at one end of a log and one student at the other," though I personally have never seen a teacher who really performs before an audience of one. Good teachers are showmen, and showmen need an audience. Some teach through the written word rather than the spoken one. This was true of both General George Marshall, the U.S. Chief of Staff in World War II, and of Alfred Sloan, the head of General Motors. Sloan's letters, some of which have been reprinted in his book, *My Years with General Motors*, are masterpieces of teaching through the written word. And of course the greatest teacher of the Christian tradition, St. Paul, taught best through the epistle.

There seems to be little correlation between ability as a performer and ability as a teacher, and none between scholarship and teaching, or craftsmanship and teaching. Of all the great painters of the European tradition, only one—Tintoretto—was, it seems, any good as a teacher; he taught El Greco. Rubens had many students, but not one of them became even a good second-rate painter himself. And all the great painters, with the single exception of El Greco, were the students of little-known and undistinguished painters who were teachers. Robert Oppenheimer, however good an administrator, was not among the great men of the age of relativity, quantum physics, and atomic physics. But he was a born teacher, who released the creative energies of a whole generation of young American physicists and kindled in them the spark of greatness. Even for a complete ignoramus like myself, to sit and listen to his advanced Princeton lectures was to glimpse vast vistas, seas, and mountain ranges. The one great teacher of musicians in the Vienna of Haydn, Mozart, and Beethoven was Diabelli, whose musical legacy consists of the most boring of five-finger exercises. And in the next generation it was not Schumann, Brahms, Wagner, or for that matter Liszt or Berlioz, who were the great teachers, but Robert Schumann's widow Clara, who by all accounts was the greatest teacher of piano ever.

Teachers, my "teacher-watching" led me to conclude early, have no pattern and no one right method. Teaching is a gift. One is born with it, the way the Beethovens and Rubens and Einsteins were born with their gifts. Teaching is personality, rather than skill or practice.

But slowly, over the years, I found another kind of teacher. Or perhaps it would be more precise to say that I found people who produce learning. They do it, not by being "teachers"—that is, not by gift of personality. They do it through a method that guides the student to learning. Each of these people does what Miss Elsa had done in fourth grade. They find the strengths of the individual student and set goals to develop those strengths. They set both long-range goals and short-range ones. Only then do they concern themselves with the student's weaknesses, which emerge as limitations on the full exercise of the student's strengths. They make sure that students get the feedback from their own performance, so they can exercise self-control and direct themselves. These people praise rather than criticize. But they use praise so sparingly that it never loses its capacity to stimulate, and never replaces the satisfaction and pride of achievement as the student's main reward. They do not "teach"; they program the student for effective learning. And those who do this can work with any student because they always work with the individual, even in a large group. In both kinds, teaching is not a function of subject knowledge or of "communications skill." It is a separate quality. For the teachers —the Miss Sophys—teaching is a dimension of the personality. For the guides to learning—the Miss Elsas—learning is a method.

In their results, the two approaches are very much the same. The end product of teaching is, after all, not what happens to the teacher but the learning of the student. And both methods produce learning.

I became fully conscious of this only years after I had first begun to watch teachers, when in 1942 I joined the faculty of Bennington College, then a small liberal arts women's school in New England. Bennington had been founded ten years earlier as an experimental college that never wanted to be large but aimed at being important. It came close to realizing this ambition for a few short years in the 1940s under the presidency of Lewis Webster Jones, who had taught economics at Bennington and had then become its president in 1941. (He moved on to the presidency of the University of Arkansas in 1946, and from there to the presidency of Rutgers University in New Jersey.) Jones recruited people with great reputations—Martha Graham in the modern dance; Erich Fromm, the psychologist; Richard Neutra, the architect. But what particularly concerned him was not reputation but teaching and learning. He succeeded in building and holding together, for a few short years, a teaching faculty of remarkable performance. It was a small faculty, no more than forty-five all told. Very few of them were not competent as teachers; the less competent did not last long while Lewis Jones was president. But fully twelve to fifteen were teachers of extraordinary performance and impact, which is a far greater proportion than I have ever heard of or seen elsewhere—and they had almost more impact than the students could absorb.

The "teachers" were as varied a lot as teachers usually are. Erich Fromm, for instance, was a truly magnificent teacher of small groups, who did indifferently with the individual student and poorly with a large class in a lecture hall. Richard Neutra was misplaced at Bennington. He was a great teacher of architects and a poor teacher of architectural amateurs such as a liberal arts college has to offer. After a few years he left, frustrated, to return to the practice of architecture.

But there was another large group who were not "master teachers" and yet produced what I can only call "master students." A fair number of faculty members knew how to guide a student to learning, and had the methods of the pedagogue. Typical of them was "the other Martha," Martha Hill, who also taught modern dance. Unlike Martha Graham, she was not a great dancer herself. She had no magnetism to her personality and did not dominate a class through sheer power as Martha Graham did. One hardly noticed her in a group. Yet her students learned as much as they learned from Martha Graham, and perhaps more. And they were as convinced of her ability as a teacher as the students of that great "master teacher," Martha Graham.

What Martha Hill applied was method. She did exactly what Miss Elsa had done in fourth grade. She watched students for a few days or weeks, thought through what each of them could do and what each of them should do. She worked out a program for each, which the student herself then ran and she only monitored. And she pushed and pushed and pushed students to do better what they already did well. She was always friendly, yet did not praise much. But she made sure that students knew when they had done a good job.

Then there was the man whom most Bennington students rightly considered the outstanding teacher on the faculty, Francis Ferguson. Himself a distinguished Dante scholar, Ferguson was not a "teacher" at all. He was a programmer of learning. But students came out of his classes with stars of excitement in their eyes, not over anything Ferguson had said or done but over what they had been induced to say or do. And very much the same method was followed by another highly effective pedagogue, Hertha Moselsio—a big German woman who ran the pottery studio—who insisted on absolutely scrupulous workmanship, and who demanded of students that they do better what they could do well.

There are two different breeds. There is the teacher who has a gift in his keeping. And there is the pedagogue who knows how to program learning in the student. Teachers are born, and the born teacher can then improve and become better. But pedagogues have a method that can be learned, probably by almost everybody. Indeed, the "born" teacher can become a great teacher most easily by adding to his gift the method of the pedagogue. Then he will also become a universal teacher, able to teach large groups and small groups, beginners and the "master class."

Miss Sophy had charisma; Miss Elsa had method. Miss Sophy gave enlightenment; Miss Elsa gave skills. Miss Sophy conveyed vision, Miss Elsa guided learning. Miss Sophy was a teacher, Miss Elsa was a pedagogue. This distinction would not have surprised Socrates, or indeed any of the ancient Greeks. Socrates is traditionally called a great teacher. He himself would have resented this as an insult. He never spoke of himself as a teacher. He was a "pedagogue"—a guide to the learner. The Socratic method is not a teaching method, it is a *learning* method. It is programmed learning. Indeed Socrates' criticism of the Sophists was precisely that they emphasized teaching and that they believed that one teaches a subject. This he thought idle and vanity. The teacher teaches learning; the student learns the subject. Learning is fruitful; teaching is pretentious and a fraud. And it was for this that the Oracle at Delphi called him the "wisest man in Greece." For almost 2,000 years, however, the Sophists have ruled—the ones who promise to be able to teach teaching. Their ultimate triumph is the blind belief of American higher education that the Ph.D., or advanced specialized subject knowledge, is the right (indeed the only) preparation for teaching. But the Sophists have ruled only in the West. Other civilizations never accepted the Western, the Sophist, idea of the teacher. The Indian word for teacher is "guru" and a guru clearly is not made but born. He has an authority which is not that of the college course, but of the spirit. Similarly, the Japanese Sensei is a "master" rather than a teacher. But in the Western tradition, we have focused on teaching as a skill and forgotten what Socrates knew: teaching is a gift, learning is a skill.

It is only in this century that we are rediscovering what Socrates knew. We are doing so because we have done more serious work and research on learning in the last 100 years than has ever been done before. We have rediscovered that learning is built into every one of us. We have rediscovered that the human being—and all living beings —are "learning organisms" who are "programmed" to learn. We do not yet know as much about learning, as a result of a century of research, as Miss Elsa perceived. But we know that what she knew and did are right and available to practically everyone.

For 2,000 years or so, since the days of Socrates, we have debated whether teaching and learning are "cognitive" or "behavioral." It is a sham battle. Teaching and learning are both. But they are also something else: they are passion. Teachers start out with passion. Pedagogues acquire it as they become intoxicated with the enlightenment of the student. For the smile of learning on the student's face is more addictive than any drug or narcotic. It is this passion that prevents that deadly and deadening disease of the classroom, the boredom of the teacher—the one condition that absolutely inhibits both teaching and learning. Teaching and learning are the Platonic Eros, the Eros of the *Symposium.* There is in each of us Plato's Winged Horse, the noble steed which seeks the mate it can only find through teaching or learning. For the teacher, the passion is inside him or her; for the pedagogue, the passion is inside the student. But teaching and learning are always passion, passion one is born with or passion to which one becomes addicted.

One more thing teacher and pedagogue have in common: they hold themselves accountable.

After World War II, I learned that Miss Elsa was still alive and destitute. I sent her a few CARE packages with a carefully typed letter. Only the signature was in my handwriting. Back, a few weeks later, came her reply in the same beautiful flowing script which I had admired so much as a ten year old, and which neither age nor adversity had marred. "You must be the same Peter Drucker," she wrote, "who was one of my few failures in the classroom. You did not learn to write the legible hand which was the one thing you needed to learn from me." There are no poor or stupid or lazy students for the real teacher and the real pedagogue. There are only good teachers and poor teachers.

Freudian Myths
and
Freudian Realities

If Sigmund Freud had not been so visible and prominent in the Vienna of my childhood, I would never have paid attention to the glaring discrepancy between the Freudian myths and the Freudian realities.

My parents had both known Freud for many years. But Freud was more than twenty years older than my father. And so my father would bow with great respect when he encountered Freud on the paths around the Alpine lake on which the Freuds had their summer villa, next to Genia Schwarzwald's resort. And Freud would bow back. My mother had had an interest in psychiatry as a medical student, and had worked for a year in the Psychiatric Clinic in Zurich headed by Bleuler, a psychiatrist whom Freud greatly respected. She had bought Freud's books as a young woman, well before her marriage. I own her copy of the first edition, dated 1900, of *Die Traumdeutung (The Interpretation of Dreams)*—one of the pitiful 351 copies which was all the first edition sold—and her copy of the definitive 1907 edition of *Zur Psychopathologie des Alltagslebens (Psychopathology of Everyday Life)* with its famous analysis of the "Freudian slips"—both with bookmarks still in my mother's maiden name. Before her marriage, she also attended one of his lecture series, whether at the University or at the Psychoanalytic Society I do not know, where she apparently was the only woman; she used to recount with some amusement how her presence embarrassed Freud in discussing sex and sexual problems.

I myself had been introduced to Dr. Freud when I was eight or nine years old. One of Genia Schwarzwald's co-op restaurants during World War I was in the Berggasse, next to the Freud apartment. In those hunger years in Vienna Dr. Freud and his family sometimes ate lunch there—and so did we. On one of those days the Freuds and we sat at the same table. Dr. Freud recognized my parents and I was presented and asked to shake hands.

But this was my only contact with Dr. Freud. And the only reason why I even remember it when I have, of course, forgotten all the other adults with whom I had to shake hands as a boy, is that my parents afterwards said to me: "Remember today; you have just met the most important man in Austria, and perhaps in Europe." This was apparently before the end of the war, for I asked, "More important than the Emperor?" "Yes," said my father, "more important than the Emperor." And this so impressed me that I remembered it, even though I was still quite a small child.

This is the point. My parents were not disciples of Freud—indeed, my mother was quite critical of both the man and his theories. But they still knew that he was "the most important man in Austria and perhaps in Europe."

Three "facts" about Sigmund Freud's life are accepted without question by most people, especially in the English-speaking world: That all his life Freud lived with serious financial worries and in near-poverty; that he suffered greatly from anti-Semitism and was denied full recognition and the university appointments that were his due, because he was a Jew; and that the Vienna of his day, especially medical Vienna, ignored and neglected Freud.

All three of these "facts" are pure myths. Even as a youngster Freud was well-to-do; and from the beginning of his professional life as a young doctor he made good money. He never suffered from discrimination as a Jew until Hitler drove him into exile at the very end of his life. He received official recognition and academic honors not only earlier than almost any person in Austrian medical history; he received at an early age honors and recognition to which, according to the fairly strict Austrian canon, he was not entitled at all. Above all, medical Vienna did not ignore or neglect Freud. It took him most seriously. No one was discussed as much, studied as much, or argued about more. Medical Vienna did not ignore or neglect Freud, it *rejected* him. It rejected him as a person because it held him to be in gross violation of the ethics of the healer. And it rejected his theory as a glittering half-truth, and as poetry rather than medical science or therapy.

The myths about Freud and his life in the Vienna of his days would be trivial and quite irrelevant to the man and to psychoanalytic theory but for one fact: Freud himself believed them. Indeed he invented them and publicized them. In his letters, above all, these myths are stressed again and again. And it was in his letters that the proud, disciplined, and very private man unburdened himself of his own concerns. These myths, in other words, were extremely important to Freud himself. But why?

Freud was a stoic who never complained, abhorred self-pity, and detested whiners. He bore great physical pain without a sound of complaint. And he was equally stoical about sufferings in his private and family life. But he complains incessantly about imaginary sufferings—lack of money, anti-Semitic discrimination, and being ignored by the Viennese physicians.

Freud was in everything else ruthlessly candid, above all with himself. He was merciless in his own self-examination and tore out root and branch what to an ordinary mortal would have been harmless self-indulgence. It is inconceivable that Freud could have knowingly created and propagated fairy tales and myths about himself. But it seems equally inconceivable that Freud could not have known that these assertions and complaints were not "facts," but pure myths. Everyone else in the Vienna of Freud's time knew it and commented on Freud's strange "obsessions."

The only answer is a Freudian one: these myths are "Freudian slips." They are symptoms of deep existential realities and traumas that Freud could not face despite his self-analysis, his uncompromising truthfulness, his stoic self-discipline. And it is Freud who has taught us that "Freudian slips" are never trivial. The Freud of official legend is a stern monolithic god—a Zeus on Olympus or an Old Testament Jehovah. The Freud of his own "Freudian slips" is a tormented Prometheus. And it was Prometheus who of all the gods of classical mythology is mentioned most often in Freud's works.

The Freuds were not "Rothschild-rich," to use the Viennese term for the super-rich. They were comfortable middle class. Freud's father was a fairly successful merchant. In the Vienna of Freud's youth—he was born in 1856, just when the rapid growth of Vienna into a metropolis began—this meant a high-ceilinged apartment in one of the new four- or five-story apartment buildings just outside the old "Inner City": fairly spacious though dark, overcrowded with furniture, and with one bathroom only. It meant two or three servants, a weekly cleaning woman, and a seamstress every month, a summer vacation in a spa near Vienna or in the mountains, Sunday walks in the Vienna Woods for the whole family, high school (Gymnasium) for the children, books, music, and weekly visits to opera and theaters. And this is precisely how the Freuds lived. Freud's brother, Alexander—he published a reference book on railroad freight tariffs for the Minstry of Commerce when my father was the ministry's head—always resented Sigmund's insistence on the dire poverty in which he grew up as maligning their dead father's memory, "who was such a good provider." All the sons got university educations, he would point out. Young Sigmund was being supported in considerable comfort in Paris for three or four more years of study, even after he had finished both his medical and his specialty training; and the young Freuds always had enough pocket money to buy books and tickets to opera and theater. Of course, they kept no horse and carriage—that was being "Rothschild-rich." But they rented one when they went for their summer vacation to Baden or Voeslau, the two popular spas near Vienna. And from the day on which Freud went into practice after his return from Paris, he had patients. For his skill in treating neuroses was immediately recognized.

But he also received official recognition very early. The title "Professor" given to an Austrian physician was a license to coin money; the holder automatically tripled or quadrupled his fees. For that reason alone, it was almost never given to a physician before he was in his late fifties. Freud had it in his late forties. A firm rule reserved this title to the medical directors of major hospitals as a way to compensate them for the substantial income they gave up in treating hospital and charity patients for free. Freud received the title, even though he held no hospital appointment and treated only private and paying patients.

But what of his oft-repeated complaint about "anti-Semitic discrimination," in that he was not going to have the title of "full professor" but only that of "extraordinary" or "associate professor" when offered the chair of neurology at the University's medical school? The fact is that university chairs at the medical school were established by law and required an act of Parliament for any change. The only clinical chairs in the medical school that carried a "full professorship" were the ones in the "old," i.e., eighteenth-century disciplines—in internal medicine, obstetrics, and surgery. Every other chair was an "extraordinary professorship." Any such professor who headed a university hospital, such as the neurological unit that was offered to Freud—

again at an earlier age than a university hospital had been offered to a Viennese physician before—received, however, within a year or two, the "personal" rank and title of "full professor." Freud was going to receive it too, had he accepted the offer instead of turning it down and then complaining that "anti-Semitism" had denied him a full professorship.

However strong anti-Semitism was becoming among the small shopkeepers and craftsmen of Vienna in the late 1800s, it was frowned upon at the Imperial court, in the government service, among "educated" people, and above all in the Viennese medical community. In the very years of Freud's professional growth, from 1880 through 1900 or so, the majority of the leadership positions in Viennese medicine were taken over by men who were Jews, if not by religion, then by birth. In 1881, at the time when Freud started on his professional career, more than 60 percent of Vienna's physicians were already Jewish, according to C. A. McCartney, the leading historian of Austria-Hungary. By 1900, Jews held the great majority of clinical chairs at the University's medical school, of the medical directorships in the major hospitals, and such positions as surgeon-general of the Army, personal physician to the Emperor, and obstetrician to the ladies of the Imperial family. "Anti-Semitism" was not the reason why Freud did not have the professorship in neurology; it played altogether no role in his practice, in his standing in official medicine, or in his acceptance by a Viennese medical community that was as Jewish as he was.

Indeed a main reason why this Viennese medical community found Freud unacceptable was that it was Jewish. For the first criticism of Freud, voiced even by believers in psychoanalysis, was always that Freud violated the basic Jewish ethics of the healer. Freud did not accept charity patients, but taught instead that the psychoanalyst must not treat a patient for free, and that the patient will benefit from treatment only if made to pay handsomely. This was absolutely "unethical" to the Jewish tradition out of which so many of Vienna's physicians came. There were of course plenty of physicians, Jewish ones included, who were out for the buck. They were called "rippers" —*"Reisser."* A physician might have to refer patients to a "ripper" if they needed the special skill of one of them—if, for instance, they suffered from some sort of skin problem or some kind of stomach ailment. But the "rippers" were held in contempt. And even the most outrageous "ripper" would serve as medical director of a hospital or as department head in one of the university clinics, and thus take care of the indigent sick. And all of them, for all their greed, would at least preach the traditional ethic of the healer, the ethic of selfless giving. Not Freud, however: he spurned it. And thus he challenged head-on the deepest, most cherished values of the Jewish tradition of the healer. He made medicine a *trade*. Worse still, the Viennese doctors came to suspect that Freud might be right. At least for emotional and psychic ailments, insistence by the physician on a good fee was therapeutic and selflessness did damage.

Even more disturbing was Freud's insistence on emotional detachment of physician from patient. The physicians knew of course that the doctor has to learn to be hard-skinned and to get used to suffering, death, and pain. They knew that there were good reasons for the rule that physicians do not treat members of their own families. But central to their creed was the belief that tender, loving care is the one prescription that fits all symptoms. Admittedly, a broken bone would knit without it—though still better with it. But the wounded *person* needed a caring physician above all. And here was Dr. Freud demanding that the physician divest himself of sympathy for—indeed of human interest in—the patient, and that for the physician to become involved with the human being meant damaging the patient, made him or her dependent, and inhibited recovery and cure. Instead of being a brother, the suffering patient became an object.

That however was tantamount to degrading the physician from healer to mechanic. To all those Jewish physicians of Vienna—and not only to the Jewish ones—this was express denial of the very reasons why they had become physicians, and an affront to what they respected in themselves and in their calling. What made this doubly offensive was again that many suspected Freud might be right, at least with respect to psychoanalysis. "But," once said the elder of Vienna's Jewish surgeons at our dinner table—Marcus Hajek, the head of the University's ear, nose, and throat hospital and one of those "extraordinary" professors with the "personal" title of full professor—"if Freud is right, then psychoanalysis is a narcotic; and for a physician knowingly to create addiction—or even the risk thereof—is both a crime and a breach of his sacred duty."

There was even more discussion of psychoanalysis as therapy and scientific method than of its ethics. Freud belonged to the second generation of "modern" medicine in Vienna. "Modern" medicine, after a century or more of slow gestation, had finally emerged fully developed—at Vienna—only a few years before Freud was born.

Freud's medical generation was therefore conscious of what had made possible the giant step from "prescientific" medicine—the medicine of the contemptible quacks of Molière's plays—to medicine that could diagnose, could heal, could be learned, and could be taught. And during this generation's own lifetime "modern" medicine had yielded its greatest gains, in the development of bacteriology, for instance, and with it in the capacity to prevent and to treat infectious diseases; in anesthesia that made surgery bearable; or in the antisepsis and asepsis that made surgery possible without killing the patient through subsequent infection.

The fundamental step from quackery to medicine—the step first taken by such revered ancestors as Boerhave in Holland or Sydenham in England around 1700—had been abstention from big theory and from global speculation. Diseases are specific, with specific causes, specific symptoms, and specific cures. The great triumph of the bacteriologist—that is, of Freud's own generation—was precisely that he showed that every infection is specific, each with its specific bacterial cause carried and spread by its own unique carriers, whether flea or mosquito, and each acting in its own specific way on specific tissue. And whenever anyone in the history of modern medicine had forgotten the lesson of Boerhave and Sydenham as, for instance, the homeopathic school of Hahnemann had done (Hahnemann was only recently dead when Freud was born), his teachings immediately degenerated into the quackery of the "humors" and "vapors." Yet here was psychoanalysis, which postulated one universal psychological dynamism for every emotional disorder; and many of its practitioners (though not Freud himself) even claimed that many psychoses too were "emotional" rather than "physical," caused by the same forces of ego, id, and superego acting out sexual repression in the subconscious. Around 1900, I was once told, the Vienna Medical Society put on a skit at one of its parties. It was a parody of Molière's *Le Malade Imaginaire* in which the scurrilous quack was made to say: "If the patient loved his mother, it is the reason for this neurosis of his; and if he hated her, it is the reason for the same neurosis. Whatever the disease, the cause is always the same. And whatever the cause, the disease is always the same. So is the cure: twenty one-hour sessions at 50 Kronen each." Of course, that was gross caricature of psychoanalytic theory and practice. But it was close enough to bring the house down; even the psychoanalysts in the audience, I was told by one of them who had been there as a medical student, laughed until the tears came.

But if the basic method was so controversial to anyone familiar with the history of medicine, what about results? The leaders of the medical fraternity had seen enough to know that medicine is not entirely rational and that things do work which no one can explain. Hence their emphasis on demonstrable results and on the controlled test. But when the Viennese physicians asked for the results of psychoanalysis, they found themselves baffled. That Freud himself was a master healer was beyond doubt. But the results of psychoanalysis were something else again. In the first place Freud and the Freudians refused to define "results." Was it restoration of ability to function? Or relief from anxiety? Was psychoanalysis "curing" anybody? If so, what explained the obvious fact that so many of its patients became permanent patients, or at the least came back to the psychoanalyst again and again? Was it alleviation of a chronic condition—and was it then good enough that the patient became addicted to the treatment and "felt better" for it? And however one defined the "results" of this strange therapy, what was the appropriate control to test its results? Every Viennese doctor saw obviously "neurotic" people in his practice; a large number of them got better without any treatment—especially, of course, adolescents. At least the symptoms disappeared or changed quite drastically. What was the natural rate of remissions in neuroses, and how significantly better did the patient of the psychoanalyst do? It was not only that all the data were lacking. The psychoanalysts, beginning with Freud, refused to discuss the question.

And then it seemed that all methods of psychotherapy had the same results, or non-results. There were some rivals in the field by 1910, offsprings of the Freudian school, Alfred Adler, for instance, or Carl Jung. There was also, in Germany, Oskar Kohnstamm—the forerunner of today's "humanist" psychologists, a respected and successful psychotherapist, and totally non-Freudian in his approach in that he stressed the therapist's personal involvement in the life and problems of the patient. But there were also all kinds of assorted faith healers and "consciousness-raisers" around: spiritualists, hypnotists, people with mysterious magnetic boxes, not to mention pilgrimages to Lourdes and Hassidic "miracle rabbis." The studies of the results of psychotherapies which began to be done around 1920 always showed the same results and still do: psychotherapies might have significant results. The data are inconclusive; but no one method has results that are significantly better than or different from any other. This can mean two things: Freud's psychoanalysis is a specific treatment for some, but not for all, emotional disorders; or emotional problems improve or are even cured by having a fuss made over them. Either conclusion was, of course, unacceptable to Freud and the psychoanalysts; it was a rejection of Freud's entire claim.

I recall a discussion of a big study of the results of psychotherapy —again at our dinner table—between Karl Buehler, a moderately pro-Freudian, who taught psychology at the University (and whose wife, Charlotte, was a Freudian psychoanalyst), and, as I recall it, Oskar Morgenstern, then probably still a student and later, at Princeton, to become the foremost authority on statistical theory. Buehler argued that the results indicated that psychoanalysis is powerful and specific therapy for a fairly wide range of psychic ailments, and that there was need to do research as to what that range encompassed. "Not so," said Morgenstern; "if you go by the figures, then there are either no emotional illnesses at all or the trust of the patient in any method makes the patient feel better, regardless of method." "In either case," said another dinner guest, an eye surgeon, "there is as yet no valid Freudian psychotherapy which a physician can recommend or use in good conscience."

But most bothersome of all for the Viennese physician was that you could never know whether Freud and his disciples talked healing the sick or "art criticism." One minute they were trying to cure a specific ailment, whether fear of crossing the street or impotence. The next moment they were applying the same method, the same vocabulary, the same analysis to Grimm's *Fairy Tales* or *King Lear.* The physicians were perfectly willing to concede that, as Thomas Mann put it in his speech at Freud's eightieth birthday, "Psychoanalysis is the greatest contribution to the art of the novel." Freud as the powerful, imaginative, stimulating critic of culture and literature, of religion and art, was one thing; it was readily conceded by a good many that he had opened a window on the soul that had long been nailed shut. This is what made him "the most important man in Austria." But was psychoanalysis then likely to be therapy, any more than were Newton's physics or Kant's metaphysics or Goethe's aesthetics? Yet this was precisely what Freud and his followers claimed. It was a claim the Viennese physicians, by and large, could not accept.

Freud himself was deeply hurt by any hint that his theory was "poetry" rather than "science." He is known to have bitterly resented Thomas Mann's birthday speech even though he himself had asked Mann to be the speaker. But, of course, whatever the validity of psy-

choanalysis as science, Freud was a very great artist. He was probably
the greatest writer of German prose in this century—it is so clear, so
simple, so precise as to be as untranslatable as first-rate poetry. His
anonymous case histories portray a whole person in two paragraphs
better than many long novels, including, I would say, those of Thomas
Mann himself. The terms he coined—whether "anal" and "oral" or
"ego" and "superego"—are great poetic imagery. Yet this made
"scientific medicine" only more uncomfortable, while praising Freud
as a poet and artist infuriated him and his followers.

All these things were being discussed and debated endlessly even
in my childhood, and far more so, I believe, in earlier years, in the
years between 1890 and 1910 when Freud's great books came out and
when he moved from being a first-rate neurologist with remarkable
clinical results, especially with women, to becoming the leader of a
"movement." Again and again the questions came up: of Freud's ethics and of the ethics of psychoanalysis; of its results and how they
should be judged or measured; and of the compatibility of cosmic
philosophy and clinical therapy. One thing is crystal-clear: Freud was
not ignored. He was taken very seriously and then rejected.

The emergence of psychoanalysis is often explained, especially in
America, as a reaction to the "Victorian repression of sex." Maybe
there was such "repression" in America but it is even doubtful
whether there was any such phenomenon in England, except for a few
short years. It did not exist in the Austria in which young Sigmund
Freud grew up and in which he started to practice. On the contrary,
late-nineteenth-century Vienna was sexually permissive and sex flourished openly everywhere. The symbol of Freud's Vienna was Johann
Strauss's comic opera *Die Fledermaus (The Bat)*, which had its first
performance in 1874 when Freud was eighteen. It is an opera of
lover-swapping and open sexual pairing in which the wife jumps into
the arms of her old boyfriend the moment she thinks her husband is
out of the way; in which the maid, one of the main stars, sneaks off to
the masked ball to pick up a rich sugar-daddy who will set her up as
his mistress and finance her theatrical career; in which another main
character—Prince Orlofsky, who gives the ball where all this takes
place—is a homosexual whose main aria, in which he invites his guests
to love "each to his own taste," must have been understood by every
adult in the audience as "gay liberation." This plot might not be
"X-rated" should it come up for approval now; but it certainly would
not be classed as healthy family fare. Yet it was set in the resort in

which the prudish Austrian Emperor spent his summers rather than in some mythical never-never land. And no one was shocked!

The popular playwright a little later, in the Vienna of the 1880s and 1890s, was Freud's former fellow medical student, Artur Schnitzler, whose best-known and most popular play *La Ronde (Der Reigen)* can be described as a game of musical beds, in which everything but the sex act itself takes place on stage.

To be sure, a woman was not supposed to have affairs before her marriage—though it was the fear of unwanted pregnancy far more than morality that underlay that rule. She married young, of course; but then she was on her own, and only expected to be reasonably discreet. And that no restriction on premarital sex was applied to men was not so much because of the "double standard"—though it did exist —as because men had to postpone marriage until they could support a wife and children, and no one had the slightest illusion that they would remain chaste until then, or that such abstinence would be desirable.

Indeed what created sexual anxieties in so many of the middle-class women, and especially the Jewish middle-class women who were Freud's early patients, was Vienna's openness of sex and its sexually supercharged atmosphere. These women came, for the most part, from the ghettos of small Jewish towns, like the Freuds themselves, whose roots were in one of the small Jewish settlements in Moravia— now a part of Czechoslovakia. In these small ghettos, sex was indeed repressed—for both men and women. Marriages were arranged by a middleman when both bride and groom were children. They married as soon as they reached sexual maturity—and until then they had never seen each other. From then on, the woman lived a domestic life in which she saw her family but few other people, and no men. Sex was deemphasized—in the synagogue, in the family, in the community. But out of this sexless atmosphere the young Jewish woman was, as the century wore on, increasingly projected without preparation into the erotic whirlpool of Vienna, with its constant balls, its waltzes, its intense sexual competition, its demand that she prove herself sexually all the time, that she be "attractive" and attract, and that she be "sexy." No wonder that these women suffered anxieties and became neurotic over their sex life and sexual roles. Freud himself never referred to the alleged "sexual repression" of Viennese society. That explanation came much later and is, incidentally, of American manufacture. No Viennese would have fallen for it.

Freud was, clearly, not in favor of "sexual freedom." He would have repudiated paternity for the sexual liberation of this century that is so often ascribed to him. He was a puritan and suspected that sex, while inevitable, was not really good for the human race. As for the claim that men have made women into "sex objects," he would have thought it a very poor joke. He was familiar with the old Jewish legend of the evil Lilith, Adam's second wife, and considered it symbolic truth. Lilith seduces Adam away from Eve and makes a sex object out of the male by changing woman into the one female among the higher animals that is at all times sexually available—whereas the females of other higher animals are in heat only a few days each month and are otherwise sexless for all practical purposes. Altogether the Freudian sex drives that create repression and neuroses are independent of culture and mores; they are structured into the relationship between adults and children rather than into the relationships between the sexes in a particular society.

Still, in the Freudian literature a constant theme is sexual anxiety, sexual frustration, sexual malfunction. But the one neurosis that is stressed in every other record of late-nineteenth-century Vienna—or indeed late-nineteenth-century Europe—is totally absent: the money neurosis. It was not sex that was repressed in Freud's Vienna. It was money. Money had come to dominate; but money had also come to be unmentionable. Early in the century, in Jane Austen's novels, money is open—almost the first thing Jane Austen tells the reader is how much annual income everybody has. Seventy-five years later, by the time young Freud begins his adult life, the novelist's characters are consumed with concern for money and wealth—and never discuss it. Dickens still talks about money quite openly, just as he talks about sex quite openly, about illegitimate children and illicit liaisons, about the haunts of vice and the training of young girls to be prostitutes. Trollope, only three years Dickens's junior but already a "mid-Victorian," is still fairly explicit about sex—far more explicit than a "proper Victorian" is supposed to be. Yet most of his novels are about money, and about money which the hero or anti-hero (or, as in *The Eustace Diamonds,* the anti-heroine) has to have but cannot mention. And in the novels of Henry James, Freud's closest contemporary among the novelists of society, money and the secrecy surrounding the lack thereof, is as much the subject as the tension between American and European.

In the Vienna of Freud's time no respectable parent discussed his income with his children; it was a carefully avoided topic. Yet money had become the preoccupation of both. This, as we now know, happens in every society where there is rapid economic development.

In Jane Austen's England—still presumed to be quite static—one's money income was a fact. It could be changed only by marriage or by the right aunt's dying at the right time—the change agents in Jane Austen's books. It could not be changed by individual effort. Seventy years later economic development had made incomes highly mobile. At the same time, however, as in any society in the early stages of rapid economic development, there were now "winners" and "losers." A fairly small group profited mightily and became rich. A much larger group, but still a minority, reached precarious affluence—the Freuds in Sigmund's youth were just a cut above that level, I imagine. A majority had suddenly much greater expectations and were torn out of the static poverty of their small-town lives; but their incomes either did not go up at all or far less than their expectations had risen. It was Adlai Stevenson who first talked of the "rising tide of expectations." But the phenomenon antedates him by 150 years. The classical treatment of it is Thackeray's *Vanity Fair,* written well over a century before Stevenson's phrase and dealing with that "less developed country," the England of 1820 rather than with Asia or South America.

No European country in the last decades of the nineteenth century developed faster—and from a lower base at that—than Austria, and especially the Czech areas (Bohemia and Moravia) from which the Freuds had come and from which the Jewish middle class in Vienna was largely recruited. Thus the secret and suppressed obsession with money—the "poorhouse neurosis," it was commonly called—had become a major affliction, and a common one among the older middle-class people of my young years. (The young people were far less prone to it, for by then Austria was no longer developing and was indeed shrinking economically; the younger people were not obsessed with becoming poor, they were poor.) The poorhouse neurosis showed itself in a constant fear of ending up poor, a constant nagging worry about not earning enough, of not being able to keep up with the social expectations of oneself and one's family—and one's neighbors—and, above all, in constant obsessive talking about money while always claiming not to be interested in it.

Freud clearly suffered from the "poorhouse neurosis"; it is etched even into the letters he wrote his betrothed from Paris while still a young man. Yet for all his ruthless honesty with himself, he never could face up to it. That he misrepresented his professional life as being underpaid, under constant financial pressure, and in financial anxiety—these were misrepresentations that evinced the anxiety neurosis which he could not and did not face and which, in a Freudian slip mechanism, he repressed. This also explains why he did not notice it in his patients and leaves it out of his case histories. It had to be a "non-fact," for the fact itself was much too painful for him.

Freud's complaints about being the victim of anti-Semitic persecution similarly covered up and, at the same time, betrayed another fact Freud could not face: his inability to tolerate non-Jews.

Freud's generation of Central European (and especially Austrian) Jews had wholeheartedly and with a vengeance become German nationalists—in their culture, in their self-identification, and in their political affiliation and leanings. And no one was more consciously a German in his culture than Sigmund Freud. Yet there were no non-Jews in psychoanalysis, or at least no non-Jewish Austrians and Continental Europeans. Freud tried hard to attract them. But those who joined were always driven out.

In the "Heroic Age" of psychoanalysis, between 1890 and 1914, Freud repudiated every one of his non-Jewish followers or associates who was Austrian, German or German-speaking, or even a Continental European male. That he broke with Carl Jung and forced Jung in turn to break with him is one example. He could tolerate non-Jews only if they were foreigners, and even then he preferred women like the French Princess Bonaparte—for women did not, of course, rank as equals in Freud's world. For all their German culture—their constant references to German poets and writers, their humanist culture of the German Gymnasium, their strong Wagnerianism, and their aesthetics of the educated German "humanist" whose taste had been formed by Jakob Burckhart's *Culture of the Renaissance in Italy*—the members of the Freud circle could not rid themselves of their intense Jewishness. Their jokes were Jewish, and it is a Freudian tenet, after all, that jokes speak the truth of the heart. The non-Jew was irksome, difficult, a stranger, an irritation—and soon gotten rid of.

This, however, Freud, grand master of non-Jewish German culture, could not admit, least of all to himself. He needed an explanation that would put the blame on others, hence the Freudian slip of "anti-Semitic discrimination" and near-persecution. It was well known, for instance, that both Wagner-Jauregg, the eminent psychiatrist who headed one neuropsychiatric hospital at the University, and the head of the other neuropsychiatric university hospital—the one that had been offered to Freud but was turned down by him—had wanted to attend the meetings of Freud's Psychoanalytical Society. Both were non-Jews, and both were made decidedly unwelcome. But in Freud's version these two men had rejected him and denied him recognition because he was a Jew. Freud needed a Freudian slip because the reality, that is, the fact of his not being able to break out of his Jewishness, was much too painful for him to face and to accept. And finally, of course, he had to make Moses into an Egyptian who was not a Jew at all—in *Moses and Monotheism,* one of his last major works.

But most important and most revealing is Freud's "Freudian slip" in respect to his being "ignored" by the Viennese physicians. He had to suppress their rejection of him; and he could do it only by pretending, above all to himself, that they were not discussing him, not doubting him, not rejecting him, but ignoring him. I suspect that Freud in his heart shared a good many of their doubts about the methodology of psychoanalysis. But he could not even discuss these doubts. For to do so would have forced him to abandon the one central achievement of his: a theory that was both strictly "scientific" and rationalist, and yet went beyond rationalism into the "subconscious," into the inner space of dream and fantasy and, in Thomas Mann's words, into the unscientific experience of the "novel," that is, into fiction.

Freud was led to psychoanalysis by his realization that the prevailing rationalism of the Enlightenment—of which modern scientific medicine was a distinguished and most successful child—could not explain the dynamics of the emotions. Yet he could not abandon the world and world view of science. To his dying day he maintained that psychoanalysis was strictly "scientific"; he maintained that the workings of the mind would be found to be capable of explanation in rational, scientific terms, in terms of chemical or electrical phenomena and of the laws of physics. Freudian psychoanalysis represents a giant effort to hold together in one synthesis the two worlds of scientific reason and nonrational inner experience. It represents a giant effort to hold together in one person the ultra-rationalist Freud, the child of the Enlightenment, and Freud the dreamer and poet of the "dark night of the soul." This synthesis made psychoanalysis so important, and yet so fragile. It gave psychoanalysis its impact. It made it timely. The systems of the nineteenth century that have had a major impact on the Western world—Marx, Freud, and Keynes—all have had in common the synthesis between the scientific and the magical, and the emphasis on logic and empirical research leading to the *credo quia absurdum*—"I believe because it makes no rational sense."

Freud clearly realized how narrow his footing was. Give one inch and you descend into the Eastern mysticism of Jung, with his invocation of myth as the experience of the race, his reliance on the magical sticks of the *I Ching* and on the fairy tales of shamans, sorcerers, and sybils. And there was the descent into the "orgone box" of another ex-disciple, Otto Reich. Give one inch the other way and you descend into the trivialities of another renegade disciple, Alfred Adler, with his arithmetic of "overcompensation" and his petty envies such as the "inferiority complex" as a substitute for the passion of the Prophets and the *hubris* of the Greek dramatists. Freud had to maintain the synthesis where he had carefully and precariously balanced it, otherwise he would have had either the pure magic of the faith healer or the pure and futile mechanism of those children of the ultra-rationalist eighteenth century, the phrenologists or the Mesmerians with their electric rods. Freud had to have in one statement both "scientific" method for clinical therapy *and* "cosmic philosophy."

Just how precarious the balance was we know today. For by now it has disintegrated. There is on the one hand the scientific, rationalist clinical exploration of the brain—and indeed, Freud's prediction that the brain and its diseases would be shown to be subject to the same approaches of chemotherapy, diet, surgery, and electrotherapy as the rest of the body is well on its way to being proven. But the phenomena with which Freud dealt—we call them "emotional" today—are increasingly being tackled by methods that do not even pretend to belong to the realm of science, but are clearly in Freud's terms "superstition": transcendental meditation, for instance, or the instant "consciousness-raising" psychodynamic techniques. Whether this is good or bad, I do not know. For unlike Freud's generation, we seem to be able to accept a split of the world into incompatible universes.

However, Freud had to hold the precarious balance. I do not know whether he thought it through. Freud was not given to writing his thought processes down for others to read; no other major thinker so carefully dismantled the scaffolding of his thoughts before presenting the finished building to public view. But he knew that he needed the synthesis. And he must have realized, if only subconsciously, that it would collapse the moment he even discussed the questions the critics raised: the question of methodology; the definition of "results" and the matter of control tests; the problem of getting the same—or similar—therapeutic results from any psychotherapy, including purely magical ones; and the hybrid character of psychoanalysis as both scientific theory and therapy, and myth of personality and philosophy of man. He could only maintain the synthesis by ignoring these questions. And so he had to pretend, above all to himself, that the Viennese physicians ignored psychoanalysis so as to be able to ignore them.

The Freud of the Freudian realities is a much more interesting man, I submit, than the Freud of the conventional myth. He is also, I think a much bigger man—a tragic hero. And while a Freudian theory that can only maintain the synthesis between the world of Cartesian rationality and the world of the dark night of the soul by ignoring all inconvenient questions may be a much weaker theory—and one that cannot ultimately stand—it is also, I submit, a more fascinating and more revealing theory, and a humanly moving one.

Count Traun-Trauneck
and the Actress
Maria Mueller

My parents were their best friends; and they lived close by, no further than a pleasant twenty-minute walk through the vineyards and fruit orchards of a Viennese suburb that was then still a self-contained village. But Count Max Traun-Trauneck and Maria Mueller came to our home only twice a year: on Christmas Day and New Year's Day. Miss Maria—as she was always called—was a leading actress at Vienna's main theater, the "Burgtheater" (originally the theater of the Imperial court) and also one of its producers and stage managers. She deemed it her duty to be at the theater whenever there was a performance, whether she played in it or not. And Christmas Day and New Year's Day were the only days during the season, other than Good Friday, at which there was no evening show.

But the two always spent Christmas Day and New Year's Day with us. They would come quite early, well before the midday meal for which they always brought the wine and the flowers. With them would come also the Count's elderly valet and Maria Mueller's equally elderly dresser. Until the meal had been eaten there would be the relaxed, comfortable chit-chat of old friends—but with a difference: we always spoke English and only English with them. Indeed the two only spoke English when alone. Maria Mueller was completely bilingual, without a trace of accent in either language. The Count, though of ancient Austrian lineage, had a pronounced English accent in his Viennese. Then, after the midday meal, Maria Mueller would yield to our importuning and begin to read or to recite from memory. And this is what all of us—not only my parents and we children, but our maid and our cook and those of the neighborhood children who were close enough friends to be admitted—had been waiting for all year.

Maria Mueller had the most beautiful speaking voice I have ever heard. It was a warm, vibrant alto, like a perfect woodwind or the *Vox Humana* of one of the great baroque organs. It was under complete control and could register every emotion, every shade of feeling, every character with the slightest change in pitch, rhythm, or cadence. But it could also maintain pitch, rhythm, or cadence while going from pianissimo to forte and back. She was one of the last great speakers of verse on the stage; she still knew how to "speak" verse rather than to declaim it, still had the breath control and diction to make verse sound like the natural voice and speech of man. She was not a "famous actress"; indeed she was hardly an "actress" at all but a "speaker." On the stage she barely moved and used few gestures, and then only small and conventional ones. She stood up and spoke. But when she first came on stage and began to speak, one was reminded of the Rushing of the Wind at the Coming of the Holy Ghost at first Pentecost. One could hear the shudder shake the audience. And from then on, nobody had ears except for her.

She knew most of the plays by heart, and all the roles in them. And so she spoke—or read—to us on these afternoons of Christmas Day and New Year's Day scenes from the main verse plays of the German repertory—Goethe's *Iphigenie* or Schiller's *Maid of Orleans* and *Maria Stuart*—from her favorite Greek plays, especially the *Antigone* of Sophocles and the *Medea* of Euripides; but above all —and always in English—she read from Shakespeare: *King Lear, The Tempest* and—her favorite as well as mine—*Cymbeline*. In between the plays she would often speak a short poem, Hölderlin or Novalis, but more often John Donne or William Blake, both then little known or appreciated. Then the lights would be turned on (while she spoke we would sit in twilight and darkness rather than interrupt her) and we would eat a light supper, usually in complete silence. Then Maria Mueller would read again, almost always from Milton's *Paradise Lost*. She finished the evening by speaking some of Shakespeare's *Sonnets*, maybe two, never more than three. Then she would pause and make as if to pick up another book. But this was the signal for her dresser, who would come forward from the seat in the furthest corner of my father's library where she had been hiding all afternoon and evening, to curtsey to the assembled company and say, "Miss Maria, you have a strenuous day tomorrow"; and the party would be over.

We were far too entranced by Miss Maria's voice to pay attention to the Count during these afternoons and evenings. And he made himself inconspicuous anyhow. He never let Miss Maria out of his sight —whenever one peeked into the corner where he always sat, one would find him looking at her. But he sat well out of the light. And he sat so as to turn only one side, the right, to the room. For the entire left side of his body was terribly maimed and disfigured. Even though he wore a black patch over it, one could see that the left eye socket had been torn apart and the eye gouged out. The entire left side of his cheek was spongy, angry scar tissue. He had lost his left hand and wore instead a prosthesis covered in black suede leather, ending in a steel hook with which he could hold a glass or into which he could screw a fork while eating. And he had a perceptible limp on the left side so that, obviously, his leg had been hurt too. He was not visibly conscious of his disfigurement and not embarrassed by it. But still he tried, whenever possible, to be in the background and to show only the good side of his face and figure.

Even small children in those years of the early and mid-1920s knew better than to show curiosity about such a disfigurement or to ask questions. One assumed that it was a World War I injury—they were abundant and all around us. But we learned early from our maid, Emmy, that the Count had received his injury rock climbing rather than during the war. In the summer of 1914, just before World War I started, he had led a party on a first ascent in the Tyrolean Alps. One of his climbing partners on the rope had been hit by a falling stone and knocked unconscious. The Count, as was his job as the party's leader, had unroped and climbed down to rescue the injured man. He had succeeded in dragging him out of the path of the rockfall onto a secure ledge when he himself was hit by falling stones. Not being on the rope, he was flung over the rock face and fell several hundred feet before he crashed into a boulder. He had been given up for dead, but Maria Mueller insisted on his being rescued; then she nursed him back to health and never left his bedside during the long months of his slow recovery.

It was also our maid, Emmy, who told us the story of the Count and Maria Mueller—our parents never gossiped about their friends and we ourselves would have considered it very bad manners to ask. According to Emmy, the Count and Maria Mueller had both grown up in England, in the Austrian Embassy—the Count's father being the ambassador for many years and Maria Mueller's father a sergeant in the embassy guard. The two had been in love since childhood; and though the Count's family was strongly opposed, they were going to get married as soon as both had finished their studies. But then, when the Count came to Vienna to attend the University, a cousin of his— a Countess, of course—fell violently in love with him and threatened to kill herself unless he married her. The young woman was emotionally unstable anyhow and given to severe fits of depression. Out of sheer pity and to save her from insanity, the Count had married her. It was to no avail, however, for the young woman went stark raving mad—Emmy said during the wedding night—and had to be kept in the closed ward of an insane asylum ever after. There was no divorce on grounds of insanity in the old Austria, and as a Catholic the Count could not have remarried anyhow. So he and Maria Mueller were living together, though for appearance's sake on separate floors of the same house, with a connecting staircase in the back. After the fall of the Austrian monarchy, divorce and remarriage became legally possible. The Count thereupon offered to divorce his insane wife and marry Miss Maria. She refused. She had long ceased to be a practicing Catholic, but the Count had remained in the Church, and she would not let him violate his religious principles for her sake.

Our maid, Emmy, was the widow of a police detective on the Vice Squad who had been killed in the war; during their short marriage she had heard enough of human depravity to have become a hard-nosed cynic about the entire race, and especially about the relationship between men and women. She was also a militant Socialist and utterly contemptuous of rank and title. Yet Emmy was prone to wild flights of fancy when it came to what she called "real quality." Then her imagination, fed by a steady diet of Ruritanian operettas, serial novels in the Sunday papers, and early Douglas Fairbanks movies, would conjure up wicked stepmothers, changelings, and clandestine romances in which the true heir would, in the end, be recognized and make the virtuous innkeeper's daughter his queen. And she clearly considered Traun-Trauneck to be "real quality." We children to whom she told the story of his injury, his marriage to a beautiful but insane bride, and his childhood romance with the sergeant's daughter, were therefore properly skeptical. But for once Emmy had not made up the tale, as I gradually found out.

Both the Count and Maria Mueller had indeed grown up in the

Austrian Embassy in London. The Count was the son of a senior diplomat and an English mother, one of the Catholic Howards and kin to the Duke of Norfolk. Maria was of peasant stock and the child of an enlisted man in the embassy guard and the embassy laundress. The Count had gone to the famous public school which the Jesuits ran in the image of Eton and Harrow for the sons of English Catholic nobility and gentry, and then to Oxford, where he had read modern history. Only then had he come to Austria to study at the University—and his English mother and upbringing still showed in his accent. Maria Mueller by that time had finished actors' school and already been hired by the Burgtheater. And there *was* a wife in an insane asylum. After her death, in the early 1930s, Traun-Trauneck and Maria Mueller married quietly, although they did not change the way they lived. And there had indeed been a mountaineering accident. It was also mountaineering that had brought the Count together with my parents, for my mother was an enthusiastic rock climber in her youth, and mountaineers then were a close fraternity in which everybody knew everybody else. Long afterwards, when my parents died, I found among their papers a snapshot that showed my mother as a young girl—probably no more than seventeen—on a rope led by a youthful Traun-Trauneck, his face still unmarred by accident, with an equally youthful Maria Mueller third on the rope. The fellow climber in whose rescue Traun-Trauneck had been so terribly maimed had, I learned, been a favorite cousin of my mother's; he was killed, only a few years later, during World War I on the Italian front.

There was enough here to make Traun-Trauneck interesting, or at least to make me pay a little attention to him. Then I began to notice that my parents, while deeply fond of Maria Mueller and as enchanted by her as all of us were, treated Traun-Trauneck with a respect bordering on deference. I once heard my father say to my mother: "Max Traun is the ablest man in Austria. What a pity that he hides himself." And my mother added—but so softly that my father probably did not hear it—"What a pity that he *has* to hide himself." Yet Traun-Trauneck's official position was minor, if not obscure; he was assistant in charge of finance and administration to the director of the National Library. He rarely said anything, and then mostly commonplace courtesies about the weather and how fast we children were growing up, or about the latest performance at the theater in which one of us had seen—or rather heard—Miss Maria. But whenever his name came up in conversation with older people, they would look up and say:

"What, you know Traun-Trauneck? You must find him very interest-ing."

There was more to Traun-Trauneck apparently than his being Maria Mueller's consort. But still whenever we saw him it was with Maria Mueller, and then we forgot everybody and everything for the magic of her bewitching voice. It was only when I was almost grown up and nearly ready to leave Austria altogether that, by chance, I came close to the Count and became his confidant for a few intensive hours.

I had known since I was about fourteen that I wanted to get out of Vienna and out of Austria altogether, as soon as I possibly could, when I finished high school. But when I was in my junior year in high school and only a year and a half away from graduation, I began to realize that I had to decide what to do. The easiest and quickest way to get out of Vienna was to take a trainee job in some business, in Germany or England—a bank, maybe, or a trading house. This would also mean that I would no longer have to sit on a school bench. By that time I had become weary of being bored by bored teachers; indeed the one point of agreement between my faculty and myself was that I had sat long enough. I would be an adult among adults—I had never liked being young, and detested the company of delayed adolescents as I thought most college students to be. I would earn a living and be financially independent. Further, supporting me for four more years would be a heavy burden for my father, even though he was perfectly willing to bear it. By the standards of the Vienna of the mid-twenties we were living extremely well, but those were the standards of the poorhouse postwar Austria had become. My younger brother, it was already clear, would go to medical school and have to be supported for years to come. I at least could help lighten my father's heavy load.

There was neither stigma nor risk attached to not going to the University in those days. Nobody called you a "dropout" if you chose not to waste four additional years sitting on your backside. You were a responsible mature adult. University in Continental Europe, more-over, had little to do with being "educated"—it gave status but was otherwise purely pre-professional. The "liberal education," such as it was, ended with graduation from high school and still does. After that one trained for the law, the priesthood, medicine, engineering, and so on.

Altogether there was still a tradition—though less strong in Austria then it was in the merchant cities such as Hamburg, Amster-dam, London, or Basel—that the ablest boys of a "good family" did not go to university; they did not need to. They went into the counting-house at age fourteen. When I was a "trainee" in Hamburg a few years later, I got to know well one of the respected patrician families. The brother who headed the firm—an old and immensely rich merchant house—considered himself the brightest and best educated of the family, and many people conceded his claim. He had gone to work at fourteen of course, and he looked down his long patrician nose on his two brothers—they were the "dumb Hansens." The joke was that one of them by that time was the president of what was considered the best court of justice in all northern Europe, the Hanseatic High Court of Appeals; and the other led the biggest Protestant congregation in northern Europe, was a leading figure in the Protestant revival and the revered preceptor of such people as Karl Barth, the Swiss theologian, and the two Niebuhr brothers, Richard and Reinhold, in faraway America.

Going into business as a "trainee" did not, I knew, even mean giving up the university degree. It was entirely possible to get a doctor's degree, especially in law, while holding a full-time job. I had seen it done dozens of times all around me. Indeed it was hard to see how one would spend the day as a law student unless one had a full-time or at least a part-time job.

A persistent American belief—only recently enunciated once again by Admiral Hyman Rickover in his educational tracts—contrasts the "hardworking European university student" with the "good-time Charlie" of the American college campus. Maybe there is some truth to this today. I doubt it. Fifty or sixty years ago, however, when this tale was universally believed in American higher education, it was pure myth and had about as much substance to it as the parallel European belief that every American was both a Baptist and a multi-millionaire. Certainly there was absolutely nothing to the myth in respect to law students in all German-speaking and Nordic countries or in Italy. Old ladies in my schooldays, when told by a young man that he was a university student, were apt to ask: "Are you a real student or do you take law?" One enrolled—it could be done by mail—and paid the fees, and even those were waived for practically anyone who applied for a scholarship. Attendance was never taken. There were no exams or papers in the courses. All one had to do was to take a final examination at the end of four years, and for that most students went to a crammer anyhow for a few months (which I tried for an evening or two but gave up as totally unnecessary; Miss Elsa's workbooks were better than any crammer). Full-time law students did not spend four years working hard and studying law. They spent four years in an agreeable haze compounded of two parts beer and one part sex. I was convinced one could get quite enough of both without being a full-time student.

But still, going into business was going into "trade." We in our family prided ourselves on having no narrow prejudices, and certainly not the prejudices of the English "gentleman" against the "lower orders." We even had a businessman in the family. My aunt had taken for her second husband—her first one, a cardiologist, having died in the "Great War"—a Hungarian who was the head and majority owner of a big timber and forest-lands company. But when we talked of him we were always careful to point out that Uncle Michael had been a professional Army officer and indeed a general, and had only gone into the family firm after 1918 when there was no Hungarian Army left. One of my parents' dear friends was an industrialist, the head of a big textile company; but when introducing him or his children to our playmates, we always stressed that he had started out to be a landscape painter and had actually had an exhibition before the early death of his father forced him to take over the management of the family company. Bankers were all right, especially if they had a university degree; but a "trainee" in a merchant or manufacturing business, that was at most "all right but."

My father very much wanted me to go to the University. We were, after all, a family of civil servants, lawyers, doctors. He also suspected, quite rightly, that I lacked the instincts and talents for success in business. Altogether the pressure on me was to try to become a university professor. I was surrounded by them on all sides, with any number of uncles and cousins and family friends who were professors in Vienna, at the German University of Prague, in Switzerland, in Germany, in Oxford and Cambridge—in law, in economics, in medicine, in chemistry or biology, in art history and music. It looked to me like an easy life, with nice long summer vacations and a minimum of duties. And of course, nothing could compare in social standing to the "Herr Professor"—in Austria, where there were no Junkers to compete with, he ranked even higher than in Germany.

But going for a professorship meant staying in Vienna, for it would have made no sense for me to go to any other university. I also felt strongly that being adequate was not good enough in an academic career, neither to obtain one of the rare paid professorships (and I knew I had to, having no private means to support myself otherwise) nor to be satisfied and contented. In business, I argued—for I was a complete prig—one could get by being second-rate. All that counted in business was to make money, after all. But in academic life one had to be first-rate as a scholar and a researcher. I knew I could write, but I was by no means sure I could do research and scholarly thinking. Before committing myself to a university career, I figured, I might as well test my abilities—and if found wanting, I'd take business.

But what research? I was sure my interest lay in such areas as government, political history and political institutions, maybe even economics. These fields were commonly taught in the law faculty in Europe. I therefore asked my Uncle Hans, an eminent legal scholar— he died only in the 1970s, in his nineties, after many years as the great man in jurisprudence at Berkeley—what the most difficult problem in legal philosophy was. "To explain the rationale of criminal punishment," was his answer. So I decided, all of sixteen years old, to go to work on criminal punishment and to write the *definitive* book on it.

For this I needed access to a library. Public libraries are an American idea. Libraries in Europe, at least in those days, were to keep books in and people out. The University Library in Vienna, for instance, did not even admit students except into special reading rooms where all they were allowed to read were assigned texts. Only recognized and tenured scholars could borrow books, and even they as a rule were not given access to the stacks. Despite all the uncles and cousins I had on the university faculty (even my father was an adjunct professor there for many years and taught an occasional course), I was flatly denied access to the library. But there was the National Library and Count Traun-Trauneck. He gladly gave me permission to come in as his personal guest, to occupy an empty small room next to his office, and to read all the books I wanted. So I began to go there each afternoon after school and to pore over legal philosophers and sociologists.

It was my first encounter with sociologists' jargon. The shock was profound and caused lasting trauma. But I also found out soon what Uncle Hans had meant when he called criminal punishment the most difficult problem in legal philosophy. It was a dense thicket and a thorny one. Every one of the great men I read, from Aristotle to St. Thomas Aquinas to Hume, Bentham, and such moderns as Roscoe Pound, Ehrlich, or my Uncle Hans, gave a different reason for punishment: retaliation or the protection of society, ritual cleansing, rehabilitation, or deterrence. But all of them, peculiarly, came out with the same punishments, no matter what they reasoned punishment was supposed to be doing. The punishments were the same throughout history and regardless of culture, civilization, or law code: death, mutilation, banishment, prison, and fines. It was also obvious that there was criminal punishment in every civilization and culture. I was not much of a logician at that age—nor am I now. But it took me only a few weeks of baffled reading to come to the conclusion that all these great men must be tackling the wrong problem. If a dozen explanations, all starting with totally different but self-evident premises, reach the same conclusion, then elementary logic would argue, they are all rationalizations rather than explanations, and beside the point. The point, it seemed to me, was not punishment at all. Punishment was, apparently, a fact of human existence in society and prevailed independent of any attempt to justify it. What needed explanation was the existence of crime—and that I knew to be well beyond my powers.

In all that mountain of literature there were only two short pamphlets that seemed to think along the same lines I was following. They were by an author of whom I had never heard—"Karl Raunt," it said on the title page. They were short, twenty pages or so each; they were comparatively recent, having been published around 1905; they were in brilliant red jackets rather than somber hand-tooled leather; and they had been published as "Tracts of the Socialist International," with the hammer and sickle on the jacket cover. They argued that crime was a product of capitalism and would cease to exist, or at least cease to be a major problem, as soon as socialism had been established or within a generation afterwards. This seemed to me to be naïve to the point of childishness. There was overwhelming evidence that crime was endemic to human society regardless of its economic, social, or political structure. And by 1925, when I read this, there was enough known about the Soviet paradise to make even a sixteen year old wonder. Indeed I could not quite figure out why these two pamphlets had been included by the librarian in the books provided for me when I described what I was after. But at least they were written in a decent style, and the author had seen what the real problem was, even though he had explained it away rather than addressing it.

By that time I had reached the conclusion that my project had failed and that I had better return all the books to the librarian, thank Count Traun-Trauneck for his hospitality, and ask my father to find me a trainee job in business. But I thought I might have another go at those two pamphlets, if only because they alone talked about what seemed to me the real issue. I was standing by the window with the pamphlets in my hands when the door opened and the Count came in. He had made a point of leaving me alone, but apparently wanted to show an interest in how I was doing. When he saw the two red pamphlets in my hand, he gave a startled look and said: "What do you think of them?" Something in his voice alerted me to be careful, so I simply said that I thought they alone of all the heap of books on the subject asked the key question how to explain crime. He seemed very pleased and smiled broadly. "I had no idea," he said, "that they are still around; do you know who the author is?" I shook my head. He pointed to the author's name and said, "Just move that last letter 't' up front. What have you got?" "Traun," I said, with sudden realization. He laughed. "Karl," he said, "is my second name—I was baptized Maximilian Karl Franz Josef. A civil servant, even a young one buried in the National Library, was not supposed to write Socialist tracts in those days. I thought everyone would have guessed that 'Raunt' was 'Traun.' But no one ever did. Would you like to hear the story?"

It was a long story and took more than one afternoon to tell. For once the Count had begun to talk, he could not stop. So much that had been bottled up in the withdrawn and wounded man came out—I don't think he knew half the time whom he was talking to or even that he was talking at all. What he told me was not just his personal story. It was the story of a lost generation and a lost dream.

"Do you wonder that a Count Traun-Trauneck was a militant Socialist twenty years ago?" he began. "Well, one way or another we were all Socialists then; I may only have been a little more articulate. I realize that these pamphlets must strike you as naïve today. I would not have written them that way a few years later; I was only twenty-three when I did. But we all expected socialism to usher in a new society. Of course, few of us had read Marx or cared about economics. What we cared about was *peace*.

"The older people, even your father's age group—and he's not quite ten years older than I am—did not believe that a war was coming. And if there was a war, they expected another picnic like the wars of the nineteenth century that were over in three months and left Europe unchanged. We knew better. Our spokesman was Jean Jaurès. Did you ever hear of him?" I said I had, but only knew the name. "He was the foremost leader of socialism in Europe, the head of the French Socialist Party, which was then the largest party in Europe and almost a majority in France, and the greatest orator I have ever heard. He was assassinated when the war started. He had been warning for years that the next war would totally immerse France and destroy Europe and civilization altogether. None of the French politicians or generals believed him, but *we* knew what he was talking about. Yet here was socialism, the first mass movement since Christianity and already the largest party—the only large party—in the main Continental countries, in France, Italy, Germany, and Austria, and of course in Russia too, even though they had no elections and no parliament. Socialism was disciplined and had leaders. It had been tested in strikes and we knew—or thought we knew—that the Socialist masses would follow their leaders' orders. And socialism was committed to peace. That's why we were Socialists in those years.

"We thought we had it made. Ever hear of the 1911 Congress of the Socialist International?" I shook my head. "It was held right here in Vienna and at it all the major Socialist parties of Europe swore solemnly to mobilize their followers against any European war and to call them out on general strike if war should break out. I ran the secretariat—of course, as Karl Raunt. There was going to be another even bigger Congress, also in Vienna, in October 1914, for which I had completed most of the arrangements when I had my accident. They were going to set up permanent anti-war machinery, probably in Brussels or in Amsterdam, and again I was to be the general secretary of the Congress. And that's why we all were Socialists."

"But who was 'we?' " I asked. "Did you have an organization, and who belonged to it?" "No, we had no organization—that's not how we worked. Your father's friend, Marcel Ray—he's now an Ambassadeur de France, as you know, but then he was a young professor of German literature at the Sorbonne—wanted to start an organization. He had a nice name for it, 'Les Chevaliers de la Paix,' and thought membership in it might rival the Légion d'Honneur as a distinction. But we were really quite informal, with no membership, no organization, and no by-laws. You just knew who belonged. Europe was a much smaller place then and the young educated people all knew each other. We climbed mountains together; we went to English house parties together; we had gone to school together. You just knew each other. Of course, there were lots of young educated well-to-do people who just drifted into pleasure: fox hunting and gaming at the Riviera, pig-stalking in India, or chasing chorus girls, which was the cheapest and least harmful of these pursuits of the idle rich. There were so many of them and they were such an offense to anybody the least fastidious that they convinced the rest of us that Europe couldn't go on the way it was and that catastrophe lay ahead. Then too, especially in Austria, France, and Russia, there were lots who just drifted into being aesthetes and who spent their time writing poor poetry and having it printed at their own expense on mauve paper. I bet your mother still has a trunkful of them; she was a very popular girl and those young Narcissuses always gave her a copy of their poems." I had to admit that I had seen some such confections around. "But then," he continued, "there were enough of us who wanted something different—and they were the 'we' I talked about. There was Marcel Ray and his wife, Suzanne. She had the right connections—you know, I imagine, that she's Anatole France's natural daughter?" I didn't know. "Well, she could get to Jaurès and persuade him to call the Peace Congress of 1911 in Vienna. He was very skeptical, as all the elder statesmen of Socialism were. They saw themselves within reach of political power and didn't want to be accused of lack of patriotism. But Suzanne went to work and convinced Jaurès. And there was a whole group of young French scholars, Marc Bloch, the historian, for instance, and a whole generation of promising young politicians like Édouard Herriot, who were rapidly becoming recognized and beginning to exercise influence.

"We even had friends in Russia, a rising young officer called von Zissermann, for instance, who was the military engineer who built the Manchurian Railroad which, I'm told, he now runs for some Chinese warlord. You know his wife; she was one of the most beautiful girls in Vienna and only recently went out to Manchuria to rejoin her husband. And there were a large number of young Germans, young professors like Franz Oppenheimer, the economist, and young graduate students, especially in Heidelberg around Max Weber and his brother Alfred, and the circle around a young philosopher whose name was Simmel, and a few bankers and economists, particularly a very brilliant young banker whose name was Hjalmar Schacht, who is now head of the German Central Bank. Most of the bright young instructors at the University and the young civil servants in Austria were in our group. Just to give you a few whose names you'll recognize, there was your mother's cousin, Arnim the historian, the one who was with me on the climb where I had the accident, and your Uncle Hans and his three brothers and his friend and colleague Alfred Verdross, the son of the lieutenant-field marshal whose aide your cousin Arnim was. The older ones, like your father or Hemme Schwarzwald, were still Liberals. But the younger ones, the ones in their twenties or so, knew that liberalism could not prevent another war. So we turned to the one force we thought could do so because it had the organization and the commitment and the mass basis: Socialism.

"In England you could still be a liberal," he continued. "You know I'm half English. My mother was still alive then and I went to England four or five times a year and saw the chaps I had been close to in my Oxford years. They were beginning their careers, some as dons, some in the diplomatic service or the Indian service, a few as barristers, and a few even in the City as bankers—and they weren't attracted to Socialism. But then they were quite sure that England would stay out of the European war as it had stayed out of the wars of the nineteenth century.

"No," he went on, "if you expected us to have a password and a secret organization, I must disappoint you. But then the small educated class of Europe was in itself an organization and everyone in it knew exactly where to go, knew everybody else, had access to everybody, so that we didn't need a password."

"And then what happened?" I interjected. "How come you failed?" "We didn't fail; Socialism did. Europe's Socialist leaders—the ones on whom we had counted—did indeed oppose the war, although none of them dared call the general strike they had committed themselves to at the 1911 Vienna Congress. But even if they had, it would have made no difference. The proletarian masses, that great powerful force for peace and brotherhood, everywhere ignited like tinder in a patriotic firestorm. You know," he went on sadly, "it's popular now to blame the military and the diplomats and the businessmen for World War I, and they were reckless. But the ones who really wanted war were the great Socialist masses. They whupped it up. They brought about the 'total immersion' of Europe of which Jaurès had warned—and that was the end of Socialism.

"Of course you'll tell me that there are more Socialist voters around in Europe these days than there were before 1914. But then Socialism was based on hope and not on numbers. Now it is based on envy. That unspeakable clown Mussolini, down in Rome, understands this. Before the war he was the most militant Socialist and always tried to make up to us and get our kind of people to write for his newspaper. At that Vienna Socialist Congress of 1911 he was the firebrand who promised to deliver 'the revolution' should war come to Europe. But then he saw what really happened—and he understood it, I'm afraid. To be sure, the Socialists here in Austria, and those in Germany and France, and the Labor Party in England are decent enough chaps; I prefer them to the clericals and priests who now rule us here in Austria. Indeed, if I had been in as visible a position in the civil service as the one your father held, I would have resigned with him when the Monsignors took over the Austrian government two years ago. But still, that's all the Socialists are today—decent chaps who won't do any good or too much harm except by timidity and stupidity. But if Socialism really should come to power anywhere in Europe from now on, it will either be a tyranny like the ones you see in Russia and Italy, or it will be government by chief clerks and paper pushers. The dream is gone.

"When war broke out," he continued, "I was lying unconscious in a hospital bed—you've heard of my accident, haven't you? When I came to and found out what had happened a few months later, I wanted to kill myself. I've often regretted that they didn't let me die on that rock wall. I often envy the ones who were killed in the war. And most of us were, of course.

"You are too young to know this, but the greatest damage the war inflicted was not even that it destroyed the one hope we had for a different world. It was that it killed off the people who could have salvaged Europe. It killed off a whole leadership generation. We were forty-eight boys graduating from the Jesuit public school I went to in England. Eighteen are still alive; the rest lie in graves in Flanders. I mentioned your Uncle Hans, the one who married your mother's sister, Greta. His three brothers were even abler than he is, yet two are buried in the officers' cemetery in the Italian Tyrol where your mother's cousin, Arnim, also lies. A fat lot of good it did my saving him a little earlier on that mountain climb. And the third brother—you know Hans's brother, Ernest?" I shook my head. "He was buried alive by a Russian mine and can barely function as a Jesuit lay brother, washing dishes and waiting on tables. Yet he was the ablest young engineer and a genius in electronics and telephony. I am the only one of my family who has survived: my four brothers, each far more able than I ever was, were all killed, and so were my poor wife's three brothers, the three young Counts Balaton. My mother came from one of those enormous English families and I grew up with dozens and dozens of cousins—there are four or five of us left. Sometimes I feel

like the Emperor Joseph—you know, the one who when he opened
the Vienna Court Gardens to the public heard a lady of the aristocracy
complain that she now had no place where she could be sure of meeting only her equals in rank. He answered that he, should he want to
make sure of consorting only with his equals, would have nowhere to
go but the Habsburg burial vault. I, if I want to meet my kind of
people, can only go to the cemeteries at Verdun and Passchendaele
and on the Russian front and the Isonzo and to all the other charnel
houses where the ones lie who should be leading us in Europe.

"You know, Peter, when the Republic came in and the Socialists
formed a government, they offered me the job of Minister of Education. It was the one office I had always wanted, the one for which I had
been preparing myself. But I just couldn't face it. I just couldn't succeed at the expense of all these dead friends of my youth and comrades
of my dreams. Sometimes I feel so guilty that I with this broken,
useless body of mine am still around that I'm ready to call it quits. It's
only that Miss Maria still needs me . . ."

That the Count was overwrought and perhaps not completely
sane even I, at sixteen, could sense. I was indeed more than a little
frightened by his outburst and tried to get away as fast as I could. That
great nonconspiracy of Europe's élite to save peace probably existed
only in the Count's imagination, although Suzanne Ray much later
confirmed that she had indeed, working with the Count and a few
other friends, persuaded Jean Jaurès to convene the 1911 Congress of
the Socialist International in Vienna at which all Socialist parties committed themselves solemnly to a general strike in the event of a European war. And an even more solemn anti-war congress of the Socialists
was planned for October 1914, with Count Traun-Trauneck (or Karl
Raunt) as its secretary general.

But whether Traun-Trauneck exaggerated his own role—and his
own guilt—is beside the point. For Socialism did indeed die with the
guns of August of 1914 when the Socialist masses rejected proletarian
solidarity and enthusiastically embraced nationalism and fratricidal
war instead. It was not the end of Marxism as a theology; theologies
do outlive faith. It was not the end of Socialism as a political force. But
it was the end of Socialism as a dream—at least for an entire generation, if not forever. Since then power has won in every conflict between the promise of Socialism and the reality of power; since then,
above all, nationalism has won in every conflict between the promise
of Socialism and the passion of nationalism. Again and again some

dreamers of the earlier dream—the best known is the American Michael Harrington—appeal to the original vision and declare that the reality of Socialism is an unnecessary and deplorable perversion of the true faith. But to no avail. This explains why Socialism has been intellectually sterile since 1914. Earlier, the ablest minds of Europe had wrestled with the intellectual promises and problems of Socialism. Since 1914, only one truly first-rate mind in Europe has concerned himself with Socialism at all: the Italian Antonio Gramsci, who could maintain his prewar innocence because Mussolini kept him imprisoned and thus protected him from exposure to reality.

The Socialist parties in Europe did have the votes in the period betwen the two world wars. But that was all they had—and it did not make the slightest difference. For they no longer had vision, belief, commitment, creed, or credence. In the sorry farce of European politics during the twenty years between Versailles and World War II, Socialism might as well not have been on the stage at all, even though in every country the elder statesmen of pre-World War I Socialism were the government. They were, as Traun-Trauneck saw, just chief clerks. And the resurgence of Socialism as a creed since World War II is, essentially, not "Socialism" at all, but nationalist tyranny and naked power-grabbing hiding behind the old slogans.

Whether these things would have been different had the leadership generation of Europe not been killed off, I do not know. But few people today—least of all in America—can realize how World War I decimated Europe's leadership. I did not realize it, despite what Traun-Trauneck had told me, until I was a few years older. Then in my early twenties I found myself a senior editor of a big newspaper, not because I was so good but because the generation ahead of me simply did not exist. There were no thirty year olds around when I was twenty; they were lying in the officers' cemeteries of Flanders and Verdun, Russia and the Isonzo. And the ones who survived were likely to be maimed for life—physically only, if they were lucky, but more likely spiritually as well. This was surely true of the Germans—of the last Chancellor of the Weimar Republic, Heinrich Bruening, for instance, an able and decent man whose willpower was fatally sapped by his deep inner conviction that it was guilt to have survived.

It is fashionable today to trace the beginning of England's decline back to Victorian or early Edwardian days. But surely a main factor was the decimation of England's leaders in World War I and the demoralization of the survivors. England lost a larger portion of its

young officers than the other countries did—the others were not committed to the code of the gentleman which demanded recklessness. As
a result England had an even greater lack of young educated men than
the Continental countries. There are few more moving accounts of
loneliness and desolation than the books by young English women of
the twenties—Vera Brittain's *Testament of Youth,* for instance—who
had lost every one of the young men with whom they had grown up.
And the survivors were broken men. Winston Churchill was already
forty when World War I started, and thus immune. But the next
generation, the generation of Anthony Eden and Harold Macmillan,
came back from the trenches with an inner crack that never healed
and caused them to shatter when, after Churchill's death, they had to
take responsibility by themselves.

But what most damaged England was precisely that, alone of all
major European countries, it had one ruling class, and one that was
generally accepted. In France there was the deep cleavage between
the ruling classes of the *Ancien Régime* before the French Revolution,
and those of the Napoleonic and Bourgeois régimes. As a result, there
was no one class to whom the nation looked for leadership. Similarly,
there were competing ruling classes in Germany: Junkers who had the
social standing but no money, and new, monied bourgeoisie without
much social standing, and the professionals and academicians, all competing with one another and none universally accepted. But England
had only the one class—a class easy to get in, a class that reached from
great nobles down to country squires and the sons of successful professional men and the grandsons of successful "tradesmen." Even those
who did not belong to that class and did not wish to behave as it did
—and neither the lower middle class nor the working class in Victorian England wanted to behave like "gentlemen"—accepted gentlemen as the legitimate ruling class. When their ranks were decimated
and their self-confidence shattered, there was thus a vacuum. It has
not yet been filled. Continental Europe was actually more class-ridden
and more class-conscious than Victorian England. The club on Pall
Mall in which a duke's son and a banker were both members would
have been unthinkable in the Paris, the Berlin, the Vienna, or the St.
Petersburg of 1890. Nor could the two have spent the weekend together at the same house party, or as the Edwardians did with such
equanimity, shared a mistress. But that was precisely England's weakness when this ruling class was decimated, broken, and discredited. In
France, the "technocrats," the intellectually trained graduates of the

"grande écoles," could move into the role of leaders. In Germany, after World War II, executives of organizations, business executives, and trade union executives could all emerge as legitimate leadership groups. In England there has been no substitute for what World War I destroyed, no one whose authority is accepted, but also no one who dares arrogate responsibility to himself.

It took me several afternoons to detach myself from Traun-Trauneck and his need to confide. After that we reverted to our earlier relationship. He never even alluded to those few hours of red-hot intensity and intimacy. He and Maria Mueller continued to come to our house Christmas Day and New Year's Day, and he would then sit quietly in a corner, looking at her with love and affection but saying very little, and then only commonplaces. But he did speak to me once more—the last time I was to see him and Maria Mueller.

It was in 1937—late February or early March—that I for the first and last time called on the two in their own home. My wife and I were then on our honeymoon but also on our way from England to the United States, and were paying a last visit to my parents and Vienna. To take my leave I went over to the modest villa where the Count and Maria Mueller—now his Countess—lived. The Count took me aside and said: "I'm worried about your parents. You know and I know that Hitler will march in at any moment; your father doesn't believe it. He thinks it can't happen here, and he thinks nothing would happen to him if Hitler came. But you and I both know this isn't true. I don't know if he ever told you that he's Grandmaster of the Austrian Freemasons?"—I did know, but not because my father had told me, since he observed the Lodge's strict secrecy. "I don't know what you think of the Freemasons," the Count went on. "I have never been one. But I'm quite sure your father's name must be high on the Nazi Secret Police wanted list. I've been trying, for several years, to get him to prepare for flight if necessary. But he won't listen to me."

I was able to reassure the Count. "Since my brother left last fall for the United States," I told him, "the house is much too big for my parents and much too hard for my mother to keep up. They put it on the market after I was here last Christmas and have just sold it, for an excellent price all in cash, and they've put the money into a bank account in Zurich. As soon as my residence in New York is established in a few weeks' time, we'll transfer the account into my name and out of the Nazis' reach, should they come. My parents are going to move into a small apartment shortly. And just now, during my visit here, I've got my father to go to the consulates of the countries next to Austria —the Swiss, the Czech, the Hungarian, and the Yugoslavian—and get an entry visa for himself and Mother at each, valid for two years." "Very good," said the Count; "I guess that's all one can do."

"And what do you plan to do when the Nazis come?" I asked. "Where will you go?" "We won't go abroad," he said. "Maria and I have no children, unlike your parents."

Less than a year later the Nazis did come and the only thing that saved my father was that they still had his old address and sent the storm troopers to the house he had sold a year earlier. By the time they had realized their mistake, he was on the train to Zurich and got through because of the visa he had obtained the year before.

Count Traun-Trauneck and Maria Mueller also escaped. On the day on which the German Army marched triumphantly into Vienna, they quietly committed suicide together.

YOUNG MAN

IN AN

OLD WORLD

The Polanyis

I came back to Vienna in 1927 for my first Christmas vacation, after four months as a trainee in an export firm in Hamburg. And I found waiting for me an invitation to attend an editorial meeting on the special New Year's issue of the weekly magazine, *The Austrian Economist (Der Oesterreichische Volkswirt)*. I had been reading the magazine since my early teens but had never met any of the editors. However my father, then in government service, had been its sponsor when the magazine was founded in 1907, and had remained a close friend and adviser, and a frequent contributor.

At that time the magazine was one of the most distinguished publications in Continental Europe. It had originally been modeled after the London *Economist* but had soon developed into a distinct and very lively journal in its own right, embracing not only business and economics but world politics, science, and technology. To be invited to an editorial meeting of *The Austrian Economist* was thus a signal honor, even though it was meant to please my father rather than me. What made the invitation even more agreeable was a penciled scrawl at the bottom, signed with the editor's initials and saying: "We here have read your article on the Panama Canal and think it very good." The thesis on the Panama Canal and its role in world trade which I had written as part of my university entrance examination the year before had been published by a German economic quarterly only a few weeks earlier—and to the intense pleasure of seeing myself in print for the first time, even with a piece that consisted mainly of graphs and tables, now was added recognition from people whom I had been reading for years. I don't think I ever received a better Christmas present.

The meeting was to be on Christmas Day at eight o'clock in the morning. I was enjoined to arrive on the dot, and did so. So did all the staff members, including the founder and editor-in-chief, a venerable, white-bearded, very deaf old gentleman. But by nine o'clock we were still sitting around, making small talk. "We are waiting for Karl Polanyi, the associate editor," I was told when I asked what was delaying the meeting. From the way this was said, it was clear that waiting for Karl Polanyi was nothing unusual.

We waited another forty minutes when I began to notice smiles on the faces of the people in the room. Then I heard a peculiar rhythmic chant, first quite faint, then getting louder and louder—it sounded as if someone was shouting out at the top of his lungs a lot of nonsense syllables like "Feng Hu-siang," "Chang Tzo-lin," "Chiang Kai-shek," and "Mao Tse-tung." Then a very large man burst into the room, carrying in each hand what looked like a small steamer trunk, and still bellowing nonsense syllables. He stopped long enough to shout: "Merry Christmas," then let himself drop into a chair that almost collapsed under the shock, all the while continuing to chant "Chang Tzo-lin" and so on.

He opened one of the trunks and an enormous mass of books, papers, magazines, letters cascaded out. In the same bellowing voice he shouted at top speed, with the words tumbling out like volcanic rocks: "For the annual review issue we'll have four lead articles. One on what goes on in China. The civil war there between Chang Tzo-lin and Chiang Kai-shek and all the other warlords," and he chanted all those nonsense syllables again, "is the most important event of the next five years. And then we'll have a piece on the fall of agricultural prices on the world markets—it foreshadows a serious economic depression in a few years' time. The third piece will deal with Stalin in Russia; Leninism is dead and with it the Communist Revolution. There is a new Oriental despotism and the reintroduction of serfdom. And finally we'll have a piece about an English economist, Keynes is his name; the man, you know, who wrote about the *Economic Consequences of the Peace* in 1919–20. He's coming out with new and exciting theories that stand traditional economics on its head." He opened the other trunk and another avalanche of books, pamphlets, and papers rushed out.

Polanyi's colleagues were more annoyed than impressed. "But Karl," said the editor-in-chief, "we can't just ignore the fair-sized civil war Austria had last summer." "Of course we can ignore it," came the answer. "We anticipated it five years ago." "But Polanyi," said another of the editors, "we surely need a lead article on the revaluation of the British pound. You yourself have told us that it was a major blunder and bound to harm both England and the world economy." "Yes," said Polanyi, "but we've said that before, and more than once." "But Polanyi, what about the stock market boom in the United States?" "And what about the final settlement of the German reparations?" "The stock market boom on Wall Street is a capitalist delusion," said Polanyi, grandly, "and the German reparations were settled five years ago. Since then it's been clear that the Germans won't and can't pay reparations whatever treaties they sign." At that point he noticed me, asked who I was, had me introduced, and said: "Do *you* have any suggestion for a subject for one of our lead pieces?" Fortunately I had been asking myself while the editors were wrangling what the most unlikely subject might be that could match Polanyi's suggestions, so I said, "What about a piece on the danger of Hitlerism taking over Germany?" "Nonsense," cried all the editors together, "Nazism was beaten to a pulp in the last German election and is as good as dead." "Yes, I know," I said, "but I'm scared of it." "Very important," said Polanyi. "Do you think you could write three pages of double-space typescript telling us why you are scared?"

Polanyi was overruled. In the end the safe, conventional topics were chosen and Polanyi's speculations (as the editors called them) were reduced to short paragraphs and relegated to back pages. But I had by that time lost interest in everyone except Polanyi. I asked him whether he would mind my riding with him to his home after the meeting so I could hear more about the topics he had been suggesting —and he promptly invited me to have Christmas dinner with him and his family. When we left the meeting, the business manager handed out the monthly paychecks. Polanyi, who had his hands full with his steamer trunks, asked me to hold his check while he fumbled for a pen to sign the receipt. I could not help but notice the amount of the check, which was open and not in an envelope. I was surprised by its size—by Austrian 1927 standards it was enormous.

We took one streetcar line to its terminal way out in a slum district. Then we took another one that ran through an industrial zone of small factories and warehouses. And then, from the terminal of that line, we walked a good twenty minutes through tumbledown shacks, abandoned-car lots, and a few city dumps until we came to a solitary old and grimy five-story tenement, the lower floors of which were boarded up. We climbed up all five stories—Polanyi all the while carrying those enormous valises that served him for briefcases. Finally on the top floor and in total darkness, the door was opened and we were greeted by Polanyi's wife Ilona, her mother, an elderly widowed Hungarian baroness, and the Polanyis' only child, a daughter then about eight years old. We sat down to dinner immediately and were served what, without exaggeration, I can call the worst meal of my life: old, badly peeled, half-raw potatoes—there was not even margarine with them. This was Christmas dinner!

No one paid any attention to me or to the food. Instead all four, including the little girl, argued vehemently how Karl could earn enough money the following month to pay the bills. The sum they mentioned as being needed was ludicrously small—a fraction of the paycheck Polanyi had just received and actually less than I, living by myself in Hamburg on a clerk trainee's stipend, found inadequate to get by in the most modest style. Finally I could contain myself no longer. "I apologize for butting in," I said, "but I couldn't help but see the amount of Dr. Polanyi's paycheck when we left the editorial meeting. Surely one can live, and very well, on that?" All four stopped talking and were absolutely silent for what seemed an eternity. Then all four turned and stared at me. And all four said, almost in unison: "What a remarkable idea; spend your paycheck on yourself! We never heard of such a thing." "But," I stammered, "most people do that." "We are *not* most people," said Ilona, Karl's wife, sternly; "We are *logical* people. Vienna is full of Hungarian refugees—refugees from the Communists and refugees from the White Terror that succeeded the Communists; and a good many cannot earn an adequate living. Karl has proven his capacity to earn. Therefore it is obviously only logical for him to turn his paycheck over to other Hungarians and then go out and earn what we need."

Karl Polanyi was the fourth of five children of equally unusual parents. The Polanyis—father and children—were the most gifted family I have ever known or heard of. They were also the most achieving family; every one of them had success and impact. But what made them truly remarkable was that all of them, beginning with the father in Victorian days and ending with Karl and his brother Michael in the

1960s, enlisted in the same cause: to overcome the nineteenth century and to find a new society that would be free and yet not "bourgeois" or "liberal"; prosperous and yet not dominated by economics; communal and yet not a Marxist collectivism. Each of the six, the father and five children—and the mother as well—went his or her own quite separate way, but each in search of the same goal. They reminded me of the Knights of the Round Table setting out in search of the same Holy Grail, each in a different direction.

Each one found an "answer"—and each then realized that it was not "the answer." I know of no family that was so successful, measured by the standards of the world, and such a failure when measured by its own expectations. But I also know of no family in which every member was so full of life, of interest, of vital energy. And Karl was the most interesting, the most vital, the most energetic—at least of the four or five Polanyis I got to know personally.

Father Polanyi I never knew, of course. He was born between 1825 and 1830 in a small Jewish settlement in the Hungarian mountains. He became one of the student-leaders of the Hungarian revolt against the Habsburgs in 1848 and one of its most effective orators. And then he became, although not yet twenty-five, a tough guerilla commander in the long losing civil war the Hungarian insurgents waged, first against the Austrians and then against the army the Czar of Russia sent into Hungary to crush the rebellion. After the final defeat, the older Polanyi escaped to Switzerland where he studied engineering and became a stern Calvinist. For ten years or so he lived in exile, building railroads all over Europe and making a name for himself as a civil engineer and railroad builder. Then in the late 1850s, when the rebels were amnestied, he returned to Hungary, determined to carry out the original program of the 1848 Revolution but by other means. Instead of waging war against the Habsburgs, Hungary was going to attain its own national destiny as a distinct, modern, but unbourgeois culture through economic development based on railroads and on a modern, highly protected agriculture. Within a few years the father had become one of the "railway kings," half financial, half political, and totally speculative. Like almost all of them—in the United States as well as in Europe—he built the railroads of his vision; and like almost all of them, he overextended himself, crashed, and died bankrupt, around 1900.

When the older Polanyi was at the peak of his career and reputed to be the richest commoner in Hungary, around 1868 or so, he met and married a girl twenty years younger than he was. Cecilia was a Russian countess and an anarchist. While still in her mid-teens she had been involved in a bomb plot—she had been making bombs in the chemistry laboratory of the Czar's School for the Daughters of the Nobility which her brothers had then used to kill a high police official. The girl had escaped and was living in hiding in Zurich when the older Polanyi met and married her. When I came to know her in the 1920s —and she was the first member of the family I met—she was still an anarchist but a shriveled-up old lady feared for her vicious tongue. Sometimes she was quite witty, as when she said upon the election of the first labor government in Great Britain: "In every other country this would be a step in the right direction; but England is the one country where the servants are even more servile than their masters." Usually she was just nasty. "What a boon for Margaret," she said when she heard that the husband of her best friend had been imprisoned for passing counterfeit currency. "She always whines about her husband's womanizing. Now he'll have to be faithful to her."

The couple had five children: two boys, Otto and Adolph; one girl, Mousie (she must have had another name but no one ever heard it or used it); then two more boys, Karl and Michael. As soon as each of the children reached school age, he or she was taken to a castle their father had bought for them in the middle of an enormous wheat plantation miles from the nearest town. There the children were educated in strict isolation, without contact with anyone, especially not with other children. They saw only their tutors, one English, one Swiss-French, one Swiss-German, one Hungarian; each tutor teaching one child a week in turn. Their father was bringing them up according to Rousseau's precepts in *Émile,* which demand complete isolation from the hypocrisy and corruption of society. He also tried to emulate the education James Mill had given to his son, John Stuart Mill, and indeed to improve on it. Surprisingly, none of the children turned into an idiot, but they did turn out different and unusual.

Otto, the oldest, born in the early 1870s, became an engineer like his father. And, like his father, he left Hungary while a young man and went to work in Switzerland and Germany. He was apparently a highly skilled machine designer and a good businessman who rose fast. He went to Italy around 1895 and took over a near-bankrupt machinery manufacturer. Otto Pol—he changed the name from Polanyi— turned the floundering firm around. It became the main supplier of brakes, steering gear, and the like to a new automobile company called Fiat. By 1910 Otto Pol had thus become one of Italy's leading industrialists and an exceedingly wealthy man. But he had also become an ardent Marxist, one of the founders and financial backers of the socialist newspaper *Avanti,* and the patron and friend of the young editor of the paper, a firebrand, more anarchist than orthodox Marxist, whose name was Benito Mussolini.

In World War I Otto Pol's Socialist hopes came crashing down and he began to look for an alternative to class war to build the nonbourgeois society of the future. It was Otto Pol who converted Mussolini —then recovering from near-fatal wounds—to the new vision of class unity based on a corporate state, neither Socialist nor capitalist, a state in which the classes would be held together by common dedication to national virtue and thereby become unbreakably strong like the bundled twigs, the *fasces* of the Romans of glorious Republican antiquity.

Karl Polanyi was reluctant to talk about his brother Otto; the family had broken with him when he espoused fascism. But he once told me that Otto was still alive in the mid-thirties, had long become disenchanted with his brainchild, had grown contemptuous of Mussolini but was also disavowed by his former protégé and forgotten by him, and had turned into a broken, bitter old man.

The next brother, Adolph, also became an engineer and, like his father, a railroad builder. Still quite young—it must have been well before World War I—he went to Brazil to build a railroad for an English engineering contractor. He fell in love with the country and decided to stay. He became Brazil's leading consulting engineer, first for railroads, harbors, and power stations, and later on for industrial projects as well. But he too was primarily interested in economic and social development. Like his father, he saw in the technological "infrastructure"—the railroads, the power plants, the ports—the engine of development and the maker of nationhood. But what attracted him to Brazil was the promise of a new society, different from the "decadent capitalism" of Europe; an interracial society in which whites, blacks, and Indians would meld to create a new civilization, modern yet tribal, free yet not individualist. He was at the center of the group of sociologists, novelists, musicians, painters, and politicans who, in the years after World War I, created the mystique of the "New Brazil" with its own distinct culture and civilization which then, after World War II, exploded in a burst of cultural and artistic creativity of modern Brazilian painting, modern Brazilian music, and modern Brazilian architecture. Adolph was tireless in preaching "Brazil's continental mission." He agitated for years for a new Brazilian capital, for instance, far in the interior and away from the seaboard with its dependence on Europe.

I never met Otto Pol. But I did see quite a bit of Adolph—he also changed his last name to Pol—in Karl Polanyi's apartment near Columbia University in New York. It was in the 1950s when Adolph was already an old man, close to eighty or older. He had come to New York for medical treatment and died within a year. But he was still tireless, an obsessive talker and a visionary. He spouted names and places, visions and promises, sounding for all the world like Karl chanting the names of Chinese warlords. Adolph foresaw then—at least ten years before anyone else—the coming North-South conflict between the developed and largely white, and the poor and largely non-white peoples of the world. But he was a defeated man. He no longer expected Brazil to be the society of the future. "It will be another Japan," he said; "westernized though not of the West, and a cultural suburb of Miami."

Next after Adolph came Mousie, perhaps the most gifted of the Polanyis but the one with the shortest creative life. As soon as Mousie married, when she was twenty-five or so, she immediately became just another middle-class matron. But when she was twenty, Mousie Polanyi had been the star of the Hungarian folk movement—the movement that is best known in the West through its musicians, Bartók and Dohnányi. It was a movement that tried to get back to the roots of Hungarian culture, to the peasant, to his folk craft, his music, and his folk tales. Mousie gave it an additional dimension—she called it "rural sociology." And she gave it a political thrust: what the peasant had to contribute was a social vision, and a community, the communal village. When Mousie was all of nineteen she founded a magazine that she largely wrote herself which had wide influence in the whole Danubian Basin and throughout the Balkans, and in particular in the non-Magyar-speaking parts of the old Hungary such as Croatia. It sparked the "Green Front," the agrarian cooperative and democratic movement that was a powerful political force in Rumania, Bulgaria, and Yugoslavia in the years before and after World War I. The man whom the world knows as Marshal Tito was a Croatian "rural sociologist" and a follower of Mousie Polanyi's before World War I when he was still Josip Broz; and the peculiarly Yugoslav concepts of the self-governing village community and the self-governing plant community are not "Marxist." Stalin was quite right to condemn Tito as a heretic; his concepts are out of Mousie Polanyi's 1900 "rural sociology."

The pamphlets, magazines, articles, and speeches that Mousie spewed out during the few years of her public life also played a part in the birth of this century's most interesting social experiment, the Israeli kibbutz. Among Mousie's friends and disciples in those years was a German sociologist and economist, Franz Oppenheimer. Oppenheimer had started as a romantic Socialist, a follower of Ferdinand Lassalle rather than of Karl Marx. He then turned to economics and sociology. Finally he had become, around 1900, an ardent Zionist and one of Herzl's closest collaborators. Herzl turned to him for the design of the first Zionist settlements in the Holy Land, the first kibbutzim. Oppenheimer—or so he told me many years later when he was an aging and ailing professor in Frankfurt—had already studied the Mormons. But it was Mousie Polanyi's tracts, with their picture of an idyllic egalitarian peasant community, with its high culture and its plain living, which he used in his design for the prototype of the kibbutz and the blueprint for a Jewish society that would be neither "capitalist" nor "Communist," but truly "Socialist."

Mousie lived to a ripe old age. She died in New York in the late 1960s. She was still a very beautiful woman—all the Polanyis were exceptionally good-looking. But she had given up sixty years earlier, around 1905; and after her short years as a youthful superstar she lost interest in anything but her children and her grandchildren. She never wrote anything again.

The youngest Polanyi was Michael, not born until 1891 and almost twenty years younger than Otto and Adolph. He is the best-known Polanyi, indeed the only one of whom more than a handful of people have ever heard. When barely thirty and a young scientist, he became Albert Einstein's assistant in Berlin. He was then, in the 1920s, considered a candidate for the Nobel Prize, the only question being whether in chemistry or physics. When Hitler came, he went to England as professor of physical chemistry in Manchester. There during World War II he changed fields and became a philosopher. At first, like all the Polanyis, he was concerned with society and social processes. He looked to science to find the way out between a bourgeois capitalism that denied community and a Marxist socialism that denied freedom and the person. But very soon he gave up on society and became instead a humanist philosopher, opposed alike to the positivism and rationalism of the traditional "Liberal" and to the anti-human collec-

tivism of the Socialists and Marxists. Human existence for Michael
Polanyi is existence as an isolated individual; and the individual is
grounded in values and ethic, rather than in logic and reason. *Beyond
Nihilism* is the title of one of his best-known papers—and it sums up
both Polanyi's concerns and his answer. Michael Polanyi became a
modern Stoic.

Between Mousie and Michael came Karl. I got to know all the
Polanyis except Otto, but Karl alone became a close friend.

Like Mousie, Karl was an infant prodigy. And like Mousie, he at
first seemed to have burned himself out at an early age. But unlike her,
he started all over again when almost sixty and entered another period
of great creativity.

Before he was twenty, as a law student in Budapest Karl Polanyi,
together with Hungary's wealthiest aristocrat, Count Michael Karolyi,
founded the Hungarian Liberal Party and soon became the party's
chief writer and the editor of its newspaper. The Liberal Party was
totally unpopular: it alone, among all the Hungarian parties, opposed
the oppression of non-Hungarians and demanded equal rights for Slovaks, Croatians, and Rumanians which, however, would have made
the Hungarians a minority in their own kingdom. The "Liberals" were
almost outlaws. Karolyi, despite his great name and wealth, was driven
into exile. But Karl Polanyi became Hungary's most popular orator
and when barely twenty-five was elected to the Hungarian Parliament. He served in World War I as an officer and was severely
wounded in action. In the hospital he met and fell in love with a very
young nurse's aide and married her. Ilona, the daughter of an old
gentry family—her father had been director-general of the railroads
which the Hungarian government inherited through the bankruptcy
of Karl's father—was only seventeen at the time; but she was already
a seasoned politician, had been arrested for anti-war activities, and was
a leader of the then underground Communist Party.

Shortly after they got married, and when Karl had barely recovered, Hungary lost the war. Michael Karolyi returned from exile, took
over as prime minister, and called Polanyi into his cabinet as Minister
of Justice. Six months later the Communists overthrew Karolyi and
Karl was a refugee in Vienna. Within another three months Ilona, who
at first had joined the Red régime but had broken with the Communists when the Red Terror began, had joined Karl in Vienna with her
old mother and a newborn baby daughter. Karl got an editorial job at
The Austrian Economist and soon became the journal's associate editor and best writer. I met him a few years later. Ilona had started to

study physics and was bringing up their daughter. And Karl, already past forty and well paid, seemed perfectly content to have a brilliant past. "Yes. Karl Polanyi," my father said when I told him of my encounter at the editorial conference. "Yes, he *was* a great promise, but he has become one of the casualties."

Karl, however, was not to grow old as political writer on *The Austrian Economist.* Six years later he was out of a job—a victim of the depression, of the ban on the magazine's circulation in Germany and on advertisements from Germany after the Nazis had come to power there, and of the rising right-wing tide in Austria itself. He went to England where he had old Quaker friends. For the next few years he made a precarious living doing odd jobs, lecturing for the Workers' Educational Alliance, writing in obscure little magazines for a few pennies, and traveling alone in near-squalor to the United States for such lectures as his Quaker friends could drum up.

These were the years when I began to see a good deal of Karl and to get close to him. I had moved to England even before Karl did, and we soon fell into the habit of taking long walks together Sunday mornings. Then, after my wife and I had moved to America in 1937, Karl visited us whenever he came there.

They were not good years for Karl. When I had first met him, at the editorial conference of Christmas 1927, he did not "speculate" as his colleagues thought. He analyzed, with an uncanny knack for seeing the importance of inconspicuous developments at an early stage. But in those years of drift after he had left Vienna he did indeed begin to "speculate"—and he had too much imagination to be good at it. Despite his own political experience he had a naïve belief in the cunning, cleverness, and foresight of our rulers that made him see conspiracies and long-laid deep plots everywhere. Instead of interpreting the news as he had done before, he began to invent it. I remember, for instance, a long talk in New York around March 1, 1938—he had just arrived from England and I was about to leave for a trip there. I told him how worried I was about Hitler's invading Austria. "That's the one thing, Peter, you don't have to worry about just now," he said. I expressed amazement, for Hitler was loudly threatening Austria and had already begun to mass his troops along the Austrian border. "Precisely," said Karl. "If he is screaming at Austria he won't invade it. The country that is in danger is the one country Hitler is not threatening—he's going to invade Switzerland." Ten days afterwards, while I was in mid-ocean on my way to England, Hitler marched into Austria.

Two years after that, during the "phony war" months in the

spring of 1940, Karl left Ilona alone in England and came to the United States for a few lectures, convinced that there would be no fighting. "It's crystal-clear," he said, "that there is a secret agreement between Hitler, Russia, the English, the French, and Japan for an attack on China and an attempt to partition it. The European war is just a feint." Whenever I heard Karl in those years discussing politics I was reminded of the old story of Napoleon's master-diplomatist, Talleyrand, who upon hearing that a colleague had died, said: "I wonder what he meant by this." Karl was, it seemed to me, becoming the victim of his own cleverness. But I may have done him an injustice; he may only have been ahead of his time. For after Karl's death the reality of politics did, finally, in Watergate, rise to the level of his imagination.

In any event, he was still a very brilliant and stimulating man, full of ideas. He also remained warm, generous, with a smile that could light up a winter's night, and possessed of an inner serenity that shone the more purely the worse his own circumstances became. When the *Blitzkrieg* that ended the phony war in June 1940 made it impossible for Karl to go back to England for the time being, my wife and I were delighted to have him spend a few weeks with us in a small cabin in northern Vermont we had rented for the summer. Our first child, a daughter, was then not quite two years old, and a warm friendship immediately sprang up between Karl and Kathleen. We listened every evening on the radio to the dreadful news of that summer of the fall of France, of Dunkirk, and the Battle of Britain. Karl could rarely sleep afterwards but lay awake all night thinking and worrying. Then in the morning, as soon as he heard Kathleen stir in her crib, he would go into her room and tell her his thoughts, ask her his questions, and test his theories out on her. Of course the child did not understand a word he said, especially as he still talked at machine-gun speed and in the rhythmic chant with which, years ago, he had intoned the names of the Chinese warlords. But she was completely captivated.

Despite the nightmare horror of those weeks, it was a very productive time for me and a turning point for Karl. A year and a half earlier, in the spring of 1939, I had published my first major book, *The End of Economic Man,* in which I had attempted to analyze the roots of Nazism and of the decay of Europe's liberal and humanist traditions. Actually, that book had been conceived years earlier—shortly after Hitler took power in German in 1933. And I myself had for quite some time been thinking of, and working on, a book that would deal with the future rather than the past, a book that would tackle the political and social integration ahead, assuming that Hitler would ultimately be defeated. By 1940 I was ready to start to write.

This book—published two years later under the title *The Future of Industrial Man*—first discerned that society was moving toward a society of organizations—we now call it "post-industrial society"—and that the questions of status, function, and citizenship in these organizations and of their governance, would become central questions of the post-World War II world. The *Future of Industrial Man* was the first book that saw what by now has become almost commonplace: that the business corporation—or indeed any organization—is as much a social organization, a community and society, as it is an economic organ. This book also laid the foundations for my interest in the management of institutions, and made it possible for me to start on the study of management. It was this work that, a few years later, led General Motors to invite me to analyze their top structure and their corporate policies. Out of this in turn came my first "management" book, *Concept of the Corporation* (published in England under the title *Big Business*), written during the final months of World War II and published in 1946. Since then I have, by and large, alternated between books of social and political synthesis and management books.

As I was working on the first draft of *Future of Industrial Man* during the Vermont summer, I would test my ideas on Karl. He was as always interested, encouraging, and enthusiastic; but he was also totally out of sympathy with what I called "a conservative approach." Yet this then forced him to clarify his own thoughts. And both of us soon realized that Karl had a major book in his head, still disorganized, disjointed, and unfocused but of real stature, provided only he could get the time and financial support to work on it for a year or two.

At this point Providence moved, and it moved through me. A few days after returning to New York—Karl had just taken off on another lecture tour in the Midwest—I got a call from the president of a small but highly visible woman's college in southern Vermont: Could I come in the winter or spring and spend a week lecturing in Bennington? And when I said I would, the president asked: Did I by any chance know anyone in the field of politics and economics who might be available for appointment as scholar in residence? The Rockefeller Foundation had given Bennington a grant on condition that the appointed scholar work on a book in economic or social history. I knew the right man, of course. So Karl Polanyi went to Bennington early in

1941, together with Ilona whom the college hired to teach physics even though she had never received a formal degree.

I myself moved to Bennington as a member of the faculty a year later, in the summer of 1942 when *The Future of Industrial Man* was finished. Karl was just starting to write his book and needed an audience and a critic. Bennington College was forced to close for three months in that war winter of 1942-3 because of a shortage of fuel oil. I was between books and had ample time. Two or three times a week that winter Kathleen, our daughter—by then a little over four and still under Karl's spell—and I trudged through deep snow to the tiny cottage where the Polanyis lived and listened to what was to become *The Great Transformation*. As it turned out, this was the only book Karl Polanyi ever finished.

In *The Great Transformation* Polanyi attempted to rewrite the history of the Industrial Revolution. What had transformed English society and economy, he argued, was not the machine, nor the explosion of world trade that had preceded it, nor even the capital surpluses created by the "agricultural revolution" of the late seventeenth and early eighteenth century. It was the extension of the market system with its "law of supply and demand" beyond the trade in goods and the exchange of capital so as to embrace the other two "factors of production," land and labor, and especially the latter, the employment and the livelihood of people. This was—and is—a novel thesis, and one that is still highly controversial.

Economic history was, however, only the vehicle for Karl's search for the alternative to capitalism and communism, and for a society that would provide at the same time economic growth *and* stability, freedom *and* equality. To Polanyi, the most important parts of *The Great Transformation* were the theoretical models of integration between economy and society that he developed. His aim was to show that the market is neither the only possible economic system nor, necessarily, the most advanced one; and that there are alternatives that harmonize economy and community, and yet permit both economic growth and individual freedom.

It was Karl's contention that a good society must use the market to exchange goods and allocate capital, but must not use it to allocate land or labor; for those either reciprocity or redistribution, that is, social and political rather than economic rationality, should apply. Indeed it was the contention of *The Great Transformation* that a good society must keep the market outside itself. The market is the right principle of integration for foreign, long-distance trade. But the community and its human relations inside must be shielded against disruptive market forces. Whether one accepts Karl's rewriting of modern history—and sociologists do, by and large, while economists do not—he was one of the few since the young Marx to raise the question of the relationship between "livelihood," the economy, and "lives," or the community; and he raised it in a new and original way, both "anti-capitalist" and "anti-Marxist." If we ever get to a structural theory of economics—and we need it badly—it will avail itself of Polanyi's identification of the social principles of economic integration: redistribution, reciprocity, and market exchange. Yet, this classification, which is the most important contribution of *The Great Transformation,* was noticed at the time only by a few.

It did however create enough of a stir to obtain for Karl an invitation, in the late forties, to teach economic history at Columbia University in New York. Karl was already past sixty then, but his energy was still undiminished. In the eight years he worked at Columbia he directed a massive research effort into primitive and ancient economies ranging from ancient Mesopotamia to the Aztecs, and from the Negro Kingdom of Dahomey to the Greece of Homer and Aristotle. He profoundly changed our understanding of early economics and of primitive economic institutions. In cultural anthropology and in economic prehistory Karl Polanyi became a big name.

But Karl himself became a deeply disappointed man. Prehistory and cultural anthropology were, to him, secondary to his quest for the viable alternative, that is, for the good society beyond capitalism and communism. What he hoped to find in economic history was the key to the future. But he found only an increasingly cryptic past. The more he dug into prehistory, into primitive economies and into classical and pre-classical antiquity, the more elusive did the good non-market society become. Karl was much too intelligent to expect the Negro Kingdom of Dahomey to have been the earthly paradise that Alex Haley's popular semi-fictional *Roots* presents it as. Yet he was attracted to the Dahomey of Haley's ancestors because it had built a stable society and a sound economy on reciprocity and redistribution, with market trade confined to exports and imports and strictly separated from the internal economy. Then he found, to his profound shock, that this stability had rested squarely on the slave trade. Indeed he found—as, incidentally, had been known for centuries—that it simply is not true that slave trade and slave raids were forcibly imposed by wicked outsiders

(Arabs in the East, whites in the West) on a freedom-loving and harmonious black tribal society. The black kings and chieftains brought in the slavers and organized, conducted, and supported the slave raids. They did so in part to weaken and destroy rivals and enemies outside their own tribe or kingdom; in part to get trade goods such as guns to maintain their sway over their own people; but in large part to maintain the stability of a community based on reciprocity and redistribution.

And when Karl then turned from West Africa in the sixteenth and seventeenth centuries to classical Greece, the Greece of Plato and Aristotle, he got the same shock. It was slavery and organized slave raids against people of their own race, their own language, their own flesh and blood, that enabled the Greek city-states, and Athens above all, to have economic development and freedom for their citizens and to set up an economic system in which reciprocity and redistribution, rather than the market forces, ruled relations within the community, with "labor" kept outside the market system.

If there was one article of the faith to which all the Polanyis suscribed—from Karl's father on—it was that the "laissez-faire" Liberals of the nineteenth-century Manchester School were wrong in their assertion that the market is the only alternative to serfdom. Indeed the market creed of the Manchester Liberals may be called the hereditary enemy of the House of Polanyi. All Polanyis searched for another alternative, whether Otto's early fascism, Adolph's romantic Brazil, Mousie's "rural sociology," Michael's stoic desire-free individual, or Karl's "social principles of economic integration." But the more Karl delved into prehistory, primitive economics, and classical antiquity, the more proof did he find for the hated and despised market creed of Ricardo and Bentham, and also of Karl's contemporary bogeymen, Ludwig von Mises and Frederick Hayek of the Austrian School. So Karl retreated into footnotes, into more and more anthropological studies, and into academic busyness.

During these years I would visit him at least once every month. He lived in a tiny Columbia faculty apartment on Morningside Heights, each of its grimy and ill-maintained rooms piled from floor to ceiling with books and pamphlets, articles and letters. The windows were shut tight and the heat turned up all the way while Karl, always cold, would be swathed in layers of frayed and threadbare sweaters. Outwardly he did not seem to have changed at all. He had the same booming, explosive laugh. He was as lively as ever, and as voluble.

Wasting no time on preliminaries such as inquiring after my work or my family—even though he was very fond of my wife—he would immediately bubble over with his own interests and concerns. He still had the old habit of chanting strange names at the top of his voice. Only where these chants years earlier had been the names of Chinese warlords about to make the future, they increasingly became the strange names of Bronze Age excavation sites in Asia Minor or the titles of local officials on a Sumerian cuneiform document 5,000 years old. He still divined the "real truth" behind the news, and was as conspiratorial, as labyrinthine, as clever as ever. Only the politics that now engaged his interest were increasingly the subterranean power struggles and intrigues in the Columbia faculty rather than those of the world's great powers. He still talked of the search for the "alternative" and of harmony between human freedom and economic development. He still expected to find the "alternative" every time he tackled the study of a new primitive or early culture. And then, for a few weeks, he was young again and enthusiastic. But soon he would turn antiquarian, concerned with minutiae, with textual criticism and emendation, and with "scholarship" for its own sake. Where earlier he had been prone to sweeping generalizations, he increasingly became a footnote hound. And yet there was always a moment when the old —or rather the young—Karl Polanyi broke through once more. "I had hoped earlier," he said at one of our last New York meetings in the mid-fifties, "that Mao would be another Confucius. He had the chance. But he has decided for power instead and will end up in Stalin's image."

Karl Polanyi retired from Columbia when he reached seventy, in 1956. He lived another eight years in Toronto with Ilona—their only daughter had married a Canadian. He was happy, or at least contented. He kept on working. He studied: the civilization of the ancient Near East, and Han China, for instance. But he wrote less and less. And even the little he wrote was only published, by and large, after his death by his friends and disciples. By the time he died, almost eighty years old, he himself may well have forgotten the promise he had held out in *The Great Transformation* twenty years earlier.

Whenever I talk of the Polanyis someone is sure to say, "Why don't you write a book about their lives?" They were indeed an unusual family, without doubt the most unusual I have known. They were also the most gifted family I have known. But still what made them matter was not their lives; it was their cause and its failure. Each achieved greatly—but not the one thing each had aimed at. They all believed in salvation by society, then came to give up on society and despair of it.

The Polyanis themselves, however gifted, were very minor figures, entertaining rather than important. But their failure is important, for it may signify the futility of the quest that has engaged Western man for the last 200 years since the French Revolution, if not since Hobbes and Locke 100 years earlier: the quest for the one absolute "civic religion"; for the perfect—or at least the good—society. It was my willingness in *The Future of Industrial Man* to settle instead for an adequate, bearable, but free society that Karl at the time criticized and rejected as a tepid compromise. In such a society—and it may be the best we can possibly hope for—we would maintain freedom by paying a price: the disruption, the divisiveness, and alienation of the market. We would pay the price of conflict, of risk-taking choice, of diversity, for the sake of maintaining the person. In such a society we would be less concerned with the greater good and more with the lesser evil. This might well mean that society itself—that Great Baal and Moloch of modern man—might become secondary, and society's organization no more important, in the end, and no more controversial, than infallible religion became in the Age of Society that is now fading. Today when the infallible society still dominates to the point where the quest for it threatens to engulf the world in intolerance, in total loss of freedom, and in self-destructive war, this might seem very remote. But just as the failure of a whole generation of brilliant thinkers to find the new synthesis between Catholicism and Protestantism in the late sixteenth and early seventeenth centuries foreshadowed the end of the Age of Infallible Religion fifty years later, so the failure of the brilliant Polanyis to find the alternative beyond capitalism and communism might well foreshadow the end of the Age of the Infallible Society.

The Man
Who Invented
Kissinger

Europe had in 1928–29 the coldest and longest winter in well over a hundred years. All the main rivers—the Rhine, the Danube, the Elbe, the Rhone, and their tributaries—froze solid and stayed frozen until late in March. When spring finally came it was miserable, with sleet and wet snow in place of the warm April showers that bring gillie flowers. Long after the solid ice sheets had broken up, ice floes dotted the roiled waters of the flooding and turbulent streams.

It was on one of these miserable days in early April with freezing winds and blinding rain squalls that I espied a kayak amid the ice floes on the Main River in the middle of the city of Frankfurt. In the little boat a cadaverous man, naked except for the scantiest of black bathing trunks and a monocle on a wide black ribbon, was furiously paddling upstream. And the stern of the fragile craft flew the black, white, and red battle pennant of the defunct German Imperial Navy.

People on the bridge who had been hurrying to get out of the cold and the wind stopped to peer. Some made the vulgar German sign for a lunatic, touching their own foreheads with their extended forefingers. I turned to a passer-by who had shouted, "Here he is again," and asked who this madman might be. "A law student. His name is Kraemer," he answered; "batty as can be, but quite harmless."

That very same evening I met Fritz Kraemer. We were both among a handful of students enrolled in the International Law Seminar; and since the professor had been sick, the start of the seminar had been delayed until April and the group met in the professor's house rather than at the University.

Even dressed, Kraemer looked odd. There was the monocle—and no one since the Junker officers of pre-World War I Germany had worn a monocle. Indeed to this day I do not know where Kraemer got his; out of curiosity I have been trying to find an optician who sells monocles and have never succeeded. The rest of his garb was as strange as the monocle, and as dated. We all dressed as students in those days used to dress, mostly in slacks and tweed jackets. But Kraemer sported the clothes gentlemen used to wear for rather formal horseback meets: a white stock, a checkered Tattersall vest, a broadcloth coat, beautifully cut riding britches, and highly polished black knee-length riding boots. Yet while clearly an affectation, these outlandish clothes looked right on him. And if anyone thought him a popinjay, he knew better the moment Kraemer opened his mouth and said something in his high-pitched, nasal, languid voice. All of us, including the professor, knew ourselves at once in the presence of a master. Kraemer was not just brilliant and knowledgeable—the seminar had more than its fair share of brilliant and knowledgeable people, most of them much older than Kraemer and I, who both were not quite twenty. But Kraemer could even then integrate political history, international law, and international politics into a consistent political philosophy. He was courteous. He was extremely modest. And he was in complete, uncompromising control.

Of medium height, Kraemer was so thin that I had been able to see his ribs when he paddled on the river in his kayak. He was of a fairly common German type, a long narrow head with sharp features. But in him this type was carried almost to an extreme of caricature: a big, triangular, sharp nose that jutted out of his face like a sail; high cheekbones; a sharp chin; and piercing, slate-gray eyes. He looked like a cross between a greyhound and a timberwolf. But at times he had also an uncanny resemblance to one of the great heroes of his younger days, the Prussian King Frederick the Great, who in the middle of the eighteenth century had converted the poor and backward Brandenburg-Prussia into a great power, and Berlin from a God-forsaken fishing village on a marshy stream into one of the capitals of the European Enlightenment. Frederick the Great's nickname had been the "Old Fritz." And so Kraemer—though only behind his back—was soon called by us the "Young Fritz."

Kraemer is a very common German name and by no means an aristocratic one, it means "peddler." There was nothing in Fritz's background to explain the monocle, the riding boots, or the languid voice that had been the fashionable affectation of the Prussian guards officer of 1900. His mother had been the sole daughter of a chemical manufacturer in the Ruhr region. She was as brilliant as her son. But she must have been quite a "problem" as a young woman in the early years of this century. She was headstrong, independent, and imaginative. Perhaps her looks were not considered downright repulsive. But she was not even what in those years was called *une belle laide,* being neither feminine, nor soft, nor submissive. She was tall—taller than her son—and thin to the point of gauntness. She looked indeed very much the way Eleanor Roosevelt looked as a girl and young woman. But she had a great deal of money. And so a husband was found for her, a dirt-poor young lawyer with lower-middle-class parents but high ambitions.

The marriage was apparently a disaster from the start. After two sons had been born—for Fritz had a brother Wilhelm, later to become a surgeon in Edinburgh—the Kraemer parents separated, Mrs. Kraemer keeping the children. The husband, buttressed by his wife's money, did very well for himself. By the time I came to know Fritz, his father had risen to the top of the legal hierarchy and lived in Düsseldorf as Director of Public Prosecution for the entire Rhineland. He had also come to realize that a plebeian but ambitious Kraemer with a small shopkeeper for a father could not afford to be a liberal in the Weimar Republic, and had established himself firmly as an ultra-nationalist with close ties to the emerging Nazi movement.

Fritz's mother meanwhile had founded, in a small mountain village not far from Frankfurt, a home and school for difficult children. She was probably apolitical. But she had values and she had taste. Her husband's Nazi friends were an utter abomination to her. They were even more of an abomination to her son Fritz, who openly despised his father as an unprincipled careerist and who stayed away from him as much as he possibly could. The ultra-nationalists and the Nazis were for Kraemer pure scum, proletarian rabble, motivated by resentment at their own inferiority and by envy of their betters, all the more contemptible for covering their Jacobin lawlessness with the rags of nationalist and pseudo-Conservative rhetoric. For Kraemer considered himself a genuine Conservative, a Prussian monarchist of the old pre-Bismarck, Lutheran, and Spartan persuasion.

A Prussian monarchist among young Germans of the Weimar Republic was simply unheard of. Even nostalgia for monarchy was confined to the old as a rule. But Kraemer believed, with Bismarck,

that the Germans require a father figure, and that they will fall victim
to a tyrant unless they have a legitimate and lawful king. Kraemer had
no illusions about the Kaiser. He knew him to be erratic, vain, and
without judgment. But he was legitimate; and so Kraemer accepted
him as his lawful sovereign and sent him a birthday telegram each year
—for William II, an old man, was still alive in exile in Holland. But
Kraemer's Prussia was even more of an anachronism than his monocle
or his wearing riding boots to law-school classes. If Kraemer's Prussia
had ever existed at all, it died before 1848 or at the very latest with
Bismarck and the founding of the German Empire in 1871. It was a
Prussia of small squires (*Junker* means "youngster," that is, the
knight's squire), each with a few acres of sandy, infertile soil and so
poor as to depend on the meager stipend paid by a stingy government
to local civil servants or infantry captains. The heroine of this class had
been the Prussian Queen during the Napoleonic Wars who with her
own hands, according to legend, had turned her ballgown so as to
make it last another season. This Prussia had prided itself on its self-
discipline and on its strict obedience to laws that bound the King as
much as the commoner. It was not educated, let alone cultured; but
it was pious, with a narrow and sentimental Lutheranism. This Prussia
had been a military state—in fact, its unity lay in its army. But it
preached and sometimes practiced the virtues of the professional soldier: truthfulness, modesty, self-control, and loyalty.

Whatever its merits and limitations, the Prussia to which Fritz
Kraemer gave his allegiance had disappeared at least a half century
before Fritz Kraemer's birth in 1908 or 1909. It had been destroyed
by money and by power; and what was left of it Bismarck had deliberately, callously, corrupted and poisoned. As Karl Marx so clearly saw,
Bismarck, for all his Junker blood and conservative gestures, was the
nineteenth century's most insidious revolutionary and a radical
through and through. By the time Bismarck had finished his work, the
old Prussia with all its virtues and vices had been totally submerged
into a vainglorious, *nouveau riche*, bumptious, and bragging empire.
The self-controlled, self-limited Junker who considered poverty a virtue and a captain's bars the height of achievement had been replaced
by ostentatious great nobles—Bismarck himself became a duke in the
end—bedecked from top to toe with diamond-studded orders and
chains of office, or by great bankers and industrial tycoons. Only the
rhetoric of the old Prussia lingered on, mainly in schoolbooks.

The old Prussia had always been more of an idea than a territory, "an idea embodied in an army," the "Old Fritz" had called it. Almost all the "great Prussians," all the way to the middle of the nineteenth century, had come from outside Prussia's territory and enlisted in an idea. Moltke, for instance, who built the Prussian Army and the Prussian General Staff that defeated first the Austrians in 1866 and then the French in 1870–71, thus imposing unity on Germany, was a Dane by birth and lineage. And the one political philosopher of the Prussian idea, Friedrich Julius Stahl—he died in the 1850s shortly before Bismarck took over—had been born a Jew in Bavaria's capital, Munich. Kraemer thus only followed old tradition when he, the Rhinelander and non-Prussian, enlisted in the cause of old Prussia. In fact, he knew precisely what he was doing. He enlisted in the cause of a Prussia that had long ceased to exist because its revival seemed to him the only salvation for Germany and for Europe. Otherwise, both would be destroyed, either by the arrogance and greed of the "ugly German" or by the fatuity and incompetence of the "good German."

With Bismarck's Germany arose the "ugly German," in turn arrogant and servile, greedy, pushy, domineering, aggressive, and a bully. His best portraits are perhaps the German cousins in E. M. Forster's *Howard's End*—Forster's greatest novel, I think, and perhaps the subtlest work of English prose written in this century. *Howard's End* is usually read as an allegory of the British class system. But it is surely just as much the novel of the dissolution of the bonds of civility that were holding together the European comity. The German cousins never appear in person in *Howard's End;* but their ugliness, arrogance, and smug aggressive superiority loom over the book. And a few years after *Howard's End* appeared in 1912, the "ugly German" became the "Hun" of World War I.

But there was all along also the "other German," the "good German"—the slightly sentimental, slightly beer-sodden German "liberal" who loved music and was *gemütlich*. He too is a stock figure; and in every generation he then becomes a reality: in Willy Brandt, for instance. His best portrait was also limned by an Englishman. It is John Maynard Keynes's masterful essay on Dr. Melchior, German patriot, Jewish banker, and true European, who committed suicide when Hitler came to power.

Kraemer hated the "ugly German." He respected the "good German," but did not believe he could win against the "ugly German." To him, the "good German"—precisely because he was a "liberal" and sentimental and *gemütlich*—lacked political strength to withstand the forces of evil, and political sophistication to hold and use power. When I once argued the point with him, he pointed to the way Bismarck had used the decency and naïveté of the "good Germans," the powerful Liberals of his time, to subvert, subjugate, and ultimately to destroy German liberalism. I had to concede. And of course the Weimar Republic, in those very years in which we argued, taught the lesson again.

And so Kraemer had decided that the "third German" alone offered self-control *and* political control, that the "third German" alone would be able both to attain power and to use it wisely. And this "third German," opposed alike to the ugliness and barbarism that was then coming up so fast behind the Nazi swastika, and to the well-meaning and decent but weak and gutless liberalism of the "good German," was the ideal Prussian of old—poor but satisfied, proud but God-fearing, wearing uniform and arms but obedient to lawful authority, self-controlled under the code of honor of an officer and a gentleman. All his mannerisms: the monocle, the Imperial Navy's battle flag on his kayak, the white stock, the riding boots and britches, were thus a deliberate manifesto.

Many years later, during World War II, I had to explain again and again why Kraemer was not a Nazi and could not be a Nazi *because* he was a genuine conservative. By then Kraemer had enlisted in the American Army to fight the Nazis; and American Military Intelligence had with some reason a difficult time understanding his story. The investigators came to me repeatedly to get an explanation and went away shaking their heads. To the American mind, especially in those years, only the two traditional Germans existed—and a self-styled "Prussian Conservative" had to be one of the wrong ones. However romantic Kraemer's notion and behavior were—and he was, of course, very young in those years—the fact remains that all effective resistance to the Nazis came from the likes of him, from men and women who were old-fashioned pre-Bismarckian "Conservatives" or pre-Bismarckian Lutherans. The men who made the desperate attempt to kill Hitler in July 1944—Count Hellmuth Moltke, Count Stauffenberg, and the former Lord Mayor of Leipzig, Dr. Goerdeler—were "old-fashioned Prussian Conservatives"; and the leader of the Protestant resistance, Pastor Niemoeller, was an old-fashioned Prussian Lutheran monarchist and former submarine commander. Kraemer was only a good deal more realistic; he knew from the very start that Hitler could not be stopped except by external force, and left Germany.

Kraemer himself did not explain his political convictions and philosophy. I had to piece the story together out of occasional hints and
references, and from his telling me that he always sent the former
Kaiser a birthday telegram. But as we got to know each other better
he came to talk quite freely about his ambitions. He had, he said, really
only two ambitions in life: he wanted to be the political adviser to the
Chief of the General Staff of the Army; and he wanted to be the
political mentor of a great Foreign Secretary. "But Kraemer," I would
say, "wouldn't you want yourself to be Chief of the General Staff or
Foreign Secretary?" "Most definitely not," he would answer; "I know
I am a thinker and not a doer. And I don't belong in the limelight and
don't make speeches."

I chuckled. It was typical Kraemer. For of course either ambition
was totally silly. There was no General Staff in the defeated and dis-
armed Germany of the Weimar Republic. And if there had been one,
Kraemer—a commoner and descendant of tradesmen—would have
had no more chance to get in than he had of becoming Pope. As to
being a Foreign Secretary's mentor, that was a role played by a great
diplomatist or a senior statesman, a Metternich maybe or a Disraeli,
not by a Fritz Kraemer, a bright boy from Frankfurt or Düsseldorf
who was studying to be a lower court judge in a German provincial
town.

Fritz himself knew how imposible these ambitions were. "This is
what I really want out of life," he said, "and I'll never attain it, never."
Fritz would, I am convinced, not have talked about his goals had he
thought that either could possibly even be approached, let alone be
attained.

Yet he attained both.

When Hitler came to power in 1933 Kraemer had finished his law
studies, had obtained his doctorate in international law, and was in the
middle of the three-year internship in the courts that German lawyers
have to serve before taking the bar examination. Still attired in riding
boots and britches, he was on duty as law clerk to a municipal court
judge in the small town where his mother had her school on the day
the Nazis ordered the dismissal of all Jewish judges and law interns.
Kraemer had then just married a Swedish girl, Britta, who for a term
or two had attended the International Law Seminar. But without a
moment's hesitation he resigned and immediately left Germany. His
code of honor did not permit him to maintain any relationship with

so dishonorable and lawless a régime. He went to Italy. When he arrived, he spoke not a word of Italian. Within the year he had taken and passed an Italian examination to validate his German doctor's degree and was teaching international relations at the University of Rome in Italian. And soon his Swedish wife joined him.

The next summer, the summer of 1934, while vacationing on the Gulf of Sorrento, Kraemer paddled around in his kayak still flying the battle pennant of Germany's defunct Imperial Navy on the boat's stern. The Nazi naval attaché also vacationed in Sorrento—and was fool enough to lodge a formal protest with the Italian Foreign Office against this "insult" to Nazi Germany, whose flag by then, of course, sported the swastika against the background of the old Hohenzollern colors. Kraemer was told to take his flag down. Instead he went into court with the claim that international law gave him the right to fly his own private flag on his own boat in territorial waters. The case went all the way up to Italy's highest court. Kraemer won it!

In those years Mussolini and Hitler were bitter enemies. Indeed Mussolini had threatened in 1934 to go to war against the Germans over Hitler's first attempt to put a Nazi government into Austria, and Hitler had backed down. Kraemer's case was therefore given wide publicity and all Italy chuckled over the Nazis' discomfiture.

However, the Nazis did not think the story funny at all. And in 1937 or 1938, when Mussolini became Hitler's ally, Kraemer was advised by his Italian friends to leave as fast as possible. The Nazis had asked for his head. By that time the Kraemers had had their first child, a little boy. Fritz's mother was still running her school in Germany. Indeed she had expanded it greatly and had changed it into a boarding school for children of parents whom the Nazi régime persecuted for their politics. And yet, perhaps because the school was hidden away in an isolated hill town, the Nazis had left her alone. She offered to put up his wife and baby until Fritz found a new job. I helped get him an American visa and an invitation to teach government at the American University in Washington.

Fritz arrived in the United States in the spring of 1939. I urged him to send immediately for Britta and his child, but he wanted to wait a few months. By the time he had decided to let them come, it was September 1939 and the war in Europe had broken out, trapping Britta and the baby in Hitler Germany.

Two years later the United States was in the war too. And within a few days after Pearl Harbor, Fritz Kraemer had enlisted in the

American Army as a private. He received a battlefield commission in his regiment's first combat action and thereafter rose rapidly. When the war ended, he was either a colonel or a brigadier general on Patton's staff and assistant commander of the division that seized the Remagen bridge and first crossed the Rhine. Four days later Kraemer was in the little town where his mother had her school and found that by sheer miracle all three—his mother, his wife, and his son—had survived. They had been threatened, arrested, and interrogated more than once, but they were alive and unhurt.

And then Fritz Kraemer attained the first of his goals. He resigned his commission, turned civilian, and became the political adviser on Europe for the Chief of Staff of the U.S. Army. His official title was somewhat more modest, "senior political analyst" or something like that. But of course "political analysts" are not sent to the U.S. War College; that's for general officers or better. And Kraemer both attended the War College and taught there. His office in the Pentagon was small and, like every office Kraemer ever occupied, filled from top to bottom with books, magazines, and newspapers in every conceivable language. But the office was in the suite occupied by the Chief of Staff, with a private connecting door to the Chief's own room. In the two hours I spent there in the early Kennedy years, the Chief of Staff put his head into Kraemer's cubicle at least six or eight times to say: "Dr. Kraemer, if you could spare me a moment?" and Fritz was finally called away to a hush-hush meeting with the Joint Chiefs. Before he left, I said half-jokingly, "Do you still prefer being an adviser, or would you rather be a commander?" "Oh Drucker," he said, absolutely serious, "you know better. There is nothing more important than making policy."

That evening, Kraemer had invited me to dinner at his home outside Washington. When he picked me up at my hotel after he finished at the Pentagon, he drove up in a white Mercedes that flew from its front fender the flag of the Thirteen States under which George Washington had fought the Battle of Trenton at the darkest hour of the War of Independence. He wore a monocle, beautifully cut riding britches, and well-polished riding boots.

This evening—the only one I ever spent at Kraemer's home— occurred several years before Henry Kissinger became Secretary of State. Then, I imagine, Fritz Kraemer might have changed his mind and considered making a Foreign Secretary to be even more important than making policy. For Kraemer largely made Henry Kissinger. He found him, he formed him, in fact he largely invented him.

The story has been published in accounts of Kissinger's early life. Young Henry, shortly after his arrival as a German refugee, was drafted as private into the American Army. During basic training he heard a lecture on the European war given by a private first class, a fellow German whose name was Fritz Kraemer. The questions which young Kissinger asked so impressed Kraemer that he sent for the boy afterwards. And from then on, Kissinger was Kraemer's protégé. When the war was over, Kissinger—whose own background was very modest—wanted to go to New York's City College on the G.I. Bill of Rights. But Kraemer said—and I can hear him say it in his most languid guards officer voice—"Henry, a gentleman does not go to City College. He goes to Harvard." He arranged for Kissinger's admission to Harvard and for his being taken on as a favorite student by the leading government professors there. And he remained Kissinger's friend, mentor, and adviser until his protégé had finished his studies and obtained his first Harvard teaching appointment, if not well beyond that time.

What has not been published is that Kissinger's thoughts as well as his actions as U.S. Secretary of State under Nixon and Ford are pure Kraemer. Kraemer, the enemy of publicity of any kind, has never written or published anything. But in those early years of the International Law Seminar at Frankfurt University between 1929 and 1933 he talked out his thoughts in great detail in countless long leisurely sessions with me. Even then his thoughts were completely formed.

Our relationship in those years was a peculiar one, both less and more than "friendship." We ran the International Law Seminar together on one evening a week; the professor was ailing and turned the job almost entirely over to us. Then Fritz and I would continue a dialogue after the others had gone home—often until daybreak when I had to go to my office and start the day's work. But we almost never saw each other on other occasions. In all my years in Frankfurt I never visited him or his rooms. I once spent a weekend as his mother's guest in the country; that was all the social relationship I ever had with the Kraemers. We never even called each other by our first names, let alone used the familiar "Du" of German friendship. We remained "Drucker" and "Kraemer" and called each other "Sie."

We knew intuitively that we were in disagreement on the answers, yet we soon found out that we asked the same questions. And both Kraemer and I knew even as very young men that the questions matter. So we used each other to hear ourselves talk and to force ourselves into defining ourselves. Kraemer contributed more than anyone else to making me understand myself as a political maverick and forcing me realize where my own concerns lay, precisely because they were not the same as his. I, in turn, probably did the same service for him. Our relationship was purely intellectual, though we respected each other and surely did not dislike each other. But I don't think we would ever have asked: "What do you feel?" The question was always: "And what do you think?"

Our talks ranged far afield, as the talks of young men in their early twenties are wont to do. But there were three points around which Kraemer organized every discussion. These three points triangulated his political philosophy, as they triangulate Dr. Kissinger's.

The first one was the primacy of foreign over domestic policy. Foreign policy deals with a nation's survival; and only after a nation has assured its survival can it concern itself with constitutions and laws, with social justice, or with economics. Kraemer may not, in those days in the early thirties, have made the point as elegantly as De Gaulle made it twenty years later; but he made it emphatically.

I conceded the primacy of survival. But I was not convinced then —and am even less now—of the absolute, unalterable primacy of foreign policy. Not only, or so I argued, had nations and empires been destroyed as often by internal decay as by foreign invasion and conquest; the very means used by the great virtuosi of foreign policy to subordinate domestic concerns ultimately caused their nation's downfall. They corrupted and deformed it. This was true of Richelieu in seventeenth-century France, of Metternich in early-nineteenth-century Austria, and especially of Bismarck in nineteenth-century Germany. My model was the first Cecil, Queen Elizabeth of England's great minister, and himself a master diplomatist, who clearly understood the need for national survival in a hostile world but who always balanced foreign and domestic policy, tried to harmonize the two, and accepted the need for trade-offs and compromises between them. Indeed, it was in these discussions that I first was forced to think through politics as the art of optimization and as the search for the "trade-off" that will do the least damage.

Kramer would have none of this. He accepted the fact of ultimate compromise. But he insisted on a pure primacy-of-foreign-policy position as the starting point and as the desirable and only honest position.

My optimization through balance and trade-off appeared to him to be sloppy, which it is, if not intellectually dishonest.

Kraemer's second fixed point was the primacy of power in foreign affairs. And by power he meant political strength and ultimately military might. The only other element to be taken seriously in foreign affairs was a great super-national idea, a religious force for instance, or a secular creed like Marxism. Kraemer, the well-trained historian, would never have made an inane remark like Stalin's "How many divisions has the Pope?" But he saw in the great ideas primarily restraints on national interest or national power. Nations did not, as a rule, act counter to their perceived interest because of their ideology. But they often—and usually with dire results—were inhibited by ideology from acting in their own best interest. Both Churchill and De Gaulle would, by the way, have agreed with Kraemer.

Both would also have joined Kraemer in dismissing or at least playing down economics, alike as motivation for and restraint on political action. Whenever I tried to inject an economic argument, Kraemer would scornfully point to the total failure of economic blockades and economic sanctions to bring about military or political surrender, whether Napoleon's Continental Blockade, the Blockade of the Confederacy by the Union in the American Civil War, or the blockade of Germany in World War I. Even economic strength and weakness, he would agree, counted for very little. The Confederacy had had no industry and was agriculturally backward except in producing tobacco and cotton, neither of which it could export during the Civil War; yet it held out for four years and had to be defeated by superior military force. Germany and Austria in World War I similarly were vastly inferior in economic production and almost without industrial raw materials; yet they too lasted four years and had to be defeated on the field of battle. Economics, Kraemer concluded, the statesman should neglect altogether or at most confine to a very small role—a walk-on rather than a speaking part—in his planning and policy.

Kraemer and I agreed that striving for hegemony is self-defeating; both of us knew and had taken to heart the warning on the folly of hegemony with which Thucydides opens his great history of the downfall of Athens. Both of us also agreed on the futility of the "bloc" in which a great power tries to buttress its position by alliances with small and weak countries. The example that was most visible to us then, in the early thirties, was the alliance between post-Bismarck Germany and a decaying Austria, which added nothing to Germany's strength but deprived it of freedom of action and ultimately sucked it into a suicidal war as a prisoner of Austrian incompetence and irresponsibility. But of course history is full of examples of the folly of "client-states" as the base for foreign policy. The policy always ends up by making the "client" the master, and a reckless one to boot.

But Kraemer concluded from this that the only foreign policy worth pursuing was that of the balance of the great powers. Others could be disregarded, no matter what their economic strength or their political ties. For weaker powers had, basically, no choice; in the language of modern politics, they had no place to go.

Again I demurred. That this or that group—labor for instance, or the American blacks—"have no place to go" has never convinced me. And it is no coincidence, I maintain, that no successful American politician has ever acted on this particular piece of conventional wisdom. Maybe these groups cannot easily defect to the other side; but they can always desert. And so I not only argued that other factors beside power and ideology, economics for instance, need to be considered in the power equation. I argued that a balance of power must integrate both, the "great powers" and the "middle powers."

This is a very old controversy. Of recent world leaders Roosevelt, Stalin, and De Gaulle would all have sided with Kraemer. But Churchill was clearly close to the position I tried to develop, and argued at Teheran and Yalta—though in vain—for a settlement in which the "great powers" would guarantee an overall balance while the traditional nations of Europe were to be full partners. This was of course the structure of the "Concert of Europe," the nineteenth-century design that alone of all the "balances of power" in history prevented major multinational war for a whole century between 1815 and 1914.

Kraemer again dismissed my attempt at compromise and qualification as unprincipled shilly-shallying and as intellectually sloppy.

Kraemer's final point, however, I rejected on principle and not out of intellectual softness. Kraemer looked for—nay, insisted on—the great man as foreign minister. To him, the conduct of foreign affairs was the ultimate challenge to statesmanship; and it required genius.

I had not in those years heard of the remark Disraeli is said to have made after the Congress of Berlin in 1878, the Congress that was Bismarck's greatest diplomatic triumph: "Poor Germany; Bismarck is old and cannot last long. And then they will try to fill the giant's shoes with a lieutenant of Marines who will either be timid and not dare do anything or so besotted as to believe that he can play Bismarck. Either way, Germany will be lost." But the more history I read, the more I became convinced that the genius foreign minister is a disaster for his country. France did not recover from Richelieu. Even De Gaulle still dreamed Richelieu's dream of hegemony in Europe rather than try to integrate France into a European Concert. And even De Gaulle, 300 years after Richelieu, still refused to adapt France's foreign policy to its resources and its needs. Austria died of Metternich's success, and Germany of Bismarck's. For the genius foreign minister is always, as Disraeli predicted, succeeded by a "lieutenant of Marines" or a chief clerk. And the successor then either abdicates or, worse, he bluffs. The very brilliance of the genius foreign minister also always leaves behind a lasting legacy of deep mistrust in the outside world. The Richelieus, Metternichs, and Bismarcks always brush aside contemptuously the old rule: "In diplomacy don't ever be clever; be simple and honest." They *are* clever—and as a result they appear tricky and dishonest.

The long talks with Kraemer those many years ago first made me conscious of the paradox of the great man in public affairs. Without him there is no vision, no leadership, no standard of excellence and achievement. And in public affairs mediocrity kills. But in public affairs, unlike the arts or sciences, individual achievement cannot stand alone. It requires continuity. The great man in public affairs requires successors of greatness. Yet almost always he leaves behind a vacuum; almost always he is being succeeded by Disraeli's "lieutenant of Marines," who knows the drill and little else.

I don't believe I realized this during the long rambling talks with an equally young and questing Kraemer. But I acquired then a lifelong interest in resolving the paradox of the great man in public affairs, and especially in organizations—whether governments, universities, or businesses. For it can be resolved. Cecil in Elizabethan England solved it, managing to surround himself with first-rate colleagues and to groom his son to become a first-rate successor. George Washington resolved it and left behind a whole galaxy of outstanding successors. General George Marshall resolved it as head of the United States Armed Forces during World War II. And many leaders—strong, powerful, articulate individuals—in other organizations such as businesses and universities have resolved it. Early business examples are those much-maligned "tycoons" John D. Rockefeller, Sr., and Andrew Carnegie, or, much earlier even, the founders of the Mitsui and Mitsubishi business empires in Japan.

These are the exceptions, however. The Franklin D. Roosevelts who do not tolerate strength in their colleagues and leave behind only used-up hacks are far more common. And one cannot count on the near-miracle of a Harry Truman, the accidental Vice-President who, chosen for his total lack of visible strength, then pulls off the ugly duckling act.

The great man who can only be succeeded by a "lieutenant of Marines," a chief clerk, or a tired servile hack, is not a necessity. But the leader who himself has strength and leaves behind strength—the truly "great man" and genuine "leader"—looks completely different and acts completely differently from the "great man" of popular myth. He does not lead by "charisma"—an abomination and phony, even when it is not a press agent's invention. The truly strong man leads by hard work and dedication. He does not centralize everything in his hands but builds a team. He dominates through integrity, not through manipulation. He is not clever, but simple and honest.

He is thus totally different from the "genius foreign minister"— the Richelieus, the Metternichs, or the Bismarcks. Yet it was precisely this kind of "genius foreign minister" that Fritz Kraemer's discovery and disciple, Henry Kissinger, tried to be.

It would be silly to see in Kissinger a shadow of Kraemer. He must have been outstandingly brilliant as a mere boy in a private's uniform to attract and hold Kraemer's attention. Fritz never had time for fools. Kissinger also has abilities that Kraemer totally lacks, as a writer and speaker, as a wit and as a politician. But Kissinger's books are animated by Kraemer's principles. And when Kissinger became America's foreign minister under Nixon, he immediately began to put into action the three axioms of political philosophy he had first heard from Fritz Kraemer in basic training way back in 1942: the primacy of foreign policy; the primacy of power in foreign policy; and the need for the genius foreign minister. In fact, these three points *were* Kissinger's policy.

There was—and still is—a crying need to free American foreign policy from its subjugation to domestic affairs. In no other country has it been so easy to forget that there is an outside world and to enact domestic policies and programs without any thought to their impact on America's international strength, its competitive position, or its friends and allies. In no other country could as serious a commitment as America's underwriting the State of Israel in the midst of a hostile Arab continent be justified with short-term vote-getting in a close domestic election—which is what Harry Truman did when he decided to recognize Israel because "there are no Arab votes in the Bronx." And surely Kissinger was altogether right in his insistence that America needs a foreign policy and cannot be content with foreign policy gestures and Fourth of July rhetoric—which is what John F. Kennedy's foreign policy amounted to, from his declaring: "I am a Berliner" while abjectly accepting the Berlin Wall, to the Bay of Pigs, to pushing the United States into Vietnam as guarantor of a "client-state."

It was also high time to cut loose from an increasingly sterile hegemony posture with dependence on "blocs" and "client-states," and to fashion a viable balance of power instead. But surely events have proven that the Kraemer-Kissinger definition of "power" is inadequate, is indeed deleterious. Only time can tell whether China is indeed a "great power" just because of its size and military potential; Mao and post-Mao China might very well end up being no different from the Manchu China they succeeded, "great" only as inert mass and impotent otherwise. But there is no need to wait in order to judge the validity of the exclusion of the "middle powers" in the Kraemer-Kissinger definition of "power," or to judge their dismissal of economic strength as a major factor. While following the Kraemer doctrine to the letter, Kissinger's brush-off of Japan—the open snub over our recognition of Communist China and the equally open dismissal of Japan as a factor in the 1971 devaluation of the dollar—were enormous and unnecessary blunders. For its industrial strength makes Japan, for the foreseeable future, the "great power" of the Pacific Basin. Kissinger's studied neglect of our European allies and his refusal to include economics in his plans and policies were equally blunders of the first magnitude. The "middle powers" had indeed "no place to go"; they could not defect. But they could desert. And the Europeans promptly did so in the first major foreign policy crisis of the Kissinger era, the Yom Kippur War in 1973. After that there was no Kissinger policy left, only the case-by-case improvisation that is precisely what the Kraemer-Kissinger approach to foreign affairs abhors, and rightly so.

If the Kissinger experience proves anything, it is the fallacy—indeed the hollowness—of the doctrine of the "genius foreign minister." The United States does need a foreign policy that is not just a cork bobbing on the waters of domestic politicking. There is need for a balance-of-power policy, but for one that integrates the "middle powers" as partners, and considers factors other than military potential in its definition of "power." And there is need for leadership in foreign policy in the United States. But this leadership had better not be based on cleverness and virtuosity; it had better be based on simplicity and honesty.

The Monster
and the Lamb

In the days of Hitler Germany's collapse, a short item on an inside page of *The New York Times* caught my eye: It ran somewhat as follows:

> Reinhold Hensch, one of the most wanted Nazi war criminals, committed suicide when captured by American troops in the cellar of a bombed-out house in Frankfurt. Hensch, who was deputy head of the Nazi SS with the rank of Lieutenant General, commanded the infamous annihilation troops and was in charge of the extermination campaign against Jews and other "enemies of the Nazi state," of killing off the mentally and physically defective in Germany, and of stamping out resistance movements in occupied countries. He was so cruel, ferocious, and bloodthirsty that he was known as "The Monster" *(Das Ungeheuer)* even to his own men.

It was the first time since I had left Germany in the winter of 1933 that I had heard or seen Hensch's name. But I had thought of him often. For I had spent my last evening in Germany in the company of "The Monster."

A year earlier, in the spring of 1932, I had realized that I was not going to stay in Germany with the Nazis in power. An old friend had come to visit me in Frankfurt where I then lived. We spent the evening together talking out our fears for the future. Then suddenly I heard myself saying: "One thing I do know, Berthold. If the Nazis come to power, I shan't stay in Germany." I had not, I think, given conscious thought to the decision at all until then. But the moment I heard myself say this, I knew that I had made up my mind. And I also knew that I had become convinced in my heart—though not, perhaps, in my mind as yet—that the Nazis would get into power.

I had come to Germany in the fall of 1927 first as a trainee clerk in an export firm in Hamburg; then, fifteen months later, I moved to Frankfurt as a securities analyst in an old merchant bank that had become the European branch of a Wall Street brokerage firm. That job came to an end in the fall of 1929 with the New York Stock Exchange crash, and I was hired as a financial writer on Frankfurt's largest-circulation newspaper, the *Frankfurter General-Anzeiger*—an afternoon paper, somewhat similar to the Washington *Star* or the Detroit *Free Press* both in circulation and in editorial policy. I made rapid progress at the paper and only two years later was appointed a senior editor in charge of foreign and economic news. Since the paper did not believe in overstaffing—there were only fourteen or fifteen writers, reporters, and editors all told to turn out a full-size forty-eight- or sixty-four-page paper every weekday and Saturdays—I also wrote three or four editorials a week and ran the woman's page for the best part of a year while the regular woman's editor was sick.

But I had a full professional life outside the job too. I had enrolled in the law faculty when I got to Hamburg and had then transferred to Frankfurt. By 1931 I had my doctorate in international and public law. Even before that I had begun to teach in the law faculty as a substitute for the elderly and ailing professor of international law, who had become a good friend. And I was due, though still in my early twenties, to be appointed "Dozent"—Lecturer—at the University, the first and biggest step up the German academic ladder.

I had begun to write outside of my newspaper job. Two unbearably "learned" econometric papers, one on the commodity markets and one on the New York Stock Exchange, were written while I was still at the bank, in 1929. They were both as wrong as they could possibly be. The premises were "self-evident," the mathematics impeccable, and the conclusions asinine—something even now by no means unknown in Econometrics. But the papers got published in a prestigious economics quarterly. My doctoral thesis came out as a book. And I wrote a fair number of magazine articles on economic and financial topics, none of which, fortunately, are still around.

When I realized that I would leave upon Hitler's coming to power —and also that I expected that to happen—I did not, of course, stop doing all these things. I did hope against hope. After all, it was not entirely wishful thinking in 1932 to believe that the Nazi wave was cresting; the Nazi vote actually did fall with every successive election. So I continued to work on the paper, teach international law and international affairs, and write for magazines. I even began to look around for another job; for I knew that I had outgrown the *Frankfurter General-Anzeiger*. I almost immediately got an offer from a prestigious German paper, the leading paper in Cologne, to take charge of everything foreign: politics, economics, literature, and culture. I was assured that with this appointment I could easily get a lecturership at Cologne University or at the neighboring university of Bonn.

But at the same time I began to prepare for leaving. I kept the offer from Cologne alive but did not act on it. I dragged my feet on the lecturership even though the international law professor urged it on me. I was officially a graduate assistant; as such I ran many of the meetings of the International Law Seminar and substituted for the professor in teaching his classes. But a "Dozent," while unpaid, had a university appointment and became automatically a German citizen, which I was not; and I had no intention of becoming Hitler's subject.

I also made up my mind to make sure that I could not waver and stay. The day after my evening with my friend Berthold, I began to write a book that would make it impossible for the Nazis to have anything to do with me, and equally impossible for me to have anything to do with them. It was a short book, hardly more than a pamphlet. Its subject was Germany's only Conservative political philosopher, Friedrich Julius Stahl—a prominent Prussian politician and Conservative parliamentarian of the period before Bismarck, the philosopher of freedom under the law, and the leader of the philosophical reaction against Hegel as well as Hegel's successor as professor of philosophy at Berlin. And Stahl had been a Jew! A monograph on Stahl, which in the name of conservatism and patriotism put him forth as the exemplar and preceptor for the turbulence of the 1930s, represented a frontal attack on Nazism.

It took me only a few weeks to write the monograph. I sent it off to Germany's best-known publisher in political science and political history, Mohr in Tübingen. Mohr accepted the little book immediately, scheduled it to come out at the earliest possible date, in April 1933, and as the key issue—Number 100—in his famous series on Law and Government. Clearly the people at Mohr, whom I had never met, felt the way I did. The book, I am happy to say, was understood by the Nazis exactly as I had intended; it was immediately banned and publicly burned. Of course it had no impact. I did not expect any. But it made it crystal-clear where I stood; and I knew I had to make sure for my own sake that I would be counted, even if no one else cared.

I was thus ready to leave when Hitler, already losing popular support precipitously, was put into power on January 31, 1933, by a cabal of nationalists and generals who were contemptuous of the plebeian Nazis and confident of their ability to control these upstarts, but who were also alarmed by the strong resurgence of the Republican and Democratic parties in the most recent election. I knew that Hitler's backers deluded themselves, though even I probably underestimated the speed with which the Nazis then would get rid of the Junkers and old-line Prussian officers who had put them into power. And from the beginning I had few illusions as to what the Nazis were up to. I knew that my foreign passport would not protect me very long and that sooner or later I would be kicked out or jailed. I was determined to leave at my own discretion, not wait until I had to.

Yet I dawdled and hung on. One reason I gave to myself was that I had to check the page proofs of my book on Stahl, promised for just about that time. I feared—perhaps not entirely without cause—that my leaving the country might give the publisher the pretext for scuttling what had clearly become a risky project. But I also gave in to my bent for postponing the inevitable.

What then decided me to carry out my intention and to leave right away, several weeks after the Nazis had come to power, was the first Nazi-led faculty meeting at the University. Frankfurt was the first university the Nazis tackled, precisely because it was the most self-confidently liberal of major German universities, with a faculty that prided itself on its allegiance to scholarship, freedom of conscience, and democracy. The Nazis knew that control of Frankfurt University would mean control of German academia altogether. So did everyone at the University. Above all, Frankfurt had a science faculty distinguished both by its scholarship and by its liberal convictions; and outstanding among the Frankfurt scientists was a biochemist of Nobel Prize caliber and impeccable liberal credentials. When the appointment of a Nazi commissar for Frankfurt was announced—around February 25 of that year—and when not only every teacher but also every graduate assistant at the University was summoned to a faculty meeting to hear his new master, everybody knew that a trial of strength was at hand. I had never attended a faculty meeting but I did attend this one.

The new Nazi commissar wasted no time on the amenities. He immediately announced that Jews would be forbidden to enter university premises and would be dismissed without salary on March 15. This was something no one had thought possible despite the Nazis' loud anti-Semitism. Then he launched into a tirade of abuse, filth, and four-letter words such as had rarely been heard even in the barracks and never before in academia. It was nothing but "shit" and "fuck" and "screw yourself"—words the assembled scholars undoubtedly knew but had certainly never heard applied to themselves. Next the new boss pointed his finger at one department chairman after another and said: "You either do what I tell you or we'll put you into a concentration camp." There was dead silence when he finished; everybody waited for the distinguished biochemist. The great liberal got up, cleared his throat, and said: "Very interesting, Mr. Commissar, and in some respects very illuminating. But one point I didn't get too clearly. Will there be more money for research in physiology?"

The meeting broke up shortly thereafter with the commissar assuring the scholars that indeed there would be plenty of money for "racially pure science." A few of the professors had the courage to walk out with their Jewish colleagues; most kept a safe distance from these men who, only a few hours earlier, had been their close friends. I went out sick unto death—and I knew that I would leave Germany within forty-eight hours.

When I got home, there, thank God, were the page proofs of my Stahl book. I went to the office—I had taken special leave that morning to attend the faculty meeting—announced my resignation, and said goodbye to my colleagues. Then I went home and read the proofs. By that time it was about ten at night; I was drained. I decided to go to bed and start packing early in the morning to catch a train from Frankfurt to Vienna the next day. But just at that moment my doorbell rang. Outside stood somebody in the uniform of the Hitler storm troops. My heart missed a beat. Then I recognized my colleague Hensch, a fellow editor at the *Frankfurter General-Anzeiger* who had not been at the office when I was there earlier in the day. "I heard that you'd resigned," he said. "I happened to pass by and did want to take my leave. May I come in?"

Hensch was not a particular friend. Indeed he was somewhat of an outsider at the office. He covered local politics, City Hall; and while important, the assignment was not of interest to most of us who were not locals and who did not expect to spend the rest of our days in

Frankfurt. He was not a particularly good journalist, and he was suspected of taking and giving political favors. Of middle height, with small close-set eyes and cropped hair that was already beginning to gray although he was not yet thirty, he came from local craftsman stock—his father was a stonemason, I believe. There were only two things noteworthy about him. First, he had a lovely girlfriend, Elise Goldstein, a commercial artist who did a lot of work for the paper—an outgoing, lively, effervescent young woman whom all of us thought most attractive. She and Hensch lived together and were going to be married; we had all attended their engagement party a year or so earlier. And second, Hensch, as everyone on the staff knew, held membership cards in both the Communist and the Nazi parties, both of course considered subversive and out of bounds for a reporter on a nonpartisan paper. When Hensch was challenged on this, he always said: "I have to get the news from them to know what goes on in City Hall—and they only talk to members of their own gang."

"I've spent most of the day," he now said, "at a meeting of the Nazi leadership in which I've been appointed adviser on the press to the new Nazi commissar for Frankfurt and the representative of the Party at the *General-Anzeiger.* Then I called a meeting of the editors to tell them that I'm in charge. That's how I learned that you had resigned earlier. I thought I'd come by to ask you to reconsider. I hope you do—we need you. Of course I have relieved the publisher. The biggest paper in Frankfurt can't have a Jewish publisher. I shan't keep the editor-in-chief very long. He's a leftist and married to a Jewish wife who is also the sister of a Socialist deputy. There would be a great opportunity for someone like you, for I won't be able to edit the paper myself; I'll be too busy supervising the press in the whole Frankfurt area." I replied that I was flattered but was sure it wouldn't work. "I thought you'd say that," he said. "But, Drucker, do sleep on it and let me know if you change your mind." He made as if to go, then sat down again and remained silent for five or ten minutes.

Then he began again. "If you go abroad, may I tell Elise where she can reach you? Of course, I had to break it off when Hitler came to power. I moved out of the apartment we had together, back to my parents, but I've paid the rent on the apartment until the end of March. I told Elise that she ought to get out of Germany as fast as possible. But she doesn't know anyone abroad. May I have your address so that she can get in touch with you when she leaves?" I agreed and he wrote down my parents' address in Vienna. Again he relapsed into silence after making as if to get up and leave.

Then he burst out: "My God, how I envy you! I only wish I could leave—but I can't. I get scared when I hear all that talk in the Nazi Party inner councils, and I do sit in now, you know. There are madmen there who talk about killing the Jews and going to war, and about jailing and killing anyone who holds a dissenting opinion and questions the Fuehrer's word.

"It's all insane. But it frightens me. I know you told me a year ago that the Nazis believed these things and that I ought to take them seriously. But I thought it was the usual campaign rhetoric and didn't mean a thing. And I still think so. Now that they're in power they'll have to learn that one can't do such things. After all, this is the twentieth century. My parents think so too; so does Elise. When I told her that she ought to get out of Germany she thought I was mad. And I probably am—they can't mean these things and get away with them. But I'm beginning to be scared. You can't imagine the things some of the higher-ups say to us when no one from the outside is listening."

I assured Hensch that I did not have to imagine these things; Hitler had written them out in great detail in his book *Mein Kampf* for anyone to read. Then I asked: "If you feel that way, why don't you leave? You aren't thirty yet and have no family that depends on you. You have a decent degree in economics and won't have any trouble finding work." "That's easy for you to say," he replied. "You know languages, you've been abroad. Do you realize I've never been away from Frankfurt, never even been to Berlin? And I have no connections —my father is a craftsman."

At that I got angry. "Look, Hensch, that's nonsense; who the hell cares who your father is? The father of the editor-in-chief was a prison guard someplace in East Prussia; Arne's father (Arne was the oldest senior editor) is a coal miner; Becker—the third senior editor—grew up as the child of an elementary schoolteacher; Bilz—the stock exchange editor—comes from a family of poor vintners with a small stony plot on the Rhine. All right, none of us would ever have been invited to a court ball by the Hohenzollerns or gotten a commission in one of their guards. But otherwise what difference can it possibly make?"

"You just don't understand, Drucker," he came back heatedly. "You never did. I'm not clever, I know that. I've been on the paper longer than you or Arne or Becker—you three are the senior editors and I still have the City Hall beat on which I started. I know I can't write. No one invites me to their homes. Even Elise's father—the dentist—thought his daughter too good for me. Don't you understand that I want power and money and to be somebody? That's why I joined the Nazis early on, four or five years ago when they first got rolling. And now I have a party membership card with a very low number and *I am going to be somebody!* The clever, well-born, well-connected people will be too fastidious, or not flexible enough, or not willing to do the dirty work. That's when I'll come into my own. Mark my word, you'll hear about me now." With that he stormed out of the room and started for the stairs. But before he slammed the door, he turned once more and shouted: "And don't forget, you promised to help Elise!"

I bolted the front door, something I had never done before in the three years I lived in the apartment. And suddenly I had a vision—a vision of things to come, of the horrible, bloody, and mean bestiality that was descending on the world. There and then I beheld as in a dream what was later to become my first major book, *The End of Economic Man.* I felt an almost irresistible urge to sit down and start typing. But I repressed it and started packing instead. I was on the train to Vienna by the following noon.

I never heard from Elise. And I did not hear from or about "The Monster" until twelve years later when I read of his end in the ruins of what had been his parents' house.

It was only a month later, in early April 1933, that I met "The Lamb." After a few weeks in Vienna I went to London where I knew nobody except for one German journalist, the London correspondent of the Ullstein publishing firm of Berlin, Count Albert Montgelas. Montgelas, scion of a Bavarian Whig family, had been in England for a good many years and was one of the most highly respected foreign correspondents there. I had been in contact with him for some time. On his last trip back to his head office in Berlin he had stopped over in Frankfurt for a few hours and we had found each other congenial despite the difference in ages, Montgelas being in his late thirties whereas I was only twenty-three. So I sent him a note from Vienna before leaving for London—and to my surprise got back a telegram saying: "Come as soon as you possibly can. I need you."

I found Montgelas packing. He too had resigned when the Nazis moved in, despite urgings by the new Nazi-appointed publisher to stay on. He was only waiting for his replacement. "I wired you to hurry up," he said, "because I'm expecting Paul Schaeffer within a day or two. He's due in from New York on the next fast boat. He's been offered the editorship of the *Berliner Tageblatt* and is inclined to accept it. But I made him stop over here and give it a final thought —it would be a tragedy if Paul took the offer. You've just come out of Germany. Maybe you can tell Paul what hell he's letting himself in for."

The *Berliner Tageblatt* had for almost half a century occupied a role in Germany and the German-speaking countries similar to that of *The New York Times* in America or The *Times* in England; not the biggest but the best and most visible daily paper. Founded in 1885, when Bismarck was still German Chancellor and the old Emperor William I was still on the throne, the paper had for all these years been run by its founder-editor, Theodore Wolff, a man renowned alike for his integrity and his independence. Wolff was getting old, of course, and so, beginning in the early 1920s, he had been grooming a successor—Paul Schaeffer, an extraordinarily incisive political writer and analyst. But before handing over to Schaeffer, Wolff sent him as correspondent of the *Berliner Tageblatt* to America in 1929 or 1930. Schaeffer decided right away that the most interesting man in the United States was a new governor of New York, Franklin Delano Roosevelt. He got to know Roosevelt well and was invited to accompany him on his campaign trips in 1932. His dispatches from the campaign were so good that they not only got reprinted in major European papers but were widely syndicated in the American press. When Roosevelt was elected, Schaeffer moved to Washington to be close to what he anticipated would become an important administration under a President who had become a personal friend and who looked upon Schaeffer as his channel to European public opinion.

Wolff had intended, as everyone in the small world of European journalism knew, to step down in 1935—the fiftieth year of his editorship and the eightieth year of his life. But Wolff was a Jew, so the Nazis threw him out two years ahead of schedule and asked Schaeffer to return to Berlin and take over the vacant position. Schaeffer stayed long enough in the United States to cover Roosevelt's inauguration. Then, in late March or early April, he sailed. But, upon Montgelas's urgings and still not totally decided, he was willing to stop over for a few days in London before making a final commitment.

Schaeffer, it turned out, did not need me to tell him what was going on in Germany. He knew, indeed much better than I did, and had no illusions. He had access, it seemed, both to the internal dispatches of *The New York Times*'s European correspondents and to the dispatches of the State Department in Washington. "It's precisely because this is such a horror," he said, "that I have to accept the job. I'm the only man who can prevent the worst. The Nazis will need me and the *Berliner Tageblatt*. They'll need loans from New York and London, trade with the West, understanding and a hearing. And then they'll need someone like me who knows the West, who knows whom to talk to and who's listened to. They'll need me because not one of them knows anything about the outside world. They are all know-nothing illiterates. They'll have to listen to me when I tell them that this or that of their barbarous policies will get them into trouble in the outside world and that they have to pay attention to public opinion in the Anglo-Saxon countries. They'll have to accept the restraints on their actions and their rhetoric that I know they need in order to enjoy a minimum of respect and acceptance. They know they depend on me and that the Americans will look to me. I had a long talk before I left with the Chicago historian whom President Roosevelt has just appointed as his ambassador in Berlin. He assured me he'd use me as his channel to the German Foreign Office and the Nazi hierarchy—and even the stupidest Nazi goon will have to respect and accept *that.*"

"But, Paul," said Montgelas, "aren't you afraid the Nazis will just use you to give them a front of respectability and to bamboozle the outside world? They haven't shown much concern for world opinion so far." Schaeffer was indignant: "I wasn't exactly born yesterday. I'm a seasoned newspaperman. If they try to manipulate me, I'll up and leave; and that would hurt them and discredit them so completely that they couldn't take the risk."

"Are you sure, Paul," said Montgelas again, "that you aren't taking the job because it's always been your ambition to be editor of the *Tageblatt*?" "I knew you'd ask that," Schaeffer replied, "and I can assure you, you're wrong. Indeed, let me tell the two of you in confidence that my wife and I liked it so well in America we'd decided to stay there and not go back. I had received and accepted this offer," and he pulled out a letter from Henry Luce on *Time* stationery in which Luce offered Schaeffer the job as chief European correspondent, located in London, for *Time* magazine, for *Fortune,* and for a new picture magazine about to be launched (the future *Life*). "Luce would have paid me twice as much as the *Tageblatt* does," said Schaeffer, "and he hinted that I'd be in line for the top job at *Time* in a few years. My wife begged me to take the job—she hates the idea of going back. But I feel I have a duty. I owe it to Theodore Wolff to continue his life's work. The old man was like a father to me when he gave me my first job on my return from the trenches after the Great War. I owe it to the *Tageblatt* to make sure that it's not going to be prostituted and destroyed by savages. I owe it to the country to prevent these Nazi beasts from doing their worst. I don't look forward to Berlin under the Nazis, but I do know that no one else can have the influence for good I shall have, because no one else is quite as badly needed as I'll be when I take that job."

When Schaeffer arrived in Berlin a few days later he was received with great fanfare. Titles, money, and honors were heaped on him; and the Nazi press pointed to his appointment as editor-in-chief of the *Berliner Tageblatt* as proof that all the stories about the Nazis and their treatment of the press that had appeared in foreign papers were just dirty Jewish lies. They immediately began to use him. He was granted interviews by Nazi bigwigs who solemnly assured him that, of course, they were not themselves anti-Semitic and had, indeed, good personal friends who were Jewish; and these interviews promptly appeared in the *Tageblatt* under Schaeffer's by-line. Whenever news of Nazi repression or Nazi atrocities filtered out, Schaeffer was dispatched to the foreign embassies in Berlin or to a meeting with foreign correspondents to assure them that these were "isolated excesses" that would not be allowed to recur. Whenever news of German rearmament appeared, it was again Schaeffer who wrote an article quoting "high-placed sources" for Hitler's intense desire for peace, and so on. For these services he was once in a while contemptuously thrown little goodies. He was allowed to keep two elderly Jewish editors on as rewrite men on the financial page, or as proofreaders—but only for two months. Or he was allowed to write a short editorial criticizing a proposed tax on oleomargarine, or on movie tickets. And when after two years the *Berliner Tageblatt* and Schaeffer had outlived their usefulness, both were liquidated and disappeared without a trace.

In her book on Eichmann, the Nazi mass murderer, the late German-American philosopher Hannah Arendt speaks of "the banality of evil." This is a most unfortunate phrase. Evil is never banal. Evil-doers often are. Miss Arendt let herself be trapped by the romantic illusion of the "great sinner." But there are a great many Iagos, trivial men of great evil, and very few Lady Macbeths. Evil works through the Hensches and the Schaeffers precisely because evil is monstrous and men are trivial. Popular usage is more nearly right than Miss Arendt was when it calls Satan *"Prince* of Darkness"; the Lord's Prayer knows how small man is and how weak, when it asks the Lord not to lead us into temptation but to deliver us from evil. And because evil is never banal and men so often are, men must not treat with evil on any terms—for the terms are always the terms of evil and never those of man. Man becomes the instrument of evil when, like the Hensches, he thinks to harness evil to his ambition; and he becomes the instrument of evil when, like the Schaeffers, he joins with evil to prevent worse.

I have often wondered which of these two did, in the end, more harm—the Monster or the Lamb; and which is worse, Hensch's sin of the lust for power or Schaeffer's hubris and sin of pride? But maybe the greatest sin is neither of these two ancient ones; the greatest sin may be the new twentieth-century sin of indifference, the sin of the distinguished biochemist who neither kills nor lies but refuses to bear witness when, in the words of the old gospel hymn, "They crucify my Lord."

Noel Brailsford—
The Last of
the Dissenters

When Noel Brailsford died, a very old man, in 1958, few people even in England still remembered his name. But forty, or even twenty-five, years earlier H. N. Brailsford had been an important man on both sides of the Atlantic, and a writer of stature. In the mid-thirties he and I were friends for a few years, despite the disparity in our ages—he was then in his sixties and actually a few years older than my own father. He was at his peak in popularity and influence, and all the more active for that. His articles in the *New Statesman* and the *Manchester Guardian,* written in a clear, simple, but graceful prose that owed more to Addison and Steele's *Spectator* in England's eighteenth century than to the seventeenth-century Puritans whom Brailsford loved, were discussed and quoted widely even by people like Winston Churchill or Anthony Eden who had little use for Brailsford's politics. The articles were immediately reprinted across the Atlantic in the *New Republic* or the *New York Times Magazine* and were read carefully in New Deal Washington. In those years Brailsford also wrote books and pamphlets in profusion for the "Left Book Club"—that peculiar mixture of Methodist brimstone and Marxist pedantry which was a "must" for educated young Englishmen of those days of upper-class "proletarian chic." These books and pamphlets almost immediately became bestsellers at every bookstall in the British Isles.

Noel Brailsford was never a power. He was a conscience. He once stood for Parliament and was roundly defeated. It was his salvation; he would have been destroyed in six months as a politician. He was very much an "insider," in that his concerns were always those of the day. But he opposed by temperament as much as on principle. He was the last of the English "Dissenters," and that made him important. What he stood for mattered far less than who he was.

Noel—he had dropped the "Henry" of his first initial in his early years—looked exactly like Puss in Boots in the traditional English Christmas pantomime. Of less than average height, with short legs, broad shoulders, and a long rump, he had closely cropped white hair that stood up stiff and bristly, twinkly eyes, and a wide generous mouth. He wore rough tweeds, a bow tie, and a blue shirt with a stiff single-piece collar, starched and rather high, that looked somewhat like a clerical collar turned around. He was a vegetarian and lived mostly on nuts and cheeses, but he enjoyed cooking a steak for his guests and liked to watch them eat it. He loved his pipe and drank dark malt whiskey and a Rhône wine or South African claret with his vegetarian meals. No one in my whole life was a better host, more entertaining, more interested, and more encouraging than Noel Brailsford, sitting after dinner by the flickering light of a country fireplace and talking with his guests until the early hours of the morning. One knew at once that he must have had a very beautiful mother. He had what the French call *douceur;* yet it was a manly charm, without a trace of sugar, let alone saccharine.

Brailsford was a deeply religious man, but the faith he professed was anti-religion. He had been born the son, grandson, and great-grandson of Nonconformist ministers, Baptists or Methodists. The zeal and rhetoric of "Chapel" stayed with him until the end of his life. But like so many late Victorians—Brailsford was born in 1873—he went through a profound spiritual crisis in his teens, lost his faith, and emerged a fiery agnostic. I never heard him say a sharp or unkind word about any one person. But when anything Christian was mentioned, this mild, warm, charitable man turned into a narrow, wrathful sectarian, damning to hell all churches, all denominations, all priests and clergymen; cursing them with the venom and invective of a John Knox denouncing Popish whoremongers and idolators. His heroes were the militant Puritans of the seventeenth century, especially the Levelers; he wrote an excellent book on them. He never forgave Oliver Cromwell for betraying them, as he put it, and for preserving the old social order of England, and especially the landowning gentry and nobility, against the Levelers' attempts at a Christian communal socialism. But the author whom he quoted most often was Voltaire, and a special edition of Voltaire's polemics against Christianity and the Catholic Church was always on his bedside table.

Brailsford had started out as a junior fellow or tutor at one of the Oxford colleges—I believe he was a classicist. He liked academic life and was well suited to it. He had the kind of wit that Oxford likes, quick but without bite or malice, and the exquisite manners that make a man a success at a college's High Table. But the Boer War pushed Noel Brailsford out of academia and into politics. He was bitterly opposed to the war as a matter of conscience; and there were far too many generations of dissenting ministers in his blood for him to be silent in a matter of conscience. So he early became a loud and articulate opponent of the war, writing pamphlets, making speeches, and organizing meetings and demonstrations. It was, of course, a highly unpopular stand, especially in the Tory Oxford of those days, and Brailsford was given to understand that he had lost all chances for academic preferment. But his anti-war writings had attracted the attention of "Old Man Scott" of the *Manchester Guardian*. The *Guardian* alone of all major English newspapers had been critical of the Boer War—indeed it was its opposition to the Boer War that made a national newspaper out of what had been a provincial one. Scott asked Brailsford to join the *Guardian* as its leader writer on foreign affairs; it was in this job that he first became a national figure. During those early years of the century, England changed what had been its fixed policy ever since the first Elizabeth and allied itself in peacetime with Continental great powers, first France and then Russia. The change was the work of a Liberal government. And the *Manchester Guardian* was the principal Liberal newspaper of England. Yet Brailsford, as the paper's foreign affairs editor, firmly opposed the new policy as likely to encourage rather than prevent war. Again he took what was a most unpopular stand. This was the period of Kipling's "Recessional"—the period in which England first became aware that its powers were waning and that it was being overtaken economically and politically. The new alliances, which promised to checkmate the rising industrial and military might of Imperial Germany, were welcomed by all parties. But while Brailsford's editorials made him unpopular, they also made him well known.

Ten years later he became the *Manchester Guardian's* war correspondent in the Balkan wars, serving with the Greeks, the Bulgarians, and the Serbs as they fought first the Turks and then each other. The Balkan wars of 1912–13 are by now no more than a footnote in the history books. But at the time they were seen as the curtain-raiser and prelude to the general European war everyone feared and expected, very much the way the Spanish Civil War was viewed twenty-five years later by the generation of the 1930s. The two years Brailsford spent in the Balkans were probably the most productive ones of his life. He hated the fighting and the suffering—and he saw a good deal of it. For in order to observe closely, he enlisted as a stretcher bearer in each of the armies whose wars he covered; he was wounded twice while serving first with the Greeks and then with the Bulgarians. But he fell in love with these romantic lands: with the wildflowers on spring hillsides and the sere stillness of summer and fall; with rapid turbulent streams in deep gorges, with rocky escarpments, towering mountains, and the lush, densely cultivated valleys in between. Above all, like so many Englishmen before him, he fell in love with simple people, people who had not yet become "civilized"; who still clung to their ancient ways of life and to rough-hewn tenets of faith and honor; who still sang the ballads and told the folk tales of yore, rather than whistle the "Merry Widow" waltz and read newspapers. Brailsford's dispatches on a cruel, protracted, and confused war were full of folk tales and fertility rites; of weddings, blood feuds, and funerals; of superstitions and folk medicines; of heroic epics on Alexander the Great, the greatest son of those wild mountains, and on guerilla fighters against the hated Turks; of comments on tribes and their traditions, on half-forgotten languages and the ruins that a succession of invaders and conquerors—Greeks, Romans, Byzantines, Crusaders, and Turks—had left behind. The books in which these dispatches were collected became bestsellers in Britain and as late as the 1930s were still being used by European foreign offices to prepare young diplomats for service in the Balkans. Many years later still, when Brailsford was already dead, I met a Yugoslav economist, a high official in the Tito government, who told me that Brailsford's books, though by then all of fifty years old, were still being recommended to young Serbs and Croats in the government service as the best introduction to those wild areas with their romantic names: Macedonia, Thessaly, Rumelia, and the Sanjak; "and," he added, "not just for areas in other countries like Greece or Bulgaria, but as introduction for the city Yugoslavs to the remote mountain lands of their own country as well."

Brailsford went to the Balkan wars a dissenting Liberal. He returned a dissenting Socialist. One cannot call him a Christian Socialist —he had earlier repudiated Christianity. But it was a religious social-

ism rather than a scientific, dialectic, Marxist socialism. Before he went
to the Balkans, Brailsford had undoubtedly been exposed to Tolstoy;
after all, Tolstoy was Europe's most widely read and admired writer
at the turn of the century. But Tolstoy's simple (or seemingly simple)
socialism of compassion and humility, of loving peasants and humble
village folk, must have seemed rather quaint to an Oxford don and
leader writer in Manchester, the capital of the Lancashire that had
been the cradle, and was then still the citadel, of the Industrial Revolution. In the Balkans Brailsford found himself among people who actually lived in Tolstoy's pre-industrial, pre-capitalist community of extended families and village cooperatives. And just at the time he
served in the Balkans, the new "rural sociology" movement began to
have profound impact there.

Hungarian in origin—indeed Mousie Polanyi's brainchild—this
movement preached a rural democracy of equal small peasant pro-
prietors with "forty acres and a mule," to use an earlier American
slogan for a somewhat similar movement. But unlike its Jeffersonian
or Jacksonian predecessors in America, "rural sociology" believed in
community rather than individualism, especially in the voluntary cooperative of extended family and joint ownership. It was not "religious" in any traditional sense. But it preached going back to the
peasant's cultural roots, his beliefs, his folk songs and folk tales, his rites
and rituals. "Rural sociology" had particularly great impact in Bulgaria, where Brailsford spent most of the years of the Balkan wars.
Stambuliiski, the Bulgarian "rural sociologist" and peasant politician,
became Brailsford's close friend and remained so until assassinated in
the 1920s while Bulgaria's prime minister, whether by right-wingers
and on Mussolini's orders or by agents of Stalin's Comintern has never
been determined.

Brailsford did not become a "rural sociologist." But his encounter
with "rural sociology" led him back to his own roots, to the communal
religious socialism of England's dissenting tradition—the Diggers and
the Levelers of the seventeenth century. They had been treated with
contempt by historians, including most Marxists. They were seen as
crude, ranting, unscientific yokels, impeding progress. Brailsford was
perhaps the first writer to see them as forerunners and pioneers of a
humane, compassionate, and loving socialism. A few years after Brailsford died, the Czechs called their attempt to reform communism
"Socialism with a human face." It is a phrase Noel Brailsford might
well have used to describe his own unsystematic but deeply felt dissenting socialism.

Brailsford was never a Fabian, nor did he have much use for what, to him, was a bunch of power-hungry ultra-rationalists out to make society over into their own bureaucratic image. He had only contempt for the brittleness and cleverness of Bloomsbury—a contempt that was amply returned. Trade union leaders he distrusted deeply. He was bored by Marx and not much interested in economics anyhow. And he loved the English language far too much and used it far too well to tolerate the illiterate jargon of the Marxists. His socialism was based on faith and morality rather than on "scientific" laws of history. His was a socialism of the heart rather than of the head or the pocketbook.

He was thus very much a "loner." But he also represented an older English tradition than Fabians or Bloomsbury or trade unionists or Marxists: a tradition going back to Wycliffe and Piers Plowman in the Middle Ages; to the Levelers and Diggers in the seventeenth century; and to the Chartists before 1850. It is a tradition that invokes the "bowels of compassion" rather than the "solidarity of the proletariat"; a tradition that asks for justice for the poor rather than for revenge on the rich; a tradition of individual conversion rather than governmental action, of dignity rather than welfare; a tradition of conscience, not of power. It is a tradition of radical dissent. Brailsford was a "loner" indeed. But he was not a "crank" or an "eccentric," he was a conscience.

The Balkan wars were over by the end of 1913, with every participant exhausted, bleeding, and frustrated. A few months later the Great War broke out. And, as Brailsford had predicted earlier, the alliances of the *Entente Cordiale,* which England had contracted with the Continental great powers of France and Russia, did not deter Germany, while they prevented England from playing the mediator. Brailsford at once decided to oppose the war. He never was a pacifist, but he made a distinction between "just" and "unjust" wars. The war the Greeks, Serbs, and Bulgarians had waged to free their compatriots from Turkish bondage had been a "just" war. The war the great powers were waging against each other—for a few strips of territory, for coal deposits, or for glory—was to him clearly an unjust and indeed a frivolous war. And so he again took the unpopular stand and went into opposition.

He had to resign from the *Manchester Guardian,* and lived for a few years in poverty without job or income. He was imprisoned once or twice for short periods. But he soon joined up with the small splinter group of Socialists who, like him, opposed the war. Most of them, men like Ramsay McDonald who later became Britain's prime minister,

were, like Brailsford, Christian rather than "scientific" socialists, and
descendants of the Chartists rather than of the Jacobins or of the Paris
Commune. None of them had come out of the trade unions, whose
leaders solidly supported the war and used it to become respectable
and powerful. The Socialists who opposed the war were thus congenial
to Brailsford. Not one of these men was well educated and not one of
them wrote well. Brailsford soon emerged as the intellectual spokesman and writer of the group. And when, within a year after the end
of the Great War, the reaction set in and the opponents to the war
became heroes rather than outcasts who triumphantly regained control of the Labor Party, Brailsford seemed about to become powerful.
He was offered membership in the cabinet of the first Labor government, or at least a major secondary post as an important junior minister—and was saved from this fate only by his inability to win election
to a supposedly safe Labor seat.

Brailsford looked around for his next unpopular cause. He found
it at once, or perhaps it found him. Within days of losing the election,
he had a caller—a young Indian lawyer who was a graduate of his own
college but sixteen years younger than Brailsford and unknown to
him. The caller's name was Jawaharlal Nehru. The reason for the call
was a request for an introduction to an English editor who might print
articles arguing the cause for Indian independence, written by Nehru
himself and by another unknown Indian lawyer by the name of
Gandhi. So Brailsford, in 1920, became the first English advocate of
Indian independence and remained its leading advocate for many
years.

Brailsford then knew practically nothing about India. He never,
I suspect, learned a great deal about the country or cared much for
it. When he finally went to India on a visit, he did not, I had the
impression, like much of what he saw. He got to know both Gandhi
and Nehru well, but distrusted both. He thought Nehru much too
clever; and Gandhi's mixture of religious rhetoric and ruthless politicking offended him. He certainly never shared the adulation of
Gandhi that became fashionable in Europe in the late twenties as a
result of Romain Rolland's best-selling book on the Mahatma. "He
sounds too much like Cromwell," he once answered when I asked his
opinion of Gandhi—and Cromwell was, of all the English rulers and
statesmen, the man Brailsford loved the least. Altogether, Brailsford
did not argue for Indian independence as being either desirable or
good for India. I suspect he doubted that the Indians would make a

go of it without the British overlords. And he rejected as pure cant the belief on the left that India had been oppressed and exploited by the British. But whether the British Raj in India was good or bad for India was, to Brailsford, entirely beside the point. Indian independence, to him, was a matter of conscience for England. Slaves, the ancient Fathers of the Christian Church had taught, may save their souls and go to heaven; their masters will be corrupted by owning slaves and will inevitably lose their souls and be damned. Brailsford argued Indian independence to save England's soul. This did not endear him to the Indians and he knew it. "They can't tell me enough how much they owe me," he once said to me. "They need me still. But I don't expect to be invited when India celebrates its independence." He wasn't. But it was precisely because he argued that Britain needed to be able to celebrate its independence from India—for the master is always more dependent on the slave than the slave is on the master—that he became in the twenties the most powerful voice for Indian independence in England, and respected for this, despite the unpopularity of his position even among his old associates in the Labor Party.

I do not remember how Brailsford and I first met. I know that he interviewed me in the summer of 1934 for an article he wrote on the Nazis' first abortive attempt to overthrow the Austrian government. And I dimly remember that he was surprised and pleased when he found out that I had heard of the eastern European "rural sociologists" and of Stambuliiski, his old friend, the democratic peasant leader of Bulgaria. But I don't believe we began to see each other regularly until the following winter of 1935. From then until leaving for the United States in January of 1937, my wife and I spent a good deal of time with him and got to know him well.

The woman Brailsford had married while still very young had become incurably insane in the early years of their marriage and had to be committed shortly afterwards. Under English law Brailsford could not obtain a divorce, but for many years he had been living with a well-known graphic artist, the etcher and wood engraver Clare Leighton, whose quietly lyrical books on country life and the English countryside were popular in both England and America. The two shared a flat in Hampstead close to where my wife and I then lived. Yet we usually did not see Noel and Clare in London but in the pleasant country house they jointly owned in Monks Risborough. It was about an hour out of London, then still well beyond the London sprawl that stopped at the market town of Princess Risborough, some ten miles or so from the Brailsford cottage. The house had a big sunny living and dining room, a large airy kitchen, a study each for Noel and Clare, and three small bedrooms. It had an old-fashioned garden—the kind of garden where wallflowers and stock grow side by side with Brussels sprouts. And it looked out over the Buckinghamshire hills and directly onto a pre-Christian landmark, the big white cross of Monks Risborough, originally according to legend a heathen horse's head, carved into the limestone of the first cliff that rises almost vertically out of the Vale of Aylesbury. There, my wife and I spent a weekend every six weeks or so during these two years. And once or twice, when both Noel and Clare went to America to lecture, they offered the house to us for weekend use. We were not the only guests Noel and Clare had at Monks Risborough, though they did not ask many people as they needed their weekends alone after the busyness of their lives in London. But I think my wife and I were among the very few friends Noel and Clare had in common and saw together.

Offices in England then still worked Saturday mornings. Both my wife and I had jobs so we usually did not get to Brailsford's country place until Saturday afternoon. By then Noel and Clare had already been in the country for two days; they always tried to leave London by the afternoon or evening of Thursday. Clare was seldom at home when we drove up. Even in the worst weather she was out sketching. But Noel was waiting for us impatiently. He was eager, almost anxious, to show his friends the precious "delights" he had discovered for them —so eager that he rarely allowed us to take our luggage out of the car and into the house, but dragged us away at once to a newly dug hole in the hillside out of which, if one waited quietly, a vixen would emerge to play with her cubs; to a sere thistle left over from the year before, in which a tiny mother tit was sitting on her newly laid eggs; or to an abandoned cart road, along which was a stand of particularly succulent hazelnuts, ready for the picking. But, above all, he delighted in flowers—in the rare, lily-like fritillary, which blooms for a few short weeks and only in a few wet meadows; in a very early crocus, blooming in a sheltered corner with new-fallen wet snow all around it; in the first cowslip on the embankment of a muddy lane; or in a rich stand of England's sweet-smelling wild hyacinth, the English bluebell, with its pure azure blooms. At those moments Brailsford particularly resembled a cat. His nose would quiver and one could almost hear him purr as he gently stroked the rough leaves of the cowslips.

Then we would return to the house and settle down for tea or sherry and, for Noel, the first of his two daily Scotch-and-waters. Clare would soon come in and join us. For an hour or so we would sit in companionable quiet listening to music. Noel and Clare lived very simply, almost frugally, but one of the few luxuries they allowed themselves was a beautifully crafted gramophone and a huge collection of recordings, mostly of chamber music. The talk began after an early dinner, and then it ranged all over: current affairs and politics; cultural anthropology—a special interest of Noel's from his Balkan days, and then much in fashion; classical history and art. Clare would be the first to go to bed; she got up early each morning to work. An hour or so later my wife would leave to go upstairs. When Noel and I were alone, he would gradually steer the talk to the one topic for the sake of which he had invited me, for the sake of which he had befriended me in the first place.

I was not yet twenty-five when Brailsford and I met. He was my senior by thirty-six years. I had been in England barely a year, and had only recently found my first decent job as the economist and securities analyst of a small, still quite unknown, merchant bank. Brailsford was an established writer and one of the leading journalists in the English tongue. I was by temperament a bystander, Brailsford an activist. My approach to political, social, and economic concerns was completely at odds with anything Brailsford stood for or practiced. By that time I had already become skeptical about salvation by society, whatever the creed or persuasion of the would-be saviour. Brailsford was a true believer by temperament, and as passionately devoted to the gospel of social salvation as his ancestors had been devoted to the Gospel of Christ. Brailsford had been moving steadily left, breaking with his old Labor Party friends when they, in 1931, joined a government of national union that soon became conservative in all but name. He had then become one of the moving spirits of the intellectual anti-establishment, the "Left Book Club." And I had never been a left-winger, or even a consistent Liberal. Indeed, I believe I was one of the very few friends Noel and Clare had in those years who was not a leftist.

But this was precisely, I think, why Noel befriended me. For his greatest concern and his constant preoccupation in those years he could not even mention to anyone on the left. Yet he had to discuss it with someone, if only to hear himself talk. The concern was his relationship to Soviet communism.

Brailsford had never felt the slightest attraction to communism, least of all in its Stalinist version. Its dogmatism, its humorless conformity, its use of secret police and of terror, and its endless theological hair-splitting were all equally repugnant to him. But he watched Fascism and Nazism steadily gain ground and came increasingly to see Soviet communism as the only effective countervailing force. Around 1930, the same man who had risen to prominence by writing against the British alliance with czarist Russia began to advocate a British alliance with Communist Russia. And then, in 1932, he published one of the first of what soon became a flood of eulogies of the Soviet Union by distinguished non-Communist Westerners. The main burden of the book was an appeal to Western Liberals, Socialists, Communists to join together in a common front against Fascism and Hitlerism. Brailsford invented both the idea and the slogan of the "Popular Front of the Left." But he not only asked Socialists and Liberals to accept the Communists as partners. He asked the Communists to abandon their ideological "purity" and to subordinate themselves to the common aim of preventing and combating fascism. He asked them, to use a term of the seventies, to become "Eurocommunists" rather than "Moscow Communists." In the process, Brailsford also went in for strong praise of the Soviet Union and of Stalin. His praise was neither as uncritical nor as fulsome as that of some later English admirers of Stalin, such as the Fabian saints Sydney and Beatrice Webb, or the pope of the London School of Economics, Harold Laski. But while the Webbs were far more powerful politically than Brailsford, the "loner," and while Laski was far more brilliant, Brailsford was first. His book was a sensation. His unequaled reputation for integrity and purity of heart also gave it an impact far beyond its intellectual weight. If Noel Brailsford, known alike for his acumen as an analyst and for his uncompromising conscience, accepted Stalin and Stalinism, then, the argument ran, the stories about terror in Russia and concentration camps, about secret police, torture, the mass murder of innocent small farmers and wholesale purges, *must* be false and nothing but malicious "Fascist lies."

By 1934, when I first met Noel, he had already begun to have doubts, and they grew steadily. Stalin eagerly picked up Brailsford's slogan of a "Popular Front of the Left." But it soon became clear that Stalin and the Communists he controlled did not mean what Brailsford had meant. To them, a "Popular Front" meant a Communist monopoly on power, and total subjection, if not destruction, of the non-Communist partners. Indeed, the Communists made it abundantly clear that they were a good deal more interested in weakening and

destroying the non-Communist left than in fighting Fascism or Nazism. Brailsford himself always believed, while I knew him, that it was
the refusal of the German Communists on Moscow's orders to support
or even to tolerate the democratic parties of the German left and
center that had brought Hitler to power. But he thought that the
failure of their policy in Germany would have taught the Communists
a lesson—only to find them pursuing the same fratricidal policy in
France a few years later, and thereby first rendering impotent Léon
Blum's government of the "Popular Front of the Left," then destroying it.

However, Brailsford was far less a politician than he was a conscience. When he wrote his eulogy on Stalin, the first reports of the
mass killing of the Russian peasants that marked Stalin's farm collec-
tivization had already filtered out to the West. But the stories sounded
too horrible to be believed, and were thus dismissed as scare propaganda. A few years later there was no longer any doubt, although even
then few in the West could accept that Stalin had cold-bloodedly
slaughtered millions of peasants whose only crime was their trust in
the promises of land ownership which the Communists had made to
them a few years earlier in order to gain power. Then the purges
began: of trade union leaders; of artists, scientists, and intellectuals; of
engineers, managers, and military men; and increasingly of old revolu-
tionaries. Many of these men Brailsford had come to know in his years
as a political writer on the left. He could not believe in their treachery
and their staged confessions. Yet how could he break with Russia when
there was no other power around to oppose the forces of darkness? His
conscience urged him to become again the independent dissenter
who opposes faith to power. But his sense of political realities whis-
pered to him, "The enemy of my enemies is my friend," and made him
condone evil, or at least close his eyes to it.

The Communists perfectly understood the war that was raging
between Brailsford's mind and Brailsford's conscience. They played
him skillfully and with care; he mattered greatly to them. Years later
a senior British diplomat in World War II Washington told me that he
was convinced that the Russian ambassador to London, Maiski, had
been chosen for the post and kept in it for years, primarily because he
was Brailsford's close friend and had Brailsford's confidence. This
probably overrates Brailsford's importance to Moscow. But to keep
Brailsford a supporter and fellow traveler was undoubtedly high
among Maiski's priorities. Brailsford meant integrity; he meant inde-

pendence; he meant selflessness, especially to the young and educated, who then—as always—distrusted politics and politicians. His
support of communism was worth many times whatever the cleverest
and best-financed propaganda campaign could have produced. And so
Maiski spent time and effort on preventing Brailsford's defection.

Maiski had lived as an exile in London for many years before
World War I, and had been befriended by Brailsford. Brailsford once
told me casually that Maiski had supported himself in those years
mainly by doing research assignments on foreign affairs for the *Manchester Guardian,* which Brailsford had been able to procure for him.
Maiski was then a Menshevik, the majority faction of Russian Socialists,
from which Lenin and the Bolsheviks had broken away. The Men-
sheviks got far more votes than the Bolsheviks in the only free election
ever held in Russia, in 1917, and Maiski had become a member of the
coalition government which then, in October 1917, was overthrown
by a Communist putsch. Many of the Menshevik leaders were ex-
ecuted or disappeared in Soviet concentration camps. Maiski was
spared only because Brailsford and other English Socialists interceded
for him with Lenin and Trotsky. Maiski threw in his lot with Stalin in
the internal party struggles following Lenin's death. He rose steadily,
to become finally Russia's ambassador to London and the man entrusted with keeping Brailsford's conscience anesthesized. He courted
Noel, sat down with him almost every week for long confidential chats,
gave him "inside information," and asked for his advice. Whenever
Noel became perturbed by a report of Communist duplicity or Communist terror, Maiski would first deny it and denounce it as a Fascist
lie. By the time he had to admit that the report was true, it had already
become stale. "And what's the use of raking up things that are over
and done with?" Maiski would ask. "No one is interested any more in
what happened six months ago." Then he would appeal to Brailsford
not to do anything that could only help the common enemy, the Nazis
or the Fascists. "Just think," he would say, "with what glee the Nazi
propaganda machine would pounce on this story if you lent your name
to it. Think how many people in England and throughout Europe
would abandon the Left as a sinking ship if they heard that Noel
Brailsford, who fathered the Popular Front idea, had deserted to the
enemy. Just think of the *damage* you'd do, and for no other reason
than to indulge in self-righteousness."

Brailsford was far too experienced to be totally taken in by flat-
tery; he was too seasoned a journalist to fall for Maiski's denials or

Moscow's lies about the endless purges and show trials. Yet Maiski's appeals not to give aid and comfort to the common enemy struck home.

Brailsford's strength had always been that he gave no thought to the consequences of conscience. This has always been the strength of the dissenter, but also, as Brailsford well knew, his undoing. And so for the first time in his life he suited conscience to circumstances. He no longer trusted Maiski, despite their old friendship, and had become deeply distrustful also of Stalinist propaganda and Communist objectives. But he shrank back from taking the ultimate step of directly criticizing Stalin and the Communists and from an open break with them. He was in perfect agony, in fact—so much so that he had to talk it out with someone. But his problem could not be discussed with anyone on the left in those days, at least not in England. And so I became the means for Noel to hear himself talk, precisely because I was not a part of Noel's problem as every leftist would have been.

And when he finally made the break, he used me as the means to make it.

A year after I had left England, I returned for a short visit to the British newspapers for which I worked as American correspondent and to the British financial institutions for which I worked as American economist and investment adviser. Noel invited me to spend my first free weekend with him at his Monks Risborough cottage.

I found him ten years older than when I had last seen him only fourteen months ago. While I was on the boat to England, Hitler had marched into Austria and annexed it by force—his first open land grab. Yet appeasement was stronger and more popular than ever in England and France. The Soviet purges and show trials had been rising toward a new peak of terror and hypocrisy. Most depressing of all was the news from Spain. The Republicans still hung on—Franco did not win his final victory until a year later—but they had been forced on the defensive. And while the Germans and Italians poured in men and weapons to ensure Franco's victory, the Western powers still maintained the embargo on arms shipments to the Republicans. Worse still was the systematic purge by the Soviet Union's commissars in Spain of the leaders of the non-Communist parties and groups on the Republican side, whether Social Democrats, Catholic Basques, Catalonian Liberals, or Anarchists. When rumor of the purge first came out of Spain in 1937, the Russians had firmly denied it and Maiski had persuaded Brailsford to write an article attacking the rumor as Nazi propaganda. Since then, however, the rumor had become verified fact, with eyewitnesses of such impeccable leftist credentials as George Orwell, Arthur Koestler, Ernest Hemingway, or the returning survivors of the American Abraham Lincoln Brigade all attesting to it. Brailsford felt that his whole life had been turned into sham and become a mockery.

On top of all this public misfortune had come personal misery. Clare was leaving him. She had already moved out of the London apartment, came to the Monks Risborough house only when Noel was not there, and was packing her bags to move for good to the United States.

It was a deeply depressed and almost despairing Noel Brailsford who greeted me when I arrived on a blustery March day. But he still was as kind and attentive a host as ever. He still had his customary small but intense "delight" waiting for me—as I remember it, the first pussy willows to come out on the banks of a small ice-bordered stream. And he refused to talk about his sorrows, but instead urged me to talk about my wife, myself, and my concerns.

I had then just finished my first major book, *The End of Economic Man*. Before leaving the United States, I had given the manuscript to an American publisher, a friend of Noel's to whom he had introduced me: He liked the book but was in two minds about publishing it. My predictions of the Nazis' "final solution"—of their plan to kill all Europe's Jews, and of the coming pact between Hitler and Stalin— were then still unthinkable for "decent people" in the free world. I spent the evening with Brailsford talking out my book and telling him of my worries about finding a publisher. Noel asked me to let him have a copy of the manuscript, which I had brought with me. When he came down for breakfast the next morning, he looked bleary-eyed. He had spent all night reading it and was enthusiastic. "This is first-rate, Peter," he said. "I've already sent a cable to the New York publisher, telling him that he *must* publish the book, and publish it as soon as possible. But please don't thank me," he said, "for I'm going to ask you a favor in return. I would like to write the preface to the book; in fact, I've cabled the publisher that I shall do so. For this way I can make a public break with the Communists."

It was a discreet way; a preface to another man's book is hardly shouting from the rooftops. But it was a clean break. For in his preface, Noel called communism a failure. As soon as the book came out a few months later (it was published by John Day in New York and by

Heinemann in London), and especially when it became the success in England which Brailsford had anticipated it would be, Brailsford's defection from communism was out and on record. And the Communists at once began to train their heaviest guns on him.

Another eight months later and war broke out in Europe. Brailsford immediately became a fervent supporter of the British war effort against Hitler. But this was the period of the Stalin-Hitler Pact, and Stalin's policy during this period was to support Hitler's war against the West, to stymie effective resistance to the Nazis by the Western powers, and especially to oppose America's entry into the war. Brailsford's influence had been particularly strong among America's intellectual left. Brailsford thus became a major enemy for the Communists and a major target of a Communist smear campaign in the United States. Bruce Bliven, an old friend of Brailsford's and editor of America's leading non-Communist liberal journal of pre-World War II days, the *New Republic,* of which Brailsford had long been European editor, told me at the time that he had never experienced anything like the pressures brought on him to deny the pages of the *New Republic* to Brailsford as a "warmonger," a "traitor," and a "Fascist agent." And when one of the leading American universities invited Brailsford to give a speech on the war and its issues, the Communists and fellow travelers on campus forced the faculty to rescind the invitation.

By the spring of 1941, the Roosevelt administration had become alarmed over the growth of isolationism amongst the very groups that had been the most loyal New Deal supporters: university faculties and university students, liberal newspapermen and intellectuals. So Washington asked the British government to send over Brailsford on a lecture tour, for the groups most affected by isolationist propaganda had been Brailsford's closest American friends and followers for years. Brailsford accepted eagerly. At last he could do something. But first he was going to spend a few weeks on a private mission of his own: to persuade Clare, then settled on Cape Cod, to return to him and to England. My wife and I had rented a house on the Connecticut-Massachusetts border for that summer. We invited Noel and Clare to come and spend July with us.

The trip to the United States was a disaster for Noel. His political mission had become futile before he even reached America. While he was on the high seas, Hitler invaded Russia; and by the time Noel landed in New York, every single Communist, fellow traveler, and leftist in America had become a fire-eating interventionist. His private mission was a total failure. Clare refused to return to him even though he offered to move to America himself if necessary. Noel cut his visit short and left after two weeks, a defeated, heartbroken old man.

A worse humiliation awaited him on his return home. He had decided, during his return trip, to forgive and forget the injustices done him by the Communists during the preceding two years, and to offer them his support during the terrible ordeal they were going through in those months of Nazi victories and Russian defeats. He made an appointment to see Maiski as soon as he was back in London. Maiski kept him waiting for three hours. When Noel was finally ushered into Maiski's office, the ambassador called him "Brailsford"— where for twenty-five years it had been "Noel," as Brailsford wrote to me. "Brailsford," Maiski said, "don't call here again. If you do, I won't see you. We don't need you any more." "Now," Brailsford wrote, "I know how the Dissenters felt when Cromwell dismissed them after they had won for him the war against the Stuart king, and when he told them that they had ceased to matter."

Stephen Blackpool, the Dissenter and the hero of Charles Dickens's most powerful and darkest novel *Hard Times* (written in 1854), is discredited, driven into exile and destroyed, because his conscience forbids him to compact with power. Even his death is defeat. It changes nothing, moves nothing, accomplishes nothing. The Dissenter of Dickens's nineteenth-century vision is not even a martyr; he is a casualty.

Noel Brailsford, the Dissenter of twentieth-century reality, tried to accommodate conscience to power for the sake of effectiveness. He ceased to matter.

Ernest Freedberg's World

I owe my career, in large measure, to a cuckoo clock, and a particularly ugly one at that. I had returned for Christmas to my parents' home in Vienna in the winter of 1933/34. When I finally decided to return to England and start on what I knew was an unpromising, and suspected would be a long, search for a job, my father asked me to take along a "small present" that an old friend wanted to send his son in London. It turned out to be a cuckoo clock, 5 feet tall and so heavy I could barely lift it. The train was crowded and I had to move the bulky clock to let people get on and off every time we stopped. I had to lug it from one station in Paris to another and get it on and off the cross-Channel boat. As soon as I reached Victoria Station in London, I called Richard Mosell, the recipient of the "small present"—it was then ten in the morning or so. "Why don't you hop into a cab and deliver the clock to me right now?" he said. "Then you won't have to carry it back home first."

I had met Mosell casually a few times in the preceding year, but knew only that he had something to do with a bank in the City. He took me to lunch, during which we chatted about my background and my plans. Then he said, "We could use someone like you at Freedberg & Co. as analyst and economist, report writer, and executive secretary to the partners. Let's go back to my office, and if my partners don't object, you can start work as soon as you're ready."

I started the following morning and stayed with the firm until I moved to New York, three years later. During the three years at

Freedberg & Co., the cuckoo clock—which Richard Mosell liked as little as I did—stood next to my desk and annoyed me every fifteen minutes by the silly noises it made.

I was told that I was a great success as a merchant banker; Freedberg & Co. certainly treated and paid me as if I were. When I finally decided to leave, they tried to dissuade me, promised me a full partnership within a few years, gave me a princely present—a first-class cabin on a two-week luxury cruise through the Mediterranean to New York for my wife and myself—and retained me for two years in a pure sinecure as their New York investment adviser. But I never enjoyed the work very much, and never felt that I was doing it well. Still, I looked forward to each day at the office. For the people were fascinating, both the members of the firm and the firm's clients.

The firm had been started during World War I by three stockbrokers who had been forced to resign their membership in the London Stock Exchange because they were of German, and therefore enemy, birth: Max Cantor, Otto Bernheim, and Ernest Freedberg. Cantor had not stayed long—there was some slight whiff of scandal, though I was never told any details. He came to the office once in a while to cadge a small loan from Ernest Freedberg, which he always got and never repaid. He fancied himself a ladies' man, wore a jet-black wig, dyed his long waxed mustaches, and liked to pinch every woman's bottom enthusiastically. Since he was almost blind—he had cataracts in both eyes and was afraid of the surgery—he usually pinched upholstered chairs instead.

Bernheim was still a member of the firm and had a desk in a corner of the partners' room. But though he was the youngest of the founders and only in his fifties, he had had several strokes, had difficulty walking and talking, and had suffered considerable brain damage. He came to the office for two or three hours one day a week, where he sat at his desk staring in the air and only coming to life for a few short lucid minutes once in a while.

Mr. Freedberg was by far the oldest of the three. A few weeks before I was hired he had celebrated his seventy-fifth birthday. But he was very much alive, indeed hyperactive. He was not the "brains" of the firm. Bernheim had played that part in the early years; after his first stroke Freedberg had brought in the Mosell brothers, Robert and Richard, to do the thinking. But Ernest Freedberg was the firm's vital energy.

The first thing one noticed when meeting him was his extraordinary nose. It was very long, pointed, and absolutely straight, exactly like Pinocchio's nose in the Walt Disney film after the first two lies. Altogether Ernest Freedberg looked and moved like a wooden puppet. He had long arms and legs, a long neck, long pointed ears, a long chin—and everything twitched, twisted, and jerked in perpetual motion, as if a demented puppeteer were pulling all the strings simultaneously. Even his half-moon reading glasses were forever sliding down his long spindly nose. When they were about to slide off altogether, he would throw his head way back and the glasses would slide up to his forehead and start their descent all over again. While he thus violently spun and jerked and twisted, he would hold one telephone cradled against one ear and talk at the same time into another telephone that stood on a special stand in front of him. Talking into both, he would turn around constantly to tell stories and to discuss business with his partners, with visitors, and with the firm's traders and managers. No one ever saw him sit still; and no one ever saw him off the telephone.

Ernest Freedberg had been born in the provincial town of Oldenburg in northern Germany when it was still the capital of an independent small duchy. The Freedbergs had been the "Court Jews," that is, private bankers, to the grand dukes of Oldenburg since the middle of the seventeenth century. But twelve years after Ernest's birth as the youngest of a large family, Oldenburg was incorporated into Bismarck's German Empire and the Freedbergs sold the family firm to one of the new large banks headquartered in Berlin; poor, turnip-growing Oldenburg could no longer support an independent bank. Ernest's older brothers had already forsaken banking, one to become a distinguished anatomist, another a historian of literature. Ernest as a boy was stricken by tuberculosis and was sent, when barely seventeen, to die in the sunny and salubrious climate of South Africa. He recovered. And before he had reached his mid-twenties he had joined up with another tuberculosis victim from a northern clime, an Englishman whose name was Cecil Rhodes. Freedberg did the financial work for the rapidly growing Rhodes empire. He also was charged with recruiting Rhodes's staff. Fifty years later, when I knew him, he still told with great glee that because of him, Rhodes, the English Jingo and straitlaced Protestant, had had only German-Jewish business partners—Oppenheimer, Beit, Barnato, and Albu. Freedberg left South Africa in the 1890s completely cured, came to London, and started a stock brokerage firm to handle the financial dealings of the Rhodes companies, the gold and diamond mines in South Africa, the copper mines in Rhodesia, and the de Beers diamond trading monopoly. He ran that firm until he had to leave the stock exchange during World War I; then he started Freedberg & Co. as merchant bankers.

Next to Freedberg's desk in the partners' room hung a full-length painting of an exquisitely beautiful young woman, a willowy girl with milk-white skin, blue-black hair that hung down to the waist, a shy smile, and flashing black eyes. It was a portrait of Freedberg's wife done in the first months of their marriage. Miranda had been a flamenco singer in a Spanish gypsy troupe. Freedberg, then already close to fifty, had seen her one evening in a London nightclub, fell in love on the spot, went backstage, bought her off her gypsy family and her gypsy husband, and married her the following morning by special license. It turned out to be a happy, or at least a durable marriage. But after Miranda had given birth to two daughters, she developed asthma; she had to leave London with its fogs and rains, and went to live in the south of France—surrounded, I was told, by cats and priests. Freedberg was still very fond of her and telephoned her almost every day around ten o'clock to wish her a good morning. But she rarely came to London, and only when one of the daughters had a new baby. The first time I saw her was quite a shock. For the beautiful girl of the portrait had turned into an obscenely obese hag with a triple chin, pendulous breasts almost bursting out of a shapeless black wrap, with an enormous cross dangling over them, and pitifully swollen legs full of varicose veins. She was sitting in a chair next to her husband's desk, placidly knitting something for the new grandchild and smiling fondly at Ernest, who smiled back at her. She left again for France within a day or two, not to return until the other daughter had a baby eighteen months later. As for the daughters, they did live in London. But though they came to the office fairly often, they only came when they wanted more money than the magnificent allowance they already received from their father. Then they went straight to Mr. Norris, the cashier, who had orders to give them whatever they wanted up to £1,000 per call—an enormous sum in those days. And if a daughter then found it expedient to look in on her father, she stayed only long enough to tell him how hard it was to make ends meet.

Mr. Freedberg lived alone in a bachelor flat on Carlton Terrace, attended only by a French manservant. But he did not want for female companionship. Once or twice a week he would go up to one of the girls in the office, a typist or telephone operator, and would openly invite her to his flat for dinner. The girl—never the same one twice in a row—would blush or giggle, and sometimes one would pretend not to hear. But while Freedberg graciously took "No" for an answer and never pressed, he was rarely turned down. He had apparently all his life been very attractive to women. He was also a considerate, courteous, and entertaining host. "He treats you like a reel laidy," the very pretty Cockney telephone operator once said when the office Lothario complained that she turned him down while yielding to the attentions of a seventy-five year old. And the dinner that the manservant served Mr. Freedberg's guest after the main event of the evening was over was legendary. The dinner was for Mr. Freedberg's guest, by the way; he himself barely tasted it. He did not seem to eat anything at all but subsisted on four to five packs of cigarettes a day and a freshly brewed pot of strong black coffee every half hour.

After the dinner Mr. Freedberg would put the girl in a cab and send her home while he went to his club to play bridge or poker for high stakes until the wee hours of the morning. For just as he did not need food, he did not need sleep—an hour or two at home after the club closed at half past three in the morning, and a half-hour's nap at lunch on an old black sofa in the partners' conference room sufficed him. He never took a vacation. "I don't know a place where I'm more relaxed than at the office," he would say; and he was always at his desk and on the telephone when I arrived in the office in the morning, no matter how early I came in.

"Speculation" was a dirty word in Freedberg's vocabulary. "Only an idiot speculates in stocks, in commodities, or in foreign exchange," he would say again and again. "If you have to gamble, play roulette; at least you know what the odds are." He prided himself on being a banker, and always stressed the 200 years of banking that were bred in his bones. But he himself was not a banker, he was a trader. He lived for the "deal." He was not even particularly interested in whether the deal was profitable or not. His idea of a "successful trade" was one in which the trader on the other end of the telephone paid a little more or got a little less than he expected to pay or to get. If there was no "deal" for as long as twenty minutes, Freedberg would get despondent, start complaining of growing old, and announce his imminent retirement from the firm. Then the telephone would ring, and he would happily start quoting, arguing, haggling. He would put the phone back with a smile of pure bliss, saying: "That chap didn't really want to pay that last eighth of a point, but he did."

To hold any asset—bonds or shares or real estate—for more than a few days was impossible for him. He had to trade. Once I found some "special situation": one of the bankrupt companies the "Swedish match king," Ivar Kreuger, had founded, the bonds of which were selling at 6 cents on the dollar even though the receiver in bankruptcy appointed by the U.S. courts had 20 cents in cash in the bank for each dollar of indebtedness, with another 20 to 30 cents about to become available shortly. Richard Mosell thereupon began quietly to buy up blocks of the bonds; they had been unsaleable for so long that the holders—mostly insurance companies—were only too happy to unload them at any price. Then Ernest Freedberg sold them all in two hectic days of "trading" for 8 cents on the dollar. Three weeks later the receiver in bankruptcy in New York announced (as we had known he would) an immediate distribution of 20 cents per dollar with another distribution of at least 10 cents to follow—and the bonds went up to 40 percent. Richard Mosell bitterly reproached Mr. Freedberg. "I don't understand you, Richard," Freedberg said; "any damn fool can sit on his rear end and wait for money from a bankruptcy court. It takes brains and hard work to sell bonds at two points above their market price. Besides, where's the fun in waiting for the postman to ring?"

For thirty years or more Freedberg had been treasurer of the Jewish Board of Guardians, the governing body of English Jewry. Then after a particularly noisy row with his fellow guardians, he called in the firm's accountant, Willy Huber, a devout Swiss Calvinist, and said to him: "I have announced my resignation from the Jewish Board of Guardians, and have nominated you, Huber, to be my successor." "But Mr. Freedberg," stammered Huber, "I'm not even a Jew." "What does that matter?" said Freedberg; "I nominated you to be treasurer, not rabbi. Besides, you aren't half the anti-Semite I am."

Quite early during my three years with Freedberg & Co. I was put in charge of the relations between the "front office"—i.e., the partners and the traders—and the "back office" of accountants and clerks. Thereupon Mr. Norris, the cashier and head of the back office, came to me and said, "I'm getting seven hundred fifty pounds a year and haven't been raised in five years, and every other cashier in every merchant bank in the City, even the smallest, makes at least a thousand pounds." I had authority to give Norris a raise and the firm had just finished an extremely profitable year. Still, Norris had been one of Mr. Freedberg's employes in the prewar stockbrokerage firm and

I thought it proper to tell Freedberg of the move. Freedberg, usually the most generous of men, exploded. "What would a clerk like Norris do with all this money?" he screamed. "He'd only SCHPEND it!" I then blundered. "Mr. Freedberg," I said, "what's two hundred and fifty pounds to you? You gamble away more than that in one night playing poker." "You mean to tell me," said Freedberg, utterly aghast, "that we have a *cashier* who gambles?" I hastily assured him that this was not what I had meant, but the damage had been done. For years thereafter—long after I had left the firm—Freedberg would call the auditors into his office each year, close the door, and say in a whisper, "As chairman of this firm, it is my duty to apprise you of a rumor about Mr. Norris, our cashier. I don't believe it, but you'd better know that he is said to gamble and to lose up to two hundred and fifty pounds a night playing poker."

It was easy to make fun of Freedberg. He himself often did. But his boast of the 200 years of banking in his bones was not altogether idle. There was wisdom in the old man, and great shrewdness. Once I brought him a proposal to underwrite the shares of a company. He took one look at it and said, "I see you expect this company to raise its sales and its profits both, by 10 percent each year for the next five years. You got this from the company's management, didn't you?" I nodded. "Any management that promises to raise both sales and profits simultaneously for any length of time," he said, "is either crooked or stupid, and usually both."

An American friend of the firm came to London with a proposal to form a syndicate to buy up U.S. railroad bonds, which were then, in those depression years of the thirties, selling at enormous discounts. "The United States government cannot afford to let the railroads go under," the man from New York said; "and then it must, according to U.S. law, honor the railroads' obligations." "Nonsense," snorted Freedberg; "never believe that any government *must* do the honorable and decent thing. Governments are instituted among men to defraud the citizenry. The only laws they *must* observe are those of nature they cannot break."

I came in with an elaborate proposal to acquire majority control of an ailing company and to reorganize it. "Very interesting," said Freedberg. "Let's call in Lewis and try your proposal on him." "But, Mr. Freedberg," I said, "Lewis is the youngest clerk in bookkeeping and, as you observed only a few days ago, a near-moron." "Exactly," said Freedberg. "If he can understand your proposal, we'll do it. If he doesn't, it's too complicated to work. Everything has to be moron-proof, for work is always in the end done by morons."

Freedberg had an uncanny perception of people. Once a promoter came to the firm, introduced by no less a personage than the Deputy Governor of the Bank of England, and with a proposal that seemed foolproof. All the major merchant banks in the City had already signed up with him. The man's background was impeccable. He had been the chief financial officer of one of the big insurance companies. The two younger partners, Robert and Richard Mosell, were ecstatic. This was the first time that Freedberg & Co. had been invited into the closed fraternity of major City banks, and to an absolutely foolproof deal at that. But Freedberg said, "No, the man is a crook." And he stood his ground, even though both Mosells threatened to leave the firm. Three months later the promoter disappeared, and with him the half a million pounds he had gotten out of the major London merchant banks. "How did you know he was a wrong one?" we asked Freedberg. "It was sticking out all over," he answered. "I really can't figure out how all of you managed to miss it. The fellow came prepared with answers to *every* question. Honest men don't, and don't have to."

Freedberg had integrity. One of my early assignments was to settle a dispute with a banking firm in Amsterdam with whom Freedberg & Co. had been trading for years. According to Freedberg's books, the Dutch owed some £80,000, which they hotly disputed. "You'll go there, Drucker," said Robert Mosell, who had been arguing the claim with the Dutch, "and fight for every penny the bastards owe us." "Oh no," said Freedberg, "you first make sure that you know what they owe us." After a few weeks of analysis I came to the partners and reported that in respect to the claims for £50,000, the Dutch were right—Freedberg owed them a small sum and they owed nothing. Robert Mosell was extremely angry. "I don't need enemies if I have you for a friend," he said, and he never quite forgave me. But Freedberg patted me on the back and thanked me. "What about the remaining thirty thousand?" he asked. "There I think we have a strong claim and I'll try to get the best settlement I can," I said.

After four weeks of discussions the Dutch and I agreed to split the £30,000, with their paying half of it. I went into the partners' room to get approval. "It's not as good as I'd hoped," I said, "but it's better than we would get were we to go to arbitration." "Does that mean," said Freedberg, "that the Dutch don't really believe they owe us the money?" I nodded. "And do you," continued Freedberg "believe they do?" "Well," I said, "I wouldn't want to prove it in a court of law." Whereupon Freedberg took the telephone, said to the operator, "Get me Amsterdam," and then told the Dutchman with whom I had negotiated so long and hard: "I'm afraid my young associate, Mr. Drucker, still has a few things to learn. I greatly appreciate your willingness to compromise. But you owe us nothing and we can't accept the fifteen thousand you agreed to pay." Then he turned to me and said, "Mr. Drucker, you are not a lawyer defending somebody else's reputation. You are a banker and the reputation you gain or lose is your own."

Above all, Freedberg was capable of great kindness—and to no one was he kinder than me. I had been working in the firm only a few weeks when Freedberg called me in. "Richard Mosell hired you," he said, "and you are not my concern. But really, Mr. Drucker, you are much dumber and far less competent than you have any business to be." I was taken aback. Richard Mosell had praised my work lavishly every day. "What am I doing that I shouldn't do, and what am I not doing that I should do?" I asked. "I understand," said Freedberg, "that you used to do securities analysis for that London insurance company you worked for last year. Well, you are still doing securities analysis. If that is what we had thought you should be doing, we'd have left you working for the insurance company. We made you executive secretary to the partners of this firm—and you haven't given any thought to what you now have to do to make a contribution and earn your salary. Today is Friday. Come back on Tuesday and give me your program in writing. What should you be doing now that you have been given so much bigger a job?" When I came in on Tuesday, he took one look at my list and said, "This is about 80 percent right; 20 percent is still missing." "What is missing, sir?" I asked. I had been slaving over the list all weekend and was quite impressed by it. His half-moon reading glasses slipped to the very tip of his Pinocchio nose and he said in a dry and cold voice, "Isn't this what you are being paid to know, Mr. Drucker?"

Only then did I look at the three partners whose executive secretary I was supposed to be, and asked what I had to do for them. The answer was obvious: I had first to make Mr. Freedberg effective in doing what he loved to do and did best, namely, trading. Whenever he concluded a deal over the telephone, he would meticulously write it down on either a "SOLD" or a "BOUGHT" trading slip, then equally meticulously fold the slip four times, tear it into sixteen pieces, and drop the pieces into his wastepaper basket. It was the first thing I had been told about him—he had been doing it for more years than anyone could remember. In the evening, the cleaning woman would empty the wastepaper basket and the records of Mr. Freedberg's deals would disappear with her. He had been asked countless times to kick the habit and always promised to do so. But after reforming for a few days, he would start tearing his trading slips into sixteen pieces and throwing them away again. Richard Mosell had tried to solve the problem by taking away Freedberg's wastepaper basket, whereupon Freedberg put the sixteen pieces of each trading slip into his pocket to flush them down the drain whenever he went to the toilet. He was quite unconscious of his habit, of course. But it played havoc with the accounting system. It was, for instance, responsible for the ludicrous dispute with the Dutch I had been asked to resolve.

Once I had accepted that it was my job as the subordinate to make the boss effective, and not my job to reform him, the solution was simple enough. I gave orders not to empty Mr. Freedberg's wastepaper basket, but to leave it for me to sort out the next morning. Within three days the accounting snarl had disappeared.

Freedberg was as proud of me as if I had been his first child and just taken my first step. I continued to work mostly with Richard Mosell. But Freedberg called me in "to teach me banking" whenever there was a lull in the office. "Mr. Robert and Mr. Richard think you'll make a banker yet," he would say. "But I see you spend most of your time with books. Maybe one can learn from books how to be an economist. But banking has to do with people, so start watching people. I'll make sure you meet some worth watching."

And the first one he had me meet was Uncle Henry.

"I want you to take the next train to Liverpool, get a first-class doctor there, reserve a good room in a nursing home, and go down to the Merseyside Docks to meet Uncle Henry first thing tomorrow," said Mr. Freedberg to me one cold March morning. "What, you don't know who Uncle Henry is? He is Mr. Henry Bernheim from America, Otto Bernheim's uncle and one of my oldest friends. He's coming over from Boston on the *Ramona* on his annual visit to England. The ship ran into the worst spring storm in the North Atlantic in thirty years, was almost totally disabled, and is being towed into port two weeks late. And Uncle Henry is in his eighties, seven or eight years older than I am. He'll be in poor shape after this horrible trip. But mind, don't you call him Mr. Bernheim; call him Uncle Henry or he'll bite your head off."

When the *Ramona* was towed into port next morning in a sleet storm, she was the sorriest sight I have ever seen in a ship, coated with heavy ice all over, her masts gone, one funnel broken off and lying across the deck, and both her propellers askew and twisted. The first person down the gangplank was a dapper little old man in a tweed suit without an overcoat. I rushed up to him and babbled: "I'm from Freedberg & Co. Mr. Freedberg sent me. I have a doctor and an ambulance and a nursing home room ready for you." Then I caught myself. "And how are you, Uncle Henry?" He looked me up and down and said: "Twelve days free food at the shipping company's expense and he asks me how I am," and strode off.

Uncle Henry had been born in the same provincial town from which Mr. Freedberg came, one of the many children of the kosher butcher of the town's small Jewish community. The family was very poor, and as more children came the older ones were pushed out of the nest as was the custom of those days, and sent off to America to make their fortune. Uncle Henry and his twin brother left when both were barely fifteen, about the time the American Civil War ended. Freedberg's father, the only wealthy Jew in town, paid their steerage fare, and that was the beginning of the friendship between Uncle Henry and Ernest Freedberg. According to legend, the Bernheim twins had one shirt between them. Before they disembarked in New York they had traded it against a wheelbarrow and were in business. Fifteen years later, Uncle Henry—the twin brother having died in the meantime—opened a small department store, the town's first, in a Midwestern city then just beginning to grow and to industrialize. In another fifteen years, by the late nineties, Bernheim's had prospered so much that Uncle Henry replaced his original store with a twelve-story building that was—and still is—the leading store in what is now a city of more than a million people. Only a few years later Bernheim's was doing so well that Uncle Henry could send his son, Irving, to the then brand-new Harvard Business School. When Irving came back with a master's degree in business administration, he was appalled at the unsystematic and unscientific way the store was being run. "But, Father," he said, "you don't even know how much profit you are making." "Come along, my boy," said Uncle Henry, and took the elevator to the top floor. Without saying a word, he walked around, looking at the shoppers, the merchandise, and the busy clerks, then went on to the floor below. He repeated this—still not saying a word —until he and Irving reached the ground floor, the basement, the sub-basement and, finally the sub-sub-basement, which had been hewn out of bedrock. There, on a rock ledge, lay a bolt of cloth. "Take away all the rest," said Uncle Henry, "it's the profit. This"—pointing at the bolt of cloth—"is what I started with." I tell this story to my graduate students once in a while, but they rarely get it.

When asked his profession, Uncle Henry would say, "I'm a peddler," and he meant it. He dearly loved a bargain. The year I met him, he had somehow found out that finished and assembled cigarette lighters paid an American customs duty of 65 percent while gold and silver imported for jewelers' use came in free. He bought 25,000 of the most expensive gold lighters from the leading manufacturer in England, at a sizable quantity discount, had them taken to pieces by a crew of unemployed women he hired in London's East End, shipped them to America as "jeweler's gold," had them reassembled by unemployed women in New York, and sold them at 100 percent profit, but still below the price at which the manufacturer offered them. Both the manufacturer and the U.S. Customs howled, but that didn't bother Uncle Henry. A true merchant, he regarded all manufacturers as thieves anyhow and knew it to be his duty to undersell them.

But the "bargain" of which Uncle Henry was proudest, and of which he bragged at interminable length, was the "Uncle Henry Bernheim Memorial Fountain." The city where he lived had contracted in the 1920s with a famous French sculptor for a handsome fountain. Came the depression, and the city could not pay for the fountain. Uncle Henry offered to donate it, but on condition that it be called the Uncle Henry Bernheim Memorial Fountain, that it bear an inscription: "In tribute to Uncle Henry Bernheim from his beloved adopted city," and that he have control of the fountain for two years after its installation. He put it under a big tent and sold admission to it for 25 cents, which then also entitled the ticket holder to buy up to $20 worth of goods at Bernheim's at a discount. He advertised widely in the region and had special trains run from the countryside to see "the only monument to an American citizen put up while he was still alive." When he turned the fountain over to the city, he had taken in more than enough in admissions to pay for what he had spent on it. He gave all the money he had taken in to a hospital. "I could afford it," he said. "Bernheim's with all these extra customers had a sizable increase in sales and profits in the two worst depression years."

Wherever he went, Uncle Henry would sniff for opportunity. He always reminded me of a little brown terrier sniffing at every lamp-post. And he would always find opportunity. One day when we walked in the City at lunchtime, he saw my name on a billboard outside a church. I was then giving a mid-week lay sermon more or less regularly at one of the City churches which, of course, had no parishioners on Sundays and tried to bring in people during the week. I explained this to Uncle Henry and also told him that one of the pleasures of doing this work were the church's splendid acoustics. "And you speak once a month on Wednesdays?" he asked. "What goes on the other days of the week?" "Nothing, I believe," I said. "Does the church have a lot of money?" he asked. "No, it just gets by and urgently needs money for repairs." "Take me to the reverend," he said.

I took him with some misgivings to the stiff, tight-lipped vicar, who was as class-conscious as only a left-wing Anglo-Catholic can be. "Reverend," said Uncle Henry, "I know how to use your church and get you the money you need to repair it. Hold concerts twice a week —there are all these people milling about outside during the lunch hour, not knowing what to do with themselves. The artists will be willing to play for free, it's good advertisement for them. Charge admissions, and you'll have the money to fix the roof or whatever needs repair in no time." The vicar was icily rude and hustled us out of his study unceremoniously. I was embarrassed, for Uncle Henry had meant well and had also, I thought, made sense. But when I started to apologize for the man's abominable manners, Uncle Henry cut me short. "Don't apologize," he said. "I know the reverend thought me a vulgar little Jew. Well, I *am* a vulgar little Jew. But mark my words, within five years he'll do exactly what I suggested."

Five years later World War II had broken out and the vicar with great fanfare started midday concerts two days a week against an admission charge, to be used for the repair of war-damaged City churches.

When in London, Uncle Henry used Freedberg & Co. as his headquarters, with a desk and a telephone in the big room where I otherwise sat alone. He would tell stories constantly, always to do with a late consignment of ladies' hats, or a shipment of mismatched umbrellas, or the notions counter. His stories would drive me up the wall. But gradually I learned to listen, at least with one ear. For surprisingly enough he always leaped to a generalization from the farrago of anecdotes and stocking sizes and color promotions in lieu of markdowns for

mismatched umbrellas. "There are only two principles to retailing,"
he would conclude the long story about mismatched umbrellas.
" 'There is no customer loyalty that two cents off can't overcome,' and,
'If you ain't got it on the shelf, you can't sell it.' The rest is hard work."
Or: "There are no irrational customers, there are only lazy merchants.
If the customers don't behave the way you think they should behave,
don't say, 'They're irrational.' And don't start 'reeducating' them—
that's not the merchant's job. His job is to satisfy customers and to
make them want to come back. If they don't behave rationally, go out
and look at the store and the merchandise through the customers'
eyes. You'll always find that they behave rationally, only their reality
is different from yours."

Uncle Henry had been a major innovator in the American retail
business. He was the first to adopt the policy: "Satisfaction guaranteed
or your money back," long before Sears Roebuck. "But what do you
do, Uncle Henry," I asked, "if a customer wears a garment, washes it,
and then brings it back for a refund?" "Why, give her the money, of
course," he said; "how else can she find out whether it's the right dress
for her?" "And if she comes back a second time with a dress she's worn
and washed?" "Then she gets nothing. The first time she does it we
put her name on a list and watch out, or else it becomes habit-form-
ing."

Uncle Henry early adopted a simple but effective way to deal with
customer complaints. Whenever a customer appeared with a complaint, the clerk at the complaints counter would make a big to-do
about calling for the "VP in charge of complaints"—and whichever
male employe over thirty-five was near the complaints counter would
answer the call. The "VP in charge of complaints" would listen to the
customer's story and appear horrified. "We can't allow customers at
Bernheim's to be treated that way. Get me the guilty clerk at once."
And the first sales clerk standing near the complaints counter would
be pulled in. "YOU ARE FIRED," the "VP in charge of complaints"
would declaim, pointing an accusing finger at the clerk. By that time
the customer, of course, was pleading for mercy for the clerk, and "if
she starts to cry," said Uncle Henry, "we give the clerk a reprieve. We
can't have weeping women in the store; it gives it a bad name." When
the customer had departed, mollified, the "guilty" clerk would get a
small payment—"I always pay extra for play-acting," said Uncle Henry
—and the complaint would be investigated. "Never take complainants
seriously," said Uncle Henry; "but always pay attention to complaints."

In World War I Bernheim's, like all American retail stores, was hit by a wave of employe pilfering. "The other stores," said Uncle Henry, "brought in Pinkertons and one-way mirrors and store detectives. This made the clerks howling mad. I'd have been mad too, and it didn't stop the pilfering. At Bernheim's we tried to figure out how much 'shrinkage' might be normal—we never called it anything else. Then we gave the clerks in each department a nice bonus if their merchandise at the semi-annual inventory-taking had no more than the normal shrinkage, and they were allowed to get free in any department in the store merchandise worth a couple of percentage points of their salary and a little more at a very good discount. And we never had even the 'normal' shrinkage in any department. The clerks policed each other and loved it."

Each of these policies Uncle Henry claimed he had discovered by going out and looking; each had come out of experience with stocking sizes or mismatched umbrellas or ladies' hats that were last year's fashion.

When Uncle Henry was in his high nineties—around 1950 or so—his grandson sold Bernheim's to one of the big chains at a very favorable price. Uncle Henry had, of course, long retired from active management; but he was still the biggest stockholder. Despite his age, he traveled to the city where the chain had its headquarters and spent a few days there visiting people in the company. Then he returned home and announced that he was selling the stock in the chain he was receiving in exchange against his Bernheim's shares. The grandson was upset. "Have you looked at their financial statement, Uncle Henry?" (even his grandson called him that). "I don't have to look at financial statements," answered the old man; "I could fiddle them every which way long before you were born. I listened to a dozen buyers for the chain. They're very bright. But they're not buying bargains for the customers; they're buying bargains for the store. That's the wrong thing to do. It means losing customers, losing sales, and losing profits." Within two years Bernheim's under the new ownership began to lose customers, sales, and profits.

There are lots of people with grasshopper minds who can only go from one specific to another—from stockings to buttons, for instance, or from one experiment to another—and never get to the generalization and the concept. They are to be found among scientists as often as among merchants. But I have learned that the mind of the good merchant, as also of the good artist or good scientist, works the way

Uncle Henry's mind worked. It starts out with the most specific, the most concrete, and then reaches for the generalization.

Long after I had left Freedberg & Co. and years after Uncle Henry had died, I served on an advisory board to the U.S. Department of Defense, the chairman of which was a successful merchant, Charles Kellstadt, then just retired as head of Sears Roebuck. Kellstadt told the same kind of stories Uncle Henry had told. Remembering Uncle Henry, I listened and always learned something. The other members of the group—it was a very high-powered committee and meant to set a new course for U.S. defense procurement and buying policies—were furious. But they were powerless to stop Kellstadt. He had the ear of President Kennedy and of Defense Secretary McNamara. He had spent most of his adult life in Atlanta, where he had been regional vice president for Sears before going to Chicago as chairman and chief executive officer, had become a power in the Democratic Party in the South and, as a Catholic, was largely responsible for getting the Southern Democrats to accept another Catholic as presidential candidate, which gave Kennedy the nomination and won him the election. And he had come to know McNamara while serving on the Ford Motor Company board—McNamara was then president of Ford—and had brought him to Kennedy's attention. But while my fellow board members could not stop Kellstadt, they suffered greatly from his interminable and apparently pointless anecdotes.

One day they learned what he was up to. The very brightest of McNamara's "whiz-kids," a brilliant Assistant Secretary, presented to the board a proposal for a radically new way of defense pricing. We were all impressed—all, that is, except Kellstadt. He began to tell a story of the bargain basement in the store at Chillicothe, Ohio, where he had held his first managerial job, and of some problem there with the cup sizes of women's bras. He would stop every few sentences and ask the bewildered Assistant Secretary a question about bras, then go on. Finally the Assistant Secretary said, "You don't understand, Mr. Kellstadt; I'm talking about concepts." "So am I," said Charlie, quite indignant, and went on. Ten minutes later all of us on the board realized that he had demolished the entire proposal by showing us that it was far too complex, made far too many assumptions, and contained far too many ifs, buts, and whens. (Alas, the Assistant Secretary did not realize this, nor did Mr. McNamara. They went ahead with what turned into one of the more expensive mistakes in defense procurement, the fixed-price contract for the Lockheed Jumbo air transport.) When we went out of the meeting, another board member, the dean of a major engineering school, said admiringly, "Charlie, that was a virtuoso performance. But why did you have to drag in the cup sizes of the bras in your bargain basement forty years ago?" Charlie was quite surprised. "How else can I see a problem in my mind's eye?"

Fifty years or more ago the Uncle Henrys and the Charlie Kellstadts dominated; then it was necessary for Son Irving to emphasize systems, principles, and abstractions. There was need to balance the overly perceptual with a little conceptual discipline. I still remember the sense of liberation during those years in London when I stumbled onto the then new Symbolical Logic (which I later taught a few times), with its safeguards against tautologies and false analogies, against generalizing from isolated events, that is, from anecdotes, and its tools of semantic rigor. But now we again need the Uncle Henrys and Charlie Kellstadts. We have gone much too far toward dependence on untested quantification, toward symmetrical and purely formal models, toward argument from postulates rather than from experience, and toward moving from abstraction to abstraction without once touching the solid ground of concreteness. We are in danger of forgetting what Plato taught at the very beginning of systematic analysis and thought in the West, in two of the most beautiful and most moving of his Dialogues, the Phaedrus and the Krito: the dialogues of the young boy Phaedrus, starting life, and of the old Socrates on the morning of his death. They teach us that experience without the test of logic is not "rhetoric" but chitchat, and that logic without the test of experience is not "logic" but absurdity. Now we need to learn again what Charlie Kellstadt meant when he said, "How else can I see a problem in my mind's eye?"

Uncle Henry lived to be one hundred and four. His mind remained clear and strong until the very end, but he became physically very frail, had not much left of lungs and kidneys, and was bedridden. One day when the weather was at its worst, he got up and started to dress himself. The nurse tried to stop him. "Leave me alone," said Uncle Henry. "I know I'm going to die anyhow." An hour later he came back, took the telephone, called the general manager of Bernheim's and gave him hell because a competitor was selling pantyhose at a lower price. Then he said to the nurse, "You see, one can do something useful even at my age," turned his face to the wall, and died.

A few weeks after he had sent me to Liverpool to meet Uncle Henry, Mr. Freedberg called me again into his office. "A good customer of the firm, Mr. Willem Paarboom," he said, "is planning to move from Holland to England. He's going to look at houses and wants you to come with him. He doesn't know the English countryside. I have told him you do. Be at his hotel at eight on Sunday morning." On Sunday I met the most peculiar-looking man; or rather, I never was quite sure whether I had met a giant raven dressed up as a man, or a man dressed up as a giant raven. Very tall—6 foot 4 or 5—and emaciated, Paarboom was clad in funereal black, black shoes, black socks, black suit, black tie with a black pearl for a tie pin, and a starched white shirt with a very high collar. He had a mouth full of crooked teeth and an enormous beak of a nose. He had a raven's croak and so heavy a Dutch accent that he was hard to understand. I always half-expected him to croak "Nevermore."

The two of us got into a black chauffeur-driven eight-seater Rolls Royce and set out to inspect the places the estate agents had recommended. We spent the whole day driving from one Victorian horror to another, all very big, very dark houses full of turrets and fake Tudor beams and cast-iron dwarfs outside the *porte cochère*. Finally, when it was already quite dark and the list was exhausted, we drove down a lane—it was in Essex as I remember—took the wrong turn, and found ourselves at the gate of the worst house of all, twice as large as the others, with even more turrets and totally dilapidated. Paarboom ordered the chauffeur to drive in. The house seemed deserted, but there was a faint light in one of the towers. Paarboom walked around the place a few times, then went up the half-rotten front steps and knocked. After a long time and many additional knocks, we heard footsteps. A very dirty and very old man opened the door with a candle in his hand. "What do you want?" he snarled. "Are you the owner of this place?" asked Paarboom. "Yes," said the old man. "What's that to you?" "How much will you take to sell me the house for immediate occupancy?" The man clearly thought he was dealing with a lunatic, but a lunatic with a big chauffeur-driven Rolls Royce. "Thirty thousand pounds," he said—the house was worth no more than a fifth of that amount—"and all in cash." "It's a deal," said Paarboom. He reached into his pocket, pulled out a huge wad of £100 notes, tied in bundles of ten, counted off thirty of the bundles, said, "What is your name, sir?" and, "Here is my card. You'll hear from my solicitor tomorrow," and turned to go. "Don't you want a receipt?" asked the dumbfounded ex-owner. "Not necessary," said Paarboom. "I have the numbers of all the banknotes." When we sat down in the car for the trip back home, he said to me: "This house has enough towers for all my wives, and even a few extra ones for the future."

A few weeks later he called me. "Mr. Drucker," he said, "could you come over again? My wives are arriving from Holland to look at the house you helped me buy and to see what needs to be done to it. Could you go with them?" "Your wives?" I asked. "Of course, all four of them," he said. When I showed surprise, he said, "Mr. Drucker, I don't think it's healthy for a woman to give birth to more than three children. Whenever a wife of mine has three children, I release her, arrange for a divorce, and marry again. But of course I still love her; we stay the closest of friends. And she and our children continue to live with me and the other wives, only each of them in a separate wing of the house or a separate tower." When I met the wives I found that they were indeed the closest of friends, only I couldn't tell them apart. They looked exactly alike, all perfect specimens of the regulation Dutch housewife—round and plump, blonde and buttery. When I apologized to Paarboom for being unable to call any of them anything but "Mrs. Paarboom," instead of "Myvrouw Maricke" or "Myvrouw Dora" as he had asked me to do, he said, "Mr. Drucker, as you get older you will learn that one sticks to the things that work. I am old enough to know the woman for whom I make a good husband and to stick to that model. And it works." And when Paarboom moved to the United States in 1939 in anticipation of a European war and settled in Dutchess County north of New York City, he brought with him all four wives and their twelve children. He found a many-turreted 1880 house on the Hudson, where they could all live together with each wife in her own quarters in her own tower.

Paarboom had been barely fourteen and recently orphaned when he left his native Holland, around the turn of the century, to voyage all alone to the distant Dutch East Indies. The only thing other than debts that his recently deceased father—a perenially insolvent small businessman—had left was a dubious claim that had been declared invalid by a lower court in the Dutch East Indies and was being appealed. Five years later Paarboom returned to Holland a millionaire. He had won the lawsuit; and he had made a fortune developing real estate in Batavia, where the rubber boom was then just beginning. But while he was rich, he was also permanently maimed. The five years of contempt, hostility, and humiliation he had had to suffer as a poor and ugly boy at the hands of the purse-proud, arrogant, and cold-hearted Dutch colonial society in Batavia had scarred him for life. He resolved never again to be vulnerable. He was going to be a "gentleman." To him this meant wearing only black suits—he had twenty-five identical suits in his closet, put on a fresh one each day, and discarded each suit one year after it had been delivered by the tailor. Paarboom also resolved never again to be beholden to anyone; he was going to be his own man forever.

He set himself up as a financial adviser in Holland, working for the large Dutch industrialists. Apparently he did very well from the outset, despite his youth. Then, in the early 1920s, he engineered the first of his major coups. As adviser to the heirs of one of the Dutch margarine and soap fortunes, he saw the need to create a European margarine and soap company to counteract the growing power of the Americans—Procter & Gamble and Colgate-Palmolive. But he also realized that the Europeans could not merge and could not sell out to each other. The British were not going to subordinate themselves to the Dutch and the Dutch were not going to subordinate themselves to the British. It was Paarboom who hit upon the solution: two companies, both called Unilever, one British and one Dutch, but managed by the same people and owning each other. A few years later he was the first to realize that the young Opel brothers in Germany could not manage the automobile company they were about to inherit, and did not want to manage it, but also would not be permitted by the German government and German public opinion to sell it to any automobile manufacturer in Europe. He conceived the idea of selling Opel to General Motors in Detroit, worked out the terms in his head, then sold the deal first to GM and then to the Opels. Thereafter he had a waiting list of would-be clients and took only the very richest, beginning with the richest of all, the Queen of the Netherlands.

However, he never talked of his deals, never mentioned his clients, never gave a newspaper interview or allowed any publicity about himself. His card said simply: "Mr. W. Paarboom"; it did not even give an address or telephone number. He was, in fact, totally anonymous. Still, he did not hesitate to call on the biggest industrialist or banker or government minister, walk into the man's office unannounced, and say, "This is what you have to do." One day he read of the financial troubles of what was then England's biggest steel company. He had never heard of it, but began to study it. Then he took the train to the northern city where the company had its headquarters, sent his card in to the chairman—who had never heard of Mr. W. Paarboom—and walked out three hours later with a long-term contract to reorganize the company and put it on its financial feet again. "Why didn't you let us arrange the proper introduction?" asked Mr. Freedberg. "We know the company and we know the chairman. And one doesn't do business in England without proper introduction." "That's precisely why I didn't ask you," said Paarboom; *"I* never do business the way it's proper for other people to do it."

Shortly after Paarboom moved to England, he rented an office in the City not very far from Freedberg & Co. and invited me over. He had taken an entire floor in London's newest and biggest office building, room after room, all empty but completely furnished with chairs and desks, all in shrouds. Finally I got to the tiny cubbyhole where Paarboom sat. Outside at a telephone sat his sole employe, a male secretary. "Why do you have all this space?" I asked. "I might in the future do a deal where I need a lot of space and a lot of clerks; and I'd hate to have to negotiate then for a lease," was his reply. "But how likely are you to go into such a deal?" I asked. "I'll never do anything, of course," said Paarboom, "that I can't work out myself alone. That's the only thing that makes sense to me." In the office he had what was then the most modern bookkeeping and accounting machinery, far more modern than anything Freedberg & Co. had just installed in its expensive brand-new quarters "What do you have all this for?" I asked. "Do you need it to account to your clients?" "My clients never get accounts," he answered; "what they want is checks, and those I write out by hand." He had, he told me, about forty "partners." Each had entrusted Paarboom with 5 percent of his fortune. "I don't work with anyone who gives me less, and I never want to be responsible for more," said Paarboom.

This money was invested in what Paarboom called "Special Ventures," such as the Unilever merger or the reorganization of the English steel company. Of the profits the investor got 50 percent, Paarboom 25 percent, and 25 percent was being put into what Paarboom called "mad money," to be invested in "Speculative Ventures," the profits of which were divided fifty-fifty between the investor and Paarboom with the investor alone carrying all the losses. "What's the difference between Special Ventures and Speculative Ventures?" I once asked. He answered, "Special Ventures must have practically no risk other than that of my not having worked out the proper solution; and they must at least double the money invested. Speculative Ventures have high risk, but also promise to return the investment at least five-fold if I can pull them off."

Paarboom took only Dutch partners. He was a fanatical Dutch patriot, but also a very exacting one. When Holland went off the gold standard in the mid-thirties—one of the last countries to do so—Paarboom wrote the Queen of Holland an indignant personal letter protesting what he called a breach of trust and a despicable act of moral and political cowardice. He then had the letter privately printed with an English translation and circulated it to all his friends. "But Paarboom," protested Mr. Freedberg, "you didn't complain when England went off the gold standard and devalued the pound. On the contrary, that's when you moved here." "Mr. Freedberg," said Paarboom, "I am not an English subject. The King of England does not owe me anything." The first thing he said when we met in his hotel before going to buy a house was, "Drucker is a Dutch name, isn't it?" I said yes. I had known all along that my family had originally been printers of religious books in The Netherlands in the sixteenth and seventeenth centuries. But this wasn't good enough for Paarboom. He traced my pedigree back, climbed up and down my family tree, and finally found out not only in what Dutch library the books printed by the family firm were still being kept, but when and where it was started, when it stopped publishing, and where in Amsterdam it had had its office and printing shop. He made me his confidant at Freedberg & Co., "because us Dutchmen must stick together." And when I pointed out that my ancestor had left Holland in the seventeenth century and I had long ceased to have any Dutch roots, he said, "Don't be modest. As long as your people didn't go to America where all the scoundrels went, you remain a good Dutchman." And he always called me Druecker, with a long *umlaut* instead of a "u", as the name would be pronounced in Dutch.

Paarboom had left for England because he expected, as early as 1934, that the Nazis would move into Holland. But he commuted between London and Amsterdam, going back to Holland at least twice a month. He became melancholy if away from Holland for more than a few weeks. "For five years in that God-forsaken Java," he'd say, "I'd lie awake nights praying for a good Dutch rain and a good Dutch fog and a good Dutch storm. And every morning I'd wake up to that same accursed beautiful sunshine." At first he went by train and boat, but got violently seasick every time. He took to flying, which also made him sick but at least was over soon. Then he discovered quite by accident that looking at a Dutch landscape painting in the seat across from him cured his airsickness. He became a collector of Dutch seventeenth-century landscapes. He knew nothing about painting and painters, but would take a painting on approval from the art dealer and try it out on his next flight. If it cured his airsickness he bought it; otherwise he returned it. Fortunately his airsickness had excellent taste and a fabulous eye—he built one of the best small collections of seventeenth-century Dutch landscapes. The three wonderful Ruysdael landscapes that to my eye are the glories of the Norton Simon Museum in Pasadena I saw first in Paarboom's airsickness collection.

"Of course he's quite mad," said Mr. Freedberg, when I told him about the wives. "Those five years in the tropics have addled his brain. But he's a genius. Just look at him studying a balance sheet." And indeed Paarboom was a financial genius. He would get stimulated by some chance remark or some item in the papers, then start digging into a company or a problem in public finance or an industry. Two weeks later he would know what to do. It was always original, always the perfect solution, and always obvious, except that no one else had seen it before. "If I have to sell my proposal," he said, "it's wrong. It's got to be so simple that people say immediately: 'That's it.' " When he first heard of the English steel company in trouble, its affairs had become so tangled that no one in England knew how to save it. After two weeks of analysis Paarboom knew which of its businesses to spin off, which ones to refinance, which ones to merge, what additional ones to acquire. What had been a dying near-bankrupt company became in eighteen months again a prosperous growing concern. He had never heard of the Austrian Phoenix insurance companies before their spectacular collapse in 1934 or 1935. He read up on them, then put in a call to the Austrian Minister of Finance and said, "This is what you have to do to refloat the companies. I'll be in Vienna the day after tomorrow and work it out with you." He was not interested in the profitable deal alone, although he reaped enormous profits. When I found the "special situation" of Ivar Kreuger's bankrupt match company, the bonds of which were so greatly undervalued, Richard Mosell tried to interest Paarboom. Paarboom studied them and said, "You're right, these bonds are worth at least six times what they are selling for. But they're not for me." "Why not?" we asked. "All you are doing by buying them," said Paarboom, "is making a sure profit. I won't invest unless I can also make a contribution and do something for the company into which I buy. I stopped long ago wanting to get paid for being clever. Now I get paid for being right."

He once told me that he looked at about forty candidates for investment a year, most of them turned up by himself, a few brought to him by friends or by his "partners." "I discard about half because they don't make sense—they usually have too much risk—and most of the others because they make only financial sense. That leaves two or three which are both profitable investments and opportunities for contribution. And that's enough for a year for my partners and myself."

When I decided to leave Freedberg & Co. and England altogether, I went to Paarboom to say goodbye. Much to my surprise, he said, "I want you to be my representative in New York on a three-year retainer of twenty-five thousand dollars a year." That was an almost unbelievable sum in those depression years. It was more than a cabinet officer in Washington was being paid or a top executive in a major company; and, of course, there was then still practically no income tax. "What would I do for the money, Mr. Paarboom?" I asked. "Probably nothing," he said, "but I'd want you just in case." I turned him down, especially as he made clear that I would have to work (or rather not work) exclusively for him. A year and a half later, when I was already settled in America, Paarboom came over and called at our home—we had had our first child and had just rented a modest house in a New York suburb. Paarboom again asked me to be his representative, and he raised the retainer fee. I told him how flattered I was, but that I was determined to make it on my own. He got up, left abruptly, and never again came near me. I had rejected him, and all the old scars from Batavia began to hurt again.

When he made his first offer, I reported it to Mr. Freedberg. "I can understand," said Mr. Freedberg, "why you don't want to take so much money without any work to do. Still, twenty-five thousand dollars for three years—you could save enough to buy into a decent small banking firm and start building it into a big bank." "But, Mr. Freedberg," I said, "I'm not at all sure that I want to be a banker." "Nonsense," said Freedberg, "what else could an intelligent young man possibly want to be?"

A good deal of the fun at Freedberg & Co. forty-odd years ago lay in the knowledge that I was watching a near-extinct species: the nineteenth-century private banker as Balzac had best described him, even though it was, of course, in the City of London that the species reached its flowering. I felt very much the way an anthropologist must feel when he observes one of our "living ancestors," a tribe of Amazon Indians, perhaps, going about their hunting and trapping, unaware of the bulldozers only a few miles away already laying down the super-highway that will destroy their Stone Age civilization. In the world of the thirties, the world of Stalin, Hitler, and Franklin D. Roosevelt, the civilization of the Freedbergs and Uncle Henrys and Paarbooms—of the "trades" and "deals"—seemed as much a Stone Age culture as that of Amazon Indians, and yet unaware of having become extinct.

Actually, these Stone Age traders and dealers have shown amazing staying power. The "gun slingers" of the "go-go" stock market of the 1960s were still living in the same world, even though it had coarsened and had little of the shrewdness, wit, and integrity of a Freedberg or a Willem Paarboom—little of the wisdom that made small-town provincial Ernest Freedberg realize that any management that promises 10 percent growth in both profits and sales for years ahead is either crooked or stupid or both; and none of the self-respect that made ugly, awkward Paarboom insist on making profits only when also making a contribution and not as a return on mere cleverness. None of the "gun slingers" would have understood what Uncle Henry meant when he decided to sell the shares of a retail chain in which the buyers bought bargains for the store rather than bargains for the customers.

Still, though it lingered on, the civilization that Freedberg, Paarboom, and Uncle Henry represented is gone or going. But our whole society has moved to the perception and the metaphysics Freedberg & Co. represented. It has shifted to seeing symbols as real: money, "trades" and "deals," interest rates, and Gross National Product. Our whole society assumes, in the words of the medieval logician, that *Nomina sunt realia:* that the symbols have substance while the objects they represent are mere shadows.

This shift in perception and metaphysics is the real meaning of the "Keynesian Revolution" in economics. The classical economists, including Marx, thought that economics dealt with human behavior. A modern post-Keynesian neoclassicist, like the Anglo-American Kenneth Boulding, speaks of economics as dealing with the "behavior of commodities." But for the Keynesian and the anti-Keynesian—the Friedmanite monetarist, for example—economics deals with symbols and their behavior, aggregates of money supply, credit, or "full-employment budgets." Unemployment is no longer a human situation; it is a target figure. Reality is created by manipulating symbols; history is made by staging "media events."

There has been a tremendous shift in perception and metaphysics from Charlie Kellstadt's brassieres in the bargain basement as ultimate reality to the pure abstraction of Gross National Product. The nineteenth-century bankers have disappeared, or at least have ceased to be the distinctive civilization they used to be in their "City." But their way of seeing reality, as a web of symbols, has become universal. Changing the name of a business from "Smith Button Company" to "Fastening Systems Corporation" can make a "growth stock" out of an old, tired buttonmaker; writing grant applications has become the most honored of the liberal arts; and a major war, the war in Vietnam, could be "won" by computer simulation and lost on the TV tube.

Dr. Samuel Johnson once said, "A man is never so innocently employed as in making money." This sounds very strange to modern ears. But one should never dismiss lightly anything the "Great Panjandrum" said about human behavior. He was the shrewdest judge—and as an old-fashioned religious moralist he could have been expected to take a dim view of moneymaking rather than endorse it. Dr. Johnson did not say that the man who makes money is doing good. He said he did the least harm. He does not seek power, he does not seek to dominate people or to make them squirm, he does not amass possessions. He is content with the symbols and lets reality go. But when Dr. Johnson said this, the man of symbols, whether those of money or those of the "media," was in a tiny minority. The great majority—bakers and shoemakers, landlords and judges, noblemen and farm laborers—were not "making money." They were making things, scheming for power, dominating people or being dominated by them. They saw in money with the classical economists the "veil of reality," not reality itself. Freedberg and Paarboom were still part of this tiny minority that was innocently employed in making money. But is the ultra-nominalism that treats symbols and images as ultimate reality, and people and things as shadows, still so "innocent" and innocuous when it has become the perception of the great majority?

The Bankers
and
the Courtesan

Robert Mosell was only thirty-two when I first met him in 1934; he was four years younger than his brother Richard, who had hired me for Freedberg & Co. But Robert had already been a partner for seven years. He had been sent to London as a trainee when only eighteen, a year or two after World War I. The intention then was that Robert would return to the family firm in Vienna after having learned the business; but he soon proved indispensable to Mr. Freedberg and stayed on. And when Mr. Bernheim, one of the founders of Freedberg & Co., had a stroke, Robert was made a partner.

He was strikingly handsome in a dark, brooding, Mephistophelian way. He looked like a portrait of the Fallen Angel by a romantic pre-Raphaelite painter. He was tall, thin, and elegant, and his clothes were so casual and hung so perfectly that it was obvious they had come from the best Savile Row tailor and been brushed, sponged, and pressed that very morning by the most accomplished of "gentlemen's gentlemen." He was moody, emotional, and brilliant. He would sit for hours saying nothing, paying no attention, not hearing what anyone said to him—then burst into an impassioned oration or give birth to a wild idea. He had insights: he could rarely explain them, but they tended to be right, spectacularly so. In the mid-twenties when everybody knew the French franc would go the inflationary way of the German mark, Robert had predicted that France would halt inflation —"Don't ask me why; I just know that's how it's going to be," he was reported to have said. This insight saved his father's bank in Vienna

213

where all other banks gambled on a continuing decline of the French
currency and sold francs short. And it had made a big profit for Freedberg & Co. A few years later Robert concluded that England would
go off the gold standard and the pound would devalue, when everyone
else "knew" that the British government was committed to the defense of the pound. He at once realized that Roosevelt's accession to
the presidency in the United States meant a stock exchange boom in
New York and had put the firm and its clients into the American stock
market in March 1933 when the banks in the United States closed
their doors. He was not impulsive. Every one of these insights was
preceded by weeks or months of silent brooding. But he despised
"studies" and analysis. He was demanding, aggressive, and so abrasive
that most of the staff were afraid of him and of the tongue-lashings he
inflicted. He also bore grudges and would remind people for years of
the mistakes they had made. But he immediately became friendly
when someone stood up to him, and he enjoyed nothing better than
a sharp verbal duel in which he would parry and thrust, then burst into
laughter, shouting: "That was good fun, wasn't it?"

But what made Robert truly interesting was his mistress, the
courtesan Marion Farquharson.

Marion Farquharson had been born into a good "county" family.
Indeed the family must have been a very good one. Not only had she
gotten Robert, a foreigner and a Jew, into a famous hunt that was
riding to hounds near Tring where she and Robert had a country
house; she herself was regularly asked to the hunt—she was an excellent though somewhat reckless horsewoman—even though she was
living with Robert and boasted openly of being a courtesan. Tring at
that time was about the most exclusive and snobbish of all areas
around London.

She had early decided on a career as a courtesan. "What else could
I have done, dahling?" she'd say. "I hated school and I didn't want to
marry one of those stupid subalterns and die of the cholera in India."
She was particularly proud of the fact that she was (according to her
story) the only person who still had the money she had made in the
Russo-Japanese War of 1905, when her protector had been an immensely rich Greek who had sold the Czar's armies poorly canned
horsemeat as prime beef at exorbitant prices. "Before I met him,"
she'd say, "I didn't hold on to my money and spent everything I got
from my first protector when I was very young. But I learned and I
haven't spent anything since." She also, apparently, decided to go for

financiers—"That's where the easy money is, dahling." She was the mistress in succession of several of the very rich men of Cecil Rhodes's circle, the men who had made their money in South African gold or diamond mines or Rhodesian copper. One of those had named Ernest Freedberg as executor in his will; and when he died, shortly after World War I, Freedberg took over Mrs. Farquharson as his mistress. Five or six years later, she was taken over by Robert as a condition of his being admitted to the partnership.

Mrs. Farquharson was about twenty years older than Robert. When I knew her she was in her early fifties and a scarecrow. Whatever her looks might have been in her youth, they were gone. She was haggard, with a long neck full of wrinkles. She suffered from some mysterious internal complaint—it might have been a tapeworm; she ate ravenously all the time but had perpetual diarrhea and could not put on any weight. Her complexion had become coarse and muddy from years of overuse of cosmetics, the skin spongy, with large pores. There were two big red spots on her cheekbones, whether from rouge or high blood pressure, I don't know. Her hair was dyed—streakily— in an improbable shade of purple. She had a peacock's rasping voice and when she got annoyed, which was often, she would drop her ladylike airs and turn pure fishwife.

And she was greedy. She would come into the office and ask one of the partners: "What's a good buy?" When the stock she had bought went up, she'd glow with pleasure. But when it went down, she would scream: "What imbecile bought this for me? I never ordered it." There were standing instructions that the shares should be quietly transferred to Mr. Freedberg's account at the price she had paid for them originally. But she also came in when a stock she did not acquire had gone up for a couple of weeks and screamed: "What happened to the five hundred shares I gave orders to buy two weeks ago? Who's stealing my profits? Why aren't they on my account?" And again Mr. Freedberg would have her account credited at his expense with the gain she would have made had she really bought the shares before they went up.

Robert worshipped her. She usually came into the office around four or so in the afternoon and drove home with him. By about half past three, Robert would begin to fidget and start worrying. "Where is Marion? I hope nothing has happened to her. Why isn't she here yet?" When she came in, he'd drop whatever he was doing, rush to her, embrace her, and murmur all kinds of pet names. Whenever he had made a deal he was proud of or had any other good news, he would first put in a call to Mrs. Farquharson to tell her.

Robert loved horses and hated motorcars. But Mrs. Farquharson liked to drive very big cars very fast. So Robert always spent his vacations touring the Continent with her in a big Daimler or Bentley. They took a chauffeur along, but Mrs. Farquharson did the driving, and at insane speeds. One rainy night in France she ran off the road at 90 miles an hour and crashed into a tree. Robert and the chauffeur, who were sitting in the back, escaped with minor scratches and bruises. Marion Farquharson was killed instantly. For weeks Robert could not be left alone for a minute. He alternated between maniacal bouts of rage and self-accusation and deep depression withdrawals. He never married and never had anything to do with another woman. Until he died, thirty years later, he spent the anniversary of Mrs. Farquharson's death in her bedroom with the shades drawn, rereading the few letters she had written him.

For weeks after her death elderly gentlemen would come to the office every day in a steady procession, dressed in cutaways, striped trousers, and top hats, would send their card in to Mr. Robert Mosell or Mr. Freedberg, and then say: "I know how you must suffer; I loved her too." And a few weeks later there appeared in the agony column of *The Times* a notice: "To the ever-lasting memory of my beloved wife Marion, who has given me nothing but perfect happiness in twenty-three years of marriage, Brigadier Nigel Farquharson MC DSO (retired)."

One person in the firm other than Robert Mosell was deeply affected by Marion Farquharson's death: Vladimir Bunin. But for him her death was the lifting of a nightmare in which he had lived for a whole year.

Bunin was a bear of a man—a Russian bear. He was enormous: tall, broad, and wide. But there was not an ounce of fat on him; it was all solid muscle throughout. He was a weightlifter, had a set of dumbbells stored in a closet in the office and practiced with them for twenty minutes every afternoon. He played the double bass semi-professionally in the orchestra that gave the popular Promenade Concerts under Sir Henry Wood's baton every week in Queen's Hall, and the bass fiddle almost looked like a violin when he carried it in his arms. He had been in the Officers Training Corps at his public school and held a commission in the Reserves. In World War II he commanded the last platoon to leave the beach at Dunkirk, received one of the very first

Victoria Crosses to be awarded, and rose to be a brigadier under Montgomery.

Vladimir Bunin had been born in St. Petersburg, the son of a cartographer in the Czar's Navy. The family fled when the Bolsheviks came in, and his father was hired as cartographer by the British. Vladimir was then about fifteen years old. When he finished secondary school, he went to work for Freedberg & Co. in the same year in which Robert Mosell came over from Vienna. The two young men became close friends, indeed Vladimir Bunin was the only male friend the saturnine and secretive Robert Mosell ever had. Vladimir was friendly, ebullient, talkative—and very Russian. He loved languages. He spoke Russian, English, German, French, Polish, Czech, Spanish, Dutch, and Italian, all equally rapidly and equally fluently, but all with a very strong Russian accent—except Russian, in which he had somehow acquired a strong British accent.

Vladimir was the firm's main trader. He had a small office near the stock exchange where he would spend the day all alone except for batteries of telephones and telegraph printers until the New York Stock Exchange opened in mid-afternoon London time, which was the end of Bunin's trading day. He would then come up to the firm's offices. First he'd practice on the dumbbells, then cast up his accounts for the day in a small and legible hand, spend a few minutes to arrange for the recording of the transactions and foreign exchange coverage for them, and finally go to the partners' room to report on the day's results. After that he would leave, either to go to a rehearsal with his bass fiddle under his arm, or to the gymnasium for a workout on dumbbells and parallel bars.

Bunin was not just a trader; he was an arbitrageur, exploiting minute differentials in price between one market and another. And he dealt essentially in only one stock: Chrysler. But Chrysler he traded worldwide, buying 10,000 shares in Shanghai and selling them in Oslo, or, on a rising market, buying in Chicago in the afternoon and holding the shares for the opening of the Amsterdam market the following morning. He had a computer between his ears and knew instantly, without conscious effort, the Amsterdam price in Dutch guilders that would give him a profit of one-sixty-fourth of a point on 50,000 shares of Chrysler bought in Hong Kong dollars, including foreign exchange rates and commissions, interest, freight, and insurance, and transfer charges and taxes. Chrysler was then among the most heavily traded shares at the New York Stock Exchange. But Bunin, day after day, traded more Chrysler shares than the entire volume bought and sold on the New York Stock Exchange. Two hundred thousand share-days were commonplace for him, and once in a while his volume would go up to 500,000 shares a day. And he would report a profit day in, day out. "We made twenty-five hundred pounds today," he'd say; or, "A very good day today, almost five thousand pounds." He was by far the biggest and most consistent profitmaker in the firm.

He used a desk in my office to sit down with the clerks and foreign exchange traders at the end of his trading day. One day when he came in, I was sitting almost invisible behind piles of reference books. "What are you working on?" he asked. "The American automobile industry, Vlad," I answered; "and you'll be interested to hear that Chrysler looks very good for the coming year." There was a long silence, then he said: "Chrysler, an automobile company? I always thought they were a railway."

He clearly deserved a partnership, so Mr. Freedberg asked the two Mosell brothers to work out the terms and to draw up a contract. When they submitted what they and Vladimir had agreed on, Freedberg said: "But it doesn't say that Vladimir will take over Marion Farquharson as his mistress. It's his turn now."

Robert Mosell was thunderstruck and protested violently. Vladimir was in despair. None of us in the firm except Robert Mosell—and perhaps Mr. Freedberg—was fond of Mrs. Farquharson. But Vladimir loathed her. He could not even bear to be in the same room with her and usually found a pretext to leave when she came in. If forced to stay in her company for any length of time, he'd develop a migraine headache, throw up, and have to lie down. Vladimir was married and deeply in love with his Masha, who was as Russian as he was though totally different; a very quiet and determined young woman, with the looks of a charming, overly serious child. Where Vladimir would have made a good Pierre in Tolstoy's *War and Peace*, Masha would have been the perfect Natasha. (What explains that Tolstoy, the woman-hater and enemy of sex, portrayed in Natasha and in Anna Karenina the two most feminine and appealing women in all European fiction?) Masha was as much in love with Vladimir as he was with her. They had been married for two years and had their first child, but still held hands when they thought no one was looking or kissed behind doors. But Masha was also quite jealous and convinced that every woman must have designs on her Vlad.

Richard Mosell, the older of the two brothers, had carefully stayed out of the discussion between the two younger men and Mr. Freedberg. But when an impasse was reached, he suggested that Mrs. Farquharson might be consulted. She was outraged. "This is an insult," she screamed. "To ask a lady to declare her affections! It's up to the man to declare himself, then he'll get my answer." And she flounced out.

But Mr. Freedberg remained adamant. "Mrs. Farquharson," he said, "comes with the job. And Vladimir has earned the job." The two young men in their despair called on Masha to argue with the old man. She had been a favorite of his since she had arrived in London after the Russian Revolution as a small child, when her father, a mining engineer, found a job with one of the South African mining companies through Freedberg's recommendation. In turn, it was Masha's father who had first introduced Vladimir to Mr. Freedberg as a fellow Russian refugee in need of a job. Masha came and was told of Mr. Freedberg's dastardly proposal. "How clever of you, Uncle Ernest," she said —she was the only one to call him that. "You always think of everything. Now I'll have someone with whom I can discuss Vladimir, someone experienced with men who can tell me what to do to please him." "But," said Richard Mosell, "you've always been so jealous of every woman who comes anywhere near Vlad." "Marion Farquharson is different," said Masha; "she's a professional."

After Masha had left, Vladimir stayed in a corner with his head in his hands moaning. And Mr. Freedberg said to Robert: "Now you see how selfish it is of you not to let Marion Farquharson become Vladimir's mistress?" "But Mr. Freedberg," said Robert, "I love her. She's *my* mistress." "No," said Mr. Freedberg, "she isn't. She's the firm's courtesan."

And so it went for a whole year. Then Mrs. Farquharson was killed and Vladimir became a partner within three weeks.

THE

INDIAN SUMMER

OF

INNOCENCE

Henry Luce and
Time-Life-Fortune

I never knew Henry Luce socially and was never invited to any of his homes. I had only two meals with him, the one at which I first met him, and the other—a big public dinner—almost thirty years later, at our last meeting. But for years Luce and I were engaged in a mild on-and-off flirtation. It was always initiated by him. And I was always interested at first. But as soon as the relationship threatened to become serious, our basic incompatibility became apparent.

I had come to the United States in the spring of 1937, as said earlier, as American correspondent for a number of English and Scots newspapers (and as American financial adviser to a number of European, mostly British, financial institutions). These were the years in which Luce and his magazines were at the peak of their success, their influence, and their fortunes. *Time* magazine was by then fifteen years old but still practically without competition, the only national news organ in the country and the only one that could properly be called an "opinion maker." *Fortune,* started in 1930, had completely changed writing and reporting on American business and the American economy; the *Fortune* "corporation" story about American businesses pioneered what is now known as "investigative journalism." And—a more lasting contribution—the *Fortune* graphics, the *Fortune* illustrations and, above all, the ads that *Fortune* designed for its customers, first made modern visual perception a part of common American experience. *Life* magazine, though only a few months old when I arrived in New York, had already become the greatest success in the history of American journalism and the embodiment of a new "life style." As a writer reporting on America to readers 3,000 miles away I was naturally interested in these magazines and wanted to do a story on them for my British papers. I did a good deal of preparatory work, but was finally turned down by my editors, who then still held to the old and honorable rule that newspapers do not write about themselves.

But I had never met Henry Luce.

After *The End of Economic Man* appeared in the spring of 1939, Luce sent me a handwritten note. He had read the book, he said, was much impressed, and wanted to discuss it. And so he and his wife Clare Boothe Luce, then Broadway's most successful playwright, took me to lunch at a fancy New York restaurant. Luce asked probing questions about the book; he had read it carefully. Clare was visibly bored. She had obviously not read the book and had no intention of doing so. She soon made sure that we stopped talking about something that bored her by turning to me and asking, with a sweet smile, "Don't you think, Mr. Drucker, that Economic Man will be succeeded by Physical Man?"

But Luce was not primarily interested in my book; he was interested in me. "We are about to change foreign news editors on *Time*," he said. I was not surprised since everyone in the newspaper world knew that Laird Goldsborough, *Time*'s foreign news editor, was sick and totally discredited after long years of praising Franco and preaching appeasement of the Nazis. "You would make a good successor," Luce continued. "Can you come in for a few weeks and work with the people there to find out whether the job suits you? If it doesn't work out, you'll do something else for us." "But, Mr. Luce," I said, "you know nothing about me except this one book." "Oh, no," said Luce, "I always do my homework." And he pulled out of his briefcase two folders, one fat and one slim. "This one," pointing to the fat one, "contains every single one of the articles you've written for your British papers since you came here, and every one of your monthly economic letters to your banking clients. And this one," pointing to the slim one, "contains all the articles of yours published in American magazines since your arrival here." He handed both folders to me, and leafing through them I saw that my articles and reports had been copiously annotated and commented upon in the margin in Luce's hand.

It was a tempting offer. The foreign news editor at *Time* had

about as important a job at that time as any young writer could hope
to get. It was also exceedingly well paid—the princely salaries of
Luce's senior people were almost a scandal in those depression days.
My own footing was still quite precarious and my income very, very
slim. But I had misgivings. I had looked at the way *Time* worked, and
I was not particularly impressed. "Group journalism," Luce-style,
seemed to me to be a misunderstanding.

Every first-rate editor I have ever heard of reads, edits, and rewrites every word that goes into his publication. Harold Ross did so at
the *New Yorker,* as did Horace Lorimer when he built the old *Saturday Evening Post* from 1910 to 1930, Scott at the *Manchester Guardian,* Theodore Wolff at the *Berliner Tageblatt,* or Walter Bagehot at
The Economist in London in the 1870s. Good editors are not "permissive"; they do not let their colleagues do "their thing"; they make sure
that everybody does "the paper's thing." A good, let alone a great
editor is an obsessive autocrat with a whim of iron, who rewrites and
rewrites, cuts and slashes, until every piece is exactly the way he thinks
it should have been done. Old man Scott of the *Manchester Guardian,*
so Noel Brailsford once told me, not only read and rewrote every line
of editorial copy that appeared in the paper; he personally read every
advertisement, including the small ads for lost pets, and rewrote them
for grammar, punctuation, clarity, and good taste.

But Luce's "group journalism" tried to make newscopy impersonal by subjecting each piece to mechanized homogenization. This,
I thought, guaranteed both bias and inaccuracy. Luce's proud invention was the "researcher"—in those days always a woman—who does
the digging and then checks every factual statement, but who does not
do the writing. This in turn means that the writer—always a man in
the early days—does not do his own digging and checking. As a result
the writer does not really understand the facts, and the researcher
does not really understand the story. Gross inaccuracy is bound to
follow. I saw a good demonstration of this years later in 1950 when
Time was doing a cover story on me and a book of mine, *The New
Society.* The story never appeared—it was pushed out of the magazine
by the outbreak of the Korean War. But in the copy that I later saw,
a senile, half-blind, and lame beagle dog of ours appeared as a "ferocious German Shepherd"; and the beat-up second-hand upright piano
in the dining room on which the kids were supposed to practice
became "a grand piano in the Druckers' music room." The researcher
had noted the pooch and asked me what breed it was. I told her it was

a hunting dog; the writer then read the notation "hunting dog" in the researcher's file as "ferocious German Shepherd." The divorce of research and writing equally transmuted our piano and our dining room. This is bound to happen in "group journalism."

I knew at the time also the reputation of the Luce magazines for internal intrigues, for backbiting and feuding, and for Luce's way of managing by setting editors against each other.

Yet the offer was very tempting and I could have used the money. So I agreed to explore.

But Luce could not deliver on his offer. The senior editors at *Time* very much wanted to get rid of Goldsborough, but, not unnaturally, they preferred one of their own people to succeed him. Goldsborough himself had no intention of resigning—and Luce could never fire or remove an old associate. Indeed, he did not remove Goldsborough until much later after the poor man had had a nervous breakdown (he finally committed suicide by jumping out of a window in the Time-Life Building). Above all, I was on the blacklist of *Time*'s strong Communist cell. When I had predicted in *The End of Economic Man* that Hitler and Stalin would get together, it was spring 1939 and the Hitler-Stalin Pact was still six months into the future. I immediately became an enemy for the Communists and the fellow travelers. The *Daily Worker* ran a long piece on me in which it "proved" that no such person as Peter Drucker existed and that this was the pen name of a sinister duo comprised of a high Nazi official and a high Washington State Department official. And Larry Todd, head of the Washington Bureau of Tass, the official Soviet news agency, personally organized and orchestrated a campaign against me, aimed at shutting my articles out of magazines and denying me any employment in newspapers or academia—and Todd, as everyone knew, never did anything except on orders from the Kremlin. Many years later Luce himself told me that this overreaction to a book by a totally unknown writer was the result of its strong endorsement by Winston Churchill. Churchill was, of course, then still very much "out" and appeasement very much "in"; but Churchill was no longer the hopeless "loser" he had been only a few years ago and a book he endorsed had to be taken seriously.

We have, properly, come to be ashamed of the "anti-Communist blacklist" in Hollywood during the McCarthy years; it was indeed shameful. But one should not forget that the "blacklist" was introduced into American academia, American journalism, and the American media altogether by the American Communists during the thirties and was made effective through their sympathizers. McCarthy, as in everything he did, simply used the Communists' own tactics in the name of "anti-communism."

Even if I had not had serious doubts about *Time*, I had no stomach for feuding and for a protracted three-front war against a Goldsborough who wanted to stay on, against *Time* editors who wanted their own man, and against the Communists in Time Inc. and their numerous sympathizers. So I told Henry Luce to forget the whole idea.

I have always known that writing is indecent exposure. By publishing a book one asks to be attacked—and mine was meant to be controversial. Still it took me a few months before I was willing to admit, even to myself, that the Communists at *Time* magazine had unwittingly been my benefactors, if not my saviours. Without them I might have taken the job; and it would have destroyed or at least crippled me. Luce hired a great many highly gifted people for *Time*, *Life*, and *Fortune*, and almost no one ever produced anything in his entire life once he had joined the staff—even after leaving it. Luce killed with kindness by overpaying and cosseting people. I doubt that I would have had the fortitude and maturity to resist. Not many did. It was not sour grapes for me to realize this; I had come to the conclusion while working with the people at *Time*. Still, I don't know what I would have done had there really been a job for me there. But at least I had learned enough to say no when Luce, greatly irked by the resistance he encountered over me, offered me a well-paid non-job on his own staff.

Luce did not give up easily. A year later he came back with another assignment, one of the most interesting, stimulating, and educational assignments of my writing career. He asked me to join him in rescuing the floundering tenth anniversary issue of *Fortune* in 1940.

Fortune was Luce's real love among his magazines. *Time* he had started in 1923 as a joint venture with his Yale classmate Briton Hadden. As even Luce's detractor, A. W. Swanberg, stresses in *Luce and His Empire* (1972), Luce did most of the work and was in charge of both editorial and publishing at *Time* from the beginning. But officially the two men were equals; and in the public eye the outgoing, showy, and effervescent Hadden easily overshadowed Luce, who was shy and who never quite got over having been born a dirt-poor missionary's kid. It was not until 1929 when Hadden died and Luce bought out his estate that Luce became the boss at *Time* in name as well as fact.

But *Fortune,* first published in 1930, was Luce's own brainchild from conception to publication. He edited it the first two years and built up its staff, its graphics, its editorial policy, and circulation, all at the most difficult time, the depth of the Depression.

Fortune also played a special part in Luce's plans for himself. *Time* had made him rich before he was thirty and Luce liked being rich, although he only learned to enjoy money after he married Clare Boothe as his second wife. *Life* made him famous before he was forty, and Luce was never entirely comfortable with fame, I always thought. But he expected *Fortune* to make him influential—and that was what he really craved. *Fortune* also suited his style. Luce never himself used "Timese"; that perversion of the language was Hadden's contribution to the joint venture. Luce himself, who wrote well and liked to write, preferred long, leisurely, *Fortune*-style essays. Nothing he did he therefore enjoyed quite as much as writing for and editing *Fortune.* Finally, Luce conceived the *Fortune* graphics, and they were probably as important to him as the *Fortune* text. He worked closely with the *Fortune* art department and spent days with the art director and the artists long after he had otherwise withdrawn from day-to-day involvement with the magazines altogether.

The issue to mark *Fortune's* tenth anniversary was therefore very much Luce's child and meant as his monument to what he himself thought his most significant and most personal achievement. He thought of it, worked out the plan in detail, and started it. And then he almost lost the child for the reason that caused so many failures at Time Inc.: Luce's inability to remove or even to move aside an old friend who could not do the job.

Russel Davenport, *Fortune's* managing editor, was a latter-day Walt Whitman, a man of expansive ideas, of a noble vision of America, and a writer of rhapsodic prose that at its best could be deeply moving. He was an excellent articles editor who had the patience to spend hours searching for the perfect word, to straighten out a sentence, or to winkle the meaning out of a bucketful of slithering tangents. And he was a very nice person: witty, stimulating, warm, and generous. But he was totally unsuited to being managing editor of a monthly magazine. He could not plan, could not delegate, and could not supervise. Deadlines to him were bogeymen to threaten naughty children with. And he was quite incapable of scheduling. The Luce magazines were first in applying to magazine editing the "Gantt Chart," which starts from the completion date and works backward. Without it these magazines would never have worked. They were exceedingly complex for their time and far ahead in structure and composition to anything anyone up to then had attempted. The new scheduling system had been Luce's own contribution, and a pioneering one. *Fortune* of course had such a schedule. Davenport never used it. "I keep the schedule in my head," he would say—but the head is the one place not to keep a schedule in. But Davenport had been with Luce for years, and so Luce put him in as managing editor and kept him in the job despite his glaring inability to do it.

The tenth anniversary issue of *Fortune* was meant to be far more ambitious than anything *Fortune* had ever done, and quite different: an issue of about twenty pieces on the American economy, a dozen major ones and about eight minor ones. Luce worked out the grand design with the editors, then turned it over to Davenport. Six months later, just a few weeks before the issue had to go to the printer, he checked. Almost nothing had been done. Some major pieces were not even assigned to a writer. It was then that Luce asked me to join in the rescue effort. He knew from the scrapbooks on me that he had assembled earlier where I had already done research and analysis, and he asked me to take on the writing of two key pieces: the one on American agriculture and the one on American labor. He also asked me to take on the editing of a few more stories for the issue, and to edit a few stories for future issues that had been lost or pushed aside in the scramble to get the anniversary issue done. For about two months we worked day and night—and beat the deadline.

Among the stories for future issues I took on as editor was one on IBM and Thomas Watson, Sr. It had been done by a young writer who had just joined; it was in fact his first *Fortune* assignment. But no one had been available to work with him. As a result the story was a disaster—brilliantly wrong and a total misunderstanding. By now *Fortune* is considered to be "pro-business." But in those days it was "about business" rather than "for business." Luce's vision of *Fortune* had been a magazine that would take business seriously as a key feature of American life and society, and would analyze it searchingly. The "corporation story" which Luce invented—and of which he himself wrote the first three or four—was the origin of "investigative reporting" and meant to be adversary. In those days, to be picked as the subject of a *Fortune* story was considered by most managements to be a noisome affliction, on a par with an attack of the shingles. I once asked Paul Garrett what his primary assignment was when Alfred Sloan had hired him as the first public relations man in General Motors, shortly after *Fortune* had been launched. "To keep *Fortune* away from GM," was his reply. And there were many tales around of attempts by managements to persuade or even bribe *Fortune* editors and writers to cancel a planned story on their company.

But the young man who had written the IBM story had not understood that investigative reporting is not the same thing as smearing— a confusion to which investigative reporters are, of course, highly susceptible. In those pre-computer days IBM was a small company, just reaching middle size. But it did some very unusual things. It did not lay off anyone, for instance, and had risked bankruptcy in the thirties rather than fire people. It paid blue-collar workers a weekly or monthly salary. It went in for continuous training for everyone in the company. It had no supervisors but had the work team itself run the job with an "assistant." IBM had been kept afloat during the Depression only by that most unglamorous product, the time clock, and had no technology of its own. Yet it managed to make itself look big and important in the public eye through such devices as Watson's slogan, THINK, and his distributing thousands of THINK stickers, through its graphics, through the THINK jokes (most of them invented by Watson and launched by him), and through judicious eye-catching publicity flashes such as the IBM pavilion at the New York World's Fair, which attracted millions of visitors, few of whom at that time had ever seen an IBM product or used it. All these traits that made IBM different, interesting, and worth writing about had been mentioned in Luce's original outline for *Fortune's* IBM piece. But the young writer had ignored it and had instead written an intemperate personal attack on Watson, in which he called him "the American Hitler," the "new-style Fuehrer," and so on. IBM itself he totally lost sight of in his indignation over Watson's greatest crime: his not allowing liquor on company premises or in the company's country club! All this was done with great brilliance—the young man went on to become one of *Fortune's* best writers.

Someone had been appointed to supervise the story. But he had had no time for it, and when pressed to approve or disapprove had simply released it unread. Thereupon *Fortune* sent it to IBM—in those days a company was always shown a pre-publication copy of a story and asked to point out factual errors (without any promise of changes).

But that was the very last step before printing and was done when the story was already in the magazine's proof copy. It was much too late, in other words, to recall the story or to do it over. I went to Luce after I had read the copy and told him that the story could not be redeemed, but the worst inanities could be changed. I would however not yield an inch to screams from the company or to threats Watson might make, though he had ample grounds for a suit for malicious libel. I would protect the writer first and edit the story afterwards. And I asked Luce to give orders to put the call from IBM through to me and not to the writer.

The call came a day or two later. As it happened, the writer was sitting across from me and we were going over the story together. "This is Thomas Watson," said the voice on the telephone. "I want to speak to the writer of the story on my company." "I am afraid, Mr. Watson," I said, "that the writer is not available. You will have to discuss the story with me; I am the editor in charge of it." "I don't want to discuss the story," said Mr. Watson, "I want to speak to the writer personally." "Give me your message," I said, "and I'll see that he gets it." "Tell that young man," said Watson, "that I want him to join IBM as our director of public relations; he can name his own salary." I thought this might be one of the "persuasion" attempts of which I had heard. "You realize, Mr. Watson," I said, "that the story will come out in the magazine whether the writer stays on the staff or not." "Of course," said Watson, "and if the story does not appear, I withdraw my offer." "Mr. Watson," I said, "have you read the story?" "Of course," he said, quite irritated, "I always read what's written about me and my company." "And you still want the writer as your director of public relations?" "Of course," said Watson; "at least he takes me seriously!"

There were many interesting people at *Fortune* at that time. But the most interesting was Luce himself. It was the first and last time I worked with him, yet for a short, intensive period I worked with him very closely indeed. In many ways he was the easiest man I have ever worked with. He is often depicted as opinionated and arrogant. He was neither. He had opinions, of course; indeed, he was so full of ideas that I had to remind him again and again that we were working against an impossible deadline. But the youngest and greenest associate could argue with him, and he or she (for Luce, unlike his editors, considered women to be members of the human race) got a respectful hearing. When it came to discussing ideas or opinions, Luce knew neither rank nor age nor sex; he respected ideas and opinions even though he did not always respect people. He was perfectly willing to be argued out of an opinion by a junior, provided the junior had done the homework and made sense. He was capable—I saw it more than once—of overruling a person and then, a few days or weeks later, calling up or sending one of his famous memoranda to say: "You were right. We do it your way."

He also went to great lengths to support younger people. When I first encountered the IBM piece and showed it to Luce, he was outraged. He wanted to pull it out of the magazine altogether. I had to argue with him that it was simply too late for that, that the story was in the issue and had, in fact, already been typeset and put into the layout. It could be corrected but that was all. Luce gave in grudgingly —he had no choice. But when the writer complained to him because I had rewritten some of the purple prose he was proudest of, Luce listened to him sympathetically and made me restore some of my cuts. "The writer," he said to me, "is entitled to his opinion as long as it is not distortion; his name will be on the piece, not yours or mine." I doubt that the writer got the slightest inkling of Luce's dislike for the story—"It leaves a very bad taste in my mouth," he said to me after the final work had been done, "and all the more so as it is so very well written."

He had a wry sense of humor and was tolerant of other people's foibles, though personally rigid and a prude. One of the first stories I heard about him (well before I met him) was that of the brilliant writer he hired for *Life*. A few months after *Life* started publication, the chief of *Life* researchers, a prim and easily shocked New England spinster, came to Luce in great agitation. "Harry," she said, "you have to do something about that writer; you cannot imagine what he does." It took some coaxing before she was even willing to tell Luce that the writer did his work stark naked lying on a rug in his office. "What about his copy, Mary?" asked Luce. "Oh, it's fine, no problem," said Mary. "Does he chase your girls, Mary?" Luce asked (and since the writer was a well-known homosexual, I can imagine the twinkle in his eyes). "Of course not," said Mary; "the very idea; I wouldn't tolerate that for one moment." "I don't understand, Mary," said Luce. "I thought all your researchers were well-educated college-bred young women." "So they are," said Mary. "Then they surely have been taught to shut a door," said Luce, and dismissed the matter. This was his general attitude: if writers and editors perform, let them do it their way whether it's my way or not.

But Luce could also be an impossible person to work for. I doubt that Davenport was ever told that Luce had taken over the editorship of the special issue, or that he even suspected it, for Luce took great care not to push Davenport aside and not to relieve him. Luce did not even attend editorial meetings, but he briefed a few of us carefully ahead of them on every article for which we were responsible. He saw the people with whom he had chosen to do the issue only one by one, and only in his own office, which was on a different floor. We only found out more or less by accident (or through the researchers' grapevine) who these other people were and what were their assignments. We were under strict orders not to tell Davenport or anyone else that we were working with Luce. This was done, in part, to make sure Davenport would not be hurt. Luce could not endure to hurt an old friend and when he finally had to do it he always moved the man upstairs, gave him a big boost in salary, and a big-sounding though meaningless "special assignment." But in large measure Luce's *modus operandi* also was meant to assure Luce's control; by that time he had already begun to spend more and more time away from the magazines. Ten years later, after 1950 or so, Luce very much became an absentee chief executive who spent long periods traveling abroad or on his plantations and ranches in South Carolina and Arizona. By having people work for him in each enterprise around their official boss; by working around the people who had the title and directly with subordinates of theirs; by seeing editors, writers, or correspondents more or less behind their superior's back—though often quite openly —Luce made sure that no editor or publisher of his would ever be in control. He almost never interfered and he practically never issued an order; but he could always roil the waters, upset, keep the infighting going, and he did. Then all he had to do—and he did it masterfully— was to come in once every six months full of new ideas, questions, suggestions, doubts, debates, and even the strongest editor-in-chief was on the defensive and kept off balance.

This explains why his magazines were so faction-ridden, beset by infighting, feuding, and mistrust. It explains why so many of his editors took to drink and why *Time* marriages were notoriously brittle. What made the human atmosphere worse was Luce's grossly overpaying people, especially in the thirties when salaries on most American papers were abysmally low while Time Inc. shoveled in the money. I doubt that Luce deliberately overpaid. I once challenged him and was told, "With the profits we are making, I could not in conscience pay anything but top salaries." But the result was that people who knew very well that they were being drained and destroyed could not leave. They had become used to a style of living where one ate lunch at a plush restaurant, traveled first-class on a big expense account, had a Fifth Avenue apartment and a "small place" in Connecticut, and got a lion cub as a birthday present from Henry and Clare Luce as Marcia Davenport (then Russel's wife) did at the one *Fortune* birthday party I attended.

It was on this birthday party, if I remember right, that I knew I would never become a Time Inc. editor no matter what Luce offered. And when he then came to me to suggest that I join *Fortune* to "support" Davenport, that is, to take over the planning, scheduling, and supervision of the magazine while Davenport kept the title of "Managing Editor," I was not even tempted. The Hollywood life has never been for me. I said "No" without hesitation.

But I also came to realize that Luce was not Machiavellian. He was something more interesting; he was Chinese. I don't think Henry Luce ever thought out his way of handling people. He applied what has been the age-old Chinese way of running any organization, from the Han Emperor of olden times on. Mao Tse-tung ran his government and party exactly the way Henry Luce ran his magazines: by creating factions; by working around people who had the title, office, and responsibility; by encouraging juniors to come to him but enjoining them not to tell their bosses; and by keeping alive feuds, mutual distrusts, and opposing cliques. This was probably the only way in which Henry Luce could imagine running anything—he may not even have realized that there are other ways.

The clue to Henry Luce as a person was his birth and childhood as a China missionary's son, who grew up 200 miles inland from the Chinese coast with almost no company except Chinese children. China rather than the America of his ancestry molded Luce—he did not come to live in America until he entered Yale as an almost grown man. And whether he knew it or not (probably not, as introspection was not his strongest trait) his human relations, his way of managing, his system of control, were those of the Chinese ruler who remains far from the scene of action and takes no direct part, but who makes sure that no one else can become a threat by organizing countervailing officials, bureaucratic factions, and competing personal networks. Every American and European I have known who grew up in rural China the way Henry Luce did has acted much the same way. And I have sometimes, wondered how much Franklin Delano Roosevelt's strikingly similar management style owed to Roosevelt's maternal grandfather, Delano, who had been a China merchant and whom Roosevelt's powerful and domineering mother had idolized.

After 1940 I saw little of Luce for a good many years. When I worked with him again it was as a consultant on a specific project. In the early 1950s Luce had become interested in the possibility of a "highbrow" magazine, a quarterly or bimonthly publication on philosophy, religion, art, history, science, and literature. He had had one of his senior staff members work up a prospectus for such a publication and had reached the point where he had to decide whether to commit people and money to it. He knew that it would be a money-loser and was prepared to subsidize the venture. But did it make sense? This was the question with which he came to me in 1952 or 1953.

By that time I had done a fair amount of such work. Indeed my very first consulting assignment had been the analysis of a newspaper prospectus in 1940 or 1941. A group of *Time* magazine editors, led by the then managing editor, Ralph Ingersoll, had decided to launch a new daily newspaper in New York—a "serious progressive tabloid"—and had come to friends of mine to obtain financial backing. These people in turn had asked me to analyze the proposal. By that time I had already learned that the first thing to look at in any kind of publication is not the financial projections. First comes editorial. Does the publication make editorial sense? And if so, are the people who propose it competent to do the editorial job? Only then does one even look at the figures. So when my friends—a substantial financial group —asked me to look at Ralph Ingersoll's prospectus and to analyze its financial projections, I analyzed the editorial proposal instead and went back to them saying, "The editorial prospectus may make sense. But the people proposing it are incompetent to carry it out." My friends backed away from the proposal. Ingersoll and his associates found other backers and brought out their newspaper under the name *PM*. It became one of newspaper history's bigger flops, editorially as well as financially.

A few years later the same people came to me with another proposal, for *Scientific American*. This one made abundant sense editorially; indeed I know of no magazine other than Luce's early ones that was timed so beautifully to fit the needs and new awareness of a large reading public. The people proposing it clearly knew what they were trying to do and were competent to do it. I therefore recommended to my friends that they subscribe an even bigger share of the magazine's capital than the one that had been offered to them, and *Scientific American* soon became an outstanding success both editorially and financially.

I thus had some experience when Henry Luce came to me. As usual he for his part had done his homework, had checked up on what I had done for *PM* and *Scientific American,* and said to me: "I've asked you in because I know that you refuse to look at financial figures for a new publication unless the editorial approach makes sense. I'm too close to the idea to be objective about it—I want you to give me your judgment."

Luce's prospectus made sense. There was a tremendous amount of first-class work being done in America in all the major areas, and little of it was accessible. At the same time there was a growing educated public and a growing interest in the American mind. But when I looked at the outlines for the sample issues—there were about five of them—I found that the emphasis on the American perspective that had made the prospectus so interesting had evaporated. One issue looked like an imitation of the *Edinburgh Review* of 1850, another like the *Nouvelle Revue Française* of 1913, another like the *Neue Deutsche Rundschau* of 1925. They were not just imitative; they were nineteenth-century European, with all the American character lost. I began to suspect after a few days musing over the phenomenon that the basic concept of a lay "liberal culture" had either never fitted the American genius or had ceased to make sense altogether in the mid-twentieth century. The success of *Scientific American,* of *Psychology Today,* of the *New York Review of Books,* of *Science* magazine, or of the magazine of the Smithsonian Institution indicates that the educated public of Luce's prospectus does indeed exist. But it is not a public for a "general culture" but for sharply segmented areas of special interest—and yet we know that the readership of these publications overlaps and is, indeed, by and large the same. And the experience of Public Television, which through its own medium has been trying to do the job Luce's highbrow magazine reached for, and for the same public, would also indicate that there has been a profound change in the meanings of "culture" and of "educated." The educated man is no longer an amateur in a number of areas, but a specialist capable of relating his own area of expertise to the universe of knowledge. For this reader the *Edinburgh Review,* the *Nouvelle Revue Française,* or the *Neue Deutsche Rundschau*—or Luce's proposed magazine, or American Public Television, or the BBC's Radio 3 (the famous "Third Programme") would be—both too amateurish and too precious.

So I went to Luce and said: "This is a beautiful prospectus but it's fifty years too late. In addition, you people at *Time* are not competent to do the job. What you have in mind is an edited magazine that finds and stimulates outside writers and helps them to project their work for a general public. But what you are good at is a *staff-written* magazine, and there's a difference." Luce listened and said: "I called you in because I suspected what you told me. But this has been my dream since I first started. I went into *Time* to get the money to do the great cultural magazine America lacks and deserves. But I know you are right . . . " and he aborted the venture.

Then, a few years later, he called me in once more. By that time *Life* had begun to show the first signs of aging. The total revenues were still going up, but *Life* had to pay more and more to get and to hold subscribers; and advertising rates and revenues therefore had to go up even faster to keep pace with the costs of acquiring or renewing a subscriber. Luce asked me to study *Life* editorial and suggest what might be done. I do not know whether my conclusions were even reported to him, for I worked through the people at *Life* and my report was unacceptable to them. I came to the conclusion that *Life* had outlived its usefulness. It could only be turned around by a change in basic editorial concept, which no magazine can do easily if at all. *Life* had been outflanked by television. It could regain its leadership only by changing itself from a photographic magazine with captions to a written magazine with illustrations—and that was unlikely to be either feasible or successful.

Horace Lorimer, who built the *Saturday Evening Post* into America's most successful magazine in the first third of this century, preached that a magazine makes its income from advertising and that subscriptions are primarily "sales promotion" to get advertising revenue. *Saturday Evening Post* in his days never lived by his maxim; until the late thirties it made a healthy profit on subscriptions with advertising revenue pure gravy. But Lorimer's dictum later became an article of the faith for American publishers and for investors in American magazines—and it is poisonous hokum. A magazine that does not at least break even on subscriptions (and newsstand sales) is headed for extinction. One can always buy subscribers at a price. *Saturday Evening Post, Look,* and *Life* all had peak circulations when they gave up the ghost; editors then always wonder out loud why their beautiful "editorial success" is not being supported by the financial or the advertising communities. But a magazine is not an "editorial success" if it pays out for a subscriber—in "special introductory offers," "premiums," and "tie-in sales"—more than it will receive back from the subscriber.

By the time *Life* folded, it paid about $15 to get $8 or $9 of subscriber revenue. This is editorial failure. The magazine bribes people to allow the editorial product into their homes. No advertiser quite knows what makes an advertisement sell, but everyone knows that an advertisement will not sell if the reader does not really want the publication. In fact, an advertisement in such a publication unsells the product and advertisers stop using it. Peak circulation that is bought rather than earned therefore always dooms a magazine. It doomed *Life* as it had earlier doomed *Saturday Evening Post* and *Look*.

The American magazine—indeed, the entire magazine concept—is facing a sea-change. It is not true, as Marshall McLuhan has been telling us, that the printed word is dead. What is dead is the mail-carried word. What matters to editor and reader is the message, not the carrier. Putting ink on heavy paper and then carrying that paper over long distances is about a hundred times more expensive and a thousand times slower than sending the same symbols electronically to have them imprinted inklessly on some sort of light-sensitive plastic or paper in the subscriber's home and at his command. To ship three pounds or so of paper in order to deliver one-tenth of an ounce of ink makes little economic sense and could only be justified as long as there was no other way. But almost everyone today has either a telephone or a television set, and both are perfect transmission and printing instruments, especially now that the paper used to record an electronic message as "durable copy" can easily be recycled. Technically, all the elements for electronic graphics exist, including the technology for color images. What stands in the way of electronic graphics are legal and political problems, including the tough one of freedom of the press. And now that pay TV is finally being accepted, the electronic magazine is bound to become reality. Even if postal transmission were not extremely labor-intensive—not even counting the hideous cost of door-to-door delivery—electronic transmission would offer enormous economic advantages and equally enormous advantages in flexibility, diversity, and editorial individuality. The British Post Office—not otherwise noted for its imagination—is already offering such a service of electronic graphics; and in the United States, an IBM subsidiary will start offering it in 1980.

Life, which was a pictorial magazine delivered the nonpictorial, mail-carried way, was therefore surely a transition phenomenon. As soon as its circulation costs began to shoot up around 1950, the exorbitant expenses of producing and delivering the message by the wrong methods were bound to threaten *Life's* survival.

I yield to no one in my admiration for the magazine. It is an important achievement of modern civilization, above all because it permits infinite variety and individuality. But it is the magazine I admire, and not the cellulose that traditionally has carried it, nor the smudges of carbon black that are mechanically deposited on the cellulose. And while the magazine will, I fervently hope, live on, the mail-carrier is obsolete and already going. Henry Luce's magazines were, in essence, the last mass magazines of the old technology. If the history of the magazine is ever written, it may well be entitled: "From Addison's *Spectator* to Henry Luce's *Life*."

But there may well be another history, 200 years hence, entitled: "From Henry Luce's *Life* to . . ." For the Luce magazines were as much the first of a new breed as they were the last of the old.

In the biographies of political figures Luce is rarely even mentioned. Good examples are the two standard biographies of the major Republican figures of his era, President Eisenhower and Senator Taft. The most comprehensive book on Eisenhower's presidency, *Eisenhower and the American Crusades* by Herbert S. Parmet (1972), mentions Luce exactly twice in its 650 pages—once as the first prominent American to speak out against McCarthy in June 1953, more than a year before anyone in Eisenhower's cabinet dared oppose McCarthy and McCarthyism, and once as a subordinate member of a group of about thirty prominent leaders whom Eisenhower organized to support the foreign aid program. James T. Patterson's *Mr. Republican; A Biography of Robert A. Taft* (also 1972) mentions the "Luce magazines" a few times but Luce hardly at all, and then only as one name among many rather than as a person of political power or influence. An earlier political biography, Robert E. Sherwood's famous *Roosevelt and Hopkins* (1948), similarly mentions Luce only twice and as a totally unimportant figure, once as a member of the "White Committee" opposed to isolationism in the pre-World War II years, and once as the writer of an editorial in 1944 that accurately predicted there would be no isolationist revival after World War II. These three books are based on the detailed diaries and papers of their subjects, not one of whom apparently thought Luce to be politically important or powerful.

But every biography of Henry Luce, whether friendly or hostile, portrays him as a major power in American politics, a major influence on American policies whether for good or evil, and as an important, if not dominant, figure in American political history from the thirties until his death in 1967. Luce's best-known biography—a bestseller when it first came out—is Swanberg's *Luce and His Empire*. It credits Luce with having invented and imposed every single policy of which the author disapproves: isolationism before World War II and interventionism at the same time; anti-Communism and America's support of Chiang Kai-shek; and so on. According to Swanberg there was only one powerful politician in America from Truman to Lyndon Johnson and his name was Henry Luce.

Obviously these two views cannot both be right. But they can both be wrong—and are.

In traditional terms Henry Luce had practically no influence on American politics, shaped no policies, and had no weight as a person no matter how vocal the "Luce papers" were. He did not even have enough political strength to achieve his own modest political ambition. It was no secret that Luce hankered after the London Embassy and put in his claim for it when his papers had helped elect Eisenhower to the presidency. But Eisenhower deftly ducked by appointing Luce's wife, Clare—former playwright and later Republican congresswoman from Connecticut—ambassador to Rome, thus shutting out her husband without slapping him down.

One reason for Luce's political impotence was that the "Luce papers" rarely reflected his own position. Luce took a most active part in the editing of the papers, at least until the early or mid-fifties. But their politics were not his major concern. He had strong political opinions—yet he allowed his editors to hold and to express totally different views. Luce was a strong "interventionist" from the beginning; as early as 1935 he established personal contact with Churchill, it seems, and began to work for an Atlantic alliance against Hitler. But he left the arch-isolationist and Hitler-appeaser, Laird Goldsborough, as foreign news editor of *Time* until well after the outbreak of the war in Europe. Luce was himself staunchly conservative. Yet every managing editor of *Time, Life,* and *Fortune* was a liberal, and some, like Ralph Ingersoll around 1940 at *Time,* were well to the left of the

liberal position. Luce opposed McCarthy almost from the start much
to the Eisenhower's administration discomfiture; but he tolerated significant support for McCarthy among the former Communists on the
Time staff who had turned vociferous "ex-commies," like the best
known of them, Whittaker Chambers.

Luce never hesitated to make his views known, in memoranda to
the editors or in one of his frequent signed editorials. But there was
only one area in which he dictated policy: China. In other areas he had
views; in respect to China he had convictions. He shared his convictions about China with a great many other "China hands"—the novelist Pearl Buck for instance—but also with President Roosevelt. All told
Luce's emotions reflected the almost mystical empathy with China
that is a feature of the American tradition, and a most puzzling one.
Surely no other country has shown less interest in America historically,
has been less receptive to American ideas and values, and has less in
common with America in every sphere than China, whether that of
the Manchus, of Chiang Kai-Shek, or of Mao. Yet there is no country
about which Americans are more misty-eyed, more sentimental, and
more romantic than China, whether the China of Chiang Kai-shek
that Luce and Roosevelt idealized, or the ruthless totalitarian dictator-
ship of Mao that Nixon and Kissinger—and the whole liberal establishment of the mid-seventies—tried to make look like a New England
town meeting.

Like all the old China hands, Luce despised Japan and imposed
an anti-Japanese bias on his magazines long after World War II was
over. It was in the mid-fifties that Luce suddenly appeared at an
editorial conference at *Fortune* to which I had been asked to discuss
a piece I had written for the magazine. Luce had a proposal: a special
issue on the recovery of Europe, then just beginning to be discernible.
"What do you think of this?" he asked, turning to the group. "An
excellent idea and very timely," all said; "but shouldn't we include an
article on Japan's recovery in that issue?" "You really think so?" said
Luce. Everyone nodded. "Then I guess we'd better drop the whole
idea of that issue," said Luce, and got up and left.

But outside China and Japan Luce was not concerned with the
political positions of his magazines or with policies at all. He was not
concerned with concepts. He was concerned with perceptions. What
mattered to him was not whether his editors were interventionists or
isolationists but whether they saw the same world he saw, the same
magazine he tried to create, the same configuration of events he

perceived, and the same *medium*. Luce was a moralist. He never sloughed off his sternly Presbyterian missionary background even though he learned to drink liquor (as a rule sparingly). But he would have agreed with Søren Kierkegaard that aesthetics is morality. And long before Marshall McLuhan, Luce had concluded that the medium is the message.

Luce's impact in terms of politics and policies was nil. It is futile even to ask where he stood on an issue, though he himself always had an opinion. His impact on the American perception of the world was incalculable. He may not have created a new perception; but he made it prevail.

Luce did not, I believe, read a word of Chinese—the mission school in Chefoo to which he went as a youngster taught only English. But at our first meeting way back in 1939 he asked me whether I knew what a Chinese ideograph was. "That's how I see a really perfect *Time* story," he said. And he clearly meant by this the ideograph's construction through architectural design rather than through stringing together in linear sequence the in themselves meaningless letters of the alphabet, and the ideograph's resulting power to convey both meaning and mood in one symbol. When he founded *Fortune* he was not concerned with being pro business or anti business. He saw that the corporation had become important and visible. He sensed that one way to get across the new configuration of which the corporation was a central motive was through brand-new graphics, both those of Picasso and those of the German Bauhaus School. *Fortune* had the first modern art director in an American magazine; and, in a daring innovation, Luce proposed that the art department actually design both the editorial graphics and the graphics for the advertiser, thus providing for the reader a total visual experience. *Life* finally was taking the new perception of the film from the movie house into the living room. There had, of course, been "illustrated papers" before; one of the greatest journalistic success of the twenties was a German illustrated magazine, the Ullsteins' *Berliner Illustrierte Zeitung*. Luce took from the Germans their printing techniques. But where the Germans had still published a written magazine with copious illustrations and photographs, Luce devised the first magazine in which the camera told the story the way it did in the best of the silent films. Cecil B. DeMille rather than Daumier was *Life*'s mentor: it was Luce who realized that the silent movie had made all Americans capable of seeing the way the camera sees rather than the way the illustrator sees.

If and when the electronically transmitted magazine comes into being, it will be the child of Henry Luce. He would not have said: "I do not care who writes a country's laws; let me write its songs," for he revered the American Constitution. But he might have said: "I do not care who shapes a country's policies; let me shape its vision"—and he did.

I last met Henry Luce six months before his death. There was an International Management Congress in New York in September 1966, with a formal dinner for the speakers and Henry Luce as one of the hosts. Luce, then sixty-eight, looked eighty-five and deathly sick. But he was as courteous as ever, greeting me warmly and pulling me down on a seat next to his. "What have you been up to lately?" he asked. "I've just come back from Japan," I said, "and Harry, you can't imagine how successfully the Japanese are once more accomplishing what they've always been so good at, how fast they're Japanizing Western culture." Luce made a face, got up, and turned his back on me. It was the last I saw of him.

The Prophets:
Buckminster Fuller
and Marshall McLuhan

No two more different people could be imagined than Buckminster Fuller and Marshall McLuhan: in appearance, in style, in manner, in speech and, it would seem, in what they stand for. Fuller is short and round and speaks in epic poetry. McLuhan is tall and angular and utters puns and epigrams. But both men became cult heroes at the same time, in the 1960s. And both for the same reason: they are the bards and hot-gospellers of technology.

Bucky Fuller and Marshall McLuhan had been friends of mine long before they became celebrities. I had met both first around 1940. For long years I was one of the few who listened to them. But even I doubted for long years that their voices would ever be heard, let alone that either man could attract a following. They were prophets in the wilderness—and far, far away, it seemed, even from an oasis, let alone their Promised Land.

To Bucky Fuller, technology is the harmony of the heavens. The road to human perfection is a technology—a "big" technology and a "hard" one—that moves the human environment ever closer to the celestial harmony of his "dymaxion" design, of his "synergistic geometry," and of his "tensegrity." Bucky is a transcendentalist, very conscious of the legacy of his great-aunt, Margaret Fuller, the last of the New England transcendentalists of the nineteenth century. Bucky's world is pantheist; man approaches his own divinity the more he identifies with universal technology.

Marshall McLuhan sees technology as human rather than divine.

244

Technology is an extension of man. Alfred Russel Wallace, co-discoverer with Charles Darwin of the theory of evolution more than a century ago, said that "man alone is capable of purposeful non-organic evolution; he makes tools." McLuhan had never heard of Wallace; but he all along shared Wallace's view. Technology to McLuhan is the self-perfection of man, the way through which he extends himself, changes himself, grows, and becomes. And just as an animal that develops a new and different organ through natural evolution becomes a different animal, so a man who develops a new and different tool, and thereby extends himself, becomes a different man.

Enmity to, and disenchantment with, technology was the ostensible "cause" of the sixties and early seventies. No less likely heroes of the decade of the "environmental crusade" could thus be imagined than those arch-technologists, Bucky Fuller and Marshall McLuhan, respectively the seer of "synergistic geometry" and the metaphysician of the "electronic media." But what went on in that decade only looked like "anti-technology." Actually, the decade discovered technology. Until then, technology was something that could be left to technologists. Engineers built dams; "humanists" read Joyce or listened to Bach or found "laws of nature." Humanists were quite willing to enjoy the "fruits of technology"—whether an airplane ride or a telephone call. But their work, its meaning, its importance, and its course, were not affected by technology or only marginally so, as when the steel-nib pen made unnecessary the trimming of goose quills, or when electric light bulbs made possible reading at late hours without eyestrain. Suddenly, in the 1960s, technology was seen as a human activity; formerly it was always a "technical" activity, carried out by God knows whom or what, presumably by "elves in the Black Forest." Technology moved from the wings of the stage of history to which the "humanist" had always consigned it, and began to mingle freely with the actors and even, at times, to steal the spotlight.

The first response to such a change in awareness is always violent rejection. It would be so much easier if the change could be made undone. If only we could return to the nice "humanist" world of hellenistic scribes and liberal arts scholars, in which ideas, values, aesthetics, and knowledge are dissociated from such grubby things as how people make their living, produce their tools, and above all in which they are divorced and disassociated from how men work. But underneath the know-nothing rejection there is then in such a period also a receptivity to new approaches, a search for a new integration.

And so Bucky Fuller and Marshall McLuhan suddenly became visible and important. To a generation which realized that technology had to be integrated with metaphysics and culture, aesthetics and human anthropology—that indeed it was at the core of human anthropology and of the self-knowledge of man—these two prophets offered a glimpse of a new reality. That their landscape was fog-shrouded and their utterances oracular only added to their appeal.

I bumped into Bucky Fuller—literally—while working on the tenth anniversary issue of *Fortune* in 1940 with Henry Luce. I backed out of an editor's office and straight into something in the hall that skittered away. A soft heavy object came crashing down, knocking me off my feet. It pulled itself up into a sitting position next to where I lay sprawled on the floor, and said in a matter-of-fact voice, "You have set back the industrial development of South America by at least ten years," got to its feet, and stalked off. Buckminster Fuller had been standing on top of a wheeled scaffolding to draw graphs of the world's future economy on the ceiling and walls.

By now, Bucky—no one has ever called him anything else, though he lists himself in all reference books as "Richard"—is a world myth. He has the longest entry in *Who's Who in America,* seventy-five lines. He has more honorary doctorates than anyone else I ever heard of, thirty-seven of them, perhaps a few more than anyone really needs. His books are bestsellers, his lectures draw standing-room-only crowds, and he is a folk hero of the young. But when I first met Bucky he was quite unknown, though nearing fifty. He had worked obsessively for two decades turning out ideas and inventions. Yet for long years on end the family had to subsist on whatever his wife could earn as a secretary. Bucky's few friends—he was always a solitary—tended to be infuriated at his single-minded pursuit of harebrained ideas when he so easily could have made a good living. For Bucky had a deserved reputation as a forecaster and analyst of technology. There was his forecast, for instance, of the developments that would make possible the airplane of the future. In 1929, so the story goes, Donald Douglas, already a leader among the younger designers, came to Bucky with a rough sketch of his "airplane of the future" for which then there was no aerodynamic theory, no engines, and no materials. And Bucky told him what was needed to build the airplane of his design—the theory, the engines, and the metals—and that it would be available ten years hence, in 1939. Ten years later Douglas built the prototype of what became World War II's most advanced bomber, the Flying Fortress, to Bucky's specifications. A few years after that Bucky performed a similar feat (to many people it smelled of witchcraft) in predicting and timing for one of the major copper companies the future emergence of what we now call "electronics." He could have had any number of similar assignments, and at good fees. Yet he only took one of them when he was desperate—when, for instance, his daughter was very sick and he needed money to pay the medical bills. Otherwise he stubbornly rode his hobby horse of geometric designs, to which he gave weird names, "Dymaxion," "Plydome," "Tetrahelix," or "Tensegrity," designs that did not seem to serve any purpose even when they worked, as they occasionally did.

Bucky was on a *Fortune* retainer as a "technical consultant" and had been hired by Henry Luce himself, though Luce, as he once told me, had no idea what Bucky was up to and did not understand a word he said. But Luce always had a good nose for the exceptional performer and was willing to bet on him. The other people at *Fortune* could not make head or tail of Bucky, neither his graphs nor his talk, which came out in a never-ending stream of words, half lyrical near-poetry, half science-fiction terms of his own coinage. I too, I admit, would have paid no attention had I not been amused by Bucky's conceit that graphs on a piece of paper determine development so that one can set back economic development by interrupting the drawing of graphs, as I had done. I thought at first that Bucky was joking. But no, he was in dead earnest; altogether a joke is inconceivable to Bucky, who is always serious and always means most literally every word he says.

The graphs were most peculiar. At a time when the best anyone hoped for was a restoration of the prosperity that had prevailed before the Depression, Bucky projected explosive economic growth for such stagnant, crisis-ridden, and backward areas as Latin America as much as for the United States, and even for a Europe that was then collapsing under Hitler's onslaught. The totally implausible results were obtained by tracing the geometric properties of curves for one factor only: energy. The curves were drawn on the assumption that energy is "organic" and will therefore expand exponentially the way a population curve does, until it fills its "ecological niche" to the limit, subject only to the ultimate—and most remote—constraint, i.e., the end of the release of energy through nuclear fusion and fission in the plasma in the sun's interior. I never was persuaded of the validity of Bucky's assumptions. But his projections for the postwar economy of the world, based on pure geometry, turned out to be remarkably accurate. Yet they were entirely based on geometric vision, devoid of analysis or "facts."

Bucky calls himself a geometer. But he sees more than the order of the earth, which is what "geometry" means. He experiences the order and the rhythm of space, or to use an old-fashioned term, the "harmony of the spheres."

Even Bucky's friends and admirers in those early years used to consider him "impractical." Bucky always denied this—indeed the accusation was one of the few things that could make him indignant. Otherwise he was singularly even-tempered. But whenever anyone hinted at his being "impractical," he would get shrill and lose his temper. People, Bucky felt, were "impractical," not he. And indeed part of Bucky's trouble was that he tried too hard to be "practical." He applied his strange designs to everyday objects in order to be practical: automobiles, houses, road maps. And he could not understand why people were not willing to shift to a three-wheeler car that had to be entered from the top or crawled into from underneath, for the sake of a little fuel-saving or "clean" aerodynamic lines. The "Dymaxion House"—a half-sphere on a slab—combines the maximum floor area with the smallest surface and therefore the lowest requirements for heating or cooling. It also combines structural rigidity and stability close to the theoretical maximum, with extreme lightness of construction that needs practically no structural supports. Bucky could not understand why people still preferred to live in geometrically imperfect rectangular houses which had wall space and into which furniture fitted.

The "Dymaxion Map" was the first to portray portions of the surface of a globe, the earth for example, on a flat plane without distortion. But the map had to be a conic section with rounded edges and triangular points at both ends—and Bucky could not understand why people were willing to accept the slight distortion of a conventional area map rather than use undistorted maps that looked like cut-out paper dolls. Actually, every one of these designs was eminently "practical," but for new and different uses. The "Dymaxion Car" has been used extensively in space design. The "Dymaxion House" became the prototype for "radomes," the automated sensing stations of the air-warning system in the Arctic, and in the last quarter century for pavilions, sports stadiums, and exhibition halls. And when the astronauts first went into orbit and needed maps without distortion, they began to use "Dymaxion Maps." But I believe Bucky still finds it difficult to understand what people meant when they called him "impractical" forty years ago.

I did see a good deal of Bucky over a ten-year span. He refused to join the faculty at Bennington College where I taught during most of the forties. But he often came to talk to the students—I believe the Bennington students were his first and for many years his main audience. For what Bucky needed above all—more than recognition, more than money—was an audience, and preferably a large one. He is awkward with small groups and uncomfortable with an individual; but give him a large group and he becomes a performer without peer.

When I introduced Bucky at his first speech at Bennington, I told the audience that he would talk for forty-five minutes and then answer questions. Four hours later Bucky was still talking, and when I tried to break in, he waved me aside and said, "I'm still on my introduction." I think we forced him to stop around one in the morning. It was a mistake. We should have let him keep on talking—later on we did. There is no point setting a time limit on a Bucky Fuller "happening." Bucky keeps on talking in an orotund monotone, rambling on without beginning, middle, or end. And the audience sits and absorbs. No one ever remembers a *word* Bucky says. But nobody ever forgets the *experience*. It is like being in a verbal Jacuzzi—a pool of warm, swirling water, relaxing yet constantly moving and challenging. And the experience is never about Buckminster Fuller. Indeed most of the people who listen to him do not remember too distinctly what he looks like, let alone how he speaks or moves or acts. What they experience —and what every audience, since those Bennington students almost forty years ago, has experienced—is Bucky Fuller's vision. Bucky Fuller calls himself a geometer, but he is in fact a seer.

I met Marshall McLuhan at about the same time as I first met Bucky, at a meeting of some learned society during which he and I read papers. I do not remember what my paper at that meeting was all about; indeed I remember nothing of the meeting, not even what learned society's meeting it might have been. All I do remember, but that vividly, is Marshall McLuhan. I was fully prepared to be bored when he started reading his paper in a flat, nasal Midwestern voice with a Canadian twang to it. He had then just started teaching as a very young English instructor at St. Louis University in Missouri, and was of course totally unknown. He looked most ordinary—tall, thin, lanky. The title of the paper—something to do with the origin of the modern university curriculum—did not sound particularly exciting either. And at first the paper sounded exactly like any first paper (typically, as in McLuhan's case, an excerpt from a dissertation) read by a young academic to an audience of bored department chairmen on the lookout for new hires for the next academic year.

But soon this ordinary-looking English instructor began to say some strange-sounding things. The medieval university, he said, became obsolete with the printed book. Everybody nodded since that much was part of conventional wisdom. But he went on to contend that the modern university came into being in the sixteenth century because of printing, which not only changed the method of instruction and the form of presentation but changed the nature of what was being taught and what the university intended to teach. The new learning, that unknown man seemed to say, had little to do with the Renaissance or with the revival of interest in antiquity and the rediscovery of the classical writers, or even with astronomy, geographic discovery, or new science. On the contrary, these great events of intellectual history were themselves results of Gutenberg's new technology. Movable type, rather than Petrarch, Copernicus, or Columbus, was the creator of the modern world view. "Did I hear you right," asked one of the professors when McLuhan had finished reading, "that you think printing influenced the courses the university taught and the role of the university altogether?" "No, sir," said McLuhan, "it did not *influence;* printing *determined* both, indeed, printing determined what henceforth was going to be considered knowledge." "This is piffle," said the man who had asked the question, and the chairman hastily called the next speaker. When we went out after the meeting, I heard the man who had asked the question, chairman of the English Department at a major university, say to a colleague: "When that long drink of water began to read his paper on the university, I was almost ready to offer him a teaching job. But I think I'd rather let an engineering school hire him." McLuhan then, almost forty years ago, did not say: "The medium is the message": he could not have said it, since the word "medium" did not then exist in its present-day meaning as the carrier of communication. But even then he clearly believed that "The medium is the message," or, at least, that the medium determines and shapes the message.

I was no more convinced of McLuhan's thesis than the English

Department chairman. I knew that movable type was not Gutenberg's "invention" but had been in use in China long before Gutenberg, reinventing or imitating, used it to print the Bible. And none of the effects McLuhan claimed for it had occurred in China; indeed there the new "medium" had had absolutely no effect on culture, learning, and perception. It remained an inferior tool that did not even make obsolete graphic reproduction of the old style, let alone traditional knowledge, methods of instruction, or what was being learned or taught. Still, that "long drink of water" had something to say, I thought.

By that time I had myself become interested in the relationship of technology to society and culture. The "assembly line," for instance, was a tool. Yet it surely had great impact on the organization of people at work and their relationship, and also on the perception society had of itself. It underlay the new view of something called "industrial society"—a term I was one of the first to use without any clear idea of what it might mean. The assembly line, as I began to realize in those years, was in itself not just "technology"; it was above all a theoretical and highly abstract concept of the nature of work. Yet, as I also began to realize in those years, the assembly line, while highly visible and a symbol in people's minds for a new and dominant reality, was in actuality a miniscule segment of manufacturing, with no more than the smallest fraction of the work force doing "assembly-line work" or ever likely to do it. Technology, in other words, was not quite as simple as the traditional view of both "humanists" and "technologists" assumed. It somehow defined to people who they were, or at least how they saw themselves, in addition to its impact on what they produced.

So I sought out McLuhan and asked him to come to visit—we were then living outside New York City, in Bronxville. And he soon got into the habit of dropping by whenever he was near us, first in Bronxville, then in Vermont, and finally, after 1949, again in the New York area in Montclair, New Jersey.

He was always good company, though absorbed in his ideas. I doubt that he asked even once what I was doing or listened to my telling him in twenty-odd years of visiting. But he also never talked of himself; he spouted ideas. He talked by preference in puns. The only time I remember him paying attention to any one *person* was when one of our children quizzed him on "Bible jokes": "When is baseball first mentioned in the Bible? When Rebecca goes to the well with a pitcher." He was enchanted and kept on repeating the feeble puns for hours. Some of his own were not much better, as for instance the pun that still graces his annual Christmas card: "Should old Aquinas be forgot?" But many of his puns had bite to them, and carried the existential shock that characterizes the really good play on words. And McLuhan was full of oddities, full of conceits, of observations that had a special quirk, a special hook, a special angle that turned the conventional world of every day into something strange, mystifying, and sometimes frightening—a surrealism of words rather than of pictures, but as truly surrealist as Dali or a Steinberg cartoon.

McLuhan dropped in. He usually came with a minimum of warning or no warning at all. Once, in New Jersey, in the midst of a tremendous midsummer storm with tropical downpours and Doomsday thunderclaps, our doorbell rang around one in the morning. There was McLuhan, sopping wet but grinning from ear to ear. "I had some business in Upper Montclair," he said (it was three miles from where we lived), "and thought I'd walk over." "Why didn't you telephone, Marshall?" I asked. "What would you have done in this weather if we hadn't been home?" "But Peter," he said, "you and Doris are much too sensible to be anyplace else in weather like this." With this he dismissed the weather, sat down in his wet clothes, and talked about his ideas until breakfast time.

This was the last time McLuhan dropped in to talk about his visions. On that stormy June night in the early sixties enlightenment had come to him. It was in that night that he, lecturing or visiting friends, suddenly realized what he had been saying all along—and rushed to tell me. What he spoke that night became, shortly thereafter, McLuhan's most important, clearest, and most original book, though by no means his best-known one: *The Gutenberg Galaxy; The Making of Typographic Man*. *Understanding Media*, the book that talked about "cool" media such as TV, and "hot" media, about the world becoming "tribalized" into a "global village" through electronics, and about the "medium as the message," came two years later. *Understanding Media* made McLuhan famous, or at least notorious. But by that time he had stopped dropping in on us, though we have remained friends. When he emerged from that storm McLuhan had finally seen his promised land. After that he did not need a listener any more.

During the twenty-odd years when I saw him frequently, he was a seer without a vision. He knew what he had to see—and could not open his eyes to see it. He must have felt these years the way all of us feel once in a while in a nightmare when we know we have to wake up but cannot do it. He had had all his vision clearly before his eyes when he answered the English Department chairman at that learned meeting that "Printing determined what henceforth was considered knowledge." But until television came, Marshall did not know that he had meant it.

It was as the prophet of television that McLuhan became a figure in the intellectual "jet set" of the sixties. This also explains, I believe, why McLuhan has not really become much more than that. To be sure, television—and the "media" altogether—have been changing what is being communicated, and not merely how. They have been changing our perception of the outside world, but also how we see ourselves and what we see in ourselves. Yet not one of McLuhan's specific predictions has come true and not one of them is likely to come true. Printing is not being made obsolete by television. There are more books and magazines being published today than there were before the "tube" invaded the living room, just as drama and poetry did not disappear once "storytelling" became "writing" and "writing" became "printing." Indeed the electronic tools are likely to become the "print media" of tomorrow, when the "printed word" is almost certain to be transmitted by some sort of electronic printer attached to a TV set or telephone. And the Xerox copier makes every man his own Gutenberg.

The interaction between the "medium" and the "message" is more profound than McLuhan's aphorism has it; neither determines the other, but each shapes the other. McLuhan knows all this, I am sure. But because his moment of enlightenment came to him over television, he has become known—and may even see himself—as the pop culture's Thoreau. This however is grossly unfair to the man and to his insight. McLuhan's most important insight is not that "the medium is the message." It is that technology is an extension of man rather than "just a tool." It is not "man's master." But it changes man and his personality and what man is—or perceives himself to be—just as much as it changes what he can do.

I do not believe that either Bucky Fuller or Marshall McLuhan can integrate technology, culture, and metaphysics. Their vision nowhere relates technology to the specific human activity that is "work." Technology does indeed not deal with tools, machines, and artifacts alone in the way the engineer defines technology, the way the monumental five-volume *History of Technology* (published between 1954 and 1958 under the editorship of the great English scholar, Charles Singer) defines technology, the way the Society for the History of Technology (founded in 1958) defines technology, and the way in which the Society's journal *Technology and Culture* deals with technology. But technology is also not just "cosmic force" or "extension of man." It is not, as Singer's *History* defines it, "how things are made or done." It is *how man does or makes.* Technology deals with the purposeful, man-made, nonorganic evolution through which man discharges that peculiarly and uniquely human activity, "work." And the way man does and makes, the way he works, then has profound impact on how man lives, how he lives with others of his own kind, and how he sees himself—and ultimately perhaps even on what and who he is. Above all, work is the specific social bond in human life and history. The organic bond that is founded in the need to take care of helpless young, man shares with many of the higher animals; elephant mothers take care of their young longer than do human mothers, and may do it better. But the unique social bond that work creates—in all its plasticity, flexibility, diversity, and demands—is the specific human dimension; it is the interface between "technology" as "tools" and "technology" as "culture" and "personality." And work neither Bucky nor Marshall ever deigned to notice.

It may be too early to come to grips with "technology" as a specific human and social dimension and as the way man does and makes. I have tried to do so in my own studies, which began about the same time—forty years ago—as Fuller moved from designing "dymaxion machines" to designing theories, and McLuhan first wrestled with the relationship of Gutenberg's technology of movable type to the curriculum of the medieval university. (What I have to say about the subject can be found in my 1970 essay volume, *Technology, Management and Society.*) I have, I realize, not gotten much beyond specific examples and generalities and certainly nowhere near a "general theory"; neither of course have Bucky Fuller and Marshall McLuhan. But at least they tried to show new and different approaches to "technology," approaches that are not "anti-technological" and may even be excessively "pro-technological," but that deal with technology as "human" and "cultural" rather than as purely "technical." The work on technology and culture is still to be done. But Bucky Fuller and Marshall McLuhan should be remembered as the forerunners, the prophets, and the seers.

Bucky Fuller and Marshall McLuhan exemplify to me the importance of being single-minded. The single-minded ones, the monomaniacs, are the only true achievers. The rest, the ones like me, may have more fun; but they fritter themselves away. The Fullers and the McLuhans carry out a "mission"; the rest of us have "interests." Whenever anything is being accomplished, it is being done, I have learned, by a monomaniac with a mission. Bucky spent forty years in the wilderness, without even the Children of Israel to follow him. Yet he never wavered in his dedication to his vision. McLuhan spent twenty-five years chasing his vision until it captured him. He too never wavered. And when their time came, both had impact.

The monomaniac is unlikely to succeed. Most leave only their bleached bones in the roadless desert. But the rest of us, with multiple interests instead of one single mission, are certain to fail and to have no impact at all.

Buckminster Fuller and Marshall McLuhan also exemplify the paradox of the prophet: his very success is failure. In one of Martin Buber's early books there is a story in which the disciple asks: "Why did the Lord let Moses die before the Children of Israel reached the Promised Land?" "Because the Lord loved Moses," the great rabbi answered. When the "Promised Land" is reached and the prophetic vision becomes commonsense, the Children of Israel should become transmuted, purified, reborn; and they stubbornly remain unregenerated and reprobates. Indeed, the moment the Prophet turns his back, they forget the vision and the Prophet and worship the Golden Calf. What to the Prophet is revealed truth, to the followers become "heuristic principle"—one insight rather than The Insight.

But worse, nothing is as powerless as a prophet whose time has come. He becomes a priest and vision turns into ritual. Or he becomes a celebrity who appears on the Late-Late Show or in the society column. The prophet whose time has come no longer shocks; he entertains.

The Professional:
Alfred Sloan

"My name is Paul Garrett," said a voice on the telephone in the late fall of 1943; "I'm in charge of public relations at General Motors and calling on behalf of the corporation's vice chairman, Mr. Donaldson Brown. Mr. Brown wonders whether you might be interested in making a study of General Motors' policies and structure for the company's top management?"

No invitation could have been more of a surprise or more welcome. Two years earlier I had finished *The Future of Industrial Man* with the conclusion that business enterprise had become the constitutive institution of industrial society and the institution within which both principles of governance and the individual's status and function had to be realized. I knew then that I needed to study a big business from within. I had never, after all, worked in one, or even in any other large organization. But my attempts to find a company that would let me do any kind of research had led nowhere.

The two years since I had finished *Future of Industrial Man* had otherwise been highly productive. When I wrote the book I was already teaching at Sarah Lawrence, in Bronxville where we then lived. I taught economics and statistics one day a week, enjoyed it, and knew that I wanted to keep on teaching. Both Harvard and Princeton had talked to me about joining their faculty. But in 1942 I accepted instead a full-time appointment at Bennington. There I was given freedom to teach whatever subjects I thought I needed learning in: political theory and American government, American history and economic history, philosophy and religion. The American Political Science Association, responding to my first book, *The End of Economic Man,* had elected me to their committee on Political-Theory Research. And I felt well launched on an academic career.

By 1943 I had established myself as a free-lance writer. I had begun to contribute regularly to *Harper's Magazine* (for more than twenty-five years, from 1940 on, I would be *Harper's* most frequent contributor, with several major articles appearing in the magazine each year). I had similarly established a close and satisfactory relationship with the *Saturday Evening Post,* then at the very peak of its circulation and popularity. After Pearl Harbor, I had gone to work for the government. But the full-time job I had been wanted for at first soon changed into a far more satisfying—and productive—part-time consulting relationship.

I neither functioned well nor felt happy as a cog in a bureaucratic machine. But to my surprise I learned that I could make a contribution as a consultant, and a far greater one than I could as a bureaucrat. If it was strenuous to commute from southern Vermont to Washington and to magazine offices in New York *(Harper's)* and Philadelphia *(Saturday Evening Post),* it was also stimulating.

My private life had developed happily. Our second child, a son, Vincent, was born in the fall of 1941, a few months before the United States entered the war. All of us liked Vermont, where we had moved in the summer of 1942. To this day Bennington, where we stayed until we moved back to the New York area seven years later, in the summer of 1949, is most nearly "home" to me of any place in the United States or indeed in the world. My parents, who had managed to get out of Austria a step ahead of Hitler's Secret Police, had joined the family (my brother was now a physician in the State of Washington) in the United States in the fall of 1938, and my father began to teach international economics at Chapel Hill in North Carolina. In 1941, at age sixty-five, he moved to Washington D.C., where he continued to teach at American University but also worked with the U.S. Tariff Commission on European economic reconstruction. And since my parents had a spacious apartment in Georgetown and my brother and I had been foresighted enough to give them one of the brand-new window air conditioners for their bedroom when they moved from North Carolina in the summer of 1941, I enjoyed the rarest of all luxuries in wartime Washington: a quiet, air-conditioned place of my own whenever I went down.

Still, I felt frustrated at my failure to do research on the political and social structure of industrial society, and on the "anatomy of industrial order." Only a few weeks before Paul Garrett called, I had decided to make one last effort to get such research going. Bennington closed for three months every winter, partly to save fuel oil in those war years, partly to allow the students to get jobs and practical work experience. And so we had rented the apartment in New York near Columbia University to enable me to spend the winter searching for a business that would permit me to study its structure and its policies, but also to work in a university library on whatever research material it might have. In preparation I had spent a good deal of time in New York during the fall months and had become increasingly discouraged. The business executives to whom I could get introductions all turned me down. Most of them, like the chairman of Westinghouse Electric, thought me a dangerous and "subversive" radical, if they understood at all what I was after. The library proved unproductive; the pitifully few books and articles that then existed in what we now call "management"—the very term was still quite uncommon—dealt either with the rank-and-file worker at the machine or with such topics as finance or salesmanship.

And so Paul Garrett's telephone call was most welcome, and within a day or two I was taken by him to see Donaldson Brown. "I've read your book, *The Future of Industrial Man,*" said Brown. "We in GM have been working on the things you're talking about—on the governance of the big organization, its structure and constitution, on the place of big business in society, and on principles of industrial order. We don't use such terms, of course; we aren't political scientists, but mostly engineers or financial men. Still, my generation in General Motors has been aware, if only dimly, that we were doing pioneering work. But we aren't going to be here much longer. Pierre DuPont, who first delineated our structure when he took over a near-bankrupt GM in 1920, is long gone; Alfred Sloan, whom Mr. DuPont put in as president of GM and who has been the architect of the corporation and its chief executive officer for twenty years, is past retirement age and only staying on for the duration of the war; and I, although much younger, intend to retire when Mr. Sloan does. The next generation takes for granted what we have been trying to do. Our policies and structure are now almost a quarter century old; there's need for a fresh look. I realize that you know nothing about the automobile business and not too much about business altogether. But your book made me think that you might be willing to look at GM as a political and social scientist, at our structure, our policies, our relationships inside and outside the company, and then report to us in top management, and especially to the able younger men who will take over from us when the war is over in another two or three years. I figure it will take you two years to do the job, working a few days a week. Would it be appropriate if we matched for that period the salary your college pays you?"

When I agreed, Brown continued: "I suggest that you start by visiting a dozen or so of our key people, just to get an impression. When you have a program worked out, I'll introduce you to Alfred Sloan. He is the most important man for the project. He is 'Mr. GM'; the rest of us are supporting cast. But there's no point meeting him until you can tell him what you intend to do."

I asked Brown whom I might see first, and he suggested Albert Bradley. "He's our chief financial officer and my successor as GM's executive vice president. He'll be chairman of GM one of these days" (indeed he became so eventually) "and he's worked more closely with Mr. Sloan and me than any of the other younger people. Get public relations to give you his biography."

The public relations people did send me the biographies of every GM officer—except Albert Bradley. "We're temporarily out," I was told. "You'll have it tomorrow." Or, "We can't find any copies. Wait until we run off another batch." Obviously there was something in Bradley's past they wanted to hide. When I mentioned this to Brown, he chuckled. "I'll give you his biography and you tell me what our public relations people don't want the world to know." And when I could not find anything that warranted being kept a secret, he said, "Don't you see that he not only went to college but worse, got a Ph.D. in economics from Michigan and, worst, *taught* at the university for a few years before I brought him here as the company's first statistician?

"Actually," Brown went on, "GM has more college-trained people in management that you customarily find in American industry, at least in the older generation. Mr. Sloan has an engineering degree from M.I.T., I have one from Virginia Polytechnic, Mr. Wilson, our president, has one from Carnegie. But we feature the people who rose from the ranks—Knudsen, the former president who now heads up the Air Force's production program as a general; Dreystadt at Cadillac, who started out as a grease monkey on a Mercedes racing team from Germany; Curtice at Buick, and Coyle at Chevrolet, who quit school in fifth or sixth grade and went to work as clerks. A Ph.D.— that's a disgrace. Bradley has lived it down, but we still prefer not to have too many people know about it." Today, thirty-five years later, GM of course hires only college graduates for managerial jobs, and stresses the number of advanced degrees its people hold. But in the forties a Ph.D.—except maybe for a chemist in a research job—was still something to hide. Bradley himself only started to wear his Phi Beta Kappa key on his watch chain after Bill Knudsen had left GM to work for the Air Force at the outbreak of World War II. "Until then, I'd only get a speech from Knudsen—who at fourteen, fresh from Denmark, had started as an apprentice machinist in a railroad shop— about spoiled rich kids who never did any honest work and who give themselves airs."

Sloan himself was proud of his record at M.I.T. He had graduated with the highest grades anyone ever earned there. He was deeply concerned with higher education, and initiated and financed a good many educational experiments, such as the first advanced management program at M.I.T. and his brother Raymond's pioneering courses in hospital administration. He left his great fortune to education: to M.I.T., to the Sloan Foundation, and to medical education and research at New York's Sloan-Kettering Cancer Hospital (which he founded together with Charles Kettering, the automotive inventor and GM vice president). Sloan also realized that the days of the self-taught man in American business—and in GM especially—were numbered, and that the future belonged to the college graduate. He therefore considered it a major responsibility of any big company to give poor but ambitious youngsters access to a college education. His favorite activity in GM, to which he gave an enormous amount of time and personal attention, was the GM Technical Institute in Flint, Michigan.

Founded originally as a school for apprentices, GM Tech had been converted by Sloan into a full-fledged engineering school. Any hourly-rated worker on the GM payroll—and only hourly-rated workers on the GM payroll—could apply and would, if admitted, go to school for half the year while working for GM the other half, with the company paying both his wages while at work and his costs while at school. "We need college-trained people," Sloan said to me; "industry is becoming too complex for people to get anywhere without formal education. We need to build open channels of educational opportunity for the youngsters who don't have well-heeled parents."

And yet whenever he was pressed to publicize GM Tech, Sloan would draw back. "I don't think we ought to give the public the impression that you need a degree to make a career in American industry," he would say. "I'd rather stress our people who started as machinists or store clerks." The only thing he suggested I ought to remove from the book that grew out of my GM study, *Concept of the Corporation* (first published in New York by John Day in 1946—English edition under the title *Big Business* published by Heinemann in London the same year)—were the two short references to GM Tech. In his own book, *My Years with General Motors* (1964), GM Tech is not mentioned at all, even though the chairmanship of the Tech board of trustees was the GM office Sloan held to the last, and the one of which he was proudest; the only ornament in his austere office was the framed announcement of his election as CM Tech's chairman.

It is hard to imagine today that less than forty years ago, higher education was still a liability rather than an asset, not only in manufacturing industry but in banking and even in government service. The prejudice against the formally schooled man as "impractical" that characterized Sloan's generation was, I think, less harmful than our present degree mania, with its prejudice against anyone who does honest work as an adolescent and young adult. Sloan would have abhorred the degree mania. But I have often thought that his refusal to offend the prejudices of his generation and to publicize CM Tech is in some measure responsible for our present overemphasis on degrees and on staying out of work as long as possible. American industry was, in those years, ready to follow his lead had he but chosen to give it. We might today have a healthier balance between working and going to school, had Sloan only been willing to have GM Tech publicized as a model.

Brown did not, at first, think of my writing a book. Far from it. Nor did I. But after my first meetings with his associates, I came back to him and said, "Your colleagues don't understand what you want me to do and see no point to it. But one after the other has suggested that a book on GM might be a good idea. Why can't we tell them that this is our intention? You can always veto publication." "I've never lied to my associates," Brown replied, "and I'm not going to start now. I don't think you'll find a publisher—I don't see anyone interested in a book on management. But if telling my associates that you're writing a book will help the project, then you're going to write one. As for our having veto power over its publication, I haven't the slightest intention of becoming a censor. We do have a duty under our government contracts to make sure that you don't publish any defense secrets—after all, we are the country's largest defense contractor. And we'll tell you if you make factual mistakes. But that's all." And that was indeed all. Neither Brown nor anyone else at GM tried to dictate to me what to write or not to write, even when disagreeing violently with my views.

I shared Brown's skepticism about the possibility of a saleable book. So did my publisher. Such few books on management as there were had been published pretty much for private circulation: as reprints of lectures, for instance, as was Chester Barnard's 1938 *The Functions of the Executive,* or as monographs for small professional societies, like Mary Parker Follett's pioneering papers on leadership and conflict-resolution. There was not then, it seemed, even a management public for a book on management; indeed most managers did not realize that they were practicing management. The general public, while very interested in how the rich made their money, had never heard of management. A book on such esoteric subjects as organization and structure, the development of managers, and the role of foreman and middle manager, was surely going to go unread.

The only dissenter from this appraisal among my friends was Lewis Jones, an economist by background and the president of Bennington College at the time. I had to tell him, of course, of my accepting an assignment from GM. Lewis was all for it. "This is the work you need to do now," he said, "and the book will be a success." He was right. *Concept of the Corporation* became an immediate success upon publication, has been reprinted many times, and is still being bought, read, and used. Yet Jones was not at all sure that I should publish the work. "You're launched," he said, "on a highly promising academic career, either as an economist or as a political scientist. A book on a business corporation that treats it as a political and social institution will harm you in both fields."

Jones was right in this too. When the book came out, neither economist nor political scientist knew what to make of it and both have ever since viewed me with dark suspicion. The reviewer in the *American Economic Review* was baffled by a book on *business* that was not "micro-economics" and complained that it offered no insights into pricing theory or the allocation of scarce resources. The highly sympathetic reviewer in *The American Political Science Review* ended by saying: "It is to be hoped that this promising young scholar

will soon devote his considerable talents to a more serious subject";
and when the American Political Science Association next met, I was
not reelected to the Committee on Political-Theory Research. Even
today, thirty years later, economists as a rule are not willing to look
upon the business enterprise except in economic terms, and political
scientists, by and large, confine themselves to dealing with overtly
"governmental" institutions and the "political process" in government.

What the book did, however, was to help establish the discipline
of management—a subject that earlier had not been known or taught.
Concept of the Corporation, for better or worse, set off the "management boom" of the last thirty years. This was largely luck; I happened
to be there first. But the main concerns of the discipline of management: organization and social responsibility; the relationship between
individual and organization; the function of top management and the
decision-making process; the development of managers; labor relations, community relations, and customer relations—even the environment—are all treated, many of them for the first time, in *Concept
of the Corporation.* Now, a generation later, we even accept the
book's assertion that "management" is not peculiar to business enterprise but is the specific organ of all institutions of modern society, with
business only one, though a highly visible, example. Now we increasingly teach "management of institutions," and the "Master in Business
Administration" (M.B.A.) is increasingly being accepted as preparation for professional work in government, hospital, research administration, labor union, school, and university, as it became accepted
around 1950 as a preparation for work in business enterprise. Now, a
generation later, we are ready to accept the premise that originally led
me to write the book.

Of the scores of executives whom I met during my work with
General Motors, no two were alike. The main impression that has
remained with me is of the diversity of personalities, characters, and
idiosyncrasies, in complete contrast to the myth of the "organization
man" with his gray-flannel conformity. But of all these characters—
some very colorful indeed—three or four stand out in my memory
even thirty years later.

One of them was Donaldson Brown himself. "He is the brains of
GM, but doesn't speak any known language," was how one of the
senior operating people put it. He had for years been GM's main ideas

man, had designed, for instance, the financial and statistical controls that held GM together, the policies for overseas expansion, the GM compensation and bonus plans, and the simple but extremely effective methods for selecting and developing managers. Each of these was a "first" at the time, without precedent in business or government and found in no book or theory. Yet while universally admired throughout GM and known as a truly wise man, most GM managers tried to have as little to do with him as possible. They simply could not understand a word Brown was saying. He completely depended on Sloan to translate him. He knew this. It underlay his decision to retire when Alfred Sloan did, even though he was only in his fifties. Actually, he was quite easy to understand once one caught on to his habits. If one waited twenty minutes or so, Brown would come to the point—with clarity and simplicity. But first he would recite, like the very worst of Germanic professors, all the footnotes, qualifications, and exceptions in a language that was half mathematical equations and half social science jargon, without any indication where he was headed.

Brown was almost pathetically grateful to me for my willingness to listen him out. He soon got into the habit of calling me in on Friday afternoons every six weeks or so, discussing my work with me, and then excusing himself for a few minutes to disappear into his washroom. When he came back, he had changed from an ultra-conservative business suit with high-collared starched shirt into what he called his "farmer's outfit"—sloppy tweeds, a woolen lumberman's shirt and the filthiest fisherman's hat with trout flies stuck in the hatband. "I'm going down to the farm," he'd say happily, "but there's just enough time for a quick drink with you." He'd mix himself a very stiff triple martini, unbend, and begin to tell wonderful stories about his youth on a rundown Maryland tobacco farm, wacky characters in his family, and the early history of General Motors.

Brown had been born the son of an old but impoverished family of tobacco planters on the Maryland east shore, just across the bay from the DuPonts in Delaware. The Browns looked down upon the DuPonts as "upstarts" and "traders." The DuPonts, in turn, looked down upon the Browns as "poor white trash." During the Civil War the DuPonts were already the biggest industrialists on the Delaware-Maryland seashore. They had a strong anti-slavery tradition inherited from the first DuPont to come to America, one of the leading *Philosophes* of the French Enlightenment. And they led the pro-Union forces in the mid-Atlantic states and became the main munitions makers for the Northern armies. The tobacco-planting Browns, who for 200 years had been the seashore's first family, were Southern Secessionists and tried hard to make Maryland join the Confederacy. So there was mutual loathing on both sides and a bitter family feud. Yet when Donaldson Brown graduated as a chemical engineer, the only job he could find was at the DuPont Company—"though I had to promise my father to quit as soon as I could find other work." He rose rapidly. During World War I he was in charge of building the new DuPont plants to make munitions, first for the Allies and then for the U.S. war effort. Then he designed DuPont's famous financial controls with their return-on-investment formula, still the most widely used system of managerial economics in the world. He was the first man to organize sales statistics and sales forecasting, long-range plans, especially for capital investment, and divisional budgets.

At this point his boss—not a DuPont—called him in and said, "Don, you realize, don't you, that you have to make up your mind whether you want to stay with the company or not?" "Does that mean that the company wants to get rid of me?" asked Brown. "Won't you young people ever learn?" said his exasperated boss. "Look, you're headed for a top management job in this company, maybe the very top. But no one gets into the top management of this company, you young fool, unless he's married to one of THEM," and the boss gave Brown a sheet listing the twenty-eight unmarried or widowed DuPont daughters, granddaughters, and nieces. " 'They' don't care which you marry, as long as it is one of those . . . and *soon*." "The trouble," Brown said to me, "was that I and one of the girls on the sheet, Greta DuPont, had been secretly married for more than a year, and neither of us had dared tell our respective families. We finally had to—Greta got pregnant. But the DuPonts never forgave me for marrying the right girl at the wrong time. 'What can you expect from a Brown?' one of their elders said to me angrily. 'They've always been sneaks.' And instead of promoting me, they exiled me to Detroit as soon as Pierre DuPont took over the presidency of a floundering and near-bankrupt GM." "And your parents?" I asked. "My father refused to meet my wife for quite a long time. Finally my mother said to him, 'Be reasonable. These days even English dukes marry for money. And at least Don doesn't work for these unspeakable DuPonts any more.' "

On a Monday, when Brown came back from two days of fishing or planting trees in Maryland, he would again be the pompous, complicated, aloof "brains" who didn't speak any known language and never took a drink throughout the week until that triple martini late Friday afternoon.

Where Brown fitted no stereotype, Marvin Coyle, the head of Chevrolet, seemed at first to be all stereotype—the stereotype of the flint-hearted bookkeeper. He looked like a stage caricature of an Irish cop (his father had been one in fact). He was big and white as a grub, ham-fisted and hard, with small, mean eyes. He was a martinet who could be very rough on subordinates. He always preached with great unction. Once when I was sitting in his office listening to his favorite sermon on the beatitudes of decentralization, the teleprinter in the corner of the office next to a big brass spittoon began to yammer. "Pay no attention," Coyle said. "It's only the Kansas City plant manager letting me know he's going out to lunch," and continued the sermon on the complete freedom enjoyed by local managers. But Coyle had thought about decentralization whereas everybody else took it for granted. He had realized that it was not, as Sloan asserted (and my book repeated) the answer to every problem of industrial structure. In the course of my GM work I had come to understand that Chevrolet itself, while half of GM, a giant enterprise in its own right, and larger than all but a handful of independent American businesses, was completely centralized. I had said so—and Coyle was quick to resent this as criticism, and eager to show me the error of my ways. But at the same time he also pointed out that decentralization, as GM had developed it—the principle I now call federal decentralization—applies only where a part of a company can be organized as a distinct business, with its distinct markets and with clear profit and loss responsibility. And Chevrolet, despite its size, was one indivisible profit center, or at least its passenger-car business was (its truck business had been organized as a separate decentralized business all along). Coyle realized that Chevrolet had to develop different concepts and structures to obtain the benefits of decentralization—without being able to use decentralization itself. "For efficiency, it should be enough that we have to compete with Buick and Oldsmobile and Pontiac, let alone Ford and Chrysler," he said; "but when it comes to developing and testing people, it's no accident that so many of the GM top executives come out of the smaller divisions and so few out of Chevrolet. There we have to simulate decentralization, and I don't know how."

General Motors then, and for many years thereafter, was contemptuous of outside courses for managers and of manager development altogether. It was almost an article of the faith that decentralization by itself, coupled with systematic placement of people within GM, would develop future managers. Coyle disagreed. He was among the first in American manufacturing industry to use outside sources to help young managers develop themselves: organized reading programs, university courses, seminars, and lectures. Though temperamentally a complete autocrat, he pushed participative management in Chevrolet, referred problems to task forces of younger managers down the line for study and recommendation, and brought managers from his plants and sales districts into headquarters to advise him. And he would sit and discipline himself not to open his mouth until everyone in the room had spoken.

Concept of the Corporation is often credited with starting the worldwide vogue for "decentralization" or, as the Japanese and Europeans call it, "divisionalization." The first company to reorganize itself on a decentralized basis was Ford, where *Concept of the Corporation* became the official text. When young Henry Ford took over from his senile grandfather, he studied my book, which had just come out, and then began to bring in executives from GM—starting with Ernest Breech as chairman and, for several years, chief executive officer—in order to revive a company that had been going downhill for thirty years and was at death's door. "Decentralization" on the GM model rapidly became the stock-in-trade of the American management consulting firms as they branched out worldwide in the fifties.

But by then I was already working on the specifications and limitations of the GM type of decentralization, and on developing alternatives for the very large number of organizations—businesses, but public service institutions like universities or government agencies as well—where we can only "simulate" decentralization. In *Concept of the Corporation* I presented federal decentralization as *the* answer, and that was how Pierre DuPont, Alfred Sloan, Donaldson Brown, and their associates and disciples in GM saw it. It is indeed the best answer where it fits; but it is only one answer and does not fit everyone. Marvin Coyle, I am convinced, would not think much of the alternative answers I have been able to develop. He would still snarl at me as he did a quarter century ago—he always tried to sound like the sheriff in an old-style Grade B Western: *"You* tell me how I could decentralize Chevrolet before you dare criticize." But I have come grudgingly, for Coyle was not a lovable man, to respect his intellectual honesty and his willingness to say unpopular things and ask disagreeable questions.

No greater contrast to Coyle could have been imagined than Nicholas Dreystadt, who was appointed general manager of Chevrolet when Coyle retired a few months after I had finished my GM study. When I met Dreystadt he was however still head of Cadillac, where he had been for more than thirty years. Where Coyle was icy, Dreystadt was warm. Where Coyle was unctuous, Dreystadt was droll. Where Coyle was feared, Dreystadt was beloved. And where Coyle was impersonal, Nick Dreystadt was concerned with people, saw them, cared for them, and understood them as individuals.

Coyle was always dressed in a tight blue serge suit and policeman's black shoes. Nick Dreystadt wore old tweed jackets with holes from his pipe's embers all over them. His secretary kept a few pairs of shoes in her closet since he often arrived at work with shoes that didn't match. He had come to the United States from his native South Germany at thirteen as the youngest apprentice on a Mercedes racing team, and he still spoke English with the broadest Swabian accent. He was happiest on the factory floor showing a machinist how to repair a tool or a foreman how to straighten out some production snarl. Yet this untidy, unschooled mechanic was generally conceded to be the ablest of the younger executives in GM, was known as the man who had built single-handedly GM's most distinct and most profitable business, and was considered almost certain to become GM's president within another ten years. Instead, he died of cancer of the throat six months after taking over Chevrolet in 1946, when only forty-eight and in apparently perfect health.

Dreystadt was Cadillac's service manager when the Depression hit, and likely to stay forever in middle management. Chevrolet did all right despite the Depression. But the three medium-priced GM cars—Buick, Oldsmobile, and Pontiac—had to be merged into one division for several years; there wasn't enough business to carry three managerial overheads. Cadillac could not sell its high-priced cars at all and was about to be liquidated. The only question was whether it would be abandoned altogether or whether the nameplate should be kept alive, with the majority of the GM executive committee, including Alfred Sloan and Donaldson Brown, in favor of giving up. It was then that Nick Dreystadt—whom none of the members had ever met —gate-crashed the meeting of the executive committee, pleaded to be given ten minutes, and presented a plan for making Cadillac profitable again within eighteen months. And he did so by marketing it as a "status symbol." In charge of Cadillac service throughout the country,

Dreystadt had come to realize that the Cadillac was the most popular car in the very small community of wealthy Negroes. An amazing number of big new Cadillacs brought in for service were owned by black entertainers, black boxers, black doctors, black realtors. It was company policy not to sell Cadillacs to Negroes—the Cadillac salesman aimed at the white "prestige" market. But the wealthy Negro wanted a Cadillac so badly that he paid a substantial premium to a white man to front for him in buying one. Dreystadt had investigated this unexpected phenomenon and found that a Cadillac was the only success symbol the affluent black could buy; he had no access to good housing, to luxury resorts, or to any other of the outward signs of worldly success. And so Dreystadt, in the depths of the Depression, set out to save Cadillac by developing the Negro market—and sold enough cars to make the Cadillac division break even by 1934.

Then he went on to make Cadillac into a moneymaker. Cadillac had sold a great many cars before the Depression, and at high prices, but it had never been profitable. It made luxury cars but made them by a luxury process, by hand, one at a time, and with high labor costs. Dreystadt saw no reason why the high quality of the car could not be maintained under mass production. "Quality is design and tooling, inspection and service," he said; "it's not inefficiency." Within three years Cadillac had become GM's most profitable car, and the market grew steadily. Dreystadt spent money on design, more money on tools, and the most money on quality control and service. But he did not spend a penny more on production than was spent on the low-priced Chevrolet. "Mass production," Dreystadt once said to me, "is not what Mr. Ford meant. It isn't the assembly line; that's a tool. Mass production is using one's brain and working smarter." Ten years after Dreystadt's death—and probably without ever having heard of him—Dreystadt's first employer, back in his native Swabia, then found the same formula. Mercedes-Benz, until the mid-fifties a small, specialty producer of hand-made expensive cars yielding little profit, made itself into a mass producer of luxury cars yielding a very high profit through design, tooling, quality control, and service combined with mass methods of production—the very policy that Dreystadt, in the mid-thirties, had used to make Cadillac into the American automobile industry's leader.

What made Dreystadt stand out was his attitude toward "persons": "Don't say people," he would object, "say men and women." Under the union contract, a new employe was on probation for ninety days; unless rejected for cause he then became a permanent employe. By the mid-forties, Cadillac was a huge business employing at least 8,000 people. Yet no foreman at Cadillac was allowed to reject a new employe except with Dreystadt's approval. Again and again foremen would come up and say: "Mr. Dreystadt, this man doesn't come up to our output standards." "How does he treat his tools?" Dreystadt would ask: "And his fellow workers? And you?" And when the foreman said, "He's all right, but he can't do the job," Dreystadt would say, "We don't hire men for ninety days here; we hire them for thirty years. During these thirty years he'll surely get up to the job standards if he has self-respect and respect for the tools and his fellow workers."

At the same time Dreystadt was willing to tackle the union and fire a long-time employe who became sloppy or who treated his fellow workers with contempt or discourtesy; even a militant shop steward yielded to Dreystadt in such a case without too much argument. He was forever fighting GM's personnel department for confining their training to new employes and stopping when they had reached performance norms. "That's when men and women begin to be able to learn," said Dreystadt. And he argued with both union and personnel department for what we today would call job enlargement, job rotation, and continuous learning. He was the only general manager in GM who put his ablest and most promising younger man into Personnel, which everybody else considered a dead-end job: "Jim Roche is good enough to be head of GM one of these days," he said; "and then he'll need to know how to deal with men and women, and not just because he has read a book." Jim Roche, who was Cadillac's personnel manager under Dreystadt, did indeed become chairman of GM twenty years later.

While I did my study at GM, Dreystadt—against the advice of GM's top management—bid on the nastiest defense job around, the production of a high-precision item (I believe it was a new bombsight, and the first one to use electronics). Everybody knew that the work demanded highly skilled mechanics. There was then absolutely no labor available in Detroit, let alone highly skilled mechanics. "It's got to be done," Dreystadt said; "and if we at Cadillac can't do it, who can?" The only labor to be found in Detroit were superannuated Negro prostitutes. To everybody's horror Nick Dreystadt hired some 2,000 of them. "But hire their madams too," he said. "They know how to manage the women." Very few of the women could read and the job required following long instructions. "We don't have time to teach

them to read," said Nick, "and few would learn to anyhow." So he
went to the workbench and himself machined a dozen of the bomb-
sights. When he knew how to do it, he had a movie camera take a film
of the process. He mounted the film frames separately on a projector
and synchronized them with a flow diagram in which a red light went
on to show the operator what she had already done, a green light for
what she had to do next, and a yellow light to show what to make sure
of before taking the next step. By now this is standard procedure for
a great many assembly processes; it was Dreystadt who invented it.
Within a few weeks these unskilled illiterates were turning out better
work and in larger quantity than highly skilled machinists had done
before. Throughout GM, and indeed Detroit, Cadillac's "red-light district" provoked a good deal of ribald comment. But Dreystadt quickly
stopped it. "These women," he said, "are my fellow workers and
yours. They do a good job and respect their work. Whatever their past,
they are entitled to the same respect as any one of our associates." The
union asked him to promise that the women would go as soon as
replacements could be found; the Automobile Workers Union of those
days was led, especially on the local level, largely by male white Fundamentalist Southerners, who did not even want white women as
fellow workers, let alone Negro prostitutes. Dreystadt knew very well
that he would have to lay off most of the women after the war when
the veterans returned and demanded their old jobs back. But though
derided as a "nigger-lover" and a "whoremonger," he tried hard to get
union agreement to save at least a few of the jobs the women held.
"For the first time in their lives," he said, "these poor wretches are
paid decently, work in decent conditions, and have some rights. And
for the first time they have some dignity and self-respect. It's our duty
to save them from being again rejected and despised." When the war
came to an end and the women had to be discharged, many tried to
commit suicide and quite a few succeeded. Nick Dreystadt sat in his
office with his head in his hands, almost in tears. "God forgive me," he
said, "I have failed these poor souls."

Everyone in GM was courteous to me, willing to see me, open to
whatever questions I might have, and altogether cooperative—it was
enough that I was sponsored by Donaldson Brown. But only one man
in senior management was genuinely interested in what I tried to do.
This man alone paid any attention to my recommendations and actually converted some of them into GM policy and action: Charles E.

Wilson, the company's president and chief operating officer. Wilson was also the one senior executive at GM who kept in touch with me beyond the conclusion of my study, through his years as successor to Alfred Sloan as GM's chief executive officer (though Sloan remained chairman well beyond Wilson's tenure) and, though less and less often, during his four years as Secretary of Defense in President Eisenhower's cabinet.

I did not meet Wilson until I was well launched into my study. When I started he was on sick leave. As the company's chief operating officer, he had been in charge of the conversion to defense production beginning on Pearl Harbor Day. For more than two years he had never taken a day off, and rarely spent even a night away from office or plant. By Christmas 1943 every single war contract General Motors had taken on was in production and on schedule, if not ahead of it, and GM was turning out three times as much war materiel as anyone in Washington had thought possible. Then Wilson collapsed— a "circulatory episode" was the official term for what was probably a stroke coupled with total exhaustion. He never fully recovered. When he was in the Eisenhower cabinet, the cartoonists had fun with the holes in the soles of his shoes. But they were there on purpose. The blood circulation in his feet had become permanently impaired and he had to cut holes in his shoes to be able to wear them at all. He suffered from blinding headaches and there was a slight speech impairment—he tended to slur his words whenever he got tired.

Wilson had been ordered by his doctor to take a six-month rest. But he came back after three months, and one of his first acts was to send for me. "Tell me about your assignment," he began. I had just at that time—maybe in late March—decided on a drastic change in my project, though I had not yet told anyone in GM about it: I was going to stress GM's "unfinished business," the organization of individual work and job, and employe relations. Wilson caught fire. "In the three months I've been idle, I've been thinking about GM's future," he said, "and I've come to the same conclusions. To design the structure and develop the constitutional principles for the big business enterprise was the great achievement of the founding fathers of GM, the last generation. To develop citizenship and community is the task of the next generation. We are, so to speak, going to be the Jeffersonians to Mr. Sloan's Federalists. Tell me what your main conclusions are so far." I mentioned two: the need, as I saw it, to develop a form of guaranteed income for the employe without destroying personal mobility and flexibility of labor costs; and the need to develop what I later came to call the "self-governing plant community," that is, the assumption of managerial responsibility by the individual employe, the work team, and the employe group alike for the structure of the individual job, for the performance of major tasks, and for the management of such community affairs as shift schedules, vacation schedules, overtime assignments, industrial safety, and, above all, employe benefits. I had been impressed by the way in which, in wartime work, the individual work team had taken over responsibility for the job and organized itself as a group to perform it, in the aircraft-engine plants, for instance, which GM was then running, or in the manufacture of complex firing and calibrating devices. There simply were neither enough industrial engineers nor enough trained supervisors available; so the workers—many of them untrained and altogether new to industry—had to be given responsibility and autonomy. In many cases this had resulted in superior productivity and performance. I felt strongly that we should not allow ourselves to lose this achievement with the return to peacetime conditions.

Of all my work on management and "the anatomy of industrial order," I consider my ideas for the self-governing plant community and for the responsible worker to be both the most important and the most original. But managements have tended to reject these ideas as an "encroachment" on their prerogatives. And labor unions have been outright hostile: they are convinced that they need a visible and identifiable "boss," who can then be fought as "the enemy." Yet what was achieved in these areas in World War II went way beyond anything that is being trumpeted today as a breakthrough, such as the highly publicized attempt to "replace" the assembly line at some Swedish automobile companies. This actually goes much less far than assembly-line practices that have been standard in American industry for thirty years, not to mention the responsibility factory-floor work teams have assumed routinely for forty years at IBM, hardly a particularly "permissive" company. And in World War II neither management nor the labor union suffered any impairment of authority, prestige, or prosperity. Naïvely, I fully expected my recommendations of a responsible self-governing "plant community" to be the most convincing part of my GM conclusions. But C. E. Wilson was the only one among top management people in any country ever to pay attention to them. Insofar as we in the United States have made progress toward income security for employes and toward a self-governing plant-community, we owe it largely to Wilson's receptivity to "heretical" ideas.

"We did," he told me, "work on guaranteed annual wages for GM workers way back in 1935" (Alfred Sloan in *My Years with General Motors* has since publicized some of these early studies). "We gave up. We could not work out a meaningful guarantee that wouldn't bankrupt any business, even GM. You have convinced me that we need to try again." Out of our discussions, and the work his staff did as a result, came ultimately the scheme now known as Supplementary Unemployment Benefits (SUB), under which workers in most American mass-production industries are guaranteed essentially their full income for any period of unemployment to be expected short of a major long-term depression. "When are you going to put this into effect?" I asked Wilson as soon as he had worked out a full plan—it must have been in early 1947. "*I* am never going to put it into effect," he replied. "I grudgingly yield to a union demand for it when I have to." I thought I understood: "You mean your associates in GM management wouldn't go along with it unless they had to?" "No," said Wilson, "my associates will accept my lead in labor relations; they have learned to trust me ever since I was proven right in the sit-down strikes. But the union leaders won't go along unless it's a 'demand' we resist and they 'win.'"

"Have you ever been a union member?" he went on. I shook my head. "Well, I was," he said, "and a union leader too, and I grew up in a union leader's home. My father came over from Wales as a toolmaker and organized a toolmakers' local in Pittsburgh. We were all Socialists and Eugene Debs was my hero—he still is. I was almost thrown out of college for agitating for him in the 1912 election; and because I was a dangerous radical, I couldn't at first find work as an engineer after graduation but had to work as a patternmaker myself, and became the business agent for the patternmakers' local. I'm still a member," he pointed to a framed membership card that stood among the memorabilia on his cluttered desk, the only thing from his GM desk other than family photographs that he later took with him to his office as Secretary of Defense in the Pentagon. "If it's to be of any value to a union, it's got to be a hard-won gain. No union can believe that what management offers can be anything but harmful to the union and its members as well. Sure, I'll plant the idea—I know enough UAW people. But we'll yield to them, after a great show of reluctance, only when it's worth something to them. The time will come." (When it did come, in 1955, and the UAW announced SUB as a great victory, Wilson—by then in the Pentagon—phoned me and said: "You've finally earned the fee you got ten years ago to make your GM study.")

"If you understand unions so well," I said, "why doesn't GM have better union relations?" For then as now the "poor union relations" in the automobile industry were complained of by everyone. "We have the union relations *I* designed," said Wilson, "and they are right for our industry and our union. They suit both of us." When I looked skeptical, he added, "The test of labor relations isn't rhetoric. The test is results. We lose fewer days to strikes than any other major company in this country or in any other unionized country. We have greater continuity of union leadership. And both the union and we get the things the country, the company, and the union need: high discipline, high productivity, high wages, and high employment security. A union is a political organization and needs adversary relations and victorious battles. And a company is an economic organization and needs productivity and discipline. At GM we get both—and to get both we need the union relations we have."

Yet Wilson was not altogether satisfied either with the union relations in America generally or in the automobile industry. "One serious problem to which I don't have the answer," he said, "is how to make all that talent in union leadership fully effective. Walter Reuther [the long-term president of UAW] is the ablest man in American industry. He, not I, should be the next chief executive of GM, and he'd love it. In fact, if Walter had only been born a few years earlier and gone to work before 1927 when the near-collapse of the Ford Motor Company destroyed opportunities for machinists to move into management, he'd be president of GM today. Yet under our union management ritual he's blocked. If we can't solve that problem, we won't have Walter Reuthers in union leadership in twenty years. The able ones will go to college and become cost accountants and members of management, and the incompetents will inherit the union"—a prophecy time has unfortunately fully borne out.

Wilson was particularly interested in the employe's job and in the plant community. "What you are telling me, Mr. Drucker," he said, "is that we in this country have succeeded in making manual work productive, well paid and middle class. And now we have to make the manual worker as effective as a citizen as he has become as a producer. Let's find out what that means." As soon as the war was over, Wilson designed a major research project to find out what areas might be the truly important ones to the GM worker. "You tell me that you know what these areas are," he said; "and the things you mention sound plausible to me. I have learned, however, to find out rather than be bright." At first he wanted to have a big employe survey and was told that he could expect a 5 percent response. "That's not enough," he said. So he and his staff people came up with the idea of a contest— "My Job and Why I Like It"—with a lot of small prizes and outside judges (I was one; George Taylor, former chairman of the War Labor Board, was another) to award them. The contest fully proved Wilson's and my assumptions. Indeed it proved all the findings that have since been made in industrial psychology, such as those of Rensis Likert at Michigan or of Frederick Herzberg on why people work. It showed that the extrinsic rewards for work—pay or promotion, for instance— are what Herzberg has called "hygiene factors." Dissatisfaction with them is a powerful de-motivator and dis-incentive; but satisfaction with them is not particularly important and an incentive to few. Achievement, contribution, responsibility, these are the powerful motivators and incentives.

The contest also showed that employes want to find satisfaction in their job and work, and that they resent nothing so much as not to be allowed to do the work they know they are being paid for, whatever it may be. They want to be able to respect the company they work for, its management and the supervisor, and—the assertion of mine Wilson was most skeptical about—they do not view allegiance to union and allegiance to the company as mutually exclusive. They want to belong to both, see the need for both (only for different purposes), and want to respect both. Wilson considered the "My Job" Contest the crowning achievement of his career at GM, and in a sense it was. Nothing else he and GM did was nearly as successful. Almost two-thirds of GM's employes, or around 200,000 people, participated. But its very success killed the contest. Not only could no one work up 200,000 essay entries, although every judge read several thousands, with a big staff at GM coding and tabulating the rest. The union got thoroughly alarmed at the contest's success, attacked it hotly, and made dropping any further work on it a condition of accepting a wage settlement without a strike in 1948.

I do not know what became of all the essay entries but GM, much to Wilson's chagrin, had to store away and forget what is the richest research material on employe attitudes and worker values ever brought together. Wilson did not give up altogether. He persuaded

Alfred Sloan to set up a separate vice president for employe relations. I was told, though not by him, that Wilson had recommended me for the job. But when he left for Washington a few years later, the employe relations vice presidency—to which the union had objected all along—was quietly abolished.

In our first meeting, Wilson asked: "What do you think of profit-sharing?" "The idea is great," I answered; "but profits are much too small to be meaningful to the employe. They amount at most to one-tenth of the wage he gets, and that's so negligible as to make him feel insulted rather than rewarded. And whenever profits go down—as they always do, sooner or later—the employes, and even more their wives, feel cheated." "That's exactly what I found out, way back around 1916," said Wilson, "when I introduced profit-sharing into the first plant I managed, a small electrical appliance plant in Dayton that later became part of GM. But there must be a way. It makes too much sense." I suggested that maybe we could find an employe need that was commensurate to the available profits, considering that profits altogether rarely run to more than one-tenth or one-twelfth of the wage bill. But I didn't know what the benefit could be.

A few months later Wilson asked me to meet him in New York. "I've thought about your suggestion that profit-sharing has to be applied where it can make an impact. What about employe pensions? There 4 or 5 percent can make a difference, and social security isn't going to provide adequate employe pensions for people whose lifetime wages have been as high as those of automobile workers are likely to be." "How will you invest those funds?" I asked. "In government bonds?" "Oh no," he said, "in the stock market. Altogether they should be invested the way a prudent financial manager would invest them." "But that would make the employes, within twenty-five years, the owners of American business," I came back. "Exactly what they should be," said Wilson, "and what they must be. For the income distribution in this country surely means that no one else can own American industry unless it be the government."

Wilson waited until employe pensions became a union demand. But when they did, in 1950, he was ready. There had been, of course, employe pension funds that invested in common shares: the one at Sears Roebuck, started in 1916, owned, by 1950, one-third or more of Sears Roebuck common stock. But Wilson's pension fund at GM was the first that invested according to sound principles of financial management, and that meant in the shares of any promising company *except* those of the company that employs the future pensioner, i.e., the company in which he already has a big financial stake through his job.

I was not convinced, and said so. When Wilson put through his pension plan in 1950, I published an article in *Harper's Magazine* in which I sharply criticized the "Mirage of Pensions," as I called it. I pointed out that company pensions would restrain individual mobility, and that vesting them, i.e., giving employes a vested right to their pensions, would make the pension charges unbearably high. I pointed out that such a plan would give the employes of rich and successful companies an unfair advantage over the people employed in small, poor, and unsuccessful businesses. And I argued—I thought cogently —in favor of a universal government pension plan based on progressive taxation. All of my arguments have, I submit, been proven right . . . but irrelevant. Wilson's scheme prevailed. By now the United States had 500,000 private pension plans. They have all the problems I anticipated. But they also control the American economy, own one-third of the equity capital of America's big and medium-sized businesses, and will in the not-so-distant future make employe control a reality by giving employes or their representatives a major voice on the pension fund board.* The pension funds may well go bankrupt, as I predicted in the *Harper's* article of 1950; but they already have made America's employes into America's capitalists. And that, I suspect, rather than employe pensions, was what Charlie Wilson—patternmakers' business agent, Eugene Debs Socialist, president of GM, and arch-capitalist—had in mind all along.

No matter how able or interesting these GM executives were, it became increasingly clear as I talked to them that they were indeed only "supporting cast." The "superstar" was Alfred Sloan. The GM executives I met—Brown and Coyle, Dreystadt and Wilson, and many others—were self-confident, opinionated, outspoken. But when they mentioned Sloan's name, their voices changed; and when they said, "Mr. Sloan agrees with this," they made it sound as if they were quoting Holy Writ. Also, in telling me their own personal histories, each one recounted an episode where Mr. Sloan had personally made the difference, and where his insight or his kindness had changed their

---

*See my recent book, *The Unseen Revolution: How Pension Fund Socialism Came to America* (New York: Harper & Row, 1976).

lives. Typical, perhaps, was the story Dreystadt told: "When I gate-crashed the executive committee way back in 1932 and pleaded to be given a chance to save Cadillac, one of the members said, 'Mr. Drey-stadt, you realize, don't you, that if you fail there won't be a job for you at GM?' 'Of course I do, sir,' I said. 'But I don't,' said Mr. Sloan quite sharply. 'If you fail, Mr. Dreystadt, there isn't going to be a job for you at Cadillac. There won't be a Cadillac. But as long as there is a GM, and as long as I run it, there'll always be a job for a man who takes responsibility, who takes initiative, who has courage and imagi-nation. Mr. Dreystadt,' Mr. Sloan went on, *'you* worry about the future of Cadillac. Your future at GM is *my* worry.' "

But when I first met Alfred Sloan I was disappointed. A slight man of medium height, and with a long horse face, wearing a large hearing aid, he seemed singularly unprepossessing. He had white hair that still showed a tinge of red, and the temper that proverbially goes with red hair. He was famous for his tantrums. His gravel voice held a strong Brooklyn accent—he had been born in New Haven, Connecticut, but his family had moved to Brooklyn when he was ten.

But he immediately showed the qualities that gave him un-challenged moral authority within his powerful, aggressive, and in-dependent team. "You have probably heard, Mr. Drucker," he said, "that I didn't initiate your study. I saw no point to it. My as-sociates overruled me. It is therefore my duty to make sure that you can do the best job you are capable of. Come and see me any time I can be of help. Ask me any question you think appropriate. But above all, let me make sure that you get all the information you can possibly use. I've thought through what you'll need. We've never done it before and shall never do it again, but you need to sit in on a good many meetings of our top committees to find out how we work and what makes this corporation run. I've cleared this for you. Of course, I expect you not to divulge any confidential matter we discuss in our committees; after all, you are concerned with how we operate and not with what we decide. And, Mr. Drucker," he concluded, "I am not going to tell you what to study and what to recommend to us. But I shall tell you one thing: Gen-eral Motors has thirty-five vice presidents. They are all quite differ-ent. But there isn't one among them who cannot make any con-ceivable compromise without a consultant's help. You tell us what you think is right. Don't worry about *who* is right. Don't worry whether this or that member of our management—including myself—will like your recommendations or conclusions. I'll tell you fast enough if what you think is right seems to me to be wrong."

He was as good as his word. He never accepted my study, never thought it worthwhile, but went all out to support it and to enable me to do the best possible job. If I had listened to his advice and not made compromises, I might even have had an impact on GM. But I was too green and inexperienced. And so I made concessions to deflect what I thought might be Marvin Coyle's objections, and only earned Coyle's contempt. Or I emphasized points on which I thought to have the support of people like Dreystadt or Wilson, only to find that they couldn't care less.

Sloan did indeed have me attend the meetings of the top committees on a fairly regular schedule. After each meeting he took me into his office and asked me whether I had any questions or comments. I once said to him, "But Mr. Sloan, you couldn't possibly care about the objections I might have. After all, you've fifty or more years of experience." "That's precisely why I do care and should care," he said; "I have been top man for fifty years and am used to having my own way. I'd better find out whether I'm an Emperor without clothes, and no one inside GM is likely to tell me."

During the years in which I attended the meetings of GM's top committees, the company made basic decisions on postwar policies such as capital investments, overseas expansion, the balance between automotive businesses, accessory businesses, and nonautomotive businesses, union relations and financial structure. The wartime operations, which had taken the bulk of top management's time before 1943, had become routine. Sloan and his associates were free to turn to GM's postwar future. Yet I soon realized that a disproportionate amount of time was taken up with decisions on people rather than decisions on policy. Moreover Mr. Sloan, while actively involved in the decisions on policy, left to others the chairmanship of whatever committee dealt with a specific policy area. But in any decision on people he was in the chair.

Once the committee spent hours discussing the work and assignment of a position way down the line—as I remember it, the position of master mechanic in a small accessory division. As we went out, I turned to him and said, "Mr. Sloan, how can you afford to spend four hours on a minor job like this?" "This corporation pays me a pretty good salary," he said, "for making the important decisions, and for making them right. You tell me what more important decision there

is than that about the management people who do the job. Some of
us up here at the fourteenth floor may be very bright; but if that
master mechanic in Dayton is the wrong man, our decisions might as
well be written on water. He converts them into performance. And
as for taking a lot of time, that's horse apples" (his strongest and
favorite epithet). "How many divisions do we have, Mr. Drucker?"
Before I could answer this rhetorical question, he had whipped out his
famous "little black book" and said, "Forty-seven. And how many
decisions on people did we have to make last year?" I didn't know. "It
was one hundred forty-three," he said, consulting his book, "or three
per division, despite all the people who went off to wartime service.
If we didn't spend four hours on placing a man and placing him right,
we'd spend four hundred hours on cleaning up after our mistake—and
that time I wouldn't have.

"I know," he continued, "you think I should be a good judge of
people. Believe me, there's no such person. There are only people
who make people decisions right, and that means slowly, and people
who make people decisions wrong and then repent at leisure. We do
make fewer mistakes, not because we're good judges of people but
because we're conscientious. And, " he emphasized, "the first rule is
an old one: 'Never let a man nominate his own successor; then you get
a carbon copy and they're always weak.' " "What about your own
succession, Mr. Sloan?" I asked. It had been publicly announced that
he would step down from the chief executive office with the ending
of the war. "I asked the executive committee of the board to make that
decision," he said. "I did not tell them whom I would recommend,
although they wanted to know. I told them that I would tell them were
they to pick someone whom I thought unqualified. They didn't pick
the man I would have picked (it was generally assumed he had favored
Albert Bradley rather than Charlie Wilson, whom he thought "a little
erratic"); but they picked a man whom I cannot object to—and they'll
turn out to have been right. The decision," he concluded, "about
people is the only truly crucial one. You think and everybody thinks
that a company can have 'better' people; that's horse apples. All it can
do is place people right—and then it'll have performance."

Decisions on people usually provoked heated debate in the executive committee. But once the whole committee seemed to be agreed
on one candidate: he had handled this crisis superbly, solved that
problem beautifully, quenched yonder fire with great aplomb. Suddenly Mr. Slaon broke in. "A very impressive record your Mr. Smith

has," he said; "but do explain to me how he gets into all these crises he then so brilliantly surmounts?" Nothing more was heard of Mr. Smith. However, he could also say, "You know all the things Mr. George cannot do—how come he got as far as he did? What *can* he do?" And when he was told, he would say: "All right, he's not brilliant, and not fast, and looks drab. But hasn't he always *performed?*" And George turned into a most successful general manager of a big division at a difficult time.

Sloan usually locked the door and gave strict orders not to be disturbed during one of his tantrums. But once when his secretary was ill, a senior executive walked in on one of Sloan's tantrums with me in tow. Sloan cursed in his richest Brooklyn truckdriver's brogue, screamed, and seemed totally out of control—one of his associates had done something unspeakably irresponsible, apparently not for the first time. The executive I was with, who was an old and trusted colleague (it was probably John Thomas Smith, the company's lawyer), asked, "If he annoys you so much, Mr. Sloan, why don't you let him go?" Sloan immediately calmed down. "Let him go?" he said. "What an absurd idea; he *performs.*"

He could also show great kindness to people. Once in a meeting a newly appointed general manager of an accessory division made a complete ass of himself. An operating man who had come up running a foundry, he found himself suddenly before Albert Bradley being cross-examined on financial and economic projections of which he knew absolutely nothing. He panicked. Instead of saying, "I don't know," he began to speculate and to make the wildest guesses. He was about to destroy himself—for Bradley rarely forgave and never forgot —when Sloan jumped in and made common cause with the general manager, capping each wild guess with an even wilder one. When we went out, I said, "You were really kind to that fellow." Sloan feigned surprise. "As chairman of this company it is my responsibility to preserve income-earning assets," he said, "and we have twenty years of heavy investment in this young man."

Sometimes he carried his consideration for people to absurd lengths. He wrote his book *My Years with General Motors* between 1947 and 1952. It was substantially finished, I was told, at the time Charlie Wilson left GM to join the Eisenhower cabinet, that is, by January 1953. Sloan showed each GM executive the section in the book in which his name was mentioned and got his confirmation of the facts quoted. But then he decided to hold the book until everyone not mentioned favorably had died. Sloan was seventy-eight years old and his greatest wish was to have the book published while still alive. Yet he waited another ten years before releasing it for publication rather than hurt former colleagues. "You can always say something noncommittal but pleasant about a person," his editor at Doubleday is reported to have said to him in the hope of getting the manuscript released. "That I won't do either," Sloan said. "You and I have to take our chances on my survival." He outlived everyone he mentioned in the book and died, aged ninety-one, a year after the book was published and had become a bestseller.

He was fair. One of the young "comers"—an executive on the corporation's marketing staff—dared, in the closing months of 1944, to raise the question whether GM in the course of postwar conversion to peacetime production might not split itself and spin off Chevrolet. Back in 1937, GM had decided that it could not take a larger share than 50 percent of the American automobile market without running into antitrust problems. "Maybe," the marketing man argued, "this implies that GM split in two would do better than GM maintained as one muscle-bound giant. And surely the conversion to peacetime production when GM can, for instance, freely allocate body plants to automotive divisions is the right time to make such a move?" In retrospect it is clear that the marketing man should have been listened to. The fact that GM has never quite dared to take more than half the total American automobile market for fear of an antitrust suit is a major reason why foreign makers have been able to make such inroads into the American automobile market in the last twenty years. But all the brass at GM headquarters were aghast. And no one was more outraged than Mr. Sloan. The young marketing man became a "nonperson." "Let's give him a decent bonus and let him go," the elders urged. "No," said Mr. Sloan. "We don't penalize people for their opinions—we want them to have opinions." And he gave the man a very big promotion, appointing him general manager of the Electro-Motive Division in Chicago, which was then at the threshold of explosive growth. For "Boss" Kettering, GM's inventor-genius, had just solved the problem of making the diesel engine light enough and flexible enough to power railroad locomotives. "This way," Sloan said, "he'll make as much money through his bonuses as if he had reached a top position at GM, or more. Yet he'll be out of Detroit, where he can't really function with all the enemies he's made, including myself."

Above all, Sloan fostered diversity. "Maybe not picking Bradley as my successor was the right decision," he once said to me years later. "I may have favored him because he did even better the things I did well. Mr. Wilson does different things, and that's what a company needs." And when I once told him that what impressed me most at GM was the diversity among its top management people, he said: "That's GM's true strength." But to obtain it, Sloan isolated himself from his fellow executives. "If I have friends among the people with whom I work, I'll have favorites," he said. "I am paid not to." He had been a gregarious person and, in his younger years, had had many close friends. But all of them were outside GM—his brother Raymond, for instance, the hospital administrator who, being twenty years younger, was in many ways a substitute son of the childless Sloan; and especially Walter P. Chrysler, the founder of the Chrysler Company, with whom Sloan spent most vacations until Chrysler died in 1938. Chrysler is the only person in his book about whom Sloan makes a personal remark, and in conversation he sometimes said: "It's been terribly lonely since Walter P. died." But his friendship with Chrysler only began after "Walter P."—who was general manager of the Buick Division—had left GM on Sloan's advice. "Some people like to be alone," he said; "I don't. I have always liked good company. But I have a duty not to have friends at the work place. I have to be impartial and must not even give the appearance of having favorites. How people perform, that is my job; whether I approve of them and the way they get their achievement done, is not." He never gave an opinion on a person, only on his performance.

But while distant, he was courteous. He was known as "Mr. Sloan," but he himself never called anyone by his first name either and did not think it wise of Charlie Wilson to be on first-name terms with his fellow GM vice presidents. Of course, he belonged to a generation —he had been born in 1875—in which first names were a sign of intimacy rather than commonplace. But he also did not use them where his generation always did, toward servants, for instance, including black servants. Whenever he noticed a new elevator man at the GM building, he'd ask: "And what is your name, sir?" "I am Jack," the black "boy" would say. Sloan would turn crimson with rage, would say, "I asked for your *name*, sir," and would thereafter always say, "Good morning, Mr. Jones," when he encountered the man. The only exception he made were women secretaries young enough to be his daughters. "I've always wanted to have daughters," he said, "but Mrs. Sloan and I haven't been able to have children." And so "Sadie" and "Rosie" and "Cathie"—all outrageously spoiled by the old man—were his "substitute daughters." He loved to be best man at their weddings, to be godfather to their children, and he showered on them presents of GM stock from his own holdings so that all of them became independently wealthy.

He was not a modest man. He valued his place in American economic and business history. But he was austere and hated personal pomp. His office was bare. When he stayed in Detroit—as he did two to three nights each week—he had neither an apartment nor a suite at a hotel, but slept in a bare cubicle in the dormitory on the top floor of the GM building. He had no private dining room, but ate in the officers' cafeteria. Since he commuted regularly each week between the two GM headquarters in New York and Detroit, he was urged by his associates to rent a private railroad car. Instead he took a roomette —or at most a single bedroom—on the New York Central's *Detroiter* each time. "All I need is a bed," he'd say. Once when I was going on GM business from Detroit to St. Louis, I had a lower berth in a Pullman which the GM travel people had booked for me. Then I noticed Mr. Sloan—seventy years old and arthritic—painfully climbing up the ladder into an upper berth; it was all he had been able to get at the last minute. I went up to him and asked him to take my lower. He thanked me but refused.

Sloan held to a high standard of honor. He had been a lifelong Republican. And while he would have preferred Taft, he enthusiastically supported the Eisenhower candidacy in 1952 as the first chance to get a Republican back into the White House. He dropped Eisenhower overnight, however, when he came out in support of Senator Jenner of Indiana. Jenner had publicly attacked Eisenhower's former chief, General Marshall, as a "traitor." Sloan was probably not much of an admirer of Marshall's. But for Eisenhower, who had been Marshall's protégé and who owed his career to Marshall's support, to court Jenner and to flatter him, Sloan thought a disgrace. When the new President offered him the position of Secretary of Defense, Charles Wilson consulted Sloan. "Of course you have to accept, Mr. Wilson," Sloan said; "one cannot turn down the President of the United States. But you'd better be prepared to be stabbed in the back—the man has no principles." Soon thereafter, Wilson found himself in need of Eisenhower's support. Wilson never said, of course, "What is good for General Mo-

tors is good for the country." It would have been totally out of
character for him. He said, "What is good for the country is good
for General Motors" which, while naïve, is something different indeed. When he was misquoted he was deeply hurt, and asked Eisenhower to make a public statement. Eisenhower ignored the request. "I am not surprised," said Sloan. "A man who has no loyalty
to his superior doesn't have any to his subordinates either."

I am often asked whether I know of a perfect "management tool."
The answer is, "Yes: Alfred Sloan's hearing aid." He was hard of hearing and had been so for many years. He had an old-fashioned hearing
aid with heavy batteries hanging down his chest and a big trumpet on
one ear. It had to be switched off before the wearer could talk, otherwise the roar blasted the wearer but also garbled his voice. Sloan had
an amplifier built into the switch. When he turned it so as to be able
to speak, it sounded like the crack of doom and everybody in the room
stopped talking immediately. But it was the only way in which he
dominated a meeting, and he never used it until everybody else had
had his say.

As I sat in more GM meetings with Sloan, I began to notice something else in addition to his emphasis on people and his treatment of
them: his way of making decisions. I think I noticed it first in the
heated discussions about the postwar capacity of GM's accessory divisions. One group in GM management argued stridently and with lots
of figures that accessory capacity should be expanded. Another group,
equally strident, argued in favor of keeping it low. Sloan listened for
a long time without saying anything. Then he turned off his hearing
aid and said, "What is this decision really about? Is it about accessory
capacity? Or is it about the future shape of the American automobile
industry? You," and he turned to the most vocal advocate of accessory
expansion, "argue that we need to be able to supply independent
automobile manufacturers with accessories they cannot make, and
that this is our most profitable business—and so it has always been. And
you," turning to an opponent of accessory expansion, "argue that we
need to confine our capacity to what our own automotive divisions and
our dealers in the automotive after-market need. It seems to me that
you argue over the future of the automobile industry in this country
and not about the accessory business, do you agree? Well then," said
Sloan, "we all agree that we aren't likely to sell a lot of GM accessories
to our big competitors, to Chrysler and Ford. Do we know whether
to expect the independents—Studebaker, Hudson, Packard, Nash,

Willys—to grow and why? I take it we are confident that they will give us their business if they have any to give."

"But Mr. Sloan," said the proponent of accessory expansion, "we assume that automobile demand will be growing, and then the independents will surely do well." "Sounds plausible to me," said Sloan, "but have we tested the assumption? If not, let's do so."

A month later the study came in, and to everybody's surprise it showed that small independents did poorly and were being gobbled up by the big companies in times of rapidly growing automobile demand, and that they only did well in times of fairly stable replacement demand and slow market growth. "So now," Sloan said, "the question is really whether we can expect fast automobile growth, once we have supplied the deficiencies the war has created, or slow growth. Do we know what new automobile demand depends on?" "Yes, we do know, Mr. Sloan," someone said; "demand for new automobiles is a direct function of the number of young people who reach the age of the first driver's license, buy an old jalopy, and thereby create demand for new cars among the older and wealthier population." "Just so," said Sloan —"we learned that twenty years ago. And what do population figures look like five, ten, fifteen years out?" And when it turned out that they showed a fairly rapid growth of the teen-age population for some ten years ahead, Sloan said: "The facts have made the decision—and I was wrong." For then, and only then, did Sloan disclose that the proposal to increase accessory capacity had originally been his.

Sloan rarely made a decision by counting noses or by taking a vote. He made it by creating understanding. Once one of the staff vice presidents—I believe it was Paul Garrett of Public Relations—made a proposal for a major campaign. Normally, any proposal of this kind evoked a good deal of discussion. But Garrett's proposal was so well prepared that everybody supported it; and it was also suspected that Sloan was heartily in its favor. But when everybody thought the proposal had been agreed upon, the old man switched off his hearing aid and said, "I take it all you gentlemen are in favor?" "Yes, Mr. Sloan," the chorus came back. "Then I move that we defer action on this for a month to give ourselves a chance to think"—and a month later the proposal was either scuttled or drastically revised.

And after every meeting, no matter how many he attended, he wrote a letter or a memorandum in which he identified the key question and asked: "Is this what the decision is all about?" Again I asked him once whether this didn't take an awful lot of time. "If a decision comes up to my level," he said, "it had better take a lot of time. If it doesn't deserve it, we'll throw it back. We make very few decisions, Mr. Drucker; no one can make a great many and make them right. But we'd better know what we are deciding and what the decision is all about."

Sloan showed me the same well-tempered courtesy he showed everyone else. He went out of his way to be helpful and to explain to me how he and GM worked. I must have gained his respect. A few years later, around 1953, he asked me to advise him on his plans for the Sloan School of Administration he was endowing at M.I.T. I spent the best part of a day with him, going over his plans. Then he said: "Would it be agreeable to you, Mr. Drucker, if I put your name forward as one of the professors at my school?"

And yet he had absolutely no use for my book and rejected it totally. He did not attack it; he simply treated it as if it did not exist, never mentioning it and never allowing it to be mentioned in his presence. Charlie Wilson wanted to send copies to his friends as a Christmas present. "I wouldn't do it, Mr. Wilson," Sloan said. "Your friends might think you endorse Mr. Drucker's book." In his own book, he refers to quite a few publications on GM. But there is no mention whatever of my book, even though it was at that time the only one that dealt specifically with Sloan's policies and his management philosophy. I was told years later by Wilson that it was primarily to present to the world an approach different from mine that Sloan decided to write and publish his own version of GM and of his role in it.

Outside Detroit my book has generally been considered as friendly to GM, sometimes uncritically so. But that was not the view inside GM. Most GM executives thought me hypercritical, and many complained that I was hostile. I criticized GM's labor policy, its treatment of the foreman, and the lack of decentralization within such big divisions as Chevrolet and Fisher Body. I dared suggest that, after a quarter century, the basic policies of GM might well need rethinking, and that was *lèse-majesté*. "If you were a GM executive," a GM friend said, "we'd have to exile you to Electro-Motive in Chicago to join that other arch-heretic," and he said it only half in jest. Donaldson Brown was severely criticized—by Albert Bradley, for instance—for his refusal to reserve to GM veto power over the publication of such an "anti-GM" book.

I doubt however that this explains Alfred Sloan's attitude, let alone his decision to do by himself what I, in his eyes, had obviously failed to do. Disagreement rarely bothered Sloan. But I had tackled what to Sloan was the wrong subject. I had written a book which, though without conscious intention on my part, established the discipline of management. What mattered to Sloan was the profession of manager, and this was what he set out to establish in *his* book.

Sloan himself still belonged to the generation of "owners." When only twenty-three he had borrowed $5,000 from his father—a middling coffee, tea, and cigar merchant—to buy a small company that was deep in the red and on the point of bankruptcy, Hyatt Roller Bearings. Within six months he had turned it around and was making a profit. For Sloan realized what the founders of the company had not seen: that the new-fangled automobile was the market for the company's products. He re-engineered the roller bearing, invented for use in locomotives and railroad freight cars, for which it was in fact ill suited, to fit the automobile. Sloan then built his company especially to supply Henry Ford. Until he sold it in 1916 to a new "conglomerate" of automobile accessory businesses, he was Hyatt's sole owner. He became the largest shareholder of the conglomerate. And when, in 1918, that company was sold to GM, he became, in turn, one of GM's large shareholders. All the men with whom he was associated during these years, including his rivals and colleagues in the early GM days, had, like him, started as owners; and when they sold their property they became "shareholders" and "directors" rather than "executives" and "managers." Sloan however left behind a GM that was run by "professional managers"; the shares they owned they had received as part of their executive compensation. During the same period most of American large business underwent the same transformation—from the "owner-capitalist" to the employed "professional manager." That to Sloan was the crucial change, and he was very conscious of being the first of the truly "professional managers," the man who had built the first large organization truly managed by such men.

Henry Ford was still an "owner." That clearly explained to Sloan why his company, after its meteoric rise, rapidly skidded downhill in the last twenty years of Ford's life. Walter P. Chrysler was in the process of transforming his company from "ownership" to "professional management" when he died; and that the transformation had not been completed explained to Sloan in large measure why the Chrysler Company began to stutter, to misfire, and to lose momentum and direction. GM, however, thanks to Sloan's example and guidance, had become "professional"—and Sloan saw it as his responsibility to leave behind him a clear statement as to what being a "professional manager" means.

My Years with General Motors became a national bestseller, deservedly so. It is a fascinating book. But the most important thing about it is what is not in the book, for Sloan defined a "professional manager" primarily by the things he did not include in the book, did not treat, did not mention. And he did so with deliberation. (All told, he did few things without clear purpose and careful deliberation.)

There are no people in the book, only names. Donaldson Brown or Charles Wilson or Albert Bradley are mentioned in connection with this policy decision or that project, but without a single word about them as people, not even a word of praise. The only time the word "friend" occurs is in connection with Walter P. Chrysler—and he is also the only person who is characterized, albeit only briefly.

But Sloan himself is just as absent. Indeed the title of the book is a misnomer; it should have been *General Motors During My Years*. General Motors is the hero, not Sloan. Sloan exists as writer of this memorandum or originator of that project, as member of the executive committee or of a party that travels to Germany to buy Opel. But of the *persona* "Alfred P. Sloan, Jr."—a highly idiosyncratic, deeply engaged, and most interesting man, with a myriad interests—there is no trace. I said earlier that he does not, in the book, so much as mention the General Motors Technical Institute in Flint to which he gave endless hours and which he considered a most important achievement. It was a "personal" rather than a "professional" interest and as such was censored out. He long refused to let his editors include even the two meager pages that tell of his family, his boyhood, and his early years. And only when the book was ready to go to press did he permit inclusion in a profusely illustrated book of one photograph— and one photograph only—that shows his family: his father, wife, sister, and brothers. Yet he was devoted to his family and happily married for more than fifty years to the same wife.

Sloan spent more time on decisions over people than on anything else; yet there is no mention of them in his book. There is no mention of the careful decision-making process he had worked out. There is no mention of his tremendous interest in automotive safety and of his active membership in the Automotive Safety Council, though an astute reader might notice that the best photographs of Sloan in the book show him at Automotive Safety Council meetings. Yet Sloan ranked the introduction of safe-driver courses into the American high-school curriculum almost as high among his personal achievements as GM Tech. There is no mention of Sloan's near-obsession with industrial safety; in fact he was a fanatic about accidents in the plant and aimed—with great success—at having GM run with "zero accidents." To achieve this goal, he early laid down a policy under which a foreman in whose section an accident occurred, but also the foreman's boss, would be instantly suspended pending investigation and would be summarily removed in the event of a second accident. He only relented under the pressure of a budding foreman's union during the years of World War II, and even then did not retreat very far.

All these things were personally important to Sloan, which is precisely why they are not in his book. A "professional" for him was not a man without interests, without convictions, without a personal life. He was a man who separated his interests, his convictions, and his personal life from the task. Anything that to Sloan was personally important was by that very fact professionally suspect. "A surgeon," he once said to me, "does not take out an appendix because he is good at appendectomies or because he likes the operation. He takes it out because the patient's diagnosis calls for it." And Sloan's book is a book on diagnosis.

Sloan the man was passionately interested in politics, a strong partisan, and active in Republican Party affairs. He had been one of the organizers of the "Liberty League" that tried to oppose Roosevelt and the New Deal in 1936, and was a generous contributor to Republican candidates until Eisenhower's "betrayal" of Marshall soured him when he was nearly eighty. His book does not mention politics or governmental affairs. He was most active during the New Deal years. But the only mention of Franklin D. Roosevelt is in one short paragraph where the name is linked with that of Harry Truman and a long-forgotten Michigan governor as supporters of the Automobile Workers' sit-down strike against GM. Sloan was an active member of the Council on Foreign Relations and the Chicago Council of World Affairs until his deafness forced him to stop attending meetings in later years. But world affairs are mentioned only as they affect GM.

When, in the years of World War II, it became clear that the Ford Motor Company was in deep trouble, Sloan became very much concerned. And when Henry Ford's son, Edsel, died in 1944 and there seemed to be no one left to rescue the rapidly sinking Ford Company except a grandson, Henry Ford II, who was a twenty-six-year-old college dropout without experience, Sloan became thoroughly alarmed. I cannot vouch for the story, but I have been told by several people that he worked with J. P. Morgan and with Morgan Stanley—GM's bankers—on setting up a syndicate that would, should the need arise, provide Ford with the necessary capital to survive while being rebuilt.

When Henry Ford II then took control and began to turn around his company by raiding GM for managers, Sloan went all out to support him. Everybody else in GM top management was bitter about the colleagues who went over to Ford, the hated competitor. Sloan did everything to enable them to join the Ford team, helped them work out their pensions and profit-sharing plans at GM so as to be able to move without financial loss, and even, I was told, got word to Ernest Breech, a former GM executive who had become Ford's chairman, where inside GM he might find hidden top talent for the Ford management team. But that, Sloan argued, was in GM's interest. The country could not let Ford go under; and the alternative to Ford's recovery as a private business was a government takeover that could only harm GM. Helping Ford's rescue was thus "professional" responsibility. But all the things I was concerned with, the employe community and the policy toward the union, for instance, were "public" responsibility.

Sloan did not argue that these things might not be in GM's interest; he admitted they might well be. But he correctly saw that I was interested in them and advocated them because of their public impact rather than because they were the right things for Sloan's "patient" and professional responsibility, that is, for GM. I urged GM to do these things to set an example—and that, to Sloan, was unprofessional conduct, "just," he said to me, "as if a surgeon were to take out a healthy appendix to show his students how to do it."

Indeed "public" responsibility was to Sloan worse than unprofessional; it was irresponsible, a usurpation of power. "We have a responsibility toward higher education," a chief executive of a major American corporation once said at a meeting both Sloan and I attended. "Do we in business have any *authority* over higher education?" Sloan asked. "Should we have any?" "Of course not," was the answer. "Then let's not talk about 'responsibility,' " said Sloan with asperity. "You are a senior executive of a big company and you know the first rule: authority and responsibility must be congruent and commensurate to each other. If you don't want authority and shouldn't have it, don't talk about responsibility. And if you don't want responsibility and shouldn't have it, don't talk about authority."

Sloan based this on management principles. But of course it is the first lesson of political theory and political history. Authority without responsibility is illegitimate; but so is responsibility without authority. Both lead to tyranny. Sloan wanted a great deal of authority for his professional manager, and was ready to take high responsibility. But for that reason he insisted on limiting authority to the areas of professional competence, and refused to assert or admit responsibility in areas outside. And for this reason he found my book unacceptable.

I admitted the strength of Sloan's position, but found myself unable to move to it, then or now. One can argue that the weakness of GM—and of business management altogether—is precisely the careful, precise, strict construction of management's "responsibility" on which Sloan insisted. GM has in one way been a huge success in the last thirty years, in the way Sloan would measure success, in terms of market share, profit, sales volume, and so on. GM has also been a huge failure, in terms of public esteem, political acceptance, and general respect. And the same thing is surely true of other "professions"— American medicine, the law, or education. The attack on them is always made specifically in terms of their failure to accept "public responsibilities," and for their insistence on limiting themselves to being "professional." In the complex society of organizations in which we live, the organizations—and that means the "professionals" who manage them—must surely take responsibility for the common weal. There is no one else around who can do it. All history teaches that a pluralist society cannot depend on the conflict and confluence of particular "interests" to produce the common good and to serve the public interest.

Yet while perhaps too strict, too pure, too principled, Sloan's position should not be easily dismissed. Today's attacks on "business"—the attacks of Ralph Nader, for instance, on Sloan's GM—are meant to be "anti-business." But by demanding that business take "public responsibility" way beyond anything my *Concept of the Corporation* would have dreamt of thirty years ago, these attacks really ask business to assert authority. The demands are meant to deprive business of power. But as Sloan saw thirty years ago, they are far more likely to make business, and the other "interests," our masters.

The Indian Summer
of Innocence

"So you only made eighteen hundred dollars last year," said the Immigration Department clerk in New York as he checked my income tax return when I applied for a reentry permit into the United States before setting off on a six-week trip to Europe early in 1938. "That's pretty slim pickings, isn't it? And look at all the work you had to do for so little money." He pointed to a gross income figure of almost $5,000. "You sure know how to work for other people—I bet you have a college degree at that, and know foreign languages! You'd make fifty percent more the first month working at Immigration and Naturalization. We pay good money here, and you wouldn't have to work half as hard or use your brain as much. You'd get three weeks vacation, overtime, medical benefits, and a pension after thirty years. Wait a minute." When he came back he carried a sheaf of papers. "If you fill these out now, I'll have my supervisor sign them today. He was my partner in the shoe store before it folded when the banks closed. By the time you get back from Europe, we'll have a job ready and waiting for you."

I didn't fill out the forms. But the middle-aged clerk with the Irish face and the Brooklyn voice still symbolizes in my mind Franklin D. Roosevelt's America, the New Deal America of the late thirties, the America of the Indian Summer of Innocence.

I was already making something like the $250 which, according to the brochure pressed on me by the clerk, the United States Immigration and Naturalization Service paid to a "Clerk Interpreter First

Class (Reading knowledge of two Foreign Languages) (College Degree or Equivalent)." For what the clerk did not notice was that the $1800 I had declared was my net income for some seven or eight months only. I had arrived in the United States in late April and had not begun work until May. And $250 a month was indeed, as the clerk asserted, "good money" then, anything but "slim pickings." My secretary, who spoke and wrote two foreign languages and had a college degree from Hunter, got only $25 a week—$100 a month—and was overwhelmed to the point of tears when I raised her to $30 six months later; a stenographer-typist was lucky if paid $15 a week, without vacation or overtime.

One of the surprises when we first moved was how much cheaper New York was than London. It was even cheaper than near-dead Vienna, with its 40 percent unemployment, where my parents still lived. The $250 I earned paid for a two-bedroom apartment in a new apartment block, and soon thereafter for the rent on our three-bedroom house and garden in Bronxville, then one of New York's plushest suburbs. We had a recent-vintage car in which we drove into the country on summer and fall weekends. For while fully prepared for the skyline, we were, like all Europeans, completely surprised by the sheer beauty and diversity of the country on all sides of New York City. We entertained quite a bit and went frequently to theater, opera, and concerts. I did not go first-class on that business trip to Europe; but I had a single-occupancy second-class cabin with bath on an upper deck of the new, luxurious, and fast *Queen Mary*.

But that the clerk wasted his pity on me is beside the point. What made him the very embodiment of Depression America was his concern, his eagerness to help, his focus on direct action.

The Depression was a catastrophe for many of the middle-aged from which they never recovered. It was a severe trauma, leaving permanent scars for children growing up in depression-struck homes where fathers suffered long years of fear or unemployment that stripped them alike of their economic security and their manhood. But for people my age—young yet grown-up, independent and healthy— it was a bracing and exhilarating time. One had to work hard, to be sure. And Depression America was no place for anyone psychologically in need of security unless he latched onto a government job. Like the Irish clerk at the Immigration Desk, Depression America was not tactful. It was not refined. It could be dreadfully smug. But it was free from envy; anyone's success was everyone's success and a blow against the common enemy. Depression America encouraged, cheered on, helped. Whoever heard of an opening looked right away for someone who needed a job. And whoever heard of someone who needed a job, right away looked for a vacancy.

When my brother arrived in New York with a brand-new M.D. degree from Vienna six months before I did, he came with only one name: that of the medical director of a big New York hospital, who, thirty-five years earlier, had been a classmate of a Vienna pediatrician, our beloved "Aunt Trudy." The medical director no longer remembered Aunt Trudy and his hospital had no job for an intern. But he lodged my brother in an empty interns' room and started telephoning. A few days later my brother had an internship in a smaller but accredited and well-known hospital in the New York area.

Concern, eagerness to help, willingness to swing into action for perfect strangers, were not confined to jobs. When we arrived in New York that late April we put up at a small midtown hotel. New York's annual April heatwave struck the same day and there was then no air conditioning. Our window opened on Sixth Avenue, where a subway was being built, mostly at night so as not to interfere with traffic. Window open or window shut, we knew after two dreadful nights that we had to get out—but where? Going down the subway steps I ran into a casual shipboard acquaintance, an elderly man of whom I knew only that he was a New York lawyer. "Hot enough for you?" he asked. When I told him that it was *too* hot and that we had to find a cooler, quieter place outside the city but didn't know where or how, he said, "Let me telephone. A nephew of mine is moving and looking, I believe, for someone to take over the lease on his Bronxville apartment." Forty-eight hours later we moved.

I had the kindness of a stranger to thank for my office. Riding in an elevator in a downtown building, I heard a voice saying: "Aren't you Mr. Drucker from London?" It was a New York stockbroker who, a few months earlier, had made a courtesy call on Freedberg & Co. in London. I told him I had moved to New York to work as financial adviser for a group of British investors, and as feature writer for a group of British newspapers. The stranger said, "You'll need an office. We're vacating three rooms on our floor." He negotiated a lease for me which gave me a spacious office at downtown's best address, the Equitable Building, 120 Broadway, at one-fourth of what I would have had to pay for the dingiest quarters anyplace else. And his firm lent me furniture without charge. "But I can't even pay you by bringing brokerage business to you. I won't have any," I said. "I know that," was the answer. "Just put us on the mailing list of your market letters so we can read what you tell European investors about Wall Street. And I'll put you on our mailing list."

I joined the Foreign Press Association and got a press card (which, incidentally, I never once was asked to show). During my European trip I had written six or seven feature stories for the Washington *Post,* which under its new owner, Eugene Meyer, was rapidly becoming the leading paper in Washington and the "house organ" of the government bureaucracy. But still I was completely unknown and had met hardly anyone in the government when, during a visit to Washington in June or July of 1938—shortly after my trip to Europe—I received a tearful call from an Austrian childhood friend now living in New York. Her father, a refugee, was in Paris awaiting an American visa and was suddenly stricken with severe prostatitis demanding early surgery. Could I get his visa speeded up so that he could have the operation in New York, where her husband was a surgeon? When I asked whom I might see, she said, "There's a Mr. Messersmith, who was American ambassador in Vienna a few years back, and is now, I think, Assistant Secretary of State. He should know something about Austria." My hotel was across the park from the old State Department building. I went unannounced, without introduction or appointment, to the State Department, looked up Mr. Messersmith on the board in the hall, walked into his office unchallenged by receptionist or guard (the State Department then had neither), and saw Mr. Messersmith, who was indeed Assistant Secretary of State, ten minutes later. He asked me a few questions, then called his secretary in and dictated a cable to a vice consul in Paris, instructing him to issue an emergency visa to Mr. X should Mr. X's papers be in order. Then he said, "If this doesn't work, here's the person to see," and gave me the name of the official I should have gone to in the first place. "But," he added, "I think it will work." And it did. Yet Messersmith, as I later learned, had a reputation as being unfriendly, a pedant and a stickler, and a person who was strongly opposed to letting refugees come in freely.

Then there was the Saturday afternoon at the very modest home of a middle-level Department of Agriculture editor in suburban Silver Springs, outside of Washington. I spent the day with Gove Hambidge, the editor, on an article I was writing for the Department's annual yearbook—incidentally, the Agriculture yearbooks Hambidge put out in those years are still, I think, among the best and most thoughtful texts on ecology and environment. Around three o'clock or so Hambidge said, "We'd better stop working and get ready for the company." "Who's coming?" I asked. "I never know," he said, "but everyone in the Department is welcome to come Saturday afternoons and pitch horseshoes; and here's Henry." The Secretary of Agriculture, Henry Wallace, drove up in a battered Ford, followed within the hour by some top people in the Department and in New Deal political life: M. L. Wilson, the Undersecretary and the head of most of the farm programs; Louis Bean, the economist, the Department's counselor and the farm programs' intellectual father; and so on. Around seven when it got dark, Mrs. Hambidge had all of us come into the kitchen and set us to making sandwiches. Wallace chatted with me, asked what I was working on, and said, "I'd like to talk with you about this. Can you and Louis Bean see me on Monday morning?" Of course he was told that I was a journalist but he never even asked what papers I worked for. I was a friend of Gove's and had asked questions that interested Wallace.

The informality was largely manners, and sometimes coarse, if not bad, manners. After forty years I still am not reconciled to the "informality" of calling women in an office by their first names while they say "Mr. Drucker." And it took a long time before my European-bred tongue was at ease saying "girls" instead of "ladies" for the women in an office. But the friendliness and the commitment to mutual help were genuine.

So was the willingness to take a chance on a person.

I got my assignment to write for the Washington *Post* during my European trip in the spring of 1938 by calling cold on the foreign editor. Somebody had mentioned that the *Post*, though not yet able to afford its own correspondents abroad, was eager to add to the syndicated dispatches it received from *The New York Times* and the Chicago *Tribune*, then still the only American dailies with an extensive foreign news staff of their own. I phoned to get the name of the foreign editor—it was Barnet Nover—and walked in on him.

Two hours later I walked out with a contract and an advance. Nover had liked my ideas, had taken me to the publisher, Eugene Meyer, who approved, had said, "We won't commit ourselves until we see the pieces, but we do want an exclusive right of refusal. So we owe you an advance: let's say the fee for two pieces," and that was it. Of course, he did not risk much. But $150 was a big sum in those days and paid for most of my European expenses other than the transatlantic fare. I similarly sold my first article to *Harper's* magazine by walking in. I had finished my book, *The End of Economic Man,* in the fall, had gotten it accepted by a publisher, and thought a pre-publication article would help sell the book. I knew the name of the associate editor, Frederick Lewis Allen, because I had read his history of the twenties, *Only Yesterday.* I called him up, was asked to come to the office, and then encouraged to write a piece for his consideration. Similarly Martin Sommers, the foreign editor of the *Saturday Evening Post,* saw me without an appointment. It occurred to me on the train from Washington to New York that I might call on him, so I got off the train in Philadelphia and took a streetcar to Independence Square. "The article ideas you're talking about sound interesting," he said. "How soon can I see the first one?" He had it five days later and called up the same morning. "I'll have to cut a few lines, but otherwise we'll run it as you sent it in."

There was the same willingness to accept the stranger on his own cognizance when I worked on a story on American industry or American education and called up people in business, the universities, or government for an interview or information; or when, a little later, I began to call casual acquaintances and even strangers to find jobs for the Austrian refugees then coming in like a tidal wave. And when there was no job for a person I was trying to place, the response would often be that of the president of one of the New York City colleges when I called on him on the slightest acquaintanceship: "No, we don't have a job for a mathematician right now. But you wouldn't know a good musician by any chance? We could use one."

Unlike the informality in manners and mannerisms that the Depression only accentuated, the commitment to mutual help and the willingness to take chances on a person were peculiar to Depression America. Whenever I discussed this with the older generation—Eugene Meyer, for instance, of whom I saw quite a bit later on in Washington during the World War II days, or Christian Gauss, the long-time Princeton dean, or Fred Allen at *Harper's* magazine, for I was tremendously intrigued by the phenomenon and discussed it with whoever was willing to listen—they all maintained that the America of the twenties, while far more informal, had been no friendlier than Europe, no more willing to help, no more receptive to the stranger. The commitment to mutual help was a response to the Depression. Indeed it was the specifically American response to the Depression. There was nothing like it on the other side, where the Depression evoked only suspicion, surliness, fear, and envy.

The American response to the Depression was the response to a natural disaster. As after an earthquake, a flood, a hurricane, the community closed ranks and came to each other's rescue. The America of the thirties talked of the Depression the way people talk about a natural disaster, with voluble personal stories of "how I managed" or "how I suffered," but also by saying at the end of a long story: "You see, I recovered from this affliction and so will you." A few years later, during World War II, everyone marveled at the spirit in the British shelters, the good nature, the *camaraderie*, the friendliness and sense of community during the London Blitz with its suffering, its dangers, its extreme discomfort. I was not surprised—I had seen the same spirit in the disaster of the American Depression.

As after every natural disaster, the "survivors" in Depression America went into gales of laughter, if only because it was so good to be alive. Above all, they laughed at themselves—good-naturedly, mostly, though with the sharp bite to the joke that also characterizes the laughter of the day after a disaster.

In the winter of 1940–41 I spoke on the monthly Saturday afternoon program of the Foreign Policy Association that CBS carried live over its national network. The Foreign Policy Association had just brought in a new president, a retired general. I noticed how nervous he was during lunch, and he told me that he had never faced a microphone before. When it was his turn to introduce the session, he froze, stumbled, and dropped all the papers he held in his hand. We picked them up, pushed them back into his hand, and pushed the poor chap, paralyzed with fright, up to the microphone. In a trembling voice he read the paper that was uppermost in his hand. But instead of the introduction to the day's program, it was the announcement for the program a month hence, with Mrs. Roosevelt as the speaker, which he should have read at the broadcast's conclusion! Somehow I got through my speech. Later I was told that CBS had never had so many telephone calls about a Foreign Policy Association program, with hundreds or thousands of people indignantly calling up to find out why Mrs. Roosevelt hadn't been allowed to talk, or concerned about Mrs. Roosevelt's health since she did not sound at all her normal self. I wrote a letter to Mrs. Roosevelt explaining what had happened and got a pleasant note back from her secretary.

Two months or so later I was lecturing in Reading, Pennsylvania. It was a luncheon speech, which meant, in those days, that one had to get in from New York the night before. At my hotel was a note from a secretary: "Mrs. Roosevelt is lecturing here tomorrow night and will spend the day visiting a hospital, a home for blind children, and a prison. Maybe you'd care to join her? She saw your lecture announced when she came to town and understands you will be here tomorrow morning." So I spent the morning inspecting a hospital and a home for the blind as part of Mrs. Roosevelt's retinue—and a most impressive performance her inspections were. I apologized again for the mishap at the Foreign Policy Association. She laughed. "I owe you thanks," she said. "From your letter I knew what to expect and introduced myself rather than let the poor general suffer again. Anyhow," she went on, "Mr. Drucker, you can't realize what a thrill it is for me to find someone who actually *wanted* to be taken for Eleanor Roosevelt."

The next spring I was working for the war in Washington and had to get security clearance. The young man whose job it was, and who was just as green as I was, had only one problem but a serious one. There was that charge of my having "impersonated Mrs. Roosevelt." I explained to him what had happened. "Why didn't you correct the mistake right away?" he asked. "Well, I probably hadn't thought fast enough in the confusion. One doesn't contradict and correct a chairman to begin with, and no one was very likely to mistake my Austrian baritone for Eleanor Roosevelt's high-pitched, New York finishing school accent." The young man was sympathetic but troubled. "If only I could see what *advantage* you derived from being introduced as Mrs. Roosevelt, I could clear you. We have to have an explanation to set aside a charge." Then he brightened. "Doesn't she draw more of a crowd than you do?" he asked. I admitted that, indeed, she did. "That'll do it," he said happily, and wrote in the margin: "Motive: to attract larger crowds and get higher lecture fees. Charge dismissed as trivial." "But," I said, "that makes me sound a perfect ass." "Mr. Drucker, this is an investigation of your loyalty, not your fitness, and besides it doesn't make *you* out to be an ass. It makes the law out to be an ass, and that's hardly news."

A "natural disaster" is nonrecurring, an Act of God for which no person is to blame, and an interruption of normal life which then, after emergency repairs, picks up as before. Few people in America during the Depression years believed in "recovery," certainly not after 1937 when the slight economic improvement that had followed Roosevelt's reelection spending proved a short-lived mirage. Fewer still believed that there would ever be economic growth again. The most honored economic prophet of those years was the Harvard Keynesian Alvin

Hansen, who in 1938 predicted—with ample mathematical proofs—
"permanent stagnation" and long-term shrinkage for decades to come
in his *Full Recovery or Stagnation*. No one then could possibly have
imagined the near-thirty years of worldwide economic expansion and
prosperity that did follow World War II, the longest and fastest period
of growth in all economic history. In fact, even the wildest optimist
would not have dared assign the slightest probability of survival to the
world economy in the event of a world war. Economically the Depression was not a "disaster"; it was a "new normalcy." But unlike Europe,
where it was felt that "the center cannot hold," the "center" held in
America. Society and community were sound, hale, indeed trium-
phant. There was plenty of violence as there has, of course, been
throughout American history, and plenty of bitterness. But the Depression was also a celebration of community, of shared values, of the
joy of life, and of common hope—as a "natural disaster" tends to be
for the defiant survivors. This, I submit, was the truly remarkable,
truly historic achievement of Franklin D. Roosevelt. And then it mattered not at all that his economic policies were outrageous failures.

But paradoxically precisely because Depression America celebrated community, it greatly strengthened the local, the parochial,
the tribal in American life. It emphasized religious and ethnic and
cultural diversities and turned them into boundaries. Depression
America was more anti-Jewish, more anti-Catholic, and equally more
pro-Jewish and more pro-Catholic than the America of the twenties
had been. And within Jewry the cleavage between "Germans" and
"Russians" widened; as did the cleavage between "Irish," "Italians,"
and "Germans" among Catholics, or that between "Yankees" and
"Southerners."

If Marxism ever had a chance in the United States, it died with
the Depression. Marxist dogma asserted that the Depression had to
make America "class-conscious," had to create the "proletariat," had
to project a "revolutionary situation." It did the opposite. There had
been plenty of genuine proletarian and revolutionary tinder in earlier
days—the "Wobblies" of World War I were a genuine movement of
revolt and class war. Eugene Debs, a little earlier, deserved to be
taken seriously as a political contender, unlike Norman Thomas, Earl
Browder, Senator McGovern, or Michael Harrington. There was, of
course, plenty of class-consciousness, plenty of hatred, plenty of class
bitterness in the Depression years. I first visited Detroit in the days of
the sit-down strikes and the bitterness and hatred on both sides were

enough to sicken even the most callous. When, on the same trip, I visited Pittsburgh and wanted to go through a steel mill, I was told by the public relations man at U.S. Steel to try another steel company— Republic perhaps—since bringing a newsman in under management's auspices might inflame an already dangerous labor situation. That ruined Wall Street brokers jumped out of thirtieth-floor windows was surely cold comfort to an unemployed automobile worker on the breadline, or to an "Okie" dispossessed from his farm by drought and sandstorms rather than by the Depression. Still, a "natural disaster" is one event that does not respect money. All the rich have is more insurance than the poor. And so in the natural disaster which America perceived the Depression to be, being of Italian or Polish origin became more important than being a contractor or a laborer, and being Jewish more important than being publisher of *The New York Times* or a pushcart peddler on Seventh Avenue.

To a newcomer from Europe this was utter bewilderment. Or rather, it seemed simple at first, then became totally incomprehensible. "Straight anti-Semitism," I would say when learning that there were "restricted" resorts or "restricted" country clubs to which Jews were not admitted. Of course, it was, as were the "quotas" for Jewish students at practically every university, or the invisible but very real bars to Jews at most university faculties. And there was Chancellor Chase of New York University who, in the midst of the Depression, managed to keep his budget balanced by cutting all faculty salaries 40 percent and then calling in his Jewish faculty members and cutting their salaries 70 percent, saying, "If you don't like it, quit. But being Jewish, you won't find another job." Twenty years later, when I joined N.Y.U. and became chairman of a major department, I still had to live with the after-effects of this "cleverness" on which Chase had greatly prided himself. Yet Chase was considered a leading "liberal" in the educational establishment, and thought himself to be one. He was indeed proud of N.Y.U.'s leadership in hiring Jewish teachers without any discrimination or quota restriction, despite strong opposition from members of his own board of what was officially then still a Methodist university.

Colleges and universities that had strict "quotas" for Jewish students and kept American Jews off their faculties, at the same time practically without exception opened their hearts, pocketbooks, and faculties to Jewish scholars from Germany and Austria. The same communities in which clubs, resorts, and apartment houses were "restricted" and closed to Jews insisted on Jewish candidates for at least one powerful office—city comptroller, for instance, or Attorney General—on every political slate. And whereas "restricted" meant "no Jews" in New York, Boston, Washington, and Los Angeles, it meant "no Catholics" in Minneapolis and Atlanta, and "no Hungarians, Slovaks, or Poles" in Pittsburgh.

In those years all of America—but particularly newcomers from Europe—became increasingly sensitive to anti-Jewish rhetoric, habits, or policies. But the American Catholic was even more subject to both kinds of discrimination, discrimination against and discrimination for; in other words, the discrimination of a tribal society.

On my first trip as a journalist to the South—probably in early 1939—the governor or lieutenant-governor of Georgia whom I interviewed about conditions in the state launched into a sharp attack on the city's leading department store, Rich's. The fact that it was Jewish was all right—department stores apparently had to be Jewish by law of nature—but Rich's had hired as its general manager a Catholic, and an Irish Catholic from the North to boot. In the next breath he talked about putting a local Catholic on his ticket so as to "balance" it.

When I once wondered whether the Catholic universities might perhaps insulate Catholic students from American life, the Jesuit father-president of Fordham University rebutted: "We don't need Catholic universities in America for the students any more. They might as well go to the state universities. We need them because Catholics can't get faculty appointments except at Catholic schools." There were Gentile law firms in New York City and Chicago, and Jewish law firms; but there were also Protestant accounting firms and Catholic accounting firms. General Motors, I was told with great emphasis, was the one and only major "Protestant" manufacturer who had both a Jew—Meyer Prentiss, the comptroller—and a Catholic—Marvin Coyle, the head of Chevrolet—in its top management. Henry Wallace, Secretary of Agriculture and the New Deal's most prominent "Liberal," had two Jews as economic advisers: Louis Bean and Mordecai Ezekiel. Though this made it only too easy to attack Wallace politically, especially in the South, on the support of which Wallace's farm program was utterly dependent, Wallace never wavered in his support of the two men. But Catholics were totally absent in the upper reaches of the Department of Agriculture. Yet only a few blocks away, at the Department of Justice, there were plenty of Catholics but practically no Jews. And the FBI under Hoover was, of course, the original "Irish Mafia."

Sears Roebuck had been built by a Jew, Julius Rosenwald, with mostly Jewish associates. In the thirties, after Rosenwald's death, Jews were excluded from management positions in Sears largely as a result of Rosenwald's doing. He laid down the rule excluding Jews from top positions in Sears after the Leopold-Loeb murder affair, the most sensational and widely publicized crime of the twenties, in which two young men in Chicago, Leopold and Loeb, murdered a young nephew just for kicks. Both murderers were sons of high-ranking Sears executives and Rosenwald kin. But Sears also did not let any Catholics into top management. Charlie Kellstadt, who ultimately became Sears' chief executive in the fifties, was, however, a Catholic who had come up the ladder during the long reign of General Robert Wood, vocally anti-Semitic, anti-Catholic, and anti-Easterner. "How come you made it, Charlie?" I asked him. "I wouldn't have," he said, "if my name were Kennedy instead of Kellstadt, and Irish instead of German."

"There are Jewish law firms in New York and Gentile law firms," I once said to a Jewish friend, "How come there are two Seligman partners in Sullivan & Cromwell?" "But they're *German* Jews, and not Russian," was the answer. And when a friend became a partner in Lehman Brothers, I was told: "He isn't really a Russian Jew, his family is Hungarian." This cleavage persisted for the older generation into the postwar years, despite Hitler. One of my students in Bennington was the daughter of a prominent New York surgeon who came from a well-known German-Jewish family. She fell in love with a young physician, one of her father's residents, and brought him to Bennington to present him as her future husband. I thought him singularly nice. But her father—otherwise a perfectly sane man—asked me to help him break up the match. "Why do you want to?" I asked in amazement. "He is a RUSSIAN Jew," was the answer. (The family managed to break up the match only to have the girl marry, on the rebound, a fortune-hunting scoundrel.) New York's Harmonie Club had been founded because J. P. Morgan had denied Jews access to the Union League Club. But the Harmonie, in turn, did not admit non-German, that is, "Russian," Jews until well after World War II.

But there was also consternation among some Catholic friends when a Polish Catholic priest was appointed auxiliary bishop of a diocese other than the Polish "fief" of Buffalo. "German Catholics," they said, "we may have to take. But a Polish bishop, that's going too far. The Pope is getting very poor advice."

The Irish in Brooklyn and the Bronx allied themselves with Jews so as to keep the Italian Catholics from getting power and patronage jobs. This then forced New York's two ablest politicians of the Depression years, whose names happened to be Fiorello LaGuardia and Vito Marcantonio, to turn "anti-establishment" and "radical," but also to become Republicans and to build their machine on an upper middle-class, white Protestant base. All of which sounded obvious and perfectly sane within the context of Depression America until one had to explain it to non-American readers 3,000 miles away, as I was supposed to do. When John Kennedy ran for the presidency in 1960, large numbers of Catholics were reported to be lukewarm to the point of not voting for him because he had gone to Harvard instead of Holy Cross. But in the Depression years of the thirties, when the young Kennedys, with their eyes fixed on political careers, went to college, they had to make a deliberate decision to alienate the Irish Catholics twenty years later rather than lose for sure the non-Irish Catholic vote which a Holy Cross degree would have entailed.

I still remember the bewilderment of a German Catholic friend of mine, an anti-Nazi and a refugee, who enrolled his son in a Catholic university and was called in by the dean and advised to put the boy elsewhere. "This is really a university for the Irish," the dean said, "and your boy won't be happy here." Among Italians a similar cleavage ran deep between "Piedmontese," whose ancestors had come from the north, and the "Sicilians."

"It's sheer madness," I reported to one of my English publishers, Brendan Bracken of the *Financial News* (now the *Financial Times*), who wanted me to write a story on religion and national origins in American life, politics, and business. Bracken was altogether the most perceptive publisher I ever worked for, and the most extraordinary one—and not just because he drank a bottle of brandy before lunch, then acquired absolute recall which enabled him to recite from memory every page in the telephone directories of London, Manhattan, and Chicago. He was a member of Churchill's inner circle and became Britain's brilliant Minister of Information during World War II. "No," said Bracken, "it's not madness. It's worse. There is recovery from madness. It's tribalism and it paralyzes society in the end."

Bracken was right, of course but he was also quite wrong. Depression America was certainly tribal in its emphasis on what divides groups, on roots and origins, its stress on where a person came from. Indeed Depression America, by all accounts, was more tribal than the twenties had been. Whether this was "discrimination against" or "discrimination for" depended, as in all tribalism, on the specific situation. It was severe discrimination against the Catholic or Jewish boy trying to get into medical school; but it could also be discrimination for the Jewish or Catholic lawyer or the Jewish or Catholic high-school teacher trying to get a court appointment as receiver in bankruptcy or a high-school principalship.

Tribalism reached a peak in the Depression years precisely because of their emphasis on community, on belonging. It was vicious and could hurt. Yet it had innocence. And for this reason the tribalism that seemed in those Depression years to have a stranglehold on American life and the American imagination could overnight become a memory rather than reality. In the early postwar years, the high-school teacher from Oklahoma who often came along with us on hikes in Colorado's Rocky Mountain National Park still raved about "Popists" and the "Roman Whore of Babylon." His attractive children have both married Catholics. Now when Jewish boys are living with Italian girls without anybody's paying any attention; when Irish accountants are taking over as chief executives of "Protestant" companies in Fundamentalist Midwestern cities; and when "discrimination" may mean appointing a Jewish male rather than a black female to a faculty position—we can with safety stress ethnic diversity, exult in "Roots," and with impunity deny that the "melting pot" ever existed.

"There are two melting pots bubbling away in America," Dr. Mordecai Johnson, the wise Negro sociologist of Fisk University, once said to me. "One boils very, very slowly. But everything that goes into it comes out three generations later as Anglo-Saxon. The other pot boils very, very fast. And everything that goes into it—and a good bit of it goes in white—comes out only nine months later as black and Negro."

Of course as a young man living in England I *knew* all about the "Negro Problem in America." But when I came over, the reality hit me as nothing has before or since. It was not "worse"; it was different. In those years it puzzled an otherwise perceptive friend, Jack Fischer —later to become the editor of *Harper's* magazine—that I held Negro slavery in the United States to have been not a mistake and not a crime, but a sin. By now, I believe, few Americans would need an explanation. And of course the Abolitionists would have understood all along. But in Depression America racial discrimination was taken for granted by the great majority of blacks as well as whites. It was seen by Marxists, but also by other heirs of nineteenth-century determinism, as a by-product of "bourgeois capitalism" and bound to disappear with it. Or, by the liberals, especially in the industrial North, it was seen as one of the things that needed "reform." To me, it needed atonement and repentance. To me, the Negro was existential fact, far more important and enduring than the Depression. It was not until many years later that I read Thomas Jefferson's words: "When I remember that there is a Just God, I tremble for the future of the Union," but after a month in New York City I felt them. And, being a coward, I knew I could not live in the South. The most attractive academic job that ever came my way was the deanship at Emory University in Atlanta. It was offered to me in the late forties, when the South was still fully segregated, and I had to say no.

The New Deal saw its mission in integrating the rural South into the nation—and it is one mission in which it succeeded. This meant making Southern farmers prosperous, competent, powerful. And "Southern farmers" were, of course, white. The Old South was the true power base of Franklin D. Roosevelt, but an Old South to be made over in the image of the Midwest. When Roosevelt took office, the Old South was an underdeveloped country not too different from Brazil's Northeast today: underdeveloped economically, educationally, in its health, infant mortality, and life expectancies, and in being predominantly rural and single-crop. By the time America emerged from World War II, the South had been transformed. It was not yet the chrome-studded "Sun Belt" of today; it was still poorer, less educated, less healthy, and more rural then the rest of the nation. But it was only "behind," it was no longer apart. Faulkner's Sartorises were indeed gone. They could never, for better or worse, have fitted into a "developed modern society." But Faulkner's Snopeses were getting ready to study to be nuclear engineers.

This however demanded acceptance by the Roosevelt administration and by the nation of the "peculiar institution" of the South, that is, of white supremacy. The Roosevelt administration was the last fully to rest on the historic, though unwritten, constitutional compact of 1876 in which the South accepted national government by Northern agriculture, industry, and labor in exchange for Northern noninterference with the South's "peculiar institution." The very success of this formula under the Roosevelt administration made it obsolete, for the South ceased to be rural and "outside." But the Depression years,

whatever their liberal rhetoric, were years of official racial discrimination far more consistent and uncompromising than earlier Northern-
based Republican administrations had to be. And anyone who then
suggested that America's internal discrimination against the Negro
and its external "anti-colonialism" were incompatible would have gotten a blank stare of total incomprehension.

Yet it was the New Deal that laid the foundations for black emancipation precisely because it made the white Southern farmer affluent.
That the Negro was rural and would remain rural was an axiom in
those days, for blacks as well as whites, and for Liberals and Conservatives alike. The great Negro scholars of the day—a Mordecai Johnson,
for instance—went into *rural* sociology. And the pitifully little the
New Deal tried to do for Negroes was inspired largely by a book by
an English economist, Doreen Warriner, called *Preface to Peasantry.*
It preached the self-sufficient peasant commune. The New Deal,
under Mrs. Roosevelt's prodding, actually built some communes for
black sharecroppers. They looked like concentration camps, turned
into instant slums, never became self-sufficient, and were deserted
wholesale the moment the black family could hitch a ride on a jalopy
to the hellfires of a Northern ghetto such as Detroit or Los Angeles.

But I too believed in Warriner's diagnosis, if not in her prescription. And it was therefore a shock I can still remember when I and
Malcolm Bryan—a Chicagoan who had become head of the Federal
Reserve Bank of Atlanta and the South's leading economist—suddenly
realized one morning in 1940 after a few days' work on population
statistics that the American Negro was becoming both a Northerner
and a city dweller, and that the "Negro problem" would, in another
twenty years, have become the problem of the Northern city.

This was directly the result of successful New Deal measures
aimed at making the Southern white farmer more productive, more
competent, and wealthier. The New Deal made the American farmer
into a good credit risk; he became entitled to secure, predictable,
steady payments for not growing stuff, for putting land into the "soil
bank," and to interest-free loans on whatever crop he did produce.
Lending to the Southern cotton farmer had always been more akin to
pawnbroking and usury than to banking. Suddenly it came to be lending to Uncle Sam, and more profitable than buying government notes.
As soon as the farmer could get credit, he could afford to farm produc-
tively—and that meant without the Negro sharecropper. For the
sharecropper, while receiving starvation wages, also represented ex-

orbitant labor costs—always the best prescription for extreme poverty, of course. He worked six weeks in the year; that's all cotton requires. But he and his wife and his children and his mule had to be fed, however poorly, fifty-two weeks a year. A weekly income that was shamefully low translated into a labor cost per bale of cotton that not even a very high price could cover. As soon as the farmer became a bankable risk he therefore bought machinery, which doesn't have to be fed unless it works. Tractors and even cotton pickers had of course been around a long time—cotton could be picked mechanically as early as 1897. It was economics that pushed the sharecropper out—the economics of affluence. He went willingly. It is only now, a generation later, that any Black can afford to be nostalgic about the Old South.

Technology did play a part, yet not in the form of the tractor and the cotton picker but of the used car. "It's no longer a question whether the American Negro will be emancipated," said Mordecai Johnson to me once. "He has been emancipated. The only question is how long it will be before the whites know it. The American Negro," he continued, "was free the day one of them realized that a white man is just as dead if run over by a car driven by a nigger as by one driven by a white." The automobile gave mobility. But above all it gave power. It put the Negro sharecropper emotionally and spiritually into the driver's seat.

Technology has been a major element in the story of the Negro in America. Whether slavery would have been abolished earlier, I do not know. But without Eli Whitney's cotton gin, it would almost certainly have become a minor factor and its territory a steadily shrinking one after mass immigration from Europe got going in the 1780s. The North American soils and climates are simply not suitable for any plantation crop other than cotton. The automobile, electricity, the tractor, the cotton picker, in the end doomed the plantation economy and with it the rural Negro. But technology also, in the mass-production industries, created the alternative employments to which an unskilled, pre-industrial Southern Negro sharecropper could migrate, start earning money, and begin having access to schools, union membership, and the political power of the ballot box.

And yet technology, I thought, was only a small part of the truth, the less important one. If, as I strongly felt, Negro slavery was a sin, then it could not be overcome by technology. It could only be affected, let alone overcome, by a contrite heart. It could not, altogether, be overcome by the Negro but only by the white freeing himself. Indeed the great advances in the status, standing, and position of the American Black were not made by and under liberals working through economics or "reforms." They were made by and under white Southerners, proud of being descendants of Confederate soldiers and acting out of conversion: by Harry Truman and Lyndon Johnson.

The New Deal years were the years in which the conversion started. They were the years in which the American Negro first produced in substantial numbers men of excellence, men of vision, men who had truly become free men. They were extraordinary people, those Negro scholars and preachers of Depression America. What made them so powerful was not just their intellect, their scholarship, and their uncompromising dignity. It was their integrity. I first met Mordecai Johnson when he talked to the students and faculty at Sarah Lawrence College in Bronxville, New York (probably in the fall of 1940). He shocked the ultra-liberal faculty by saying that the greatest problem of the American Negro was not oppression and discrimination; it was the fact that, alone of all peoples in human history, the Negroes in Africa had been willing, indeed eager, to enslave their own kind and to sell them off into slavery with Arabs and whites. "Unless the American Negro is willing to confront the guilt and mystery of his own roots, he'll never be truly free," Johnson said. Nothing less popular could have been said then or now. I went to Dr. Johnson after the meeting and said: "You are wrong. The classical Greeks—especially the Athenians of the Golden Age—did exactly that. Look at the horrible story of Athens' enslavement of the Melians in Thucydides." "I know all about it," he said, "and *you* are wrong. The Greeks enslaved their own kind, but they sold them to other Greeks, not to foreigners or invaders the way only we did."

This was the integrity out of which Martin Luther King arose, the integrity that gave the Negro leaders their inner sovereignty and moral authority, not only among their own people but also in white America.

But perhaps the black voice was even more important. The "Negro Problem in America" requires a change of heart as much as a change of policies, and even the best rural sociology does not reach the heart. I learned a great deal from Mordecai Johnson even though I did not see him often, for he was a busy man. But I was shaken and moved by the voice of Howard Thurman, the chaplain at Howard, the Negro university, into whose church I sneaked whenever I spent a weekend in Washington. Thurman's was the last generation of the great Negro preachers' voices—the microphone and the loudspeaker have killed them off. The sheer power and beauty of these voices reached the inner core of one's being. In the Depression years the radio made us singularly voice-conscious. And the radio got the great Negro voices, such as Thurman's, out of the black church and into the white living room.

The true emancipation of the American white from the bondage of Negro slavery began perhaps on that Depression day when the Daughters of the American Revolution, shocking even bigots, denied the use of Washington's Constitution Hall to Marian Anderson— thereby making a fine Negro musician into a major national figure. It was Marian Anderson and her voice—that beautiful and totally spiritual force—that, having become a "celebrity" through bigotry, suddenly reached every American living room when she sang "Let My People Go." It was Marian Anderson's voice which made White America recognize that the "Negro" problem concerns the conscience of the white far more than the rights of the black.

A few days after I had joined the Foreign Press Association (not more than six weeks after I had arrived in New York), a letter from Columbia University arrived, signed by the provost, a Mr. Fackenthal. "President Nicholas Murray Butler," it said, "remembers with pleasure meeting you earlier in Geneva at the League of Nations and would like to renew the acquaintance. He hopes you can join him for tea next Tuesday at four in his office at the Low Library." I had heard of Dr. Butler. I had definitely never met him, however, and could not imagine what he might want of me.

Mr. Fackenthal ushered me into an office where a very old man sat huddled in a chair looking at the floor. "Here is Mr. Drucker, Mr. President," said Fackenthal. "You remember you met him earlier in Geneva and had such interesting talks with him?" The old man in the chair did not look up and only held out a limp hand. "I'll leave you two alone," said Mr. Fackenthal cheerfully. Not a word was said until the tea came. Then the old man poured a cup and asked, "One lump or two?" "Thank you," I said, "but I don't take sugar." There was no response—and another five minutes of silence. Then the old man asked again, "One lump or two?" and I, thinking that he might be hard of hearing, repeated what I had said earlier. Again nothing happened for five minutes, then I was asked again how many lumps of sugar I might want. This time I said, "One." Dr. Butler promptly put one lump into my cup and pushed it across to me, still staring at the floor.

Twenty minutes of total silence, broken only by his pouring me another cup and asking again how many lumps of sugar I would want, then Mr. Fackenthal bustled in and said cheerily, "I hate to break in when you and Mr. Drucker are having such an enjoyable chat but, Dr. Butler, your next appointment is waiting." When I got back to my office downtown, I found out what Fackenthal wanted, although not why he wanted me to meet the poor old man. No sooner had I left my office to go to Columbia than a messenger had arrived with an enormous box containing Dr. Butler's collected speeches and papers and fifty envelopes, already stamped and addressed to Mr. Fackenthal, with a note: "Please use these envelopes to mail any dispatches in which you refer to President Butler or quote him."

I never had occasion either to refer to President Butler or to quote him. But I did follow up Fackenthal's parting words: "I hope you'll pay some attention to American higher education in your dispatches to your British papers. It is a most interesting subject." This, I soon found out, was an understatement. Higher education in Depression America may well have been *the* most interesting subject. The 1960s are today considered to have been the "golden age" of academia in America, but they were only the era of riches, numbers, and grants, and maybe, of arrogance. The "great age" of American higher education was the 1930s. Colleges and universities were not rich then, though they did amazingly well in the Depression as costs went down sharply while both tuition fees and charitable donations held up strongly. But the thirties were years of thinking, of venturing, of excitement and innovation.

Nicholas Murray Butler's senility—despite which he stayed on as titular president until 1945, with Fackenthal running the show as provost—was highly symbolic. For the university that Butler had built and stood for had, by the early thirties, become so successful as to outlive itself. Butler was the last of the giants who, beginning with Charles Eliot (who became president of Harvard in 1869), had created the modern American university on the ruins of the eighteenth-century "seminary." Butler became a college president earlier than anyone in the history of American higher education and stayed president longer. He was only twenty-six when, in 1888, he proposed that teachers' education should be "higher" education rather than "normal school," and founded Teachers College and with it the concept of "education" as a subject of research and university study. He had moved on to the Columbia presidency in 1902, merging Teachers College into Columbia in the process. When I met him he had been a college president for forty-nine years; he hung on for another eight, until he was finally forced out, eighty-three years old and totally incapacitated. He had been a firebrand in his youth and earned his nickname, "Nicholas Miraculous." But everything he had fought for: higher education for teachers and systematic research into education; attention to educational administration; civil service reform and systematic university-level preparation of public servants; systematic preparation for university teaching with the Ph.D. as a prerequisite and work as a teaching assistant as a supervised apprenticeship; the graduate school as a distinct and separate unit—but also systematic money raising and organized publicity—all this had become reality by World War I and commonplace by the mid-thirties. And so had Butler's idea of the university as itself a public service institution, which not only prepares students and fosters research but provides a focus of leadership, responsibility, and expertise in public affairs, both within the community and for government. Butler's ideas had become old as he was becoming senile. The Depression then unleashed a turbulent abundance of new ideas, new experiments, new directions.

In the Depression the university was "news." The quickest way to break up a dinner party was to express an opinion, whether favorable or unfavorable, of Robert Hutchins's attempt to make the University of Chicago over into the image of Plato's Academy, or to ask for an opinion on Harvard's equally controversial attempt to abolish any kind of educational coherence altogether and to become education's highest-quality delicatessen store. Husbands and wives fought over the virtues or vices of "progressive education"—whether that meant no rules for students, small classes, or the lavish use of field trips, movies, and guest lecturers from the "real world," no one quite knew. Every college or university, no matter how small or undistinguished, was at work on curriculum reform, developing new ideas, testing new courses.

This ferment centered on teaching and on the student's learning. I had long harbored the prejudice that school has to do with teaching and learning; I had after all been engaged in "teacher-watching" as a favorite pursuit since encountering Miss Elsa and Miss Sophy in fourth grade. But teaching and learning were not particularly important in the universities of Europe, with their emphasis on preparation for professional careers, and on research and scholarship, that is, on the study and the laboratory rather than the classroom. Higher education in Depression America was passionately concerned with teaching, engrossed in teaching, obsessed by it. The first thing the visitor was told on any campus was who the first-rate *teachers* were.

When I mentioned that I was going to the University of Minnesota at Minneapolis to give a lecture, I was told at once, "You have to go and hear so-and-so, he's their best *teacher.*" "What's his field?" I'd ask. "It's statistics," was the answer, "and he's not particularly good at it, just average. But he is the one first-rate statistics teacher in the country." And he was indeed outstanding. I learned more statistics from him in five minutes than I ever learned before or since, including even the course I myself taught in the subject. A little bald-headed bearded man, almost a dwarf, he ran a doctoral seminar in which he projected tables and graphs onto a screen without any legend or explanation. "Look at the figures," he'd say, "and tell me what they tell you." The students would point out this irregularity in a distribution or that periodicity, this pattern or that internal contradiction, and the little man would nod, smile, argue, and get across a great deal about numbers as a grammar without ever belaboring the point. Then he'd flash on the screen two series of figures that obviously belonged together; they showed a close correlation, almost one to one, over long time periods. "Clearly," all the students said, "these two series are causally related." "That's what every statistician would say," the little man responded, "but perhaps you can tell me what the relationship could be. This series," pointing to the table on the left, "is the annual herring catch off Newfoundland; and that one," pointing to the right, "is the number of illegitimate children born the same year in North Dakota."

"Publish or perish" was not, of course, entirely unknown even during the Depression years, despite their emphasis on teaching and learning. But even at the big "research" universities—Harvard, Columbia, or Chicago—the first question was not: "What has he published?" It was: "How good a teacher is he or she?" The clinching argument for whatever educational philosophy one favored—Hutchins's Neo-Thomism at Chicago, "progressive" education, or the "fix-your-own-educational-hero-sandwich" approach of Harvard—was always that it best fitted student needs and student abilities and enabled students to learn.

There was also great interest in the role and function of the university in society. It was a surprising topic for someone from Europe.

It had, one assumed, been settled long ago, certainly by the time the University of Berlin was founded in 1809 as the first of the "modern" German universities, which then became the prototype. But no, in the America of the Depression years the question was wide open, and very controversial indeed. These were the years in which the state university and the state college attained maturity and became "national" institutions rather than parochial ones. Of course, some state universities (North Carolina at Chapel Hill, "Mr. Jefferson's University" in Virginia, or Michigan) had long achieved distinction, but by being "as good as the leading private schools." Now the tax-supported public American university emerged as a distinct type and *sui generis*. There was Iowa State College at Ames, different equally from Germany's "technical university" and the traditional land-grant "aggie" school: a top-level, research-focused school of applied sciences, but also at the same time the very center of policy-making in agriculture.

But above all there was Monroe Deutsch—"American education's best-kept secret," as Christian Gauss, the dean at Princeton, once called him. Whenever one talked about the university, its structure and its function, someone would eventually say, "The one man who has thought the most about this is Monroe Deutsch." Deutsch himself never appeared in public, never showed up at meetings or conferences, never made a speech, never gave an interview, never had his picture in the papers. If one called the University of California where Deutsch was provost, one got a secretary on the line who wanted to know what the call was all about. If she found out that it was a newspaperman calling, she hung up. Otherwise she said, "Please write a letter; I'll see that it gets to the proper place." It took persistence to penetrate to Deutsch's lair—his office literally was a "lair," in the basement of an old building on the Berkeley campus and without a name on the door to help anyone find him.

Deutsch was then quite willing to talk about the university and particularly about the University of California, which was his whole life. But he never talked about himself. He had been born into one of San Francisco's wealthy families and decided early to spend his life in public service. But being pathologically shy, he was unable to endure public exposure, let alone run for office. And so he had invented for himself the role as *eminence grise* of the California university system, or rather he decided that it would become a "system." He made himself "Provost" and went underground, literally as well as figuratively. Then he designed the multi-campus university which California became after World War I when UCLA was first started; and he designed California's multi-tier system of university, state colleges, and junior colleges, which would maintain the scholastic excellence and exclusivity of the university and yet enable every high-school graduate in California to attend a tuition-free state institution of higher learning. Deutsch also largely designed the ingenious system that gave the university fiscal autonomy by guaranteeing it a fixed sum from the state for each student admitted. He pushed for state commitment to higher education as California's first political priority, and commitment to excellence as the university's first educational priority. "I didn't know that there would be a Hitler and that we would suddenly be able to hire fifty or sixty first-rate scholars and teachers," he said; "but I started fifteen years ago to make both the state and the university ready for manna from heaven, should it ever rain down."

An entirely different kind of excitement was the bitter political fight within American higher education in those Depression years. By that time the Communists had already lost their influence in, and control over, the American labor movement. They had failed to organize the American Negro. They then aimed their efforts at the American university. The fight was particularly vicious in New York; and as always, the Communists and their fellow travelers concentrated on destroying Social Democrats and ousting them from any position of influence. Their main targets were non-Communist leftists, like the New York University philosopher Sydney Hook, the economist Harry Gideonse, then president of Brooklyn College, or Lionel Trilling, the literary critic at Columbia. But the fighting—the threats, manifestos, proclamations, denunciations, and far too many outright Communist attempts to silence, defame, and intimidate faculty, administration, and students alike—reached into colleges and universities throughout the country. Fifteen years later American academia, cowed and silent, left the defense of freedom against McCarthy largely to outsiders—mainly old-line Liberals and especially Conservatives—and in the end to the U.S. Army. The reason in large measure was a massive case of bad conscience; far too many professed believers in academic freedom had knuckled under and signed Communist denunciations of non-Communist collegues, declarations of support for the purge trials, or Communist-inspired political manifestos of all kinds. Indeed everyone except a tenured full professor who dared refuse to sign these documents might be told bluntly that he need not expect to be reappointed or promoted. And there were far too many institutions where the

Communist cell had enough power for the threat to be credible, perhaps even real.

Into all this turbulence—some joyful, some corrosive, all strident —came the refugee scholars from Germany, Austria, Hungary, Czechoslovakia, and—though many fewer—Spain and Italy. It was, of course, the turbulence that in large measure made it possible to absorb them and put them to work in such numbers. And it was also the turbulence in American higher education in those Depression years that gave the newcomers such impact. Britain, after all, also took in many refugee scholars especially of the older, already well-established generation; yet they had no impact at all on the British university. The refugees in America arrived at the very moment when the universities there were eager for new values, new ideas, new methods, new voices, and new faces. And in turn the American universities had incredible impact on the refugee scholars—a story that would make fascinating reading although by now it is probably too late to get it together.

America made first-rate scholars and teachers out of many men and women who would probably have become at best competent mediocrities in their own countries. They found themselves forced to move beyond narrow departmental boundaries so as to satisfy students' needs or to teach in an "integrated" curriculum. They had opportunities that would have been denied them forever by the rigidity of the European university. In Italy Enrico Fermi would not, after having received the Nobel Prize, have been allowed to teach physics to liberal arts freshmen, or Leo Szilard—another physicist of Nobel Prize status—to switch to teaching biology. All told the Europeans would not have been forced to become active members of a *university;* They would have stayed encapsulated in their "specialty" or, at best, remained in confinement in one "faculty." But in Depression America even the biggest university and the one most clearly focused on graduate school and on "research," Harvard, for instance, was still a common venture, still a corporate body, still—despite all feuds, all backbiting, all politicking—a community, and not just an office building.

In public press and public discussion, the spotlight was on the "big name" universities (although some of them, Princeton, for example, were then still quite small by present-day standards). But I found myself drawn more and more to the small undergraduate college. It was a specifically American institution. There was nothing like it in Europe, where one found either state universities (and even a small state university in Germany, France, or Italy is part of a big central-ized system) or the very big cluster-universities that Oxford and Cam-bridge had already become. The small American college—meaning in those years anything between 150 and 700 students—also seemed to me to have unique properties and virtues.

I saw a good many of the smaller colleges in those years. It was clear to me fairly early that my work for European newspapers and financial institutions would not survive the coming of a European war. I therefore tried to shift my base to America as a writer and, increas-ingly, as a lecturer. By the time America went to war, I was giving as many as fifty or sixty lectures a year all over the country. At least half of them were at small colleges.

Lecturing was strenuous, if only because travel in those years meant spending nights in old Pullman cars on rough roadbeds, being shunted from one siding to another all the way from Dubuque to Fargo or from New Orleans to Jacksonville. It meant getting snowed in in such places as Gratis, Ohio, and Beatrice, Nebraska—still my favorites among American place names. It meant a lot of odd experi-ences. There was, for instance, the lecture for the Colonial Dames of America in a charming eighteenth-century clubhouse in New York. "Who or what are Colonial Dames?" I asked my lecture agent. "I don't know myself," she said, "but they pay the highest fees." The lady who greeted me said, "I'm the club secretary and the only member under seventy-five. We'll put all the members who can hear into the first two rows. But you better speak up; most of them can't hear too well. Don't bother about the others. They don't hear at all." After my lecture an old woman—the only person I've ever seen wearing a diamond stom-acher—slowly made her way forward, held up on both sides by sturdy maids. "I am sorry I didn't hear well enough to get your talk," she said. "But don't you think, Mr. Drucker, that the world is getting to where the poor will soon demand their place in the sun?" Or there was the evening in Rochester, New York—at the University Club, I believe—where, ten minutes before the start of the program, I was told to split my talk in half, "one half before the music, one half after." "What music?" I asked. "Didn't they tell you? We'll have two students from the Eastman Conservatory doing the death scene from *Aïda* between the first and second half of your talk." And when the star-crossed lovers had finally died at my feet, the chairman turned to me and said: "Your last sentence before you stopped was . . ."

Lecturing was the best way to get to see and know the country.

And while I spoke in most of the larger cities in those years, I lectured more and more in the small colleges. They were hungry for someone from the outside, receptive, hospitable, and also fascinating. They were as diverse as the country itself. Some prided themselves on having higher academic standards than any of the "name" universities; others still clung to the simplicities of the early-nineteenth-century "seminary." Some were so conservative that the lights were switched off at nine o'clock, except for a nightlight in the toilets. Others were ultra-permissive and worried about the "sexual repression" of their students. Not all of them had the scholarship, the discipline, the high standards of Oberlin, Wesleyan, Pomona, Grinnell, or Mills, but there were enough of them to make the visitor realize how committed the country was to learning and to teaching. And even the poorest and most benighted "cow college" tried.

Altogether it was in small schools that most of the experimentation took place, for they were still small enough to respond to a courageous administrator. In the small town of Yellow Springs, Ohio, for instance, an engineer-educator called Arthur Morgan, the president of Antioch College, introduced "cooperative education" in which students combine work in regular full-time jobs for five months of the year with regular full-time college attendance during the remaining seven months. And it was a small school, Bennington, started in the darkest days of 1932 as a "progressive" women's college, which at the end of the Depression years asked me to join in developing an integrated liberal arts curriculum that would combine the intellectual rigor Robert Hutchins aimed at in Chicago with the student self-management of Harvard and with a faculty freedom to learn and teach that neither had.

In many ways the small schools were better off in those days than the big universities. Bennington, which limited itself to an enrollment of 325 students, was economically and educationally viable. Yet it had no endowment. It matched the highest faculty salaries paid everywhere. It had a particularly high faculty-student ratio, with 50 faculty members for the 325 students. To be sure, it charged even then very high tuition; but no qualified applicant was turned away because she could not pay. And all the money the college had to raise to pay its bills (other than capital funds for new buildings) was scholarship money; otherwise Bennington broke even. For costs in those years were very low, and far lower in the small school than in the big university, with its heavy graduate school overhead, its expensive labs, and its old faculty in place and tenured. The small places could often outbid the "big name" universities for talent, especially in the humanities and the arts.

There were some wonderful characters around in those small schools. Aurelia Reinhardt, for instance, the president of Mills, the women's college in Oakland, California, was the very picture of a spinster bluestocking. She had been an outstanding historian at Stanford and Herbert Hoover's first love, but had turned down marriage to pursue an academic career. When I got to know her, in the course of a three-day stay as a lecturer, she had been the president at Mills for thirty years and had built the school into the leading women's college in the West. She was very tall, raw-boned and gaunt, with a voice to match her figure, but clad in yards and yards of flowered pink organdy. At a reception for me at her house there was a lull in the conversation, and a student's voice could suddenly be heard: "I'll remain a virgin until I marry." Miss Reinhardt turned around and said in her booming basso voice, "You are wasting your college years, my child," then went on telling me about the Versailles Peace Conference where she had been a member of the American delegation.

But my most poignant small-college memory is of a very small and totally obscure one: Friends University in Wichita, Kansas. I got there in June 1941 on a team which the Foreign Policy Association was sending to a number of small colleges to run week-long foreign affairs institutes. The president of the school, which was (and is) affiliated with the Kansas Quakers, tried to be kind to us. "You're only going to be here a week," he said, "so we shan't attempt to reform you. I know you're all from the godless East. Gentlemen," pointing to a magnificent copper beech outside the building, "under this tree you may smoke." Then he told us the secret password to get a drink in any drugstore on Main Street, for Kansas was still officially bone-dry. "If you order a double mumbo-jumbo Southern ice cream soda," he said, "you'll get a shot of bourbon; but please don't order it until after your day's talk. You are going to lecture under our proudest possession. Carry Nation's hatchet, with which she smashed the saloon furniture in her campaign against the Demon Rum, is mounted above the speaker's podium and I'd rather you respect her memory. We do." Friends University, despite its grandiose name, was tiny. It then had about 150 students and was losing enrollment (although now, I see, it has almost 900 students). Nevertheless we attracted large crowds from the town and had a successful week. But I was puzzled by the president's obvious attempts to make us stay below the fourth floor of the five-story building. Finally, on the last day of our stay, I asked him why he did not want anyone to go upstairs. "We only have our museum up there," he said in obvious embarrassment, "and you people from the big city are used to much better museums."

I pried the story out of him. The college did not need the two top floors; it could barely fill the three lower ones. And so when two retired old employes—a teacher of Spanish and the college carpenter—asked for the loan of the upper floors for a museum, they had gotten them and, in addition, a grant of $50 a year from the Kansas Society of Friends. This, they wisely decided, did not enable them to buy anything. But it did give them enough money for postage on begging letters all over the world to the college's alumni and friends—which yielded the contents of their "museum." I have rarely seen a more fascinating magpie's nest. There was a large and beautiful set of Plains Indians baskets, of the Kiowas, the Poncas, and the Winnebago—the finest I've ever seen. Today it would be worth a king's ransom. There was also the world's largest collection of Hungarian counterfeit money, and an enormous Imperial Russian double-headed eagle made entirely of mother-of-pearl buttons. There was the first sod house built in Kansas. You crawled in on all fours, only to find yourself up against the first Ford Model T driven in Kansas. "We had no other place to put it," the old carpenter explained somewhat sheepishly. The two old men had seen in a magazine that the American Museum of Natural History in New York had built "habitat groups" with stuffed animals and artificial palm trees; as they had several stuffed African animals, a lion, a zebra, even a giraffe, they had built one too. The lion—a most majestic beast—was standing there, aroar; but he carried in his open mouth the first typewriter used in Kansas. Again, there was no other place for it.

I was enchanted and would have loved to linger. But I had to catch a plane. As I got downstairs, I found my colleagues huddled around a radio. Hitler had invaded Russia.

"Are you working for *The New York Times* or the Chicago *Tribune,* and where in Europe are you stationed?" William Waymack, editor of the Des Moines *Register,* asked when I was introduced to him as a foreign correspondent. When I told him that I was a foreign correspondent in the United States and wrote for British newspapers, he got so excited that he called his editorial staff together. "A foreign correspondent, as we all know, is an American newspaperman reporting on Europe. But here's a foreign correspondent who is reporting on the U.S. to British papers." And he wrote a feature story on me for next day's front page of the *Register*. Yet Waymack was no yokel but one of America's most distinguished newsmen. He had received Pulitzer Prizes for editorial excellence in 1936 and 1937. He was the best source of information on the Midwest and on agricultural conditions and problems, but also deeply interested in foreign affairs and knowledgeable about both Europe and Asia. He was the moving spirit behind the growth and upgrading of both the University of Iowa and Iowa State College at Ames. After the war he became a member of President Truman's first Atomic Energy Commission. And the Des Moines *Register*, which he had edited since 1921, would have been included in any list of the ten best American papers; it was singularly well informed about the outside world.

Waymack knew, of course, that there were foreign newsmen in the United States. He made it a point to look them up when he came East every two or three months. After our first meeting in Des Moines he always, for instance, had lunch or dinner with me on these Eastern trips. But foreign newspapermen or indeed foreign visitors did not normally get to Des Moines. They stayed on the East Coast. They went to Chicago when forced to by such quaint American folk rituals as a presidential nominating convention. They went once during their tour of duty to Detroit, and wrote a piece on Ford's River Rouge Plant which, by the thirties, had taken the place as a "must" tourist attraction that Niagara Falls had held for the visiting European in the nineteenth century. And, of course, there was a standard piece on Hollywood—it always read as if supplied by Central Casting at a half-hour's notice. But the country between New York and Hollywood was wasteland "where the buffalo roam"; and why bother with it when all one needed to know had been said by Sinclair Lewis and H. L. Mencken? So a "foreign" correspondent who appeared in Des Moines to learn about the Midwest, the corn country, Iowa University and Iowa State College, the New Deal's farm program, and the American people, was really something to write about.

But it was not just foreign correspondents who thought Iowa "isolated." Iowa, like most of America, saw itself as isolated—different from, outside of, and far away from, the world of the great powers, of European national rivalries, and petty boundaries; different in values, in culture, in basic commitments. Not "better," necessarily. "Europe" as a symbol of refinement, of "culture," of the "higher things in life," rated more highly and was venerated more piously in those years than ever before or since in American history. These were the years, for instance, when Midwestern cities—Detroit and Toledo, Cleveland, Chicago, and Minneapolis—vied with one another to fill their newly built museums with European masters, and when a "Western Civilization" course that rigorously excluded anything American became the core of the college curriculum from Columbia University in New York City to Stanford on the Pacific. Few Americans in those years had ever heard of Kafka—the cult began a few years later, in the mid-forties— yet their picture of their own country was not too different from the fantasy of Kafka's *Amerika*: a realm apart, free from the vices, the hatreds, the constraints, and the guilt of the Old World. "America Was Promises" said Archibald MacLeish in a poem of 1939 that sold by the thousands, if not the hundred thousands. What set America apart, in the minds of Americans—and of Europeans such as Kafka—was precisely that it was not a "country" but a "Constitution." The promises were political and social. The "American Dream" is an ideal *society;* and the American genius is political.

America is a territory, to be sure, and occupies a specific area on the earth's surface. But this place is the spatial location of principles held to be universally valid, without which there would perhaps be an "America" but surely not a "United States." America was, and is, the only country that has a politician for its public saint: Abraham Lincoln. There is only one genuinely native American art form: politics. And one becomes an American citizen by swearing allegiance to abstract principles, to a "Constitution."

Europe was not all that far away geographically from Iowa in the Depression years, or from the Department of Agriculture in Washington, or the General Motors headquarters in Detroit. Following World War I, in which large numbers of young Americans had been taken on a conducted "Grand Tour," the European trip became the thing to do for anyone moderately well off. Even in Faulkner's Yoknapatawpha County the young uncle who represents civilization in all its helplessness has been to Heidelberg; and Temple Drake in *Sanctuary,* Faulkner's small-town anti-heroine, is taken to Paris to forget the horrors and thrills of a Memphis whorehouse. But spiritually the distance between Europe and America was never greater than in the Depression years.

For the New Deal was a conscious reaffirmation of the distinctive

ness, the uniqueness, the American-ness of America. Above all, it tried
to reestablish the basic American commitment: America is not a "nation" like any other, not a "country"—it is a creed. It was the one point
on which the New Deal and its enemies agreed. The crucial debates
in the New Deal years were not over whether this or that measure was
right but whether it was "American" or "un-American." What Henry
Wallace, the Secretary of Agriculture, or his bright young regional
administrators of Soil Conservation Districts and Farm Security Programs throughout the country, always stressed first, was the "uniquely
American character" of the farm program. And indeed no other country could have imagined anything like the New Deal's farm program,
with its aim of creating millions of profitable agricultural businesses,
each of them a high-technology, capital-intensive, and education-
intensive enterprise rather than a "farm"; and yet each of them self-
reliant, independent, and the home of a family. To be sure, after
World War II Japan adopted a somewhat similar program, but largely,
of course, under American prodding and on the New Deal model.
New Deal America was equally conscious of the uniqueness of the
American labor union: militant but nonideological, and a countervailing power to management rather than the "class enemy" of "capital."
The New Deal itself saw its essence in the uniquely American concept
of regulation under due legal process by quasi-judicial organs such as
the Securities and Exchange Commission (SEC), as against the "European" alternatives of arbitrary and political, and therefore essentially
unregulated, nationalization, and equally arbitrary and unregulated
laissez-faire.

This consciousness of being different can lead to stupidity and
blindness. It underlies the unthinking assumption that anything that
happens in the United States must be uniquely American and have
distinct American causes. In the last few years, for instance, it has
become unquestioned "fact" in the United States that the "explosion"
of health care costs is a uniquely American phenomenon that has its
causes in peculiarly American habits, policies, or conspiracies—in the
American payments mechanism for health care, for instance, which,
we are told, is biased in favor of hospitalization, or in the tendency to
overbuild hospitals resulting from the private and local character of
the community hospital, or in a conspiracy to do unnecessary surgery.
No one in the United States seems to realize that every other developed country—Japan, Great Britain, Sweden, France, Germany—is
undergoing the same "explosion" of health care costs, even though

none of them has the American payments mechanism, the American community hospital, the "over-supply of unneeded hospital beds"—in Britain, for instance, "under-supply of hospital beds" is considered a main cause of the "explosion" of health care costs—or the American prevalence of surgery. No one, in other words, is willing to realize that we are dealing with a general phenomenon that cannot possibly have peculiarly American causes. To do so would put in question the belief in the uniqueness of America as a society and polity. Similarly, the student unrest of the late sixties and early seventies is explained with peculiarly American causes: the Vietnam war, or the black ghetto. But again the phenomenon occurred in every developed country, and first in Japan and France, none of which had a Vietnamese war or a black ghetto.

The American Creed can also easily degenerate into bathos, bragging, and populist ranting, and often has. Charles Dickens in *Martin Chuzzlewit*—published in 1843—wrote during the years of the Jacksonian "New Deal" what is still the funniest and most biting satire of American populist bragging. And though Dickens himself, twenty-five years later, apologized and retracted his satire as exaggerated, one can still find the braggarts and charlatans he caricatured at every American political convention and in every American political campaign.

But the American Creed is also Lincoln's "Last Best Hope." And it is the American Creed, of course, that again and again has attracted the European to this country. Only the European so attracted soon ceases to be a European. After I told him why I had come to Des Moines, William Waymack smiled and said, "You won't be a foreign correspondent long. You'll soon be an American writer." A few years later, when I moved to Bennington College and had to choose which of the curriculum's basic courses I wanted to teach, I did not pick "Western Civilization." I picked American history and American government.

But by the time I first met Waymack (probably in the early fall of 1938, at the time of the Munich crisis), the American Dream was already encountering the one awakening it cannot face: international affairs.

The America of the American Creed must be "isolationist." Indeed what historically has been known in the United States as "internationalism" is as much a form of isolationism as the avowedly isolationist version. It attempts to relieve the United States of the need for concern with international affairs and foreign politics through an automatic, self-governing, perfect mechanism that will maintain peace and order in the world without policy decisions, and indeed without anyone's active intervention: an International Court of Justice, a Wilsonian League of Nations, a United Nations. For the "American Dream" to be meaningful, foreign affairs must become a "non-event." Thus Arthur Schlesinger, Jr., in his celebrated *Age of Jackson*, managed to avoid any mention of foreign affairs and of the outside world altogether, even though foreign politics were a major preoccupation of the Jacksonian period when the foundations were laid for the annexation of Texas and the War with Mexico a few years later. To Schlesinger the "Age of Jackson" was the heroic age of American history precisely because it reaffirmed and redefined the "American Creed." *The Age of Jackson* was published in 1945 with the professed aim of recalling the American people and the American government to their mission of building the Universal City of Man on the American continent, a mission from which the international crisis and World War II had deflected them. Arthur Schlesinger was an "internationalist" in those years and had to believe that the United Nations would make the world "safe," thereby enabling America to return to its own business and its own mission. But for that, foreign affairs had to become "non-affairs."

The reality of international politics, however, always demands that foreign affairs be given primacy. It always asserts loudly that creed, commitment, values, ideals are means rather than ends. It always makes survival paramount over vision. It always treats the United States as one country dependent on many other countries, rather than as the "Last Best Hope on Earth" by itself.

In 1932, when Roosevelt ran for office the first time, his platform was completely isolationist. One of the main charges against Herbert Hoover, especially on the part of the "Liberals," was his undue concern with the outside world, his attention to foreign—that is, alien—affairs, whether the Japanese invasion of China or the Italian invasion of Ethiopia, and his willingness to consider the impact on a world economy in turmoil when shaping American domestic policies. And one of the very first actions of Roosevelt was the deliberate, highly publicized sabotage of the London World Economic Conference, by which the newly inducted President served notice of the New Deal's commitment to the denial of foreign affairs, foreign responsibility, and international cooperation.

Four years later, in 1936, when Roosevelt ran for his second term, foreign affairs still did not exist, and "isolationism" was still unquestioningly accepted by him and his administration. The "internationalists" were Wall Street bankers, or "Merchants of Death," or "tools of British Colonialism"—and in any event all "malefactors of great wealth."

A year after that the world was changing rapidly. And by 1938 it had become clear that the United States faced a major foreign affairs crisis and a radical international policy decision. The question had already become how—if at all—America could be maintained as the "Last Best Hope" while having a foreign policy. Increasingly America moved in its politics from being Depression America to being Prewar America. And the basic positions developed then still dominate our domestic and foreign policies, forty years later.

One of these positions was that of Herbert Agar, like Waymack a distinguished writer and journalist, and editor of an equally distinguished newspaper, the Louisville *Courier.* In the early New Deal years, Agar had established himself as the preeminent historian of the American Dream, especially in *The People's Choice,* a book on the American presidency that had won the Pulitzer Prize in American history when it appeared in 1933. Its heroes were those presidents—all Democrats—who had emphasized the uniqueness of America as a political vision, and the separation of America from the vices, the nationalism, the power politics, the "colonialism" of Europe. Yet Agar at once and without hesitation decided that the United States had to lead the crusade against Hitler.

I first met Agar in the early summer of 1939 when, following the publication of my book *The End of Economic Man,* he invited me to stay for a week at his home in Louisville. Appeasement was then still riding high in London and Paris; and Washington was still convinced of, and committed to, staying out of a European war at all costs. But Agar knew that there would be war. And he had decided for himself that the United States had to be in it, must indeed be in it. America's values, its principles, demanded active participation in, if not leadership of, what to Agar was the last possible attempt to prevent the worldwide destruction for all time of everything America stood for. Agar lived in an old rambling farmhouse in the midst of cornfields. There we sat every evening on the porch in the long twilight of a Kentucky June. And Agar, sipping mint juleps, talked out a blueprint for a "Pax Americana," under which the American vision would be extended to an "Atlantic Community," which, in turn, would wage war against anyone threatening peace and freedom. John Foster Dulles's aggressive defense treaties of the 1950s were direct descendants of Agar's ideas, as was John F. Kennedy's policy in Vietnam. Agar himself soon became the most vocal advocate of American intervention in Europe, and, after Pearl Harbor, head of America's Office of War Information in London and one of the key links between the Americans and Churchill.

William Waymack also had become an "interventionist" before Roosevelt's Washington did. Or rather he had never been an "isolationist." He and his paper were Republican and had been strongly opposed to Roosevelt and the New Deal. One of Waymack's main points of criticism was precisely Roosevelt's disregard and neglect of foreign affairs—which, it needs to be repeated, tended to be a complaint of Republicans in those days, and especially of Republicans like Waymack who had been close to the internationalist Herbert Hoover. But Waymack, unlike Agar, still hoped that American intervention could be limited to economic and financial support to the countries threatened by Hitler. The political organization he helped found was called "Committee for the Defense of America by Aiding the Allies." Beyond this immediate policy, Waymack envisaged a return to the Wilsonian strategy of a self-policing world order of law, buttressed by American economic strength. It was this position to which Roosevelt moved when he had to give up his original isolationist stance. And it was this position that largely determined American foreign policy in the immediate war and postwar years. Lend Lease, the United Nations, but also the Marshall Plan, all were logical developments from a position that was, in the main, first developed by people like Waymack: Midwesterners and "liberal" Republicans. Waymack's committee was known as the "White Committee," after its chairman, William Allen White, perhaps Mid-America's best-known journalist, Republican sage, editor of the Emporia, Kansas, *Gazette,* and friend of Teddy Roosevelt, Taft, Coolidge, and Hoover. Where Agar was out to save Europe, Waymack and White were out to save America and to make possible again America's uniqueness and separateness, if not its isolation.

But to me, the most ominous response to the international storm that was rapidly blowing up was that of John L. Lewis, the labor leader, head of the United Mine Workers Union, and founder of the Congress of Industrial Organizations (the CIO) and of industrial mass unionism in the United States altogether.

Herbert Agar had me stay with him as a houseguest. Waymack took lunch or dinner with me whenever he came East. But Lewis I saw only three or four times in all, and then at formal "interviews" in his Washington office a year apart, each no more than a few hours in length. Agar and Waymack wanted to know my opinion. Lewis made speeches. And he made them on the topic that interested him. I went to Lewis to interview him about labor relations and unionism; he orated instead on foreign policy. Foreign policy was his obsession and personal devil, on which he blamed all evils: his own isolation and downfall, the corruption of the labor movement, and the downfall and destruction of the Republic. Foreign policy—any foreign policy other than the strictest isolationism, in which intercourse with the world outside would be limited to the barest minimum—was evil, incompatible with American ideals, and certain to corrupt, to distort, and to deform.

When I first met Johnn L. Lewis in mid-1937, his name was a household word. Few Americans, then as now, knew the names of their senators, of their state's governor, or of any member of the President's cabinet. But everyone knew two names: Franklin D. Roosevelt and John L. Lewis. Everyone also knew what John L. Lewis looked like—his massive body with the big head, the heavy eyebrows, and the mane of gray hair were a cartoonist's delight. And in those days of radio, his voice was as familiar as his looks: a big voice formed in the days before loudspeakers and public-address systems, and meant, like a bullhorn, to be heard over the roar of the wildest labor riot. It was a distinctive voice with a Welsh lilt to it, even though Lewis himself had been born in a coal town in Iowa. The voice was sonorous and at its best reciting Shakespeare, the Bible, Milton, or *Pilgrim's Progress,* all of which Lewis knew by heart and quoted constantly at great length.

Lewis was then considered the second most powerful man in America, next to Franklin D. Roosevelt alone. He retained this reputation for another ten years, until President Truman called his bluff and broke the coal miners' strike of 1946 by taking over the mines. But where press and public saw Lewis as too powerful, he himself, from 1937 on, could see nothing but impotence, rejection, and repudiation. He perceived himself as the King Lear of American politics, driven out into the wilderness and shamed by the two ungrateful and treacherous "children" who owed their power to him but had then turned on him: Franklin D. Roosevelt and Phil Murray, his chosen successor as head of the CIO. Both had deserted him and betrayed him because they had signed themselves over to the devil of foreign policy and become corrupted by it.

Like Shakespeare's *King Lear,* which he constantly quoted and paraphrased, Lewis had both his Cordelia and his Kent—and they were as interesting as Lewis. His daughter, Kathryn, was Cordelia, and she served her father faithfully to the end. John L. and Kathryn looked more like twins than father and daughter, even though Kathryn was still a young woman when I knew her. She stood the same way, she moved the same way, she spoke the same way. She was by all odds the most gifted, ablest person in the American labor movement of that time, and there were then giants in the land of labor! No one knew as much about American industry and American labor, understood as much, had thought as much and as deeply. And she was, like her father, a moving and stirring orator. She was the one to whom I learned to go to get information about unions and labor relations. One could also see in her the charm for which her father had been famous in his younger years, before vanity and power had eaten into him. Yet she completely subordinated herself to her father. She had wanted to marry more than once, according to Washington gossip, but had always broken off the engagement to stay with her father. She was always present when he saw a newspaperman, but never spoke unless her father directed a question at her. And when Lewis disappeared from public view, she disappeared with him.

Lewis's "Kent," the faithful vassal who serves his master without thanks, recognition, or reward, was another remarkable woman: Josephine Roche. The same age as Lewis—they were both born in 1880 —she had been the daughter of one of America's richest men, the owner of one of the biggest coal companies in the West. Lewis's first pitched labor battle had been fought against her father's mines when Josephine was in college. She had become a convert to the cause of labor and a disciple of her father's adversary. She made a distinguished career in her own right as a social worker, but also as an industrialist, managing, most successfully, the large mining company her father left her. But her first allegiance was always to John L. Lewis and his United Mine Workers, to whom she devoted both her life and her great fortune. President Roosevelt made her Assistant Secretary of the Treasury. But when Lewis broke with Roosevelt in 1937, Josephine Roche resigned. She had been beautiful and was still a very good-looking woman when I met her in Lewis's office. It was evident that she worshipped him, and she never married. Lewis—every inch a Lear in the presence of the faithful Kent—did not even notice that she was around and paid no attention to her; yet he also took it for granted that she would come running to sit in on his interviews whenever he called.

When I first met him in 1937 Lewis was only in his late fifties. He was in perfect health and would live another thirty years, dying in 1969 at age eighty-nine. But he fancied himself an old, broken man. He was very much alone and complained bitterly about it. Of course, it was his own fault: he had driven out anyone who might conceivably have become a threat to his absolute domination of his union. But Lewis blamed his loneliness, as he blamed any misfortune, on the one arch-villain in his world, "foreign policy" or, more precisely, "internationalism" or "interventionism."

Lewis—with some exaggeration—claimed full credit for Roosevelt's nomination and election. Lewis's defection from labor's oldest and truest friend, Al Smith, and his switch to Roosevelt, whom labor earlier had always distrusted and disliked as a spoiled, rich "aristocrat," had indeed clinched the nomination for Roosevelt at the 1932 convention. And during Roosevelt's first term Lewis had reaped the rewards. Roosevelt's administration had supported labor, and especially the unionization of the mass-production industries that Lewis had started through the CIO, of which he was founder, chief financial support, and chairman.

But then, in 1937, Lewis had decided to strike "Little Steel"—the four steel companies which, while very big, were still smaller than U.S. Steel—against the advice of everyone in the labor movement. He had counted on Roosevelt's support to give him victory. Instead, the administration stayed on the sidelines and Lewis had to call off a strike that neither the steelworkers in the mills nor the public had supported. This, of course, was the reason why Roosevelt had not pulled Lewis's chestnuts out of the fire. But Lewis felt betrayed. And the cause of his betrayal, he was convinced, was Roosevelt's abandoning "neutrality" in favor of an "interventionist" foreign policy. "Whenever a President in the United States gets ready for foreign adventures," he said to me, "he abandons the workingman and sucks up to the bosses. He deserts the quest for social justice and embraces production and profits. He betrays America and becomes an imperialist." Within the year Lewis had broken openly with Roosevelt and moved to a rigidly isolationist position. "When we go to war—and we will—" he said to me in 1939 when I called on him just as war was declared in Europe, "the President will ask the worker to buckle under in the name of patriotism. I shan't cave in."

In 1943 Lewis made good on his threat. American troops were fighting in North Africa and in the Pacific; yet the country was not geared for full war production and was dangerously short of supplies for the men at the front. But rather than accepting the wage restraints of the War Labor Board, Lewis pulled the coal miners out on strike, thus threatening the collapse of the entire production effort. President Roosevelt chastised him for putting the self-interests of the miners above national survival. "The President of the United States," Lewis retorted in a public speech, "is paid to look after national survival. I am paid to look after the selfish interests of the miners"—and he kept the miners out on strike until he had won his demands.

He similarly blamed the lure of foreign adventures for Phil Murray's "desertion." Murray had for many years been Lewis's faithful lieutenant in the Mine Workers' Union, and perhaps the only man ever close to him. Lewis considered him his son rather than a colleague, even though Murray was only a few years younger. When Lewis plunged into the Little Steel strike, he had boasted that he would resign from the chairmanship of the CIO should he lose the strike—and he had lost it. As everyone in Washington knew, he confidently expected his resignation to be refused. It was accepted. Then he engineered Murray's election to succeed him, confident that Murray would be his lieutenant, if not his stooge, as he had been all those years at the United Mine Workers Union. But Murray soon proved to be very much his own man, and indeed quietly, without fanfare and without a strike, got from the Little Steel companies the very union recognition Lewis had unsuccessfully struck for. Finally Murray, in early 1938, came out in favor of an "internationalist" foreign policy. Lewis broke with him, publicly consigned him to outer darkness, and pulled his mineworkers out of the CIO.

"Why are you so sure that a war is the end of the labor movement?" I once asked him. "It seems to me that unions and union leaders have profited from every war in this century and gained standing and acceptance." "No," said Lewis, "they have only been corrupted. Labor leaders become respectable in a war. They get offices and titles and are made much of. But they sell out their members in the name of patriotism and national unity." "An internationalist foreign policy in America," he once said, "means taking money out of the pockets and food out of the mouths of the poor and putting it into totally unproductive weapons and munitions. It means that emphasis shifts from workers' rights to workers' duties. It leads to supporting greater profits and lower wages and longer hours, and it means public support for the bosses and a heavy hand on the workers in the name of the national interest. It means giving up the dream of building Jerusalem in America's green and pleasant land so that generals and politicians can garner glory." The last time I saw him—in 1941, shortly after Hitler had invaded Russia and only a few months before Pearl Harbor—he ranted about the power-greedy politicians who were dragging us into war, predicted that Roosevelt would somehow manipulate an attack on the United States by Hitler (he paid just as little attention to the Japanese as everybody else), and declared that the entire war was a conspiracy of bankers, munitions makers, intellectuals, and of "the bosses" in general, to destroy freedom, justice, and equality in America forever. "We already," he said, "have taken over the French and the Dutch colonies—and when England goes, we'll take over the British Empire in the name of defending freedom. Then we'll forget all about America being the Last Best Hope and applaud that tyrant Roosevelt when he proclaims that to save the world America must become *the* imperialist super-power."

Lewis was clearly not entirely sane in his vanity, in his need to dominate, and in his suspicion of anti-Lewis conspiracies everywhere. He was motivated as much by a pathological hatred of the English as by concern for America and the American Dream. He was indeed Lear, and a Lear who never awakens to his own folly. But he anticipated in his suspicions and fears everything that since has been put forth as "revisionist" history. And as in the case of the "revisionists," there was just enough truth to his delusions to make them convince himself.

A few months after my last meeting with John L. Lewis I found myself in Minneapolis in early winter, to speak on the world scene during the Sunday service at the city's largest Lutheran church. After my talk the elderly minister, who still had a Swedish inflection in his English, said: "We do live indeed in horrible times. But let us remember that the forebears of everyone in this congregation came to this country to get away from the incessant wars, the insane hatreds, and the sinful pride of Europe. Let us remember that the forebears of everyone here hacked a farm out of the howling wilderness amid blizzards in the winter and sandstorms in the summer, so as to live as free men and women, innocent of the wickedness and folly of national honor and the tyranny of government disguised as military glory. Let us remember that the forebears of every one of us came to build a new nation subservient to laws rather than to men. Let us pray that this cup will pass us by and that America will remain the Last Best Hope, and not succumb to being just another entry in the long and vain list of empires."

I was deeply moved. No one before—or since—had summed up what the American Dream really means more succinctly, more clearly, more movingly. And yet, as I drove to the airport, I knew that the prayer was in vain. Goodness by itself no longer sufficed. The fight between "internationalists" and "isolationists" was by then tearing apart the American Dream as much as any war possibly could, or more. Even so, America seemed no closer to a decision. Indeed the fight between the "internationalists" and the "isolationists," each intent on saving the American Dream his way, was paralyzing the national will and was, I thought, endangering America's very survival and cohesion.

We were half an hour out of Minneapolis when the pilot in an excited voice came in on the intercom and asked us to put on the earphones with which every seat was equipped and listen to the radio. The Japanese had attacked Pearl Harbor! When we landed in Chicago two hours later in the early darkness of a December evening, soldiers with fixed bayonets were already guarding the hangars and patrolling the corridors. The Age of Innocence was over.

Only a few weeks later America did indeed betray its promises and beliefs to opt for being just another "power" when Roosevelt, to appease the Californians, ordered all Americans of Japanese descent interned.

But innocence still lingered on in a few corners for a little while. Six or eight weeks after Pearl Harbor I went to work on my first Washington wartime job. We were housed in temporary quarters in an old apartment hotel that had been closed for years and was about to be torn down when the government took it over. The staff was crammed into the two-or three-room apartments while the "big shots," such as I was supposed to be, had each a private office in the apartment's former bathrooms, with their seat on the toilet and a board over the bathtub for a desk. We were all green—not one of us had ever been in government service or in any big organization before. And we were still such hopeless civilians that none of us knew the insignia of rank on a uniform or could tell a corporal from a three-star general. Great was our excitement therefore when the first staff car any of us had seen pulled up outside. We all crowded around the window to watch. First a man sitting in front next to the driver got out. He opened the door in back on his side and another, younger man got out. The young man in turn went around the car and opened the rear door on the other side, and a fat older man got out—all were in uniform, of course. The older man gave a big bundle to the younger man, who in turn gave it to the soldier who had sat in front and got out first. Then all three marched in. When they reached our office, the older man introduced himself as a colonel come to bring us a super-secret report—so secret that it could only be lent to us for a few days. After he had left, we opened with great trepidation the bundle he had brought and found a book inside: the first intelligence study of a European country. Then we read the opening sentence: "The Estonians are by nature monogamous," and collapsed in laughter, none louder than the Estonian on our staff.

One of the girls in the office who had been a commercial artist, suggested that we inscribe this magnificient sentence in proper calligraphy on a sheet of paper and hang it over a badly discolored mildewy spot on the wall of the dilapidated room. Then we went back to our work—we had more urgent things to worry about than sex on the shores of the Baltic. A few days later the colonel came back to pick up the report. He chuckled when he saw our poster, then asked. "Where does this gem come from?" "It's the opening sentence of the report you brought us the other day," He turned white. "Take it down at once," he said, "and shred it. It's classified top secret."

Index

Adler, Alfred, 31, 90, 98
Africa, slave trade in, 137–138, 311
Agar, Herbert, 328–330
Allen, Frederick Lewis, 299
American Economic Review, 262
American Political Science Association, 257, 263
American Political Science Review, 262–263
Amsterdam, 105; Drucker's ancestors in, 208
Anderson, Marian, 312
Anglo-Austrian Bank, 37
Annette, friend of Schwarzwalds, 48–51, 54, 60, 61
Antioch College, 320
Anti-Semitism: of European Jews, 32–33; Freud said to be victim of, 84, 86–88, 96–97; in U.S. in 1930s, 302–304
Aquinas, St. Thomas, 108
Arendt, Hannah, 168–169
Aristotle, 108, 138
Athens, ancient, 138, 152, 311
Austen, Jane, 49, 94, 95
Austria: Army, social class in, 49–50; currency, 15–16, 35–36; Department of Foreign Trade (Commercial Museum), 28–31, 33, 50; Freemasonry, 29, 118; German alliance with, 152–153; Ministry of Finance, 28–31, 33, 35, 36, 50; Nazi invasion of, 60, 118–119, 133, 183; "poorhouse neurosis," 95; "prewar" obsession, 58–60; refugees from, in

U.S., 299, 303, 318; Socialists, 114, 115; universities, 105–107; women in universities, 39–41; in World War I, 35–36, 152
Austrian Academy of Science, 52
Austrian Economist, The, 123, 132, 133
Austrian National Bank, 51
Austrian School of Economists, 50, 138
Automotive Safety Council, 290
Avanti, 129

Bagehot, Walter, 225
Balkans, 173; rural sociology movement, 174
Balkan wars (1912–13), 172–173, 175
Balzac, Honoré de, 210
Bank of England, 37
Barnard, Chester, 262
Barth, Karl, 106
Bartók, Béla, 130
Batavia, 205–206
Bauhaus School, 242
Bay of Pigs, 156
Bean, Louis, 298, 304
Bennington College, 68, 78–80, 135–136, 249, 256–258, 305, 320
Bentham, Jeremy, 108, 138
Bergson, Henri, 32
Berlin, 43–44; University, 316; Wall, 156
Berliner Illustrierte Zeitung, 242
Berliner Tageblatt, 166–168, 225
Bernheim, Henry, 196–203, 211
Bernheim, Irving, 197–198, 203
Bernheim, Otto, 188, 196, 213

337